MIAMI ICE:
Winning The
NHL Rat Race
With The
Florida Panthers

by
Dave Rosenbaum

Publisher's Cataloging in Publication
(Prepared by Quality Books Inc.)

Rosenbaum, Dave.
    Miami ice : winning the NHL rat race with the Florida Panthers / Dave Rosenbaum
      p. cm.
    Includes index.
    Preassigned LCCN: 96-78068
    ISBN 0-9653846-6-7

    1. Florida Panthers (Hockey team) 2. National Hockey League. 3. Hockey—Florida. I. Title.

GV848.F6R68 1997   796.962'64'09759
                                      QBI96-40553

Cover photo: Bruce Bennett Studios

Interior design and typesetting: Sue Knopf, Graffolio

Published by McGregor Hill Publishing, Inc., Tampa, Florida

Printed in the United States of America

Contents

Acknowledgments v

Prologue: Father Knows Best 1

1. A Snowball's Chance in Hell. 5

2. Wayne and a Prayer 9

3. Home Is Where the Heat Is. 24

4. Jumping Head-First. 44

5. Gone Fishing 58

6. Feels Like the First Time 74

7. Where No Team Has Gone Before 90

8. Taking a Bruising 123

9. The Season That Almost Wasn't 141

10. The Summer of Our Discontent. 168

11. The Year of the Rat. 188

12. The Ultimate Warriors. 223

Epilogue: Going Home. 271

Index 275

Acknowledgments

Warm thanks to my publisher, Lonnie Herman, for opportunity, confidence, constructive criticism, support, ideas, friendship, and making this a far more enjoyable experience than I had ever anticipated. Before I started writing this book, a few people told me to beware of publishers. I'm still trying to figure out why.

Several people played key roles in the creative and editing process. Gary Stein, my editor at McGregor Hill, used the big red pencil with care and helped shaped the final work.

My wife, Jacqui, not only endured living with a hermit for five months, but offered suggestions and made comments that were more helpful than even she knew. For example, "Stop sounding like Mickey Spillane" after reading the original version of Chapter One.

My parents, Irving and Blanche Rosenbaum, and my brother, Alan, read and proofread, and, as always, provided support and offered encouragement. My friends, Kisha and Kell Ciabattari, generously gave their time and loaned their playoff tapes. And Ron Chawkins offered his comments from the Gulf Coast.

When writing an unauthorized work, an author is somewhat at the mercy of his subjects. In this case, the Florida Panthers had no financial stake in the book, nor any control over its content, yet their cooperation was complete and unconditional. Grateful thanks to Chuck Fletcher, Wayne Huizenga, Dean Jordan, Doug MacLean, Bryan Murray, and Bill Torrey, all of whom selflessly gave hours of their time. And to Stu Barnes, Tom Fitzgerald, Mark Fitzpatrick, Mike Hough, Jody Hull, Ed Jovanovski, Paul Laus, Tim LeRoy, Bill Lindsay, Dave Lowry, Scott Mellanby, Gord Murphy, Rob Niedermayer, Lindy Ruff, Ray Sheppard, Brian Skrudland, Bill Smith, Martin Straka, Duane Sutter, Scott Tinkler, John Vanbiesbrouck, and Rhett Warrener.

Thanks to the Panthers' staff, whose contributions, large and small, were invaluable: Greg Bouris, Steve Dauria, Kevin Dessart, Jon Kramer, Aza Krotz, Marni Share, and Tom Ziermann.

And to Mike Barnett, Jim Devellano, Bob Dittmeier, Rob Franklin, Lloyd Friedland, Dave Joseph, Mike Kane, Mark Kiszla, Sam Laroue of the Coral Gables Historical Society, Jim Lites, Barry Meisel, Steve McAllister, Bryant McBride, Andy McGowan, Barry Melrose, Ray Murray, Dave Neal, Roger Neilson, Dennis Patterson, Craig Peters, Jeff Rimer, Rick Rochon, Denise Rubin, Ed Snider, the people at the Miami Sports and Exhibition Authority, Gil Stein, Godfrey Wood, and John Ziegler.

The quotes from Bob Clarke in chapter eight were generously contributed by Jay Greenberg, author of *Full Spectrum: The Complete History of the*

Philadelphia Flyers Hockey Team (Dan Diamond, Toronto).

   And, finally ... Back in June 1996, when the Panthers were in the Stanley Cup playoffs, Damian Cristodero from *Florida Sportsfan*, called to say that "some guy from a publishing company" was looking for me. "He probably wants you to write a book," he joked. To my surprise, that's exactly what some guy wanted, so I'll end this by thanking Damian for passing along the message.

Dave Rosenbaum
Parkland, Florida
November, 1996

For Jacqui and Adam,
Mom and Dad,
With Love

Prologue:
Father Knows Best

John Vanbiesbrouck was already thinking about tomorrow night's game as he sat in the passenger seat of his father's van and rode down I-95 to the Fort Lauderdale Jet Center. A plane would take him and his teammates the rest of the way, to Pittsburgh for Game 7 of the 1996 Eastern Conference finals, and Vanbiesbrouck allowed himself to dream about where they might go afterwards.

"Wouldn't it be great if we could win this game?" he asked his father.

"That would really be something," said Robert Vanbiesbrouck, a man of few words.

That understated reply stayed on his mind after his father dropped him off at the airport, during the flight to Pittsburgh, and all that night. He could've blocked out the importance of the upcoming game, but he wanted to think about what was at stake and the reward for victory.

A third-year National Hockey League team getting to the Stanley Cup finals. That *would* be something, he realized. Vanbiesbrouck, cast out by two teams, was the Florida Panthers' first pick in the 1993 Expansion Draft, and three years later he and nine more of those rejects were on the verge of eliminating superstars Mario Lemieux, Jaromir Jagr, and the powerful Penguins from the playoffs. It was unbelievable! South Floridians were driving around with plastic rats on their dashboards and Panthers flags flying from their cars. Television newscasters were wearing Panthers jerseys on the air, and the owner, who had months earlier threatened to sell the team, was acting just as silly as everyone else.

But Vanbiesbrouck realized everything would be quickly forgotten if they didn't win one more game. He had been to the Conference finals 10 years ago with another team that wasn't supposed to be there, the New York

1

Rangers, and remembered the empty feeling of shaking hands with the
Montreal Canadiens when that series ended with a loss. Third-year teams
had come this far before, but none were able to take the final step. Here
was their chance at making history.

Vanbiesbrouck began his game-day ritual the next morning: Breakfast
with a few teammates, the morning skate, and then isolation. His teammates
knew not to speak to him on game days, and Vanbiesbrouck focused on
his task: *What am I going to face tonight and how will I react to certain
situations? Lemieux likes to do this. Jagr likes to go there. What are their
tendencies on the power play?* He thought about what the Penguins had
done in the series and what would likely happen in Game 7.

As game time approached, Vanbiesbrouck wandered around the visitors'
locker room at the Civic Arena, sat in front of his stall, and was nearly oblivious to the commotion around him. Teammates conducted pre-game interviews and taped their sticks. He'd occasionally laugh at a funny remark
before returning to his private world, which consisted entirely of the
Pittsburgh Penguins making plays and taking shots. *What's the best way
to go about winning this game?*

Then the game started and his focus switched to the present. Just 3:15
had expired when he blocked Lemieux's quick wrister from close-range.
Jagr loomed on a wraparound, but couldn't find the open far side of the
net. Lemieux and Brad Lauer threatened with a two-on-one, but Terry
Carkner broke up Lemieux's pass. By the mid-point of the period, the
defenses tightened up and most of the action took place in the neutral zone
or along the boards.

That's good, Vanbiesbrouck decided. *We're getting into the same flow
as some of our other games and if we can get into our game, then we'll
have a shot at winning.*

Having held off the Penguins' early charge, Vanbiesbrouck watched as
the action went the other way. Francois Leroux, the Penguins' lead-footed
defenseman, fell down at center ice. Mike Hough and Svehla moved in on
a two-on-one and worked a give-and-go. Hough scored. Svehla danced
around the ice. The Panthers on the bench celebrated. Vanbiesbrouck forced
himself to remain focused, knowing how tenuous a 1-0 lead could be against
this team.

They're really going to turn it on now, Vanbiesbrouck figured, and he
was right. He liked how the defense allowed him to see the puck and eliminated second chances, but at some point the Penguins were going to test
him. They were just too good. Dave Roche had two chances from in front
of the net. Joe Dziedzic couldn't finish off a two-on-one. Kevin Miller and
Jagr swiped at the puck in the slot, but Vanbiesbrouck made both saves.

The Penguins kept getting power plays and Vanbiesbrouck kept turning them away. As the second period continued and the Panthers' 1-0 lead grew more meaningful, Vanbiesbrouck braced for another Penguins onslaught and weathered that, too. He realized he got lucky when Kevin Miller's shot with 52 seconds left in the period found his glove. *You have to have some luck,* he thought.

The second period ended and the Panthers still had their lead.

Vanbiesbrouck liked the Panthers' chances. The game was down to one decisive period, and that meant the fans would be too nervous to get involved and the Penguins would start pressing if they didn't score in the first five minutes. But he was aware that the Penguins are dangerous in the first five minutes of a period and, as he skated to his crease, he prepared for another flurry on yet another power play.

This time, the Penguins cashed in. Petr Nedved scored to tie the game with 1:23 gone, and Vanbiesbrouck knew the next few minutes were key. His teammates were coughing up the puck, and the Penguins were getting one scoring opportunity after another. The checking line was tired after being on the ice for nearly a minute and desperately in need of a change. Tom Fitzgerald took a pass from Gord Murphy in the Panthers' defensive zone and headed toward the Penguins' end. Fitzgerald was merely buying time for a line change when he wound up and fired a slapshot, but the puck deflected off of defenseman Neil Wilkinson at the blue line, past goaltender Tom Barrasso, and into the net. The Panthers had a 2-1 lead.

Vanbiesbrouck was as excited as he was surprised. It looked like Barrasso would never break; he had been the Penguins' key player in several games. Now Vanbiesbrouck's job was making sure he didn't break, either. With 12 minutes remaining, he stopped Jagr from point-blank range. Lemieux offered his bid. Vanbiesbrouck turned him away. With each passing minute and spurned opportunity, Vanbiesbrouck felt the Penguins losing their will to win. And, with 3:37 remaining, he watched Bill Lindsay and Johan Garpenlov race into the Penguins' zone, and Garpenlov's shot pop over Barrasso's glove and into the net.

The Panthers had a 3-1 lead. Vanbiesbrouck knew his team was going to win and tried to chase away the thought. *It's not over yet. It's not over yet. Stay focused,* he kept telling himself, more anxious than he had ever been in his life for a game to end. Then it did and Vanbiesbrouck happily succumbed to his emotions. He watched his teammates joyfully jumping over the boards, and saw the elation on their faces. Heck, some of those guys were leaping 12 feet! *And they're all coming at me!*

Teammates surrounded him, hugged him, and patted him on the head. Some of them yelled, "We did it! Can you believe we did it?" Every memory in Vanbiesbrouck's hockey life started rushing through his mind like a videotape on fast forward: all of the games in his friends' backyards; the three years in Florida that led up to this moment.

Everybody knows, he thought. The kids in Florida with the smiles on their faces, his family, every friend he knew from the time he was a child, all knew that the Panthers had won. He realized that, as much as he had dreamed about this moment, he never really believed it would happen to him. Then he thought about his brother, Frank, who had died three years earlier, and how his life had been changed by the man he idolized: *If Frank hadn't played goal, I wouldn't have played goal, either.*

He felt like Frank was with him as he lined up and shook hands with the Penguins. But this wasn't a dream, this was for real! The Panthers were going to the finals! He thought again about what the team had been through, from the very start, and enjoyed the sense of accomplishment of being with these teammates who had different stories, but felt the same way he did.

Then he remembered his father's words the previous day. *That would really be something.* And it really was!

CHAPTER 1

A Snowball's Chance
in Hell

Wayne Gretzky stepped onto the ice at Miami Arena and immediately realized there was a problem. Here he was, the greatest hockey player of all time, but even he hadn't figured out a way to skate on water.

On second thought, Gretzky considered when his skate sank a couple of inches into the Miami slush after the second intermission, *maybe I won't play the third period.*

On the evening of September 21, 1990, it was 90 degrees and humid outside Miami Arena and not much cooler inside. The temperature was even hotter under the collar of Tim Wendt, whose job was creating a solid sheet of ice for the NHL pre-season game between the Los Angeles Kings and the New York Rangers. This was supposed to be the first National Hockey League game in South Florida but, at the current rate of meltdown, it was fast becoming the first ice water hockey game.

Less than two minutes into the game, the Arena repair crew had made its first appearance and patched a hole in front of the Rangers' bench. A dozen more interruptions followed. The second period was called 47 seconds early for more repairs. The final period was cut short by five minutes. The Kings were declared the winners, 6-4. The sellout crowd of 14,596 booed.

"A lot of players were hitting cement," said Mike Krushelnyski of the Kings. "This was probably the worst ice I've ever seen."

"MIAMI ICE" taunted the headline the next day over a front-page photo in *The Miami Herald*. The photo showed Arena workers spraying dry ice over a shallow portion of a surface that refused to stay smooth and solid.

Nature was taking its course. In hot, steamy South Florida, ice was returning to its original state: Water.

▲ ▲ ▲

Nearly three months later, Godfrey Wood sat in a conference room at the historic Breakers Hotel in Palm Beach, listened to the words coming out of his money man's mouth, and realized that he, too, was about to return to his original state: Massachusetts.

Empty-handed. Without the NHL team he so desperately wanted to bring to Miami.

Wood, 49, a former goaltender at Harvard University, had been optimistic from the start, even after the ice melted under Gretzky's skates, but there was no overcoming this latest obstacle: John Henry had just told the NHL's 21 governors that he had no intention of paying their price of $50 million for an expansion franchise.

Yet wasn't this to be expected? After all, nothing had gone right in Wood's dreadful year. First, there was his failed effort to place a Global Hockey League franchise in Providence, Rhode Island. The League folded before it started and Wood walked away $100,000 lighter.

Then he was presented with an even grander opportunity: Being the point man for a deal to get an NHL expansion franchise for Miami.

South Florida's interest in hockey became stunningly apparent when every ticket for the Kings vs. Rangers exhibition game was snatched up in less than two hours. Hockey and Miami looked like a perfect, though unlikely, match, but as game night approached, Wood kept having nightmares about everything that could go wrong. None of them involved the ice melting.

Even that fiasco wasn't a total loss. Miami Hockey Inc. accepted its first deposits for season tickets and, within a few months, Wood had collected nearly $500,000. The League recognized the Arena's first-night ice problems as commonplace. Gretzky praised the crowd's enthusiasm.

The real complications were behind the scenes, where Wood was having a hard time talking some rich South Florida businessman — any rich South Florida businessman — into paying $50 million for an NHL franchise. The opportunity was enticing: the NHL planned on adding two teams for the 1992-93 season and groups in five other cities, including St. Petersburg and Tampa across the state, weren't scared away by the asking price.

But in Miami, the major television market in Florida, and to many the most attractive location for a franchise, finding an investor with that much money was no simple task.

Elliott Barnett, a Fort Lauderdale attorney, thought he had one. Barnett's money man was going to be H. Wayne Huizenga, the multi-millionaire who owned the Blockbuster Entertainment Corp. This solid financial rock, who had proven his entrepreneurial genius numerous times, would make the Miami bid a cinch for approval.

"Barnett told me that he represented Huizenga and Wayne had other investors with him," Wood said. "I really believed that Wayne and his people were going to do the deal."

That was far too optimistic a view of the situation. Rick Rochon, the President of Huizenga Holdings, met twice with Barnett, but Huizenga never had any real interest in actually joining the group.

"They came and talked to me about it, but I didn't get involved," said Huizenga, who had applied for a Major League Baseball franchise. "I think Barnett was just going around trying to raise some money. I wasn't interested in being a part of the group."

By then, it was mid-November and the Governors' meeting was scheduled for December 5. Wood was in a precarious situation and getting dozens of calls every day from the local media, demanding the names of the owners. The problem was, he had no names to offer.

Then John Henry, a 41-year-old commodities adviser from Boca Raton, surfaced and said he'd put up the $50 million. The bid was saved. Wood had his money man, or so he thought. He had no idea his money man was going to come up short until Henry tried to negotiate the franchise fee at the Governors' meeting.

Wood nearly swallowed his tongue. If possible, he would have dove across the room, picked Henry's words out of the air, and stuffed them back into the man's mouth. He looked at the governors for a reaction, something. Nothing. But no reaction was necessary. Several of them had already said that the League would never accept anything less than $50 million in a cash payment.

Wood and Henry, along with Jeb Bush, the son of the former President, and Tony Ridder, the president of the Knight-Ridder newspaper chain, were a somber foursome as they addressed the media afterward. The Ottawa contingent had brought a pep band. The other bidders gushed their optimism. Wood and Henry barely mustered a smile.

That night, a reception was held at the Palm Beach home of Boston Bruins owner Jeremy Jacobs. A grim Henry and Wood sat at a table with their group. At an adjoining table was the Tampa contingent, celebrating as if they had already won the game.

"They were having a lot better time than we were," Wood said.

But there was one remaining hope. Peter Pocklington, the owner of the Edmonton Oilers, approached Wood and Henry and offered them a chance to save the bid.

"If you'll pay the money, I can guarantee you're in," Pocklington said.

"No, I'm not going to do it," Henry replied. "I'm not going to be the first one."

Wood returned to his room at The Breakers and didn't sleep a wink. Henry went home to Boca Raton. By now, Wood realized the only way the bid could be saved was if all of the other groups had taken the same position as Henry's.

The following morning at 11:00, Wood received a call from an NHL official asking him to come down to a conference room for a 1:30 briefing. Wood contacted Henry, who said he'd get there as quickly as he could. When Wood went downstairs to the meeting, he saw the groups from St. Petersburg, San Diego, and Hamilton, Ontario.

Jeez, I wonder if they took four of us, Wood thought.

"The NHL has decided to expand to Tampa and Ottawa," NHL President John Ziegler announced.

Wood was crushed.

He soon learned that Tampa and Ottawa were the only groups that agreed to pay the $50 million fee without negotiating a longer payment schedule. The Tampa bid, for months the butt of jokes, had come together just weeks earlier when former NHL great Phil Esposito and David LeFevre pieced together a Japanese ownership group. No arena was attached to the bid, but $50 million was. Nothing else mattered. The governors didn't bother voting on any cities but Ottawa and Tampa, and the vote was unanimous.

As the League held its press conference, Wood stood in front of the hotel with a crestfallen look on his face, waiting for the late-arriving Henry. A reporter approached and asked how he was doing.

"They just granted Ottawa and Tampa franchises," Wood replied. "Can you believe that?"

When Henry drove up and got out of his limousine, he didn't ask what happened. He knew by Wood's expression.

"We chatted for a while," Wood said. "I told him it was because of the fee, that they were the only two teams willing to pay the lump sum. Then he drove home. I went back north the next day."

The entire effort was finally perceived as a disorganized, ill-conceived, and poorly prepared fiasco which ended with many people questioning whether South Florida either needed or wanted a hockey team. In one of the rare times when Miami was outdone by Tampa, the disappointment wasn't softened by the fact that Tampa's outsiders outdid Miami's outsiders.

Tampa had a hockey team. Miami didn't.

"The questions are all academic now," wrote Bob Rubin in *The Miami Herald,* "but perhaps there's a lesson to be learned from this abortive bid to bring hockey to Miami. Study this effort, and the next time the NHL expands, do the opposite."

Next time wouldn't arrive for another two years.

CHAPTER 2

Wayne and a Prayer

If the NHL's governors had stepped back and taken an objective view of their accomplishments at the 1990 meetings in Palm Beach, they would have realized nothing had changed except the quality of their tans and the size of their bank accounts. Sure, Tampa Bay and Ottawa anted up a total of $100 million, but what did it mean for the League's future?

Having finally discovered Florida, they chose for expansion the third largest city in the state and one that didn't even have a hockey arena. The Ottawa expansion made sense only from a traditionalist's standpoint; Edmonton and Winnipeg, Canadian franchises in similar-sized markets, were struggling to fill their buildings and stay financially afloat, despite the area's fervor for hockey. Ottawa would spend most of its first four seasons playing in a 10,500-seat building. Tampa Bay would convert a 10,400-seat State Fair hall into a hockey arena just in time for its first season.

The time it took for the governors to recognize South Florida as a major hockey market was a testament to their lack of vision. It was already the 16th-largest television market in the United States. Many of the governors owned homes in the area. The mid-winter meetings were held in Palm Beach County every December. Had the League's not-so-wise men spent all their waking hours walking on the beach and hitting golf balls? Didn't they realize the tri-county area of Dade, Broward, and Palm Beach, was one of the fastest growing regions in the country? Had it really taken Godfrey Wood to open their eyes?

Indeed, it had.

A few months after the NHL completed its sixth expansion in 1990, League President John Ziegler and Chicago Blackhawks owner Bill Wirtz visited Wayne Huizenga while on business in South Florida. Wirtz knew of Waste Management, the company on which Huizenga built his fortune, from its operations in Chicago and had spoken with several people who formerly worked with Huizenga.

The meeting was a friendly social call with a little business thrown in. The three men discussed Huizenga's application for a National League Baseball franchise, his investment in Joe Robbie Stadium, and the rapid growth of Blockbuster Entertainment. Wirtz and Ziegler asked Huizenga if he had any interest in owning a hockey team.

Huizenga was cordial, yet direct: He was too busy and his application for a Major League Baseball franchise took precedent over any other sport.

"Well," Ziegler asked, "would you be interested if an opportunity came about in the future?"

"Right now, I couldn't say yes," Huizenga told them. "Let's see what happens if and when you people start expanding again."

If and when ... Before it could even think about a seventh expansion, the NHL wanted to make certain the new franchises in San Jose, Tampa Bay, and Ottawa were established. But South Florida impressed many of the governors as an area where the NHL could thrive. They liked the demographics, not so much of one particular city, but of the three-county area.

"The market offers a lot and we know it," Ziegler said. "And, as everyone knows, we're planning to expand by four more teams by the year 2000."

Huizenga forgot about the meeting. South Florida's sports life went on. There was football, pre-season baseball, even horse racing, dog racing, and jai-alai. Hockey faded in and out of the news. A rumor, repeatedly denied at the time, turned out to be true: In 1991, Huizenga explored the possibility of buying the financially ailing Hartford Whalers and moving them to Florida.

"We spent a fair amount of time trying to make something happen," said Rick Rochon of Huizenga Holdings. "We were serious about checking it out, but the deal died after a while. Also, the Hartford owners wanted to keep them in town."

From a financial standpoint, buying and relocating an existing team made more sense than purchasing an expansion franchise. The market price for an established team was approximately $30 million (the Whalers were sold three years later for $47.5 million, slightly lower than the price for an expansion franchise). Unfortunately for prospective buyers, there was a catch: no existing teams were for sale.

Besides, Huizenga couldn't waste time shopping for a hockey team when a Major League Baseball team was on his list. Another battle between Miami and the Gulf Coast was taking shape and, unlike the Wood-Henry hockey effort, this one had the solid financial backing of Huizenga and the emotional support of the South Florida community.

In late March, two exhibition games between the Baltimore Orioles and

New York Yankees attracted 125,000 fans to Joe Robbie Stadium in northern Dade County. Momentum was building; fans, the media, and local politicians were solidly behind the effort. On July 5, Miami was unanimously voted into the National League, mostly because Huizenga made a highly favorable impression on the owners.

With South Florida turning its attention to baseball, and deeply in love with football, interest in hockey waned. Although the Miami Sports and Exhibition Authority reconfirmed its desire to bring an NHL team to Miami Arena, only 8,836 fans showed up on September 21, 1991, for a pre-season game between the Rangers and Capitals. Fans booed when the attendance was announced. The building was far quieter the following night, when 4,255 watched a game between the Red Wings and Flyers.

"There'll be no more back-to-back games in the same city," said promoter Michael Halbrooks, who didn't find it necessary to add the words, "especially in Miami."

The only good news from those two nights was the ice: It didn't melt.

With Tim Wendt, the overseer of the 1990 Meltdown, now contracting stagehands for concerts in Orlando, the Miami Sports and Exhibition Authority brought in Mr. Ice: Doug Moore, a 61-year-old Canadian from a Toronto firm called Jet Ice.

"They won't get in the trouble they did last year," Moore said. "They just have to follow a few basic rules."

Like keeping the doors shut on game day — anybody who has made ice cubes in their freezer would know that — and not turning off the air conditioning.

Having perfected the art of ice, Miami Arena didn't get another chance to make it until October 2, 1992 for a pre-season game between the Whalers and the Islanders. Hardly a marquee attraction, the game drew only 8,049 fans. Many of those in the crowd were members of the Florida Hockey Club, a fan club formed by former NHL player Rosaire Paiment.

"I guess you can call it a booster club," Paiment said. "The difference down here is, since there's no team, you can root for whoever you want."

Hopes were occasionally lifted, only to be dashed. The NHL reconfirmed its assessment of Miami as a potential member city, while at the same time saying there were no plans for expansion in the near future. Huizenga said he'd be willing to buy an expansion team, although not by himself. One of his concerns, he said, was the seating capacity of Miami Arena, which was below NHL guidelines. Blockbuster was a sponsor of the Whalers vs. Islanders exhibition game and Huizenga attended solely as a guest.

That was it. Huizenga had so much work to do with the Marlins and Blockbuster that he didn't have time to think about hockey.

▲ ▲ ▲

Meanwhile, the usually stagnant NHL was going through a period of turmoil and change. A players' strike in early April, 1992, just weeks before the start of the post-season, resulted in union solidarity and increased rights for the players. The dispute was settled and the playoffs went on.

Ziegler, under whose leadership the League went nowhere fast, stepped down as president in June and was replaced on an interim basis by Gil Stein, 64, the vice president for 15 years. Under Stein's watch, the League returned to national cable TV in the United States, leaving the regional SportsChannel for ESPN. More importantly, the NHL took an important step toward improving its image by instituting rules that curbed fighting.

With Bruce McNall, the 43-year-old owner of the Los Angeles Kings, replacing the financially and ideologically conservative Wirtz as Chairman of the Board of Governors, the NHL was finally open to new ideas and moving toward becoming a major sport in the United States, instead of a poor fourth brother to baseball, football, and basketball. The League was actively seeking its first commissioner, preferably someone with a strong background in marketing. Most governors didn't care if the right person came from inside or outside the game. Change was needed.

"The key issue for this League is this: Are we prepared to be led?" McNall asked.

Despite an expiring collective bargaining agreement, and another players' strike or owners' lockout looming, the League was moving forward, having finally realized it was losing the fierce competition for the sports entertainment dollar in the United States.

But Stein and McNall knew of two companies that had been winning the competition for quite some time: The Disney Corporation and Blockbuster Video.

"I took over as president in June 1992 and the first thing I did was go on a missionary trip. I visited every NHL city, met with fans, editors, held news conferences, and beat the drums about the positive aspects of hockey," Stein recalled. "I sensed that everybody was starting to feel that hockey was upbeat and on the way up. I took the message to the media. We worked very hard at building the positives of hockey. We made significant rule changes, cutting down on the wrong kind of violence. People were beginning to recognize our efforts. Then we worked on bringing in these two significant new teams."

Never in his wildest dreams could Stein have imagined his work would proceed so smoothly or so quickly.

According to legend, Huizenga went shopping for an airplane and ended up buying a hockey team. The story sounds good. It's just not entirely true.

Owning a hockey team or another airplane were among the last things on Huizenga's mind in early November 1992 when he flew to Southern California for a meeting with executives from the Walt Disney Company. Upon arriving at Burbank Airport, Huizenga's pilot, David Linnemeier, mentioned that the Los Angeles Kings were selling a 727 that might be perfect for the Marlins.

"It's at this airport," Linnemeier told Huizenga. "Do you want to take a look?"

Huizenga was hesitant. "I don't know if I want a 727."

"Think about it," Linnemeier said. "It's right close by."

Huizenga didn't think about it. After his meeting at Disney, he returned to the airport and was ready to fly back to Florida when Linnemeier again brought up the plane.

"Let's just go over there and take a look," Linnemeier suggested.

"So we went over and there was a guy walking around in the plane," Huizenga recalled. "It was the pilot. We walked in, talked a little bit, and he showed it to us. It had first class seats all the way back, pretty nice. We looked around, but it was nothing special."

Huizenga's inspection was short and to the point. He knew enough about airplanes to check for legroom and make sure the upholstery wasn't torn, not enough to kick a tire or check out the instrumentation in the cockpit. He walked to the rear of the cabin and back to the front, and was ready to go home when a man he never met walked in. The man was relatively young and portly with razor thin eyes and thick jowls.

"Hi," the owner of the plane said. "I'm Bruce McNall."

▲ ▲ ▲

Could it be so easy, that all a person had to do was be on the right plane at the right time and meet the right man to wipe out hockey's 54-year history of failure in South Florida?

Fifty-four years. Can that be right? All the way back to 1938, when most of the region was still swampland and sawgrass infested with mosquitoes, alligators, and poisonous snakes?

Yes, it's true, but the evidence is long gone. You'll never find it. Not at the intersection of Douglas Road and 16th Street in Coral Gables, where all four corners are lined with thriving restaurants and businesses. None of them date back to 1938, when the four-team Tropical Ice Hockey League made its debut in one of the hottest, most uninhabitable parts of the United States.

The Miami Clippers, Miami Beach Pirates, Coral Gables Seminoles, and

Havana Tropicals played all of their games at the Ice Palace, the converted name of a converted auditorium with $50,000 worth of modern refrigeration equipment. The players came from Canada and the northern United States, a few of them had even played in the NHL and, on opening night, a crowd of 3,500 came out to watch Miami beat Miami Beach, 3-2. *The Miami Herald* called it the "wildest, goriest evening of sport seen for many a Miami moon."

Coral Gables won the league's first and only championship. Low attendance, spurred by high ticket prices — from a low of 25 cents to a high of $1.10! — led to the league's demise after one season, and builder George Merrick's Ice Palace never hosted another hockey game. It housed World War II flight simulators, then a health club, and finally a bowling alley, before it was torn down in 1994. By that time, just about everyone had forgotten hockey games were ever played at the corner of 16th and Douglas. Used to be a hockey rink, right there. Now there's a Service Merchandise.

In 1971, businessman Herbert U. Martin failed to bring a World Hockey Association franchise to South Florida. In the mid-1970s, season ticket deposits were accepted and never returned for an attempt to land an NHL expansion team. Jerry Saperstein took his shot early in 1979. He signed a deal to move the San Diego Mariners of the WHA to the Hollywood Sportatorium and rename them the Florida Icegators. Then the WHA was swallowed up by the NHL and Saperstein's Icegators were left behind in the muck.

The Wood-Henry effort came next and that failed, too.

By the early 1990s, somebody should have heard the message: Destiny would never allow South Florida and ice hockey to get together.

▲ ▲ ▲

Then, one day, aboard a grounded 727 in Burbank, California, Bruce McNall and Wayne Huizenga met for the first time and talked about airplanes. Huizenga told McNall he wasn't sure if he wanted to own a plane or simply charter the Marlins from city to city. Ever practical, Huizenga didn't like the idea of an acquisition sitting on the runway all winter collecting dust. McNall suggested a joint venture: He'd get the plane in the winter for the Kings, Huizenga would run it in the summer for the Marlins.

"I'll work up some numbers," McNall said. "Heck, if we can own the plane together and share the costs, we'll work out."

"By the way," Huizenga asked. "When are you guys going to expand again?"

McNall knew Huizenga was referring to the NHL.

"Why do you ask?" he responded.

14

"Well, I think hockey would do good down in Miami. I really don't know if I want to own a team myself, but I'd have somebody bring it down there."

With the idea quickly taking shape, Huizenga explained to McNall that South Florida is filled with transplanted New Yorkers and northeasterners who were already familiar with the game.

"If you're really serious," McNall told Huizenga, "the next time you get into New York, why don't you see our president, Gil Stein."

The conversation ended. Huizenga said good-bye, returned to Florida, and once again forgot about hockey.

A few weeks later, Stein called Huizenga.

"I bumped into Bruce McNall, and Bruce was telling me of your conversation," Stein started. "He said you were going to come by and see me."

Huizenga didn't recall his conversation with McNall finishing quite that way, but agreed to meet Stein the next time he was in New York. There was no urgency. Huizenga had plenty of other deals to keep him busy.

"When are you coming?" Stein pressed.

"I'll be up there next week or the week after."

"Come see me," Stein said. "We're working on something that you might be interested in."

And again, Huizenga pushed hockey to the back of his mind.

▲ ▲ ▲

What if they built a sports arena and nobody showed up to play in it? That was the problem facing the City of Anaheim with its sparkling new, state-of-the-art, indoor facility, the Anaheim Arena. The 19,400-seat building, located just a few miles from the gates of Disneyworld, was scheduled to open in June 1993 but, as of October 1992, all it had planned were concerts, ice shows, and the circus. No home team.

The Disney Company already had one: The Mighty Ducks, the fictional team on which a fabulously successful hockey movie of the same name was based. Disney chairman and CEO Michael Eisner was a hockey fan whose children had taken a liking to the sport. He frequently attended Kings games with his family and knew McNall from the movie business.

One day, Eisner told McNall he was impressed with the direction the NHL was headed because of the rule changes regarding violence. He suggested an interest in discussing the acquisition of an NHL expansion franchise, either for himself or Disney.

McNall, delighted by the idea of bringing in a major name such as Disney, initiated the process. He contacted Stein and set up a meeting at a small restaurant in Hollywood, California. The three men exchanged small talk and then got down to business: What would it take, Eisner asked, to get a team?

"First of all, there was the money," Stein said, recalling the conversation. "Michael felt that Disney would bring so much to the table that it shouldn't be charged for a franchise. Bruce and I told him that it must pay $50 million, the same price as the last expansion. We felt there was no way the Board of Governors would come down on that price. It had been established. Eisner didn't balk. He was just taking a shot, but he said he wouldn't pay a penny more than $50 million."

But McNall owned the territorial rights, and Norman Green, who owned the Minnesota North Stars, had offered McNall $25 million to approve his move into Anaheim. Stein suggested a plan under which Eisner would pay $50 million for the franchise, split evenly between McNall and the other owners.

That was fine with Eisner, who realized he'd be getting a $25 million bargain. The terms were certainly acceptable to McNall, who needed the money. Although the Kings had reached the finals the previous spring and played to sellout crowds, McNall's other business ventures were sputtering. The Toronto Argonauts, the Canadian Football League team he owned with Wayne Gretzky and actor John Candy, had lost $7 million in the past two years. Not only would Disney's involvement be good for the NHL's image, it could increase franchise values.

The plan was simple but unprecedented. Eisner would submit a letter offering to purchase an expansion franchise for $50 million under the outlined terms. Stein would take it from there.

Then Stein said to McNall, "We ought to present the same opportunity to Wayne Huizenga."

▲ ▲ ▲

Huizenga knew from his experience with Major League Baseball that expansion was typically a one or two year process, so there was no use rushing to New York or making a special trip. Hockey could wait. He just happened to be in town a few weeks after his phone conversation with Stein when he stopped by the NHL's offices.

Huizenga and Stein discussed the Marlins, Joe Robbie Stadium, and Godfrey Wood's failed NHL expansion bid of two years ago. Stein told Huizenga the NHL was interested in the South Florida market. Huizenga said he'd be interested in owning a team or putting together an ownership group.

"We're working on something," Stein revealed. "We're looking to do an expansion on a special circumstance and it doesn't make sense for us to expand by just one team. We could do it, but it would be better to expand with two teams."

Sure, Huizenga thought. *In one or two years.*

"We won't go through the normal process," Stein said. "We'd go at the same price as the last expansion, $50 million. But you've got to tell me, do you want it or don't you?"

Said Huizenga: "Let me think about it."

Stein never mentioned Michael Eisner or Disney.

Shortly after his face-to-face with Huizenga, Stein met with Billy Cunningham at his Villanova, Pennsylvania home. Cunningham, then a part-owner of the Miami Heat of the National Basketball Association, was a basketball star with the 76ers around the same time that Stein, a Philadelphia native, was working for the Flyers. They were friends and Cunningham wanted to know what it would take for him and Heat majority owner Louis Schaffel to acquire an NHL expansion team.

Stein hesitated.

"Maybe you oughta speak to Wayne Huizenga," he said.

Cunningham never discussed a possible deal with Huizenga and Stein didn't press him further. Stein says Huizenga rejected the idea of working with the Heat partners. Huizenga remembers it differently.

"My impression was that they [the NHL] didn't want the Heat to have a team," Huizenga recalled. "Gil Stein said to me, 'The Heat wants to have this franchise and Cunningham is a friend of mine. You have to be careful this doesn't get out because if it gets out, Cunningham is going to come back and put the pressure on me.'"

When he returned to Florida, Huizenga discussed the NHL deal with three of his closest consultants: Rochon, attorney Jim Blosser, and Carl Barger, the new president of the Marlins and Huizenga's best friend. Although Huizenga knew hockey people, such as Pittsburgh Penguins owner Howard Baldwin and New Jersey Devils owner John McMullen (who also owned the Houston Astros baseball team), he never discussed the deal with them or anybody else. The team would play in Miami Arena — there was no other choice in South Florida — but nobody from Huizenga's office discussed possible lease arrangements with Arena officials.

"We just kept it in the office," Huizenga said. "I never discussed it with any hockey people. We weren't even sure if it would work. I asked some people, 'Do you think hockey would work down here?' and some would say yes, some would say no. And I felt comfortable that the Latin community, even though they're perceived as being big baseball fans, would also like hockey."

Stein kept the deal quiet, too, both out of his desire to prevent the Heat people from finding out and because of Eisner's almost comical anxiety: The CEO of the most famous entertainment company in the world was worried the NHL might turn him down.

Eisner and Huizenga didn't realize they weren't courting the NHL, the

NHL was courting them. If anybody was going to do any rejecting, it was Disney and Huizenga.

In mid-November, Huizenga called Stein and told him he wanted to go through with the deal.

"We'll probably put a group together," Huizenga said.

"This is going to happen fast," Stein replied.

"That's OK," Huizenga assured him, still thinking fast meant a year.

One week later, Huizenga and Stein spoke over dinner in New York.

"Wayne, I think we're moving along," Stein said. "I think we could get you a team. We're meeting at the Breakers in December. I talked to a couple of our Board members and this is something we could get done at the December meetings."

Huizenga was startled. Although he was used to working as many hours as it took to get a deal done quickly, this one was moving at an incredible pace with hardly any work being done on his end. Stein instructed Huizenga to send along some financial information and write a letter officially requesting a franchise. He would handle the rest.

"We didn't need any security checks or to check out their finances," Stein said. "The truth is, we didn't do any checking at all. I felt I could get the governors' approval, but Michael was concerned. He didn't want it out that he was seeking a franchise if there was any chance of the Governors turning him down. He didn't know what he was dealing with."

In short, Huizenga and Eisner were dealing with a league desperate for both the credibility Blockbuster and Disney could bring them, along with the $75 million in franchise fees. For Eisner, the major decision was whether he or Disney would purchase the franchise; Disney ended up being the owner.

The issue was a little more complicated for Huizenga, who didn't truly desire sole ownership of a hockey team. But the problem was timing. It was already late November. Stein knew the easiest and quietest way to do the deal was with Huizenga or Blockbuster as the sole owners, so the League wouldn't have to run security checks on minority investors. Huizenga agreed to buy the team now and possibly sell pieces of it later. There was another element: Huizenga had privately hatched the idea for a Blockbuster-owned sports and entertainment theme park in South Florida, complete with a hockey arena, baseball stadium, movie studio, TV studio, and shopping arcade. Who would own the team: Huizenga or Blockbuster?

"If we did Blockbuster Park, it made sense for Blockbuster to own the programming, just like Turner owns the Braves," Huizenga said, explaining his decision to purchase the team privately. "We owned Spelling Entertainment, so we would have moved some of Spelling there and done television shows from Blockbuster Park. But it didn't make sense for

Blockbuster to own the team if we weren't going to get the park done. I knew I couldn't put Blockbuster in that position."

In early December, shortly before the Board of Governors meeting at The Breakers, Huizenga received another phone call from Stein.

"Could you be at the meetings?" Stein asked.

Huizenga, whose offices were less than 45 minutes away, said he could.

"Come to my suite first," Stein instructed. "Then I'll send for you to come down and meet with the Governors. Michael will be there, too."

Michael?

One phone call confirmed Huizenga's suspicion. Michael was Michael Eisner. The NHL's seventh expansion would be a multi-media event.

▲ ▲ ▲

Harry Wayne Huizenga III describes himself as a "fat" (not quite), "bald-headed" (just about), "rich guy" (no doubt about it). He has a ruddy complexion and a little boy's smile, piercing ice blue eyes, and he looks like somebody's uncle. If there's one thing that gives away the businessman in him, it's that he appears so much more natural in a suit and tie than in a rolled-up, open-at-the-neck dress shirt or even shorts and a polo shirt. The Florida Marlins program once ran a picture of Huizenga wearing a team jacket and seeming as comfortable as a little boy who had been forced by his parents into wearing a stiff pair of wool pants.

He arrived into the world with a broken leg on December 29, 1937, in Evergreen Park, Illinois, but barely broke stride from that point on. At 16, Wayne and his family moved to Fort Lauderdale, where he played for the Pinecrest High School football team (the team's nickname was the Panthers) and developed a love of fast cars and hard work. Although never much of a student, Wayne was intense about the things that interested him, and one of those things was making money.

In 1962, Wayne borrowed $5,000 from his father-in-law and purchased a second-hand garbage truck. He built a garbage route in Pompano Beach into Waste Management, a billion-dollar waste collection company and the largest in the world. In 1984, Huizenga sold the company and, shortly afterward, acquired Blockbuster Entertainment Corp. from a Dallas, Texas entrepreneur. Huizenga's seven-year success story was front cover news in all of the financial magazines: He built a 19-store, $7 million regional chain into a $4 billion leader of the video rental industry with over 3,700 stores in 11 countries.

Huizenga was purely a businessman who kept score by how much money he made. He was making a business deal in 1990 when he bought half of Joe Robbie Stadium and 15 percent of the Dolphins, and it was business again when he plunked down $95 million for the Marlins. By that time, Huizenga had amassed a personal fortune of $800 million.

"I bought the Dolphins because I wanted to make a profit," Huizenga said. "Bringing in the Marlins was a business deal because it brought more activity to Joe Robbie Stadium. But the hockey team I did not do for business reasons. The hockey team I did because it was the right thing to do for South Florida. I didn't want to lose money, but I didn't care if I made money. To me, it was the right thing to do."

Although Huizenga's office walls are decorated with the magazine covers he has appeared on, he claims to detest the public spotlight. After completing the Dolphins-Robbie Stadium deal, Huizenga didn't understand why there had to be a press conference; in the past, buying half of a building and 15 percent of a company was worth a few lines in the newspaper or a short interview. The Dolphins and Marlins purchases were small potatoes compared to the multi-billion dollar deals he consummated and surely of less importance. Huizenga didn't think any differently about buying an NHL team.

"It was very anti-climactic compared to the Marlins," Huizenga said. "With the Marlins, it was a long waiting period. The community was involved. It was on-again, off-again. The newspapers were doing all sorts of things. We weren't talking about hockey, then all of a sudden — boom! — a hockey team. So it wasn't big excitement."

For Huizenga, there was only sadness. On December 9, one day before the NHL Board of Governors convened in Palm Beach, Carl Barger died while attending the baseball owners meetings in Louisville, Kentucky. A grief-stricken Huizenga received word late that afternoon that the friend who was going to help him build the Marlins and the hockey team had suffered a fatal heart attack.

Huizenga, who usually operates at warp speed with no distractions when a deal is nearing completion, was in no mood to do anything but mourn. The following morning, December 10, after a sleepless night, he got out of bed, dressed for work, and put on the strongest public face he could.

He had no choice. At his moment of personal despair, Huizenga had to conduct his business for the day. The NHL couldn't wait. On his way out the door, Huizenga looked down and saw the newspapers on his patio.

The sports pages contained nothing about Huizenga's meeting with the Board of Governors.

The front page had a picture of Carl Barger.

So began what a *Miami Herald* headline would call Huizenga's "worst good day."

▲ ▲ ▲

"It is still a fantasy," wrote Dave Joseph of the Fort Lauderdale *Sun-Sentinel* on December 10. "A beyond-your-wildest-dreams wish that South Florida will one day have an NHL team. For those hoping for that one day, Wednesday evening's game ... will only make the wait that much longer."

As part of its strategy to spread interest in hockey and test potential expansion sites, the NHL scheduled two neutral-site games for each team during the 1992-93 season. Miami got its turn on December 9 and 12,842 fans turned out for the first regular season NHL game in Florida, not knowing that in less than 24 hours, they'd have their own team. Even the press didn't know what was taking place behind the scenes.

Still, there were rumors and hints the wait might be shorter than expected. Two days before the Board of Governors meeting, Wirtz told the *Chicago Tribune* the Board would vote on Huizenga's application for a conditional franchise. The story didn't make front page news in Chicago or South Florida; the *Sun-Sentinel* buried it within its measly hockey coverage. Mel Lowell, the Tampa Bay Lightning's vice president, said he would welcome a rival on Florida's east coast. Jerry Bernfeld of the Miami Sports and Exhibition Authority revealed he had heard Huizenga would appear before the Board.

Stein and McNall did their best to keep a secret. When the governors looked at their agendas for the meetings, they saw expansion listed as a general issue, not an immediate possibility to be voted upon.

A few days before the meetings officially convened, Stein had appeared before the League's 10-member advisory committee and outlined the proposal to bring in Huizenga and Disney. They granted unanimous approval. With that step completed, Stein turned to his next problem: getting Eisner to fly in from California for the meetings.

"I told him he should be there, but he didn't want to come," Stein recalled. "He kept saying, 'What if they turn me down?' I told him the chances of the Board turning him down were zero if he was there. If he wasn't there, who knows? Maybe a few noses would get out of joint. Finally, he hopped on a plane and came down."

On the day of the meetings, Huizenga and Eisner were secretly ushered into Stein's suite. Mickey Mouse and Minnie Mouse dolls holding Blockbuster video cases had been placed on a chair. Stein greeted his guests, then went downstairs and made his presentation to the full Board of Governors. Huizenga and Eisner stayed behind and talked hockey.

While Huizenga and Eisner chatted, Stein filled in the governors on what had happened over the past two months. He told them about his initial meeting with Eisner in Hollywood and Huizenga's introduction to McNall at Burbank Airport. As the story continued, a sense of excitement built among the governors. They realized this expansion was happening now, before their

21

very eyes, with no time to meet with their consultants, study the applicants' backgrounds, or consider the consequences.

"What surprised me was that it was more of an immediate possibility, rather than a long-term possibility," recalled Bill Torrey, the New York Islanders' governor. "South Florida was definitely a long-term objective of the League, to put a team in here. To do it as quickly as that, the immediacy of it, was a surprise. This was the first time that expansion came out of the blue. There was big excitement."

Only the governors of the new franchises in Tampa Bay and Ottawa contained their excitement, and for good reason. The amateur draft, held every June, is conducted in reverse order of finish, with the worst team picking first and the best team picking last. In expansion years, the new franchises get the top picks. The Lightning and Senators, well on their way to finishing at or near the bottom, were concerned that the new teams would pick ahead of them. Tampa Bay Governor Phil Esposito worried that having another team in Florida would hurt his team at the gate or in terms of TV audiences.

"Some negotiating had to be done," Torrey said. "But for the overall long-term good of the League, you just couldn't reject them."

Less than an hour later, without meeting the applicants, the governors voted unanimously in favor of awarding conditional franchises to Huizenga and Eisner.

"It was the fastest expansion in the history of sports," Stein said. "It took less than an hour."

By that time, Huizenga and Eisner had been moved to a room adjoining the Governors meeting. Huizenga was joined by Rochon and Blosser, as well as his father, Harry. Finally, Huizenga and Eisner were ushered into the conference room, where they were questioned by the governors. Eisner wore a Mighty Ducks hockey jersey from the movie and a Goofy hat. Huizenga, who was in no mood to laugh the day after his best friend's death, wore a suit.

"We don't think Miami's the right place for you to play," the governors told Huizenga. "We think you should play in Broward."

"I agree," Huizenga said.

"We've been down to the Miami facility," they said. "It's not really adequate for two teams. It's imperative that you build a new arena."

Huizenga said that was fine with him.

How about Tampa and possible infringements upon its territory? The Lightning owned the NHL's TV rights for the entire state and would have to hand over a portion of those rights to the new team.

Huizenga agreed to help the Lightning with advertising, promoting hockey in Florida, and with the building of an arena if the proposed one in Tampa fell through.

The governors asked Huizenga and Eisner more questions, and then took another vote. Once again, their approval was unanimous.

"There's no question in my mind that had it not been for the quality of the two candidates, it wouldn't have been done so quickly," Torrey said. "It wasn't a planned expansion, but when the opportunity came to bring in Michael Eisner and Disney, and Wayne Huizenga and Blockbuster, that changed. If it had been Godfrey Wood and company a second time, it wouldn't have happened."

The governors were thrilled. McNall called it "probably the most important thing I've ever done." Maple Leafs general manager Cliff Fletcher called the expansion "great for the game. These guys are major league." Stein called it a "great day for hockey." The hockey media was surprised, but nearly unanimous in its approval and interpretation of the day's events: If Disney and Blockbuster were involved, then hockey was becoming major league.

Huizenga wasn't as happy as he might have been. The death of his friend pained him and this was no time for rejoicing. South Florida wanted him to smile. He couldn't.

"You try to forget about Carl's death for today, and try to get up for the occasion," Huizenga said as tears welled in his eyes.

The day that was 54 years in the making for South Florida should have been joyous for everyone involved. It might have been a time to reflect on the failed efforts of the Tropical Hockey League, Herb Martin, Jerry Saperstein, and Godfrey Wood. Huizenga had succeeded where everyone else failed, as if all he had to do was snap his golden fingers. Miami had become the fourth city in the United States with all four major professional sports and Huizenga owned all or part of three of them.

Before leaving The Breakers, Huizenga wrote a check for $100,000 as a down payment on the franchise and promised to pay the remaining $49.9 million when the franchise officially entered the League. Driving down I–95, he called Dean Jordan, the Marlins' director of marketing and broadcasting, from his cellular phone.

"Dean," Huizenga said calmly. "We've got a hockey team."

CHAPTER 3

Home Is Where
the Heat Is

A few minor adjustments to the Emma Lazarus inscription at the base of the Statue of Liberty is all it takes to sum up the NHL's theory on welcoming new owners. "Give us your $50 million," the revised version would read. "We'll give you our tired, our poor, the wretched refuse of our teams!"

The governors would assure there would be no superstars playing for the new franchises in Anaheim and South Florida, merely outcasts from the existing 24 teams. Huizenga and Disney had been courted, and if the past was any indication, they would now get slapped in the face.

Approving Huizenga and Disney was the easy part for the NHL Board of Governors. There remained issues to be settled, primarily when the new franchises would play their first games and in which divisions they would be placed. With only six months before the Entry Draft and, if necessary, an expansion draft, a 1993-94 startup would give the new owners little time to build their organizations. And there was the matter of arena leases on both coasts, no simple matter.

"It would be better for us if we didn't go this season," Huizenga said in December. "It's a big job. If we want to do it right, we should follow the trend of baseball. Have a name contest, unveil the uniform, build enthusiasm so we can sell season tickets. That would be much better than jamming everything into a couple of months in a hit or miss arrangement."

Timing aside, there was at least one very good reason for moving forward as quickly as possible: the 1993 NHL Entry Draft crop was considered one of the strongest in decades with the top seven prospects — Alexandre Daigle, Chris Pronger, Chris Gratton, Rob Niedermayer, Viktor Kozlov, Jason Arnott, and Paul Kariya — all potential stars.

That was on the minds of Ottawa Senators President Bruce Firestone and Tampa Bay Lightning General Manager Phil Esposito when they questioned what the order of the 1993 Draft would be if Disney and Huizenga joined the league next season. The Senators, Lightning, and San Jose Sharks were bound to pick one-two-three from this inviting pool and didn't want their bounty usurped by the incoming teams. The issue was easily settled: Anaheim and South Florida would select after Ottawa, San Jose, and Tampa Bay, but no other teams could pick ahead of the expansion clubs. Anaheim and South Florida would pick one-two, with the order to be determined, in the 1994 Draft.

"We've been assured that if we finish last overall this year, we will have the first choice," Firestone said. "That was our No. 1 concern and my No. 1 question to the committee."

But the general managers, especially those with dual roles as governors, had a hard time grasping this "one for all, all for one" concept regarding the expansion draft when they met in Toronto in mid-January.

"Here, you can have our garbage," is basically what they wanted to say to their new rivals.

"That's not right," said Gil Stein and several other governors, who were watching the Senators stumble through a season in which they would win only one road game. They were concerned the rapid expansion of five teams in three seasons would destroy the competitive balance of the League and negatively affect attendance (bad teams, especially bad expansion teams, are low road draws).

"I gave my word to Eisner and Huizenga that they would have a fair draft, that it wouldn't be like an Ottawa draft," Stein said. "But I knew the battle I'd be taking on."

Battle? That's an understatement. Players are a team's most valuable commodity, so treasured that millions of dollars are spent each year on developing minor leaguers who have little hope of ever reaching the NHL. But player evaluation is a tricky business; many first round draft picks have never played a game in the NHL and numerous NHLers were once deemed career minor leaguers. Nobody is always right and nobody wants to give away anything on the chance they're wrong.

For the Tampa Bay and Ottawa expansion drafts the previous year, each existing team protected 14 skaters — forwards and defensemen — and two goaltenders; players with fewer than two years NHL experience were exempt, so teams didn't have to protect their youngest prospects.

That's why the Lightning and Senators had very little from which to choose in the 1992 Expansion Draft and ended up with the dregs. Ottawa got Peter Sidorkiewicz, a struggling backup, from Hartford, and Mark LaForest, a career minor leaguer known by the inspired nickname, "Trees."

25

Tampa Bay got career backup Wendell Young and Frederic Chabot, who was rotting in the Canadiens' system.

True to form, both teams had miserable goaltending and were well on their way to predictably bad first seasons by the time the Disney and Huizenga franchises were awarded. The Senators were so awful that a national hockey magazine compared them to the best team in the minor leagues and decided there wasn't much difference.

But when the expansion committee recommended that each existing team be allowed to protect only one goaltender and a split of nine forwards and five defensemen — and exempted only players with less than one year of NHL experience — the general managers reacted as if their first-born was being taken away. Worse!

The "let them eat cake" charge was led by Chicago Blackhawks owner Bill Wirtz and General Manager Bob Pulford and Toronto Maple Leafs General Manager Cliff Fletcher.

"They were furious," Stein recalled.

The "give the dog a bone" side was led, surprisingly, by Boston Bruins owner Jeremy Jacobs and General Manager Harry Sinden. Surprisingly because Jacobs and Sinden had a reputation for having the tightest wallets in the League.

Goaltending was the main battleground. Most teams want two solid goaltenders: a top man to play 50 or 60 games and a backup to play 20 or 30 games and fill in if the top guy gets hurt. In many cases, the No. 2 goalie is a prospect who will some day be a No. 1. No team carries more than two goaltenders, so by protecting two goalies in the 1992 Expansion Draft, the teams exposed only veteran minor leaguers. A similar draft would place Anaheim and Florida in a similar situation as Ottawa and Tampa Bay.

"There was great leadership on the committee and they thought the teams brought in should have a chance to be competitive, and the key was goal-tending," Stein recalled. "The plan that came up was that every club could protect only one goaltender."

That didn't sit well with the Leafs, whose goaltending tandem consisted of veteran Grant Fuhr, a future Hall of Famer, and the outstanding rookie Felix Potvin. The Blackhawks, who had Ed Belfour and Jim Waite, were suddenly high on Waite and didn't want to lose him. At least four other teams had a lot to lose: the Sabres (Dominik Hasek and Daren Puppa), the Rangers (Mike Richter and John Vanbiesbrouck), the Devils (Chris Terreri and Craig Billington), the Canucks (Kirk McLean and Kay Whitmore), and the Islanders (Glenn Healy and Mark Fitzpatrick).

"Any team that had two good goalies wasn't very happy," Bill Torrey said. "Anybody that had one goalie was very happy. And remember, this came out of the blue. Teams didn't have two years to set themselves up for the expansion draft."

The old school general managers promised a revolt. Sinden and Jacobs reasoned with them.

"Is it better for the established teams if these teams stay weak for 10 years?" Sinden asked. "Let's think in terms of the League. A new team coming in has a right to be competitive."

Stein tried swaying the governors, but had lost much of his persuasive power. The day after the governors voted in Huizenga and Disney, they named Gary Bettman, the former vice-president of the National Basketball Association, as the League's first commissioner; Stein stayed on as president in a limited role until Bettman officially took office. The expansion committee, whose recommendation the governors accepted so easily in December with $75 million from Disney and Huizenga at stake, was now being attacked.

The governors' problem was that they had promised favorable expansion draft rules to Huizenga and Disney when the franchises were granted. Of course, that didn't mean the governors' general managers were happy about it.

"All of a sudden, there was money made available to the owners that they wouldn't have had otherwise," Torrey said. "Maybe the general managers didn't like protecting only one goalie, but I think their bosses liked getting five million bucks."

The peacemaker was Ottawa Senators Governor Bruce Firestone, who knew firsthand how desperately a first-year team needs good goaltending. Rather than cry over his misfortune and wish the same upon the new teams, Firestone insisted that what happened to the Senators wasn't in the best interests of the League.

"We have to do it the right way," Firestone said.

Firestone wasn't being completely objective in this view. As part of the plan, the Senators and Lightning could each select two players chosen by the new teams in the expansion draft.

"I think we really looked at it as being in everybody's best interest, short and long term, for the expansion teams to be competitive early on," said Brian Burke, the Hartford Whalers general manager who went on to become Bettman's hockey man in the NHL office. "We supported the plan, even though we hoped teams that lost goalies in last year's draft wouldn't be subject to losing one this year."

The final vote, though not unanimous, sustained the expansion committee's recommendation.

"We could've had a fight," Stein said. "I felt that we had already given approval to whatever the committee came up with, but I didn't want that. I wanted a consensus."

The decision reached that day, January 14, turned out to be the most important in the early history of the two new teams. Outstanding goaltending would, indeed, keep them competitive in their first three seasons and the tandem that ended up in South Florida was arguably the best in the League.

For the first time, the NHL's new owners would actually get something for their money.

▲ ▲ ▲

Huizenga was dealing with other issues, too. For scheduling purposes, the NHL needed to know by March 1 whether the new teams would begin play in the 1993-94 or 1994-95 seasons. But unlike in baseball, where Carl Barger handled the startup process, Huizenga didn't have a single hockey man on his staff. Of greater urgency, he didn't have a lease.

Huizenga wavered on this decision. Ultimately, his course of action would be dictated by Disney; if they went forward, he'd go forward. If they didn't, he wouldn't. Huizenga didn't want Disney getting a head start on his team, and the League didn't want to hold two expansion drafts.

"I would've preferred to wait a year because we were busy with baseball," Huizenga said. "But Disney's deal was ready and they wanted to get going. Gil Stein was pushing, and then Michael [Eisner] called me and said, 'Can we get it done this year?' And there were some people in the NHL who wanted it to happen."

Good reason for that: The new teams wouldn't pay the balance of their expansion fees until the June before they started play and several franchises, including Peter Pocklington's in Edmonton, dearly needed the money immediately.

Huizenga also worried about the future. He was committed to building an arena that met the League's guidelines regarding capacity and luxury suites. The arena site search began soon after the franchise was granted and several South Florida communities bid for Huizenga's attention.

The City of Hallandale offered land near Gulfstream Park racetrack. Officials from Hollywood, Miramar, Pembroke Pines, and Pompano Beach proffered land deals and tax incentives while virtually salivating over the money a sports arena could bring into their cities. They assumed the arena would be built with Huizenga or Blockbuster money. Bad assumption.

They didn't know that Huizenga was already envisioning one of his grandest plans: Blockbuster Park, a combination sports and entertainment complex with a hockey arena, baseball stadium, Little League stadium, movie studio, shopping arcade, and TV studio. A concept that started as a sports complex for the Marlins and his hockey team was growing by the day and if the plans ever became reality, they would require far more land than was being offered; a mini-city, as it turned out.

In early January, Huizenga began looking for hockey men to run his team. One of the first candidates for general manager was Mike Keenan, who had just been fired as general manager of the Chicago Blackhawks. Keenan, a fiery, independent soul who has been known to step on toes, including those of his superiors, interviewed for positions in both South Florida and Anaheim.

"I met with him, but we never made him an offer," Huizenga said. "His asking price was way up. He wanted to be general manager and coach and I thought the right guy could do that."

The right guy wasn't Keenan, and it's easy to see why: Huizenga hires company men who are loyal to their employers. Keenan certainly did not fit that description. Keenan says he dropped out of the running because there wasn't enough time to properly prepare a team for the 1993-94 season. Logic said he was right, time proved him wrong.

Time was not on Huizenga's side in January 1993. He hadn't decided whether he wanted a separate general manager, coach, and president, a combination general manager/coach, or a combination general manager/president. With no background in hockey, he knew very little about the men he interviewed for the jobs: Keenan, Bob Clarke, Jack Ferreira, David Poile, and Pierre Lacroix for general manager; Bill Torrey and Jack Diller, formerly of Madison Square Garden, for president.

Thousands of potential buyers inquired about season tickets, but the team didn't even have a marketing and sales department, or a public relations department. Don Smiley, Dean Jordan, and Jonathan Mariner from the Marlins helped as much as possible, but opening day of the baseball season was only three months away.

Huizenga finally settled on a novel solution to these problems: Forget about them.

"Wayne said we can't worry about it until we get the Marlins started," Jordan recalled.

But he needed a general manager, a president, and a lease, and those problems couldn't wait.

▲ ▲ ▲

If Robert Rosenthal, Stephen Walsh, Ralph Palleschi, and Paul R. Greenwood had glanced away from the bottom line and studied their hockey history, they would have known that William A. Torrey was one of the few people in the NHL who could be called a legend because of what he accomplished in the front office.

They hadn't. In 1992, the new management team of the New York Islanders only saw a team slipping in the standings, failing to qualify for the playoffs in three of the past five seasons, and playing in front of an increasingly large number of empty seats at Nassau Coliseum.

So one day, they called Torrey into their office and asked how he planned to change the franchise's fortunes.

"I'm going to continue to operate the way I have," Torrey told them, firm as ever in his convictions.

That wouldn't do, they said.

"If you want to make a change," Torrey said, "then there are no hard feelings. I've had a good run."

Which was, in typical Torrey fashion, vastly understating the truth. Torrey didn't merely have a good run. He had one of the greatest runs by any team builder in sports history.

In 1972, after spending five seasons in Oakland as executive vice president of the California Golden Seals, working under eccentric owner Charles O. Finley, Torrey faced a career decision. Long Island and Atlanta had been awarded expansion franchises and Torrey was offered the general manager's job with both teams. Torrey, unsure over which job to accept, sat down for lunch one day with Pittsburgh Steelers owner Art Rooney.

"He told me two things," Torrey recalled. " 'Bill, don't go to Atlanta, go to New York, because you won't have to sell tickets. Long Island's a market unto its own. And second, if you're successful in New York, you'll be a big success. In Atlanta, nobody will know you exist. You've been through that in Oakland. You don't need that.

'However, if you're not successful, or if you make a mistake, you're going to hear about it.' "

Torrey, then 38, chose the New York Islanders and from the day he was hired, February 14, 1972, he made very few mistakes.

That June in the expansion draft, Torrey selected goaltender Bill Smith, who went on to a Hall of Fame career with the Islanders, and Ed Westfall, who became the team's first captain. In the Islanders' first amateur draft, Torrey picked Lorne Henning, Bob Nystrom, and Garry Howatt, all three of whom went on to play key roles on the Islanders' four Stanley Cup championship teams.

The Islanders won only 12 games their first year, but Torrey knew he'd have to be patient and smart. He was both.

In June, Torrey hired Al Arbour as his coach. Over the next five years, Torrey would draft three future Hall of Famers — Denis Potvin, Bryan Trottier, and Mike Bossy — and several of the key players on the Islanders' championship teams: Clark Gillies, Ken Morrow, Dave Langevin, Stefan Persson, Duane Sutter, and John Tonelli (he also drafted Neil Smith, who never played in the NHL, but went on to win a Stanley Cup as general manager of the New York Rangers).

What Torrey couldn't draft he stole from other teams in one-sided trades: J.P. Parise from the Minnesota North Stars, Bob Bourne from the Kansas

City Scouts, and, in one of his greatest coups of all, Butch Goring from the Los Angeles Kings. In their third year of existence, the Islanders upset the Rangers, their cross-river rivals, in the first round of the playoffs, and came within one game of reaching the finals. The Islanders were one of the elite teams in the NHL for the next four seasons and won their first of four consecutive Stanley Cups in 1980.

From nothing, Torrey had built a dynasty. The Islanders were so popular on Long Island that fans camped in front of the Coliseum the night before individual game tickets went on sale. Extra seats were shoehorned into every reasonable open space in the building, and some that weren't so reasonable. Cablevision, the Long Island cable company, picked up subscribers by the thousands thanks to one hot attraction: the Islanders.

The Islanders were Long Island's only professional sports team. Torrey and the winning team he created were its only sports heroes.

But the Islanders, like every great team, couldn't stay on top forever. The great players got older and either stuck around past their prime or retired.

"I was second-guessed the year after we lost the Cup," Torrey recalled. "I didn't trade four or five guys. Well, two of them were hurt. Second of all, I thought that after we won 19 or 20 series in a row, it wasn't right to break up the team right away.

"I remember a meeting we had with the scouts. We spent all day talking about the future. How do we move out certain guys? When do we move out certain guys? We were always competing against another team [the Rangers] in our own market, so to take the team back totally to where we were in 1972 was unacceptable. So we tried to do it in steps."

Winning had its rewards and its drawbacks. A disadvantage was picking late in each year's amateur draft. After choosing Pat LaFontaine with the first pick in 1983, the Islanders had seven consecutive drafts in which they either picked poorly or unluckily. None of their first-rounders made an impact. Few of their late rounders ever played in the NHL. Duncan MacPherson and Bruce Melanson, the Islanders' first two picks in 1984, died before playing in a single NHL game; MacPherson died in an avalanche, Melanson of a heart disorder. Two other first rounders, Dean Chynoweth and Kevin Cheveldayoff, suffered career-hindering injuries shortly after they were drafted. Torrey was accused of being too loyal to his scouting staff, led by Gerry "Tex" Ehman, whose bias toward big Western Canadians who couldn't skate became a running joke in hockey.

Suddenly, the genius was perceived as an old, bow tie wearing, bumbling fool, ready for the junk heap. The game had seemingly passed him by and Torrey's image didn't get any better when LaFontaine, the only remaining superstar on the Islanders, refused to report to training camp for the 1991-92 season because of a salary dispute.

31

The fans sided with LaFontaine.

"It seemed as if every night this one guy had a different sign putting down Bill," recalled Greg Bouris, who at the time was the Islanders' Director of Media Relations.

Torrey, as is his way, refused to take the dispute public. Gerry Meehan, LaFontaine's agent, didn't have the same approach and criticized team owner John Pickett.

"We're tired of hearing for a year and a day that the assets are frozen," Meehan said. "If that's not the case, maybe Pickett should call up Bill Torrey and get their signals together."

Which is what Pickett and Torrey did after Meehan blasted Pickett during a TV interview on SportsChannel.

"He went on our television one night in our own building and personally criticized the owner," Torrey recalled. "Once that occurred, Pickett called me the next day and said, 'That's it. I don't care what it is. It's over.' From that time on, it was a matter of figuring out the best way to salvage the situation."

The LaFontaine dispute ended on October 25, 1991, a Black Friday that will never be forgotten by Islanders fans and symbolically marked the end of Torrey's welcome on Long Island: He traded LaFontaine and two others to the Sabres, and also dealt Brent Sutter, a two-time Cup winner with the Islanders and one of their most popular players, to the Blackhawks. Meehan later said he would have accepted the four-year, $6 million offer from any other team but the Islanders.

When LaFontaine returned to Long Island later that year, the fans gave him a standing ovation. Torrey got another sign: Let's Hang Billy Bow Tie.

The Islanders limped through their fourth straight sub-.500 season and missed the playoffs for the second straight time. They were no longer the hot team and there was no demand for tickets. The Islanders couldn't give them away.

In August, Rosenthal, Walsh, Palleschi, and Greenwood took over the management of the team and replaced Torrey with Don Maloney. It was an insult; Maloney was too young, too inexperienced, and Torrey's assistant for only one year. He was also a former member of the Rangers, the Islanders' hated rivals.

"These guys came in and said, 'Geez, you haven't won a Stanley Cup in seven or eight years,'" Torrey said. "I figured if that was their impression of me after meeting me five or six times, it wouldn't work if I stayed. So why, at this stage in my life, should I drive myself crazy?"

But Torrey, too proud to complain and loyal to the franchise, continued in his limited role as a consultant to the team and its alternate governor. He scouted the Islanders' minor league players, attended Board of Governors meetings, and offered advice when it was asked for. For a man who had spent 20 years overseeing every aspect of the Islanders' operation, this was like telling the president of a major corporation that he was now working in the mailroom.

"It was tougher on him than he let on," said Nelson Doubleday, the New York Mets chairman and a friend of Torrey's. "The Islanders were his franchise. He built them, and he built them again."

The time had come to move on, but to where? With four years remaining on his contract with Nassau Sports, the Islanders' parent company, Torrey had enough work to keep him reasonably busy. He was 58, unmarried, and had four children on Long Island. Other teams were calling and an unfounded rumor had Torrey becoming Vice President of Hockey Operations for the NHL. His Hall of Fame credentials were firm and nothing, not even these four men from Long Island, could keep him out.

Despite this impressive résumé, the name Bill Torrey meant nothing to Huizenga until Doubleday called and suggested he speak with Torrey about any job openings. In January, Huizenga invited Torrey to Florida to watch an NFL playoff game between the Dolphins and San Diego Chargers at Joe Robbie Stadium. Standing in a luxury suite overlooking the field, they discussed the new hockey team and Huizenga's plans. Over the following month, they spoke on the phone and met several times. The admiration was mutual.

"My interest in the job didn't hit me until I had a couple of meetings with Wayne," Torrey said. "I liked Wayne. I liked his personality. He interested me as much as the job did. The project interested me. Building a team and building a building at the same time in this market kind of got my juices going."

Huizenga wasn't sure what kind of challenge he was offering Torrey. He needed a person to run the team and help build a new arena. Some of Huizenga's candidates for the general manager's job, including Keenan, had expressed interest in coaching, too. A few others thought they could be GM and President. Torrey figured it was a two-man job.

"My experience told me there was no way you could do both," said Torrey, who was involved in the building of Pittsburgh's Civic Arena in the early 1960s. "I advised him to find somebody to be general manager."

Huizenga immediately recognized Torrey for what he is: a loyal, knowledgeable hockey man, respected around the business, who could work within Huizenga's corporate structure.

"The name Bill Torrey didn't mean anything to me," Huizenga said. "It was his personality, his knowledge that came out just by talking to him. I deal a lot on first impressions and gut instincts. What's the chemistry? What's the personality of this guy and is he going to fit into my organization? Some guys might be smart as hell, but they don't fit in.

"My people checked him out. Everything always came back good."

And what might Huizenga's people have found out about Torrey?

He is the last man a reporter would approach to find out what's going on behind the scenes. He detests speaking off-the-record and will say what he wants on-the-record, but nothing more. He appears stern in his trademark bow tie, rumpled shirts, and simple sport jackets, but he is quick with a joke or story, almost always about hockey. He does not rip his employees in the media and if they want to question him, he expects them to do it to his face, not through the newspapers. He has spent countless hours on countless occasions sitting with a wayward young prospect or disgruntled veteran in a cold, darkened arena, talking through a problem. To agents, he is a tough negotiator who is respectful of his owner's wallet and won't throw around money the team doesn't have. They'd call him tight-fisted. He'd call himself prudent. Many detractors have questioned him, but he doesn't answer them unless asked, and then only if pressed. The most striking aspect of Torrey is that those who rip him are treated no differently than those who don't.

Some view him as pompous but, if anything, he is grandiose in his gestures. When Torrey stands, he seemingly unfolds his body, then hikes up his pants, folds his arms across his chest, and finally begins speaking. He is a big man who can fill a room with his presence, not because he is loud, but because he is there.

His allegiance to the man who signs his paycheck can never be questioned and his life revolves around hockey. If he's not at the rink or in his office, chances are he's at a meeting or sleeping. And, after all of these years, he still takes winning and losing the same way.

After a loss, "How're you doing, Bill?"

"Could be better."

And, after a win, smiling through tight lips, there is no need to ask.

He has won far more than he has lost, and this bottom line makes him confident.

Asked why he never responds to criticism, Torrey said, "There are days when you say, 'What the hell,' but, in the long run, when you resort to that it's an indication that you're trying to justify yourself."

Torrey's last official duty with the Islanders was casting their vote in favor of Huizenga and Disney at the Board of Governors meeting in Palm Beach. Although he couldn't have known it at the time, he was moving along to the third stage of his hockey career.

In late January, Torrey told the Islanders' managers that he wanted to settle his contract at the end of the season. They readily agreed. In mid-February, he came to terms with Huizenga and unofficially began the next part of his career as president of the South Florida hockey team, acting on a consulting basis while still occasionally scouting for the Islanders. The official announcement wouldn't be made for another two months, but

Torrey's new job was the worst-kept rumor in hockey. Insiders snickered that Torrey was going to Florida to play golf.

"They probably thought I was ready for the ash can," Torrey cracked.

No way. For Billy Bow Tie, it was February 14, 1972, all over again.

▲ ▲ ▲

From Day 1, the same problem had always kept South Florida and hockey from getting together: A place for the team to play. So when Huizenga Holdings President Rick Rochon and attorney Jim Blosser went to negotiate the new team's lease at Miami Arena, they confronted a Miami Sports and Exhibition Authority dealing from a house deck.

That was a take-it-or-leave-it problem in which one side knew the one pertinent, cold fact of the matter: Huizenga couldn't leave it. He had to take it. In the South Florida major league arena business, the City of Miami had a monopoly. There was no other suitable arena for an NHL team.

"Our thought was that there wasn't hockey down there," Rochon said. "We assumed that we could play in the Arena, but we were pretty sure of the fact it wouldn't be a great lease because the Heat had a fair amount of the revenue streams. As it turned out, there was nothing left."

Huizenga and his men looked enviously to the west, where the Walt Disney Company received an entirely different reception from the City of Anaheim. Like Huizenga, Disney had only one place to locate its new hockey team: the 17,250-seat Anaheim Arena. Unlike Huizenga, Disney could dictate the terms.

Miami Arena had a team: the NBA's Heat. Anaheim Arena didn't have a sporting tenant and the city had taken a huge gamble by constructing the $103 million building on $26 million worth of public land. Like St. Petersburg, which built a Major League Baseball stadium without first having a team, Anaheim owned what could turn out to be a white elephant, and a costly one, too, politically and financially. Under its operating agreement with Ogden Entertainment, the city owed Ogden up to $2.5 million annually for eight years if neither a professional basketball or hockey team played in the arena; with one franchise, the debt was reduced to $1.5 million a year.

With $1 million at stake, the City of Anaheim was willing to negotiate a sweetheart deal to get the team into its empty building for the 1993-94 season.

The City of Miami would have waited forever. The Heat, perhaps feeling slighted by Huizenga acquiring the franchise they wanted, were not in a charitable mood and didn't want to give away what was contractually theirs: all revenue streams from advertising and luxury suites under a generous eight-year lease negotiated in 1988 when the building opened.

"There's no doubt the Heat didn't want us there," Torrey said. "They viewed us as a competitor."

The MSEA, represented by Leisure Management, wasn't playing Santa Claus when the lease negotiations began shortly before Christmas 1992. Because of the Heat's lease, the Arena was losing money with little hope of reversing the bottom line under the status quo.

The Heat was paying the Arena approximately $350,000 a year for all advertising rights within the building and, in return, receiving nearly $4 million a year in advertising revenue, a startling return on their dollar of more than 1,000 percent! For about $300,000 a year for exclusive rights to 16 luxury suites which hang from the Arena ceiling, the Heat was pulling in about $1.6 million. The City of Miami had given away the store.

Worsening Huizenga's bargaining position was his desire for a short-term deal. He never intended to make Miami Arena the hockey team's permanent home and figured he'd have a new arena ready for his team in a minimum of two years.

"We wanted a short-term lease and they said, 'Bullshit. Take a long-term deal,'" Huizenga said. "Then we said, 'No.'"

Robert Franklin, general manager of the Arena, offered Huizenga three packages: a 10-year deal, a five-year deal, and a three-year deal with three one-year options. Huizenga said he wanted a two-year deal with four one-year options. The Arena made him pay the price; the longer the lease, the better the terms.

"To my recollection, Rick Rochon volunteered the fact that they only wanted a short-term deal because they were planning to build an arena in Broward County and they were willing to pay for it," Franklin said. "It's not like they were innocent little lambs coming to slaughter. They knew the reality.

"We took the position that since we weren't going to enjoy the long-term benefit of a hockey team, and they were going to add injury to insult by not only withdrawing the team, but were in the process of building a competitive arena, we felt we had to make hay while the sun shines."

Rochon says very little give-and-take occurred during the three months of lease negotiations. Much of the bargaining was on minor items; MSEA couldn't offer what the Heat already owned, but it drove a hard bargain on even negotiable items, such as game night staffing and share of concessions.

Huizenga signed a lease that would end up costing him $2.5 million a year for use of the Arena, nearly twice what the Heat pays, with little chance of recouping his investment on anything other than ticket sales. The costs of upgrading the playing surface and locker rooms would all come out of his pocket.

"It's not what you pay the arena, it's what you get back from the arena,"

Huizenga said. "The difference between what the Heat pays and gets back and what we pay and get back is about seven or eight million dollars in one year."

This was a win-win-lose situation.

The winners: the Heat, which could now offer their luxury suite subscribers NHL games, and MSEA, which has operated the Arena in the black since Huizenga signed the lease.

The loser: Huizenga.

"We knew we were going to lose money when we signed the lease," Dean Jordan said.

Even the conditions of the four one-year options weren't advantageous to Huizenga; each option would have to be exercised 14 months in advance. The option rules, which seemed meaningless at the time, would cause trouble for both sides three years later.

Disney had a far more satisfying negotiating experience with Anaheim. Under its 30-year contract, Ogden paid half of Disney's $25 million indemnity fee to the Kings. But because the indemnity fee was included in the $50 million franchise fee, Disney paid $12.5 million less for its franchise than Huizenga. Figuring it should have paid a $25 million indemnity in addition to the franchise price, Disney got a half-price deal!

The negotiating conditions couldn't have been more opposite. But by late February, with the League's March 1 deadline approaching, it was a foregone conclusion that South Florida and Anaheim would start in the 1993-94 season. The City of Anaheim wanted Disney in its building immediately. Disney wanted to squeeze as much as it could out of its bargaining position. And if Disney began play in 1993-94, the League wanted South Florida at the same time, thereby avoiding expansion drafts in four consecutive years. Only one man was reluctant.

"We went back and forth as to whether to play that year or the following year," Huizenga said. "We went along with it, but it wasn't something we wanted to do."

Either way, Huizenga was going to end up with the worst lease in the NHL.

▲ ▲ ▲

According to the official version, Bill Torrey was named President of the team 50 days after Bob Clarke was named General Manager. In reality, Torrey advised Huizenga in the hiring of a GM and recommended Clarke, 43, who at the time was doing nothing but pushing pencils across his desk as Senior Vice President of the Philadelphia Flyers.

For Clarke, who'd have more fun pushing pencils into an enemy's eye, that was no kind of job at all.

Until Bob Clarke came along, Gordie Howe was generally considered the greatest cheap shot artist in NHL history. The difference between Howe and Clarke was that after slashing an opponent behind the knees or high sticking him in the face, Howe dropped his gloves and settled matters on his own. Far more often than not under the same circumstances, Clarke skated back to the bench and let one of his goon teammates, usually Dave Schultz, fight the fight. Schultz grew to despise Clarke.

Despite this seeming cowardice, Clarke was considered one of the bravest players of all time, partly because he overcame diabetes to have a Hall of Fame career, and partly because of hockey's convoluted value system, under which men such as Clarke are viewed in the positive light of willing to do anything for their team. And he is.

Clarke's signature moment came in the 1972 Summit Series between the NHL and the Soviet Union. Much to Canada's dismay and embarrassment, the Soviets were leading the series after five games and a wondrous Russian named Valeri Kharlamov was having a glorious time, skating circles around the stunned NHLers. Then, in Game 6, Clarke took matters into his own hands. He slashed Kharlamov across the back of the leg, breaking his ankle. Kharlamov was neutralized, the NHL won the series, and Clarke was canonized.

No matter that if Kharlamov did to Clarke what Clarke did to Kharlamov, he would have been vilified as a cheap shot artist beyond reproach. According to the lore, Clarke went out and did whatever it took to ensure victory. In this case, it meant injuring the other team's best player.

"It's not something I was really proud of," Clarke said, "but I can't honestly say I was ashamed to do it."

Clarke was a little more ashamed when he speared Rod Seiling, one of his best friends, in front of the net during an NHL game in Toronto. His contrition didn't last long.

"Clarke is always hitting guys after the whistle," said Garry Howatt, the former Islander. "He's always sticking guys."

Philadelphia, so desperate for sports heroes that it eventually lionized a fictional one, movie boxer Rocky Balboa, had no trouble adopting a native of Flin Flon, Manitoba, as one of its own. When Clarke joined the Flyers in 1969, they were a bad team being bullied on a nightly basis. But led by Clarke, Bill Barber, Rick MacLeish, Bernie Parent, and a supporting cast of goons, the Flyers won the Stanley Cup in 1974 and 1975. Clarke was their leading scorer and captain and, in an era when players were already moving from team to team, he spent his entire 15 year career with the Flyers. Perhaps Philadelphia was the only place in which this odd battler with the crooked, toothless grin and scarred face would be welcome.

In Philadelphia, he was hockey.

"In the 1970s, only two players could dominate a game," Ken Dryden wrote in his acclaimed book, *The Game.* "One was Bobby Orr, the other Bobby Clarke. Clarke, a fierce, driven man, did it by the unrelenting mood he gave to a game, a mood so strong it penetrated his team and stayed on the ice even when he did not."

Although still a competent player, Clarke retired in 1984 and advanced to the next chapter of his Philadelphia Story: He was named General Manager of the Flyers.

Clarke couldn't have picked a better time to continue his legacy. The Flyers were already built to win and didn't need much grooming. They won three straight Patrick Division championships and reached the finals in 1985 and 1987, pushing the dynastic Edmonton Oilers to seven games in one of the most memorable series ever.

But the Flyers' talent camouflaged Clarke's lack of a manager's magic touch. He made a series of bad trades and oversaw disastrous drafts: from 1984 through 1989, the Flyers drafted only one player who went on to make an impact in the NHL: Scott Mellanby. It remains one of the most dismal runs by any GM in NHL history and in 1989-90, when the Flyers missed the playoffs for the first time in 17 seasons, the unimaginable happened. Clarke and Jay Snider, the president of the Flyers and the owner's son, had been disagreeing on the direction of the franchise, and Clarke didn't realize what he was walking into when he left his house on April 16, 1990, for a meeting with Snider. His wife knew.

"I was prepared for the worst," Sandy Clarke would tell *The Philadelphia Inquirer.* "I just had this uneasy feeling since the meeting they had the week before. I don't know what it was."

The meeting with Snider lasted 15 minutes. When it was over, Clarke didn't have a job.

Clarke handled the news better than his friends and family. Jody, his oldest daughter, removed her Flyers jewelry. Wade, their oldest son, stopped wearing his Flyers cap and jersey. Clarke wouldn't show any bitterness, although he later admitted to feeling hurt.

"I certainly don't consider myself a tragic figure," he said. "My career here has been outstanding. Most people, especially in pro sports, either get fired or change jobs once or twice in their careers. I just happened to go 21 years before it happened to me and I'm thankful for that."

Fortunately for Clarke, there were teams even worse than the Flyers. One of them was the Minnesota North Stars, who couldn't draw a crowd in one of the hockey hotbeds of the United States. There was a simple reason for that: They were awful. After losing most of their games that season, they also lost their general manager, Jack Ferreira, who signed on with the expansion San Jose Sharks. So, on June 8, 1990, six weeks after he was fired, Clarke became a member of an NHL team other than the Flyers for the first time. Now he was vice-president and general manager of the Stars.

In Clarke's first season in Minnesota, the Stars had one of the most unlikely runs by any team in any sport: Despite winning only 27 of 80 games and finishing fourth in the Norris Division, the Stars qualified for the playoffs and didn't lose until the finals. But Clarke was working under difficult circumstances. Most of the scouts and front office staff had departed to start up the San Jose Sharks, leaving Clarke virtually on his own. His draft record improved over the Flyers years, but not by much. He grabbed Derian Hatcher, who became an impact defenseman, in the first round of the 1990 draft, and then came up empty. So did the Stars, who floundered.

Now an unfortunate pattern was forming in Clarke's managerial career. Perhaps he wasn't cut out for the job. Maybe he was surrounding himself with the wrong people. Clarke didn't give himself the chance to find out. Saying he was tired of dealing with agents and players who cared about nothing but money, Clarke decided he no longer had a taste for being a general manager. In late May 1992, he requested and received permission to speak with the Flyers and, on June 10, returned to Philadelphia, this time as Senior Vice-President and limited owner of the team.

Clarke and the Flyers were joyous.

"You'll never know how happy this makes me and my family," Clarke said. "We had two good years in Minnesota but, for me and for our family, this is home."

Clarke's family knew Philadelphia was where he belonged.

"He was like an extra piece of furniture," Sandy Clarke said of their time in Minnesota. "He was there, but his mind was always back here."

Now that he was back in Philadelphia, Clarke was as comfortable as an old sofa and felt about as useful, too. All of the good hockey jobs with the Flyers were taken: Bill Dineen was coach and had two assistants, Russ Farwell was general manager, and Jerry Melnyk ran scouting. There was nothing to satisfy his hunger for competition and hard work. No authority and very little input, other than teaching the Flyers' young centers, including budding superstar Eric Lindros.

"For a lot of people, it was the best job in the world," Clarke said. "Somewhere along the line, I was getting out of bed and was not happy with what I had to do. I didn't feel I was contributing to the Flyers."

Out of the corner of his eye, he saw an opportunity in Florida, a chance to become a meaningful part of an organization once again. So in late January 1993, he asked Jay Snider to call Wayne Huizenga and recommend him for a job.

"Bobby's not happy here," Snider told Huizenga. "Why don't you do something with him? He'd be a good guy for you."

Thankful for any hockey input, Huizenga arranged to meet Clarke a few days later. They met again on February 6 while attending the All-Star Game in Montreal. Impressed, Huizenga placed Clarke on a short list of three candidates for the GM's job and showed it to Torrey, who by that time was living almost full-time at his home in Palm Beach.

"He [Clarke] was by far and away the best candidate," Torrey recalled. "His personality, competitiveness, and he had enough experience as a manager. He was through his ex-player early stages. It's not easy changing from player to executive, although he did a good job in a tough situation in Minneapolis. I thought the whole aura of Bob Clarke here would be positive."

Hungry for competition, Clarke wanted the job, even if it meant leaving Philadelphia. He was hired on March 1, the same day Huizenga told the League his team would be ready for the 1993-94 season.

Now it was full speed ahead.

▲ ▲ ▲

Clarke had absolutely nothing to work with when he started his new job on March 2. He had built a hockey career out of scratching and clawing his way to the top, and now he would build a hockey team from scratch.

The team didn't have its own office, so Clarke worked at a spare desk in the Blockbuster building. He had no secretary, no assistant, no scouts, no training facility, no minor league affiliation. But there was no time to worry about what he didn't have. The expansion and amateur drafts were less than four months away and Clarke, who had done some scouting with the Flyers, had to act fast.

At least he had a telephone, which was ringing like crazy.

Fans wanted season tickets, but there were none to buy. Scouts and candidates for assistant general manager sent in their resumes; Clarke read them, but he already had some names in mind. Dennis Patterson had spent most of his scouting career working for Clarke, and was named chief scout on March 25. Ron Harris, the former player who was working for the Central Scouting Bureau, was hired as Eastern Scout.

"There were only just the two of us, Ron Harris and myself," Patterson recalled. "We were working with a short staff and it was different. I usually like to have a western guy and a European guy. I went over to Europe five times that year and then we went over to the World Championships because we wanted to see Paul Kariya play. There was a chance we were going to pick fourth in the amateur draft and we possibly could've taken him."

Clarke and Huizenga succeeded in their first combined task, lobbying the NHL governors to place their team in the newly-named Atlantic Division with Tampa Bay, creating a cross-state rivalry, and five Northeast teams: the Islanders, Rangers, New Jersey Devils, Flyers, and Washington Capitals. This involved some rearranging and negotiating by the governors, but the objective was reasonable: Hundreds of thousands of people from the Northeast had relocated to South Florida.

"Tampa Bay expressed a strong desire to be in the same division as Florida," Bettman said. "Based on all the information we had, we thought it would enhance the rivalry, fan interest, and attendance. If you look at a map, it also makes the most sense."

Clarke was thrilled. So was Huizenga, who sported a perfect record in Board of Governors meetings. *Franchise. Expansion draft. Divisional placement.*

Ironically, the son of the man most opposed to South Florida and Anaheim getting a break in the expansion draft was among Clarke's first hires: Chuck Fletcher, whose father is Maple Leafs general manager Cliff Fletcher. Fletcher, 26, had spent two years working for agent Don Meehan in an administrative role when Clarke interviewed him for assistant to the GM. He was hired after two interviews.

"In six weeks, I went from having nothing to having a dream job," Fletcher said.

While Patterson and Harris were on the road, Clarke and Fletcher stayed back and spent their days going over scouting lists and preparing for the entry draft. They had no players, so they couldn't work on contracts. They had no schedule, so they couldn't work on travel arrangements. At night, over dinner at an outdoor restaurant along the Intracoastal Waterway, Clarke would tell old hockey stories and discuss the day's work; uncomfortable when speaking about himself, he was a reluctant story teller. Clarke was more at ease discussing the future.

Both men took a liking to their jobs. Here they were, in the middle of hockey season, sitting outside, taking in the warm breeze, watching yachts cruise past on the Intracoastal, and building a team. After dinner, they'd return to Blockbuster Plaza for a few more hours of work. They operated out of one spare office on the 10th floor while David "Sudsy" Settlemyre, the trainer, would find a spare corner from which to order washing machines, dryers, and equipment for the training facility.

Only the team didn't have a training facility. It didn't have anything. Not even a name.

▲ ▲ ▲

The name South Florida Hockey Club Limited might look good on corporate ledgers, but it's not exactly appropriate for a professional hockey team, nor would it fit on the front of a jersey. What are the fans supposed to chant, "Let's Go Limited"?

Huizenga's team needed a real name and the public gladly offered its advice. *The Miami Herald* and Fort Lauderdale *Sun-Sentinel* both held "name the team" contests and received over 1,000 responses each. The results were remarkably similar: Ice won both contests, followed by Blades, with Panthers and Stingrays far behind.

Huizenga didn't like that. What he really needed was another poll, because he had already decided upon a name: Panthers, preceded by Florida or South Florida. The regional designation would infuriate the Tampa Bay Lightning and their fans, who couldn't understand why the second team into Florida took the entire state for itself. But Huizenga had a rationale: He had no intention of keeping the team in Miami and planned on attracting fans from Dade, Broward, and Palm Beach counties. Miami was too limited a regional designation, South Florida too bulky. Florida made sense.

Naming the team finally became serious business in April, after Huizenga signed a lease and decided the team would begin play the following season.

"Wayne told me that when he did the Marlins, he considered using the name Panthers," said Torrey, who wasn't yet officially on board. "His football team in high school was the Panthers, but Marlin fishing happened to be something he really likes and had done for years in Australia. I said the best thing to do is to run a contest for 10 days in the papers, let the public vote, and see what they think."

The results of this second newspaper poll were almost too good to be true. Out of more than 6,000 entrants, 2,900 voted for the Panthers; Manatees came in second. Huizenga couldn't have been happier had he stuffed the ballot box and, on April 19, he called a press conference at Burt and Jack's Restaurant in Port Everglades and made two announcements.

South Florida Hockey Club Limited had embraced the state animal, an endangered species, and would be known as the Florida Panthers. And Bill Torrey, formerly an endangered species of hockey, would be the team's first president. Now it was official.

CHAPTER 4

Jumping Head-First

Roger Neilson was at his low point. A month earlier, he had been fired by the New York Rangers, the team he coached to the best regular season record in the NHL the previous season and, a few days later, his 14-year-old dog Mike died. He was all alone and, at age 58, he figured his prospects for again coaching in the League couldn't be much bleaker. *I might as well jump*, Neilson figured.

So he did. Two hundred feet, straight down, over the edge of a cliff in Taupo, New Zealand. As he fell, he saw the scenery rushing by and a river running straight below. He felt exhilarated, almost rejuvenated, and any second now, his fall would be over and he would be free of his troubles.

Then, with the ground just feet away, he felt the yank of the bungee cord on his ankle and dangled upside down from the mountain. Which was, at the same time, perfectly appropriate for a man whose life had just been turned upside down, and ironic considering his reputation as a man who always had to be in control.

This seeming refusal to take chances ... that's what got him fired by the Rangers, wasn't it? He was hired by General Manager Neil Smith nearly four years earlier to coach a team that hadn't won the Stanley Cup since 1940, and helped them recover from the disastrous, quick-fix era of Phil Esposito. Neilson was brought in to give the team stability, because that's what he does best, and that's what he did.

In 1989-90, his first season in New York, Neilson installed a conservative defensive system. The Rangers cut a half-goal off their goals-against average and won the division championship. The following year, the Rangers finished second behind the eventual Cup-winning Pittsburgh Penguins and then acquired Mark Messier in a deal that would change the franchise's fortunes. Neilson's too.

The strong-willed Messier and Neilson got along well, at first. The Rangers won a franchise-record 50 games in 1991-92 and ran away with the League's regular season title. When the Rangers won their first-round series against the Devils and took a two-games-to-one lead over Pittsburgh in the Conference semifinals, it looked like they could be on their way to ending the Cup drought.

But it all came apart in Game 4 during a third period that perfectly illustrated both Neilson's coaching philosophy and its potential drawbacks. Leading 4-2 with 15 minutes remaining, the Rangers were given a five-minute power play. Here was a chance to put away the game and the series but, instead of going for the kill, Neilson had the Rangers treat the penalty as a chance to take time off the clock. The Penguins scored shortly after the power play expired, won the game in overtime, and went on to win the series. Neilson's defensive, go-into-a-shell philosophy had backfired.

"We should've won the Cup," Neilson said of his team that fell three rounds short.

Even though none of the Rangers publicly blamed Neilson for the debacle, Messier decided Neilson's system was too conservative for a team with so many offensive weapons. Rather than playing Neilson's beloved dump-and-chase, he thought the Rangers should take advantage of their talent. The rift between the coach and his strong captain widened when the Rangers got off to a mediocre start in the 1992-93 season and quickly became unsalvageable. Clearly, one of them had to go and it certainly wasn't going to be Messier, even though Neilson had signed a three-year contract extension that made him the highest-paid coach in the League. The relationship became so acrimonious that Neilson, in an act of desperation that probably cost him his job, called Kevin Lowe, Mike Gartner, and Adam Graves into his office and discussed Messier's apparent lack of leadership. Word of this meeting leaked to an infuriated Messier. Neilson was fired three days later, on January 4, 1993, with the Rangers in third place and having lost three in a row.

"Last year, Mark came in and gave us all hope for the Stanley Cup," Neilson said. "He was as good a leader as you could get on a hockey team. This year, he just didn't lead us."

So, with nowhere else to go because the only job opening was the one he had just created, Neilson loaded his bags and his dead dog into the car and drove home to Bridgenorth, Ontario. When he got there, he buried his canine friend and got down to the difficult task of putting New York behind him.

"I was closer to the team in New York than any of my previous teams," Neilson said. "Prior to New York, I always felt a coach should keep aloof from the team but, when I got to New York, I decided not to bother with that anymore."

Neilson knew his situation wasn't entirely hopeless. Money wasn't a problem because he was still being paid by the Rangers. After returning from New Zealand, he was invited by Mike Keenan to help coach Team Canada at the World Championships in Munich, Germany. And, he knew, there were new teams in South Florida and Southern California that would need coaches for the upcoming season.

Anaheim wasn't interested, Florida was. Clarke and Neilson discussed the job while in Munich and Clarke told him to send a résumé when he got home. For the first time in months, things were finally looking up for Neilson. Which wasn't bad for a man who had been hanging upside down.

▲ ▲ ▲

Bill Torrey didn't need a résumé to get the scoop on Neilson. Neither did Clarke. Neilson's record was well established and by no means clean.

Torrey knew. This guy was Captain Video, the space cadet who was one of the first coaches to use video as an instructional tool. He might as well have used rock 'em sock 'em robots when he dealt Torrey one of the most crushing defeats of his career.

In 1978, Neilson was the rookie coach of the Toronto Maple Leafs and Torrey's powerhouse Islanders were supposed to reach the Stanley Cup finals. The teams met in the second round and Neilson's Leafs were heavy underdogs, trailing two games to none, when he turned loose his goons on New York's stars. One of those goons was Dave "Tiger" Williams and whatever remaining respect he had for the rules was wiped out by Neilson's marching orders: Go get 'em, Tiger!

The series turned into a free-for-all. Jerry Butler charged Mike Bossy from behind, sending the Islanders superstar to the hospital. In another game, Williams speared and high-sticked Bossy. He fought at every opportunity. The Leafs won the series, four games to three, on an overtime goal by Lanny McDonald in Game 7. Torrey hadn't forgotten the pain of that loss.

"Mike Palmateer, their goalie, had his career series," Torrey recalled. "We had chances to win the series, but we just missed the net. Billy Harris had a breakaway before MacDonald scored and had Palmateer beat. It was going to the far corner of the net, but it hit the shaft of Palmateer's stick. I can see it going in now."

A more pleasant memory was of 1982, after the Islanders had won two Cups. Neilson, fired by the Leafs and Sabres, was on his third job in five years, having taken over behind the Vancouver bench for Harry Neale at the end of the 1981-82 season. The Canucks were a mediocre team in the regular season, finishing three games under .500, but reached the finals in one of hockey's all-time Cinderella stories. Cinderella with a black eye, that is. Reunited with his old coach in Vancouver, Williams put on one of the most disgraceful exhibitions of goonery in NHL playoff history. This time, the Islanders' talent overcame Neilson's thugs and swept the series for their third straight Cup.

Torrey knew all about Neilson's reputation: He was a coach whose teams often overlooked the rules and would do anything to win, obviously at their coach's behest. Players behave the way their coaches tell them to and Neilson obviously hadn't changed in the past 11 years. Just that winter, when Neilson was coaching the Rangers, Tie Domi had his much anticipated boxing match with Bob Probert of the Red Wings: Anticipated because Domi vowed to take on Probert for the undisputed heavyweight championship of hockey when the teams met on December 2 at Madison Square Garden.

Neilson could've stopped the nonsense by ordering Domi not to fight Probert. Instead, Neilson sent out Domi the first time Probert skated onto the ice. The expected happened and NHL President Gil Stein punished the perpetrators: Domi and Neilson. They were both suspended for two games.

"The only instruction [Domi] received from Neilson was to make sure he did not get an instigator penalty," Stein ruled. "Neilson was the person most directly responsible for what occurred. During our interview, Neilson stated he did not know Probert was on the ice when he sent out Domi's line. I find that statement unworthy of belief. During our personal interview, Neilson displayed no regret, remorse, or contrition."

The other half of Neilson's reputation was more appealing to Torrey and Clarke: His mediocre teams always overachieved and his highly talented teams always underachieved.

The Panthers were not going to be a highly talented team.

"The one thing we learned about expansion is that it's best to select a coach that fits the kind of team you're going to have," Torrey said. "Roger has a certain philosophy and theory. There was no way we were going to have a high-octane team, so we might as well get somebody who could work within that system. I'm a full believer that guys are successful because there's a fit."

The choices for coach were limited because Torrey promised the Islanders he wouldn't pursue the man he really wanted: Al Arbour, whose contract expired after the 1993 playoffs. When the Islanders agreed to set Torrey free, they wanted to make sure he wasn't going to take half the franchise with him.

That left Clarke and Torrey with a short list of two candidates: Andy Murray, who worked for Clarke as an assistant coach in Philadelphia and Minnesota, and Neilson. Clarke considered both men patient teachers who could get the most out of the talent they'd be given, but Neilson had far more experience; Murray had never coached in the NHL.

"After I talked with Bob, I felt pretty good about getting the job," Neilson said. "He just wanted to get to know me a little more and some of my ideas. It wasn't a difficult interview by any means. We talked at the airport in Toronto, then he said he'd get back to me."

Although Torrey never forgot the Toronto series, he agreed with Clarke that Neilson was the right man for the job, easily the best available. The only remaining hang-up was Neilson's contract with the Rangers. Neilson was making $375,000 a year and the Panthers were looking to pay him $250,000. Neilson didn't want to take a pay cut but, on the other hand, the Rangers didn't want to keep paying a coach they had fired. After about a week of three-way negotiations between the Panthers and Neil Smith, then between Neilson and Smith, the Rangers agreed to pay the additional one-third of Neilson's salary for the remaining two years of his contract in a lump sum of $250,000.

Neilson didn't care how he was paid. His friend, Gary Green, a part-time hockey consultant for Huizenga, had told him how much he would love coaching in South Florida and Neilson welcomed a situation with less pressure than in New York. At 58, he wasn't exactly in a position to pick his spots. Anaheim hadn't returned his calls and neither had Philadelphia for its job opening. Florida beckoned. Neilson answered.

Nobody could have guessed how happy Neilson was when he was introduced as the Panthers' first coach on June 2. With Torrey and Clarke at either side, Neilson sipped gently from a glass of champagne and wore the look of dread that had become his permanent mask.

"You look nervous," a reporter told Neilson.

"Naw," he said. "That's the way I always look."

▲ ▲ ▲

Dean Jordan wasn't a baseball man. He wasn't a hockey man or even a sports man. Dean Jordan, 32, was a TV man who spent three years as Director of Broadcasting and Advertising Sales for baseball's Pittsburgh Pirates before coming on as Vice President of Communications for the Marlins. Jordan worked his way into Huizenga's confidence and when Huizenga bought a hockey team, he naturally turned to Jordan for assistance in selecting a general manager and president. That's about all Jordan had time for. The Marlins, priority No. 1 around Huizenga Holdings, had everybody busy worrying about baseball until the season-opener.

"Two weeks," Huizenga told his staff. "You have two weeks to get baseball started, then we have to worry about hockey."

Less than a week after the baseball season started, Huizenga summoned Jordan to his office.

"What are your thoughts on the future?" Huizenga asked.

"Well," Jordan said, "I wanted to come down here and get our TV company started."

"One of these days we're going to get around to doing that," Huizenga replied, "but right now, we've got to get this hockey team started. I'd appreciate it if you'd go over there."

Jordan was selected by Torrey, who recognized there wasn't time to bring in and educate a marketing expert from outside the area.

"I went to Wayne one day and said, 'I have good news and bad news,' " Torrey recalled. "The good news is I think I found our marketing guy. The bad news is he's already working for you."

Just like that, Jordan went from broadcasting expert to hockey salesman. With less than 180 days remaining until the start of the 1993-94 season, not a single ticket had been printed or sold. Everything done with the Marlins would have to be repeated, and Jordan felt like he was running on a treadmill.

Running fast. There was no choice but to assemble a staff as quickly as possible. With Torrey's advice, Jordan hired Greg Bouris, formerly of the Islanders, as Director of Media and Public Relations. Declan Bolger, who worked with Jordan in Pittsburgh, came in as Director of Promotions and Special Projects. Kim Terranova defected from the Miami Heat to head corporate sales and sponsorships. Steve Dangerfield, the former assistant athletic director at the University of Miami, was Director of Tickets and Game Day Operations. Ron Dennis was in charge of merchandise.

Jordan contracted an advertising agency, Crispen and Porter, and, at the first creative meeting, told them to make the ads fresh and snappy. Humorous, if possible. Maybe people didn't know anything about hockey, but they knew what was funny.

"We felt we had to educate people on what hockey is and in order to make it sell right away, we had to make it unique," Jordan said. "We had to give it an attitude that it's cool to be involved with hockey. *You're with it.* We came up with some crazy slogans."

South Florida residents who inquired about season tickets received brochures in the mail. "The Florida Panthers are about to put 25 NHL teams on the endangered species list," the cover read. Wallets would be placed on the endangered species list, too. Season ticket prices stretched from a low of $860 for 42 games to a high of $3,215 for seats in rows three through six. No matter that nobody would want to sit in the first six rows for a hockey game. How many people in Florida knew that? These Panther Club Founder seats offered cocktail receptions with the coaching staff and Wayne Huizenga, a sweater, hockey clinics, and a media guide, all for the everyday low price of $55 a seat for each game, plus an $850 annual fee. Join the club! Lots of people did.

The Panthers sold over 6,000 season tickets the day they went on sale and the entire lower bowl of Miami Arena by mid-June. But after the initial rush, sales slowed to a crawl.

The only cheap ticket wasn't available to season subscribers: $8 Panther Pack seats, located in the last three rows of the upper deck, which would go on sale the morning of each home game. The idea behind this bargain fare wasn't so much to fill the house as to hook new hockey fans. The thinking went, *Will anybody pay $40 to sample something they had never seen before?*

At the time, nobody knew if anybody would pay eight bucks to sample something they had never seen before.

The entire staff was assembled between May 1 and July 1, and if it's true that adversity brings people together, they were on their way to becoming a tight-knit group. On June 1, the Panthers moved into their new offices in downtown Fort Lauderdale on the 10th floor of 100 Northeast Third Avenue, a building with a view: To the east, a panorama of Fort Lauderdale Beach; To the south, downtown; To the west, Broward County, all the way to the Everglades. The view was perfect, the atmospheric conditions jungle-like. The air conditioning didn't work for the first 10 days and people were putting in 16 hour days, seven days a week, under sweatshop conditions, with perspiration dripping from their faces and sweat-soaked sleeves rolled up.

"It was miserable," Jordan recalled, "but in hindsight, it was a real good time because it brought everybody together. Nobody knew anything about hockey, except Bouris."

So they started picking Bouris' brain. He spent most of the first staff meeting teaching Hockey 101 to his co-workers: the names of the divisions, the teams within the divisions, the names of the trophies and what they were for. *This is a hockey rink. This is icing. This is off-sides. This is a stick. This is a puck. This is the Stanley Cup.*

The miserably sweating people who would sell hockey to South Florida's happily sweating, football-crazy public had no idea what Bouris was talking about.

▲ ▲ ▲

Shortly after the team name was chosen, the small staff got down to the business of creating a logo, team colors, and a uniform. These were serious debates over serious issues. Once simply a question of what looks best, a team's logo and uniform is the focal point of its multi-million dollar merchandising efforts. Encouraged by the marketing consultants they hired, teams in all four major sports have changed their colors and uniforms simply so they can sell more stuff.

The market had become remarkably lucrative. During the 1991-92 season, the San Jose Sharks were by far both the worst team in the NHL and the best dressed. The Sharks sold more merchandise than any team in the League and finished second in sales behind the NBA's Chicago Bulls in all of professional sports. It was an unheard of achievement for a hockey team; the Sharks' merchandise sales of $150 million represented 27 percent of the League's total.

The Sharks didn't merely stumble upon the right logo and uniform. From the time the franchise was granted on May 9, 1990, the staff spent well over a year brainstorming ideas, creating and discarding designs, and interviewing 14,000 fans about their preferences. The Panthers had about a month.

The logo design took shape during a conversation Torrey had with his son, Rich, a cartoonist on Long Island. Rich pointed out that most team logos of animals are done in profile.

"I want our panther to be aggressive," Torrey said. "I want him to be in your face."

Rich Torrey drew a few rough sketches before his father turned the design effort over to Sean Michael Edwards, a fledgling studio in New York City that had created the Seattle Mariners' and California Angels' new uniforms. By trial and error — in one of their first renderings, the cat's paws were two times the size of its head — they came up with the team's unique logo: a roaring panther that leaps right at the viewer.

Now the cat needed some color and there was no time to waste. The manufacturer, CCM, couldn't guarantee the uniforms would be ready for opening night. Sean Michael Edwards sent the Panthers a folio of uniforms in every possible color scheme. A lime green rugby-type sweater — they had horizontal stripes on the arms and were perfectly ugly — was eliminated early in the discussion, as were a number of other wild, unconventional colors and designs. Bob Clarke, who spent his entire career wearing the orange and black Halloween colors of the Flyers, favored a scheme of purple, black, and white. He was about the only one.

Huizenga's Florida Marlins were already a hit in their teal and black uniforms. The Miami Dolphins also wore teal, an appropriate color for an area whose dominant geographical feature is the Atlantic Ocean. Huizenga thought teal was perfect for his hockey team, too, and pushed for a color scheme with teal as the dominant color trimmed in black and purple.

"They had become hot colors," Torrey said. "And I didn't like them. I wanted something more aggressive."

Just about everyone involved in the debate was thinking in terms of merchandising, money, and fan appeal. Huizenga didn't see this as a one time, life-or-death decision: He figured the team could go with a color scheme for three or four years, then switch to a new one if necessary.

"Wayne, you can't do that," Torrey explained. "You want to establish a tradition."

"All you hockey guys are too traditional!" Huizenga shot back. "You have to loosen up and be a little more aggressive."

Torrey, about as traditional a hockey man as you'll ever find, finally got the conversation onto the track he wanted.

"Just remember one thing," he said. "None of us in this room are going to pull this jersey over our heads and play in it. You've gotta design a uniform that a player is going to feel good about pulling over his shoulders. Just remember: Somebody has to play in it. It's not like they're billboards or neon signs. They're hockey players."

Torrey's concern for what the players would wear came from his first NHL job as Vice-President of the California Seals. Charles O. Finley, the owner of the Seals, was one of the most colorful sports owners in history — meaning he'd do anything to draw attention and make a buck — and Torrey's frequent discussions with Finley often concerned the outlandish uniforms and accouterments the owner wanted his players to wear.

When Finley decided the Seals would look good in white skates complementing their California gold, kelly green, and wedding gown white uniforms, Torrey was aghast and resisted for as long as possible.

"I just wouldn't allow it and Freddie Glover, our coach, wouldn't wear them," Torrey said, gleefully telling the story. "Then in exhibition season we were playing St. Louis up in Sudbury and at the end of the first period I got a message that Charles O. Finley had just walked in the building and was looking for me.

"I found him and he said," — here, Torrey goes into a baritone Charles O. Finley voice — " 'Bill, I'm here to see my white skates.' And I said, 'Charlie, they're terrible.' And he said," — that voice again — " 'Bill, I've come all the way from Chicago to see my white skates.' So I went down to the dressing room and I said, 'Freddie, we've got to get somebody to wear those white skates the next period.' And Freddie Glover said, 'Screw you. I'm not going in there and telling somebody to put them on. You can go into the dressing room.'

"So I went into the dressing room and said, 'Mr. Finley is here. We have a pair of white skates. He wants somebody to try them out the next period. Do I have any volunteers?' And I waited and I waited and I waited and nobody volunteered and I said, 'If I don't get a volunteer, I'm going to have to designate somebody, because somebody is going to walk out of this dressing room with a pair of white skates.'

"Finally, I think it was Gary Jarrett who volunteered to wear them, so he wore them for the rest of that game and, like I said, white skates on white ice is just nothing. So I said after the game, 'Charlie, the reason your white baseball shoes look good is because the players wear them on green grass. There's a contrast. White skates on white ice … ' So he agreed with me that white skates were horseshit."

Aided by Torrey's wisdom, the choices were narrowed to the teal, black, and purple favored by Huizenga and Jordan, and the red, blue, and gold favored by Torrey, Greg Bouris, Chuck Fletcher, and just about anyone else who had a vote.

Although Huizenga was outvoted by a wide margin, his ballot carried the day. Panthers colors were teal, black, and purple when Torrey and Jordan flew to New York for the purposes of presenting the uniform and logo to NHL Enterprises. But Torrey wouldn't give up without a fight and used the flight to sway Jordan.

Jordan wavered when he contemplated merchandising from a different perspective: South Florida sports fans whose tastes were in black or teal already had plenty of Marlins merchandise from which to choose. Why not come up with a unique color scheme for the Panthers? Although the Heat were already wearing red, they had done a poor job at merchandising and fans were not attracted to their logo.

"I think Bill's biggest move was to separate Dean and Wayne," Bouris recalled.

Back in Florida, Bouris had spent a sleepless night. He was convinced teal and black were the wrong colors for the Panthers and red was right. That morning, as he walked from the Panthers' offices to the Blockbuster building across town, Bouris sulked and thought, *I can't believe we're going to be teal. I can't believe we're going to be teal.*

Then Bouris walked into Huizenga's office and saw his boss looking down at the two color schemes. *There's still time*, he realized.

"You know," Huizenga said, "that red's pretty good, too. It's starting to really grow on me."

Clarke said he liked the red, too. Bouris, recognizing his opportunity, exclaimed, "It's new again! It's dynamic! It fits the ferocity of the Florida Panthers."

"It's red," Huizenga agreed. "Go with the red."

Huizenga then paused.

"What do we tell Bill when he calls?"

"Lead him on," Bouris said. "Make him believe he's persuading you to change."

The conference call began and Huizenga asked NHL Commissioner Gary Bettman which colors he preferred. Bettman voted for red. Then Huizenga asked Jordan.

"I like them both, Wayne," Jordan said.

Finally, it was Torrey's turn to make his final pitch. Huizenga never let him finish.

"You're right, Bill," Huizenga said. "Let's go with it."

▲ ▲ ▲

Nice uniforms. They looked great in *USA Today* and fans who attended the unveiling at Miami Arena agreed they were a hit. A little traditional, maybe, not quite what everybody expected, but certainly not offensive. At least there wasn't a duck on the front! Huizenga was there for the fashion show. So was Bettman. Now all the Panthers needed were some players to wear those handsome new clothes.

If only Clarke and his scouting staff knew who those players would be. All they could do was guess, and that's exactly what Clarke, Dennis Patterson, Ron Harris, Chuck Fletcher, and Bill Barber — on loan from the Flyers — did for one week in June at Clarke's beach house in Ocean City, New Jersey. They reviewed scouting reports, projected which players teams would leave unprotected in the expansion draft, and compiled lists of the players they most desired.

"Bob told us we want character players," Patterson recalled. "He wanted guys who have done something on the teams they were on. His theory was that if we took character guys, then the younger players in the amateur draft, those veterans would show them how to win, and it would continue."

Clarke wasn't stating the obvious. There are various theories on selecting players in an expansion draft and all of them had been tried. Some teams go for the youngest players available and hope they'll develop into stars. Others go for veterans, regardless of salary, and hope they still have something left. Another option is going for skill. By Clarke's way of thinking, the first few years of this franchise were not going to be easy on the players. If the Panthers were a typical expansion team, there'd be plenty of close losses and quite a few blowouts. He wanted players willing to work through the tough times and maybe turn some of those close games into wins.

Clarke's task was identifying these players and hoping some would be available. Already, the general managers of the existing teams were preparing their rosters for the draft. The more talent a team had, the more likely it was to trade its excess talent — a quality second goalie or solid prospects after the first 14 protected skaters — prior to finalizing its protected list.

The less-talented teams were willing to trade for these players at a bargain price and place them in their available protected spots. Rather than lose Paul Ysebaert, a two-time 30-goal scorer, for nothing, the Red Wings traded him to Winnipeg for prospect — and exempt player — Aaron Ward. The Wings had one of the most talented teams in the League, but few unprotected players anybody wanted.

Clarke and his staff paid special attention to the teams with two quality goalies, knowing one of them would have to be exposed. Would the Rangers expose John Vanbiesbrouck or Mike Richter? Vanbiesbrouck had the better season, but Richter was younger. Would the Islanders expose Glenn Healy or Mark Fitzpatrick? Healy was their playoff hero, but Fitzpatrick was younger and a former second-round draft pick.

"We were guessing which players would be made available," Fletcher said. "We ended up being relatively close, but there were some surprises. We didn't anticipate John Vanbiesbrouck being available."

The Panthers would play this guessing game until June 21, when the final lists of unprotected players were released, just three days before the expansion draft in Quebec City.

Clarke gathered his staff, which now included Neilson and Associate Coach Craig Ramsay, at the Sheraton Center in Montreal on June 19 for the final pre-draft meetings. The Panthers still didn't know which players would be available but, with only two days remaining until the deadline, they had a pretty good idea and reviewed medical records and contracts. Talking to the players was out of the question; the Panthers didn't want to reveal which ones they coveted.

Another consideration was the Anaheim franchise, nicknamed the Mighty Ducks. Which players did they want? What type of player did Ducks GM Jack Ferreira prefer? The Panthers had a few clues because they knew the Ducks were asking around about certain players. Of course, the Mighty Ducks were getting the same messages about the Panthers.

There were few surprises when the final list of unprotected players was released.

The Canucks had settled upon 27-year-old Kirk McLean as their No. 1 goalie of the near future, but had high hopes for Kay Whitmore, 26, a former second-rounder acquired from the Hartford Whalers. Anxious over having a powerful goaltending tandem broken apart by the expansion draft, Canucks General Manager Pat Quinn had made a shrewd trade four days earlier, sending defenseman Doug Lidster to the Rangers in exchange for goaltender John Vanbiesbrouck. This was a rare case of a trade looking good for both teams: the Rangers, knowing they would have lost Vanbiesbrouck for nothing in the expansion draft, got Lidster as compensation. The Canucks exposed Vanbiesbrouck and Whitmore, the Rangers exposed only minor leaguer Boris Rousson.

The Islanders also made a deal, sending goaltender Mark Fitzpatrick to the Nordiques in exchange for veteran goalie Ron Hextall. The Islanders exposed Glenn Healy and two rookies. The Nordiques exposed five goalies, including Fitzpatrick.

The list included no current stars, but some enticing veterans: Defenseman Mark Howe, a three-time All-Star who was 37; J.J. Daigneault, who played an important role on the Canadiens team that had just won the Cup; Guy Carbonneau, the Canadiens captain and one of the best checking forwards in the League; Denis Savard, the speedy center; and Dave Poulin, the former 30-goal man whom Clarke once traded in a disastrous deal for Ken Linesman.

Most of the youngest players available seemed destined for careers in the minor leagues; the oldest players came with big contracts and injury concerns. The Panthers were aiming somewhere in between.

Each member of the Panthers' staff had a player preference.

Torrey wanted forward Tom Fitzgerald and Fitzpatrick, his former players on Long Island.

Neilson wanted Vanbiesbrouck, center Randy Gilhen, and defenseman Joe Cirella, all of whom played for him in New York. Although some of Neilson's difficulties in New York stemmed from an unworkable platoon with Vanbiesbrouck and Richter, both of whom wanted to be the No. 1 goalie, he thought getting them separated might be good for both careers. Besides, Vanbiesbrouck was clearly the best goalie available.

Ramsay knew Wayne Presley, a checking forward from Buffalo and felt he fit the "character" definition.

Clarke wanted Scott Mellanby, who played for him in Philadelphia.

The Panthers ranked goalies, defensemen, and forwards separately. The staff divided into two teams and held three mock drafts. The key was getting the desired player at the right time; not taking him too early, but not waiting too long and losing him altogether.

They kept returning to the same determining factor: that intangible called character.

"Being around as long as Bob and I had been around the League, we knew who the character guys were," Torrey said.

They decided upon Vanbiesbrouck over Whitmore for a first choice and Fitzpatrick over Guy Hebert for a second goalie. Four veteran forwards were targeted: Dave Lowry, Mellanby, Mike Hough, and Presley. The Panthers knew they probably wouldn't get all four, but hoped for at least two. And with Hough traded from Quebec to Washington at the deadline, the Panthers could go after another Nordiques forward, 22-year-old Bill Lindsay. They also decided to take Brian Skrudland, the former Canadiens checking forward now playing for the Flames, if he was available later in the draft.

Unknown variables made the mock drafts a guessing game: Who did the Mighty Ducks really want — there was no way of knowing for sure — and who would pick first in the goaltenders phase? What if the Ducks selected a goaltender from a team with a defenseman the Panthers wanted? Then they'd have to readjust their thinking. The three mock drafts had limited value because the real draft could play out in a million different ways.

The Panthers knew they couldn't answer all of their questions until the draft was underway. After arriving in Quebec City the day before the draft, Clarke, Neilson, and Torrey spent the rest of the day relaxing, going over final expansion draft plans, and entertaining trade offers for players they hadn't yet drafted. Neilson kicked off his shoes and socks and pulled on a baseball cap. The mood was relaxed, jovial. They were as ready as they were going to be.

CHAPTER 5

Gone Fishing

On a beautiful, warm, early summer day in Quebec City, the Panthers' hockey men gathered with Wayne Huizenga and Dean Jordan in a suite at the Loews Le Concorde Hotel for the short walk to the site of the 1993 Expansion Draft. They planned on making June 24, 1993, an historic day in South Florida sports, but the Marlins beat them to the punch.

Just as the Panthers' brass prepared to leave, word came that the Marlins had acquired star outfielder Gary Sheffield from the San Diego Padres. This wasn't merely a trade, it was a blockbuster.

Great, Bouris thought. *Here we are, our sister organization. Couldn't they have postponed it a day?*

Jordan, who was in a joking mood anyway, immediately phoned Marlins General Manager Dave Dombroski in Miami.

"Dave," Jordan said. "Next time you're going to make a trade, tell us first!"

There couldn't have been a clearer, or more annoying, example of how independently of each other Huizenga's teams would operate. The Panthers left knowing they'd be sharing the front page of the sports sections the next morning.

The expansion draft remained the big story in Canada, where even war doesn't overshadow hockey news. Television camera crews and newspaper reporters followed the Panthers onto the street. Heads turned at the impressive sight of Bill Torrey, Bob Clarke, and Roger Neilson, three famous men in Canada, leading the way. When they arrived at the Grand Theatre du Quebec, the Panthers and Mighty Ducks brass were herded into a room, where an NHL official explained the draft rules. Then they marched out into a dimly lit theater, framed on three sides by six rows of occupied spectator seats, and prepared for action.

Panthers and Mighty Ducks officials sat at long banquet tables set up in the open end of the horseshoe-shaped room. The Florida table was covered with a Panthers red cloth; the Anaheim table with a Mighty Ducks purple cloth. Facing the tables were two empty selection boards that would soon be filled with the names of the players selected. The media, representing newspapers, TV, and radio stations from throughout North America, took their seats at 2:30 p.m. and prepared to witness what could be an exercise in futility for both teams.

Although it sounds exciting — new teams stocking their rosters with real players for the first time and filling those new uniforms with bodies — the expansion draft is one of the dullest exercises in sports. Unlike the amateur draft, the players aren't present. Again unlike the amateur draft, a day full of promise for the future, most of the players selected don't have a future. The expansion draft isn't televised in the United States and fans aren't allowed to attend.

And who would want to? Representatives from each team take turns walking to a podium and announcing their selections. Then they sit down. Then they stand up. Finally, both teams are stocked with players only astute hockey fans could identify.

Despite the League's new and liberal rules regarding how many players each team could protect, it was widely agreed the Panthers and Mighty Ducks would pick up a few good goaltenders and little else in the draft. After all, an expansion draft was held one year earlier, and hadn't the Lightning and Senators taken whatever halfway decent players were out there?

Even so, the 1992 Expansion Draft showed why this exercise should not be taken lightly. The Lightning found themselves an eventual 42-goal scorer (Brian Bradley) and a defenseman who would score 39 points (Shawn Chambers). The Senators, in disarray from Day 1, made one bone-headed selection after another at the draft table, picking players who weren't even available. The result was 24 points for the Senators in their first season, a respectable 53 for the Lightning. In 1992, the difference between drafting right and drafting wrong was 29 points; in 1972, Torrey found goaltender Bill Smith, a future Hall of Famer, in the expansion draft.

Most importantly, the expansion draft represents a starting point in a team's history. The shaping of its identity.

The first order of business, and in retrospect the most important, was the coin toss. Because the two teams entered the League simultaneously, the NHL needed a series of tosses to decide the order of selection in the expansion draft and, two days later, in the amateur draft. For the expansion draft, each team would pick 24 players in the following order: three goaltenders, then eight defensemen, then 13 forwards. The team that won the toss would decide whether it picked first, fourth, and fifth, or second, third, and sixth in the goaltenders phase.

Two things were certain: the team that won the toss would pick first and the first goaltender selected would come from the Vancouver Canucks. But which goaltender? The Mighty Ducks reportedly wanted Kay Whitmore. The Panthers didn't hide their desire for John Vanbiesbrouck. Had the trade between the Canucks and Rangers not been made, both teams could've had the goaltender they wanted. Not anymore. Each team could lose only one goalie in the expansion draft, and the coin toss was crucial.

So, as Panthers President Bill Torrey and Mighty Ducks President Tony Tavares were called to the middle of the room by NHL Commissioner Gary Bettman, the immediate futures of these two franchises — or at least their 1993-94 season — was at stake.

▲ ▲ ▲

Practice makes perfect, Torrey knew, and he had gone through great pains to make sure he didn't blow the toss. Talking on the telephone in his office during the weeks before the draft, Torrey tossed a Stanley Cup commemorative Canada silver dollar, checking for angles, the proper height at which to toss the coin, and how much force to use. A person who happened by Torrey's office during those practice sessions would have mistakenly thought he was idling away the time. Truth was, Torrey was getting ready for his big day.

"You're under the lights and it's nerve-wracking," Torrey said. "I wasn't nervous, except that it was important to us. We had a strategy set up that we knew who we wanted to draft first."

Torrey only made the first toss, which determined who would call Bettman's subsequent tosses for the goaltenders and forwards phases of the expansion draft, the supplemental draft, and the decision on picking fourth or fifth in Saturday's amateur draft. Torrey's practice paid off. He won the pre-toss, then called heads in the air on the goaltenders toss and won. The Panthers chose to make the first, fourth, and fifth selections of goaltenders and could now follow their Plan A. Torrey did his job: He got lucky.

Luck had nothing to do with what happened next. Clarke, sitting at the head of the table wearing a navy blue summer suit with white dress shirt and red power tie, was the decision-maker who ran the show. To his left sat Chuck Fletcher, Huizenga, Jordan, Neilson, Jonathan Mariner, and Ron Colangelo of the media relations staff. To his right sat Torrey, Dennis Patterson, Ron Harris, Craig Ramsay, Greg Bouris, and Kevin Dessart. Neilson and Ramsay, the most informal men at the table, had taken off their jackets. All wore conservative business ties except Neilson, who had on one of his many colorful, floral numbers. The table was covered with papers, notebooks, and pitchers of water. Photographers formed a ring around the area where the teams sat. The room was quiet, except for the constant hum of an air conditioner. If Clarke and Torrey needed reminding about what was at stake, all they had to do was look across the table at the bald guy, the one who placed his $50 million purchase in their hands.

"He was right there," Torrey said. "It's not like he knew the players, but he knew he had spent 50 million bucks."

Huizenga didn't want his hockey men feeling pressured and the day before had told Clarke, "Don't worry about money. Take the best player available, even if he's making a million."

At 2:37 p.m., Clarke was called to make the first selection. Striding purposefully to the podium, he took his place in front of a Panthers banner. With his voice rising ever so slightly, and betraying little excitement, Clarke pronounced, "From the Sunshine State, the Florida Panthers select, from the Vancouver Canucks, John Vanbiesbrouck."

Indeed, Vanbiesbrouck was making nearly a million: $950,000 a year.

The Ducks went next. Pierre Gauthier, their assistant general manager, announced the selection of Guy Hebert from St. Louis and Glenn Healy from the Islanders. The Panthers didn't reveal their happiness; these were two goalies they didn't plan on taking. The next two picks belonged to the Panthers. They selected Mark Fitzpatrick, whom Torrey once traded for on Long Island, from the Quebec Nordiques, and Daren Puppa from the Toronto Maple Leafs. When Anaheim finished the goaltending round by picking Ron Tugnutt from the Edmonton Oilers, the Panthers knew their day was going well.

Before the draft, the Panthers had prepared two lists for the goaltending phase: One for if they won the toss, another list for if they lost the toss. Knowing the Mighty Ducks would pick a Vancouver goalie with the first pick, the Panthers had Mark Fitzpatrick at No. 1 on their alternate list. The Panthers ended up with their 1 and 1a.

One goaltender not selected was Dominik Hasek of the Buffalo Sabres. Hasek would go on to become a two-time Vezina Trophy winner with Buffalo but, in June 1993, he was a 28-year-old who had spent three straight seasons as an NHL backup.

"Craig Ramsay was unbelievably high on Hasek," Fletcher recalled. "I don't think he was pushing him ahead of Vanbiesbrouck, but he wanted him in there. I think Hasek was in our top five for goalies, but we knew our third goalie would get drafted back by Ottawa or Tampa Bay."

Actually, Clarke already knew the Panthers' third goalie would get drafted back by Tampa Bay, as long as that third goalie was Puppa. When the Lightning won the toss to pick first in Phase II of the Expansion Draft, General Manager Phil Esposito offered Clarke a third-round draft pick if the Panthers picked Puppa and left him unprotected. To Clarke, this was like getting something for nothing, and he happily agreed.

During the long days and nights spent on the New Jersey shore and in a Montreal hotel room, the Panthers could have never expected reality to play out so according to plan. The mock drafts, the debates, the arguments, were preparation for any eventuality. So far, they were three-for-three.

"They're going to end up with Vanbiesbrouck and Fitzpatrick and there are not many better duos in the League," said Toronto Maple Leafs General Manager Cliff Fletcher, realizing the new team in Florida had better goaltending than his 77-year-old club.

Anaheim had the choice of picking first and fourth or second and third in the defensemen stage of the draft, but what was a meaningful decision in the goaltending phase was meaningless this time. There were no standouts available, not a millionaire in the bunch. The Ducks chose second and third. Again, the Panthers went first.

Clarke, finally breaking a smile over the surprise he was about to unveil, selected Milan Tichy from the Chicago Blackhawks.

"Milan who?" asked any reporter in the room who wasn't from Chicago.

Milan Tichy, a 6'3" defenseman from the Czech Republic, had accomplished little in his professional career since being selected by the Blackhawks in the sixth round of the 1989 Entry Draft. He scored one point in 13 games during an unpromising call-up by the Hawks during the 1992-93 season and looked like a project, at best, but the Panthers liked his age, 24.

The Ducks went next and selected an experienced hand, Alexei Kasatonov, and Sean Hill, a Canadiens' prospect considered more promising than Tichy. He had already played in 35 NHL games. The Panthers came back with the fourth pick and pulled another surprise.

"From Pittsburgh, Paul Laus," Clarke said, so unfamiliar with his new defenseman that he mispronounced the name "Louse" instead of "Lawz."

Laus, a 22-year-old goon, had spent three seasons fighting his way through the minor leagues and was still awaiting his NHL debut. Scouts thought he had borderline major league skills, at best, and was a borderline psychopath on the ice; Laus fought Darryl Williams three times in two International Hockey League games simply because the man had looked at him the wrong way. Psychopathic behavior wasn't a concern to the Panthers; they were looking for some toughness and liked Laus' youth, too.

"We thought it would be wise to take the younger defensemen first," Clarke said. "Obviously, there are only so many young prospects available and we considered these two as good, young prospects with a chance to play for us next season. We looked at the veteran defensemen available. It seemed to be fairly similar to what we would be able to get from free agents."

The Panthers gambled the veterans they desired would be available later in the draft. They were.

By this time, the talk at the Panthers' table was animated. Neilson, separated from Clarke by Huizenga and Jordan, seemed to be off in his own world. Jordan was looking all over the room, as if he couldn't sit still for another moment. Huizenga, acting like the manager of a fantasy league hockey team, took notes, looked through the media guide for information on his new players and, with each pick, asked Fletcher, "How much does he make?" For a man who told his staff not to worry about money, he sure was worried about money.

Anaheim took Bill Houlder from Buffalo. The Panthers, holding the sixth and seventh picks, prepared to pick their veterans. Clarke was pensive. All of the hockey men at the table made their final recommendations. They settled upon Joe Cirella, who played for Neilson in New York, and Alexander Godynuk, a Russian. Dallas' Gord Murphy, an offensive defenseman whom Clarke drafted in 1985, was taken with the eighth pick overall. Murphy, 26, twice led the Flyers' defensemen in scoring before his career went downhill in Boston. The Bruins had traded Murphy to Dallas four days earlier and the Stars unhesitatingly exposed him in the draft.

With their three remaining selections, the Panthers decided upon Steve Bancroft from Winnipeg, Stephane Richer from Boston, and Gord Hynes from Philadelphia. None of them reminded anyone of Bobby Orr, Denis Potvin, or even Gord Murphy.

Hardly an all-star cast, the Panthers' new eight-man defensive unit had scored a total of 15 goals the previous season. No wonder Neilson, the conservative coach who didn't want his defensemen joining the offense, was the only man at the table still smiling.

▲ ▲ ▲

As the draft proceeded and the Panthers and Mighty Ducks went from being just logos to logos with players, rival general managers called the draft tables to inquire about the availability of some of their more talented players. Several offers were for Vanbiesbrouck, who Torrey believed the Mighty Ducks might have drafted and traded if they had won the toss. Other GMs used draft picks and money to bribe the Panthers out of taking certain players. Moments before the forwards phase began, an exasperated Torrey picked up the phone.

"Hello, Fulton Fish Market," he said. "Fish speaking."

The caller hung up, Torrey offered a quizzical look, and Clarke broke out in pained laughter.

Torrey and Tavares were called front-and-center again for another coin toss, this time to decide which team would select the first forward. The Mighty Ducks won — the only toss they'd win all weekend — and as Tavares walked away, he quipped, "Finally, we won one."

The forwards phase was crucial, with skilled veterans and genuine prospects available in the pool of unprotected players. The Mighty Ducks went for a prospect: Steven King from the New York Rangers. King, a right wing, had torn up the American League the previous season and scored 12 points in 24 games for the Rangers, who couldn't find room to protect him on a roster loaded with veteran talent.

The Panthers, preparing to make the next two selections, loved the pick. King was never in their plans.

"We were drooling because the two young players we identified were Jesse Belanger and Tom Fitzgerald," Fletcher recalled. "Fitzgerald just had a big playoff, two shorthanded goals on the same shift against the Penguins, and we wanted those two players badly."

Fitzgerald went second, Belanger went third.

"Then we started just ticking them off," Fletcher said.

"We thought if they took the first pick, they would likely take one of the Montreal prospects," Clarke said. "Then we were going to take [Brian] Skrudland and [Tom] Fitzgerald. But when they took King, we decided to get the young guys and hope to get Skrudland after that."

Anaheim took Tim Sweeney from the Bruins. Neilson conferred with Clarke, who chose Scott Levins from Winnipeg. Anaheim took Troy Loney and enforcer Stu Grimson. The Panthers pounced on Edmonton's Scott Mellanby, a four-time 20-goal scorer.

The Mighty Ducks drafted a few of the players the Panthers had on their lists but, for the most part, the teams were approaching this exercise with different philosophies. The Panthers finished the draft by selecting Skrudland from Calgary, Mike Hough from Washington, Dave Lowry from St. Louis, Bill Lindsay from Quebec, Andrei Lomakin from Philadelphia, Randy Gilhen from Tampa Bay, Doug Barrault from Dallas, Mark Labelle from Ottawa, and Pete Stauber from Detroit. Among those not selected were several high-salaried veteran stars, such as Guy Carbonneau, Denis Savard, Michel Goulet, Bob Carpenter, and Dave Poulin. Goulet was a former 50-goal scorer, Savard a former 40-goal scorer.

When the draft ended, one hour and 22 minutes after it began, the men at the Panthers' table shook hands and knew they had accomplished their goal.

"The only player we wanted that we didn't get was Wayne Presley, but they took Bob Corkum from Buffalo," Fletcher said. "We were ecstatic. I think every team has that same sense of elation at a draft because, inevitably, teams pick the guys they rank the highest. I'm sure they got what they wanted, too."

A realist might have wondered why these guys were so happy. The 21 positional players drafted by the Panthers had scored a total of 78 NHL goals the previous season. Maybe this team had character, the great intangible, but it sure didn't have much skill, the greater tangible. Neilson was asked who on his team would be the go-to goal scorer next season and hesitated before answering. This might have been the most difficult question he was ever asked.

"Nobody on that list," he said after scanning the board.

Anaheim's offense was even worse: Their players had scored a total of 77 goals and one could easily wonder if they'd take to the NHL like Ducks to water.

Gauthier explained the Mighty Ducks' philosophy.

"Our priority was to go for talented players, and then from there try to get some character on the team," he said.

Clarke explained the Panthers' philosophy.

"We want to be a team that's not easy to play against every night," Clarke said. "You go against Brian Skrudland and you'll know you're in a hockey game."

Later, one general manager would remark, "There were a lot of character players available. The Panthers got all of them."

Who could have known how accurate his comment would be? Certainly not Jordan and Huizenga. As Jordan looked up and down the Panthers' selection board, he recognized only one name: John Vanbiesbrouck. The other Panthers were complete unknowns to him and one name struck him as particularly comical.

Jordan nudged his boss.

"Wayne," he said, "You just paid $50 million to draft Brian Skrudland. How do you feel?"

▲ ▲ ▲

Brian Skrudland felt pretty good for a guy who had been traded from the eventual Stanley Cup champions during the season and, at 30, was now expected to be the leader of a first-year team. Skrudland's misfortune was the Panthers' good fortune. He had a reputation as one of the best checking centers in the League, but tore up his knee in the first game of the 1992-93 season when he ran into another player. Suddenly, he was damaged goods.

The season was an ordeal for Skrudland. The knee injury was followed by a broken thumb and a sprained ankle. In January, after nearly eight seasons in Montreal, the Canadiens traded him to the Calgary Flames. His wife, Lana, was five months pregnant with their second child and the first, Simon, was barely two. But, with no other viable choice, they moved to Calgary and purchased the dream home in which they saw themselves settling down. Surely, the Flames wouldn't have traded for a player they didn't plan on keeping.

Unfortunate assumption. The Flames exposed Skrudland in the expansion draft, a clear indication of how far his career had fallen.

"Al Coates [the Flames' assistant general manager] called and told me they weren't protecting me for this and that reason," Skrudland said. "I thought, 'Oh, Jesus.' I was considered to have a big contract. I was making $650,000 Canadian at the time and I'd played a total of 80 games in two and a half seasons. Any time a player is not protected, they're sort of telling you that the back door is unlocked. Whether you get pushed out or not is a whole different thing."

Upon hearing he hadn't been protected, Skrudland was perfectly willing to sell the house, walk out the back door, and join either of the expansion teams. All he had to do was take a look at the names of some of the other players the Flames hadn't protected — career minor leaguers Rick Chernomaz, Kerry Clark, Todd Harkins, and Patrick Lebeau — to figure out where he stood with this organization. The Flames obviously weren't interested in taking any more chances on a guy who was missing more games than he was playing.

"If he had a full season, he wouldn't have been available," Torrey said.

The expansion draft meant a change of fortune. Bouris phoned Skrudland with the news he had been picked by the Panthers and rattled off the names of his new teammates.

"Pretty good," Skrudland said when he heard the names of the goaltenders. His enthusiasm didn't wane when Bouris reviewed the rest of the list.

"He was excited, pumped up," Bouris recalled. "I remember thinking, *This is pretty good if the other players come in with this guy's attitude.*"

Excited wasn't the word. He was absolutely ecstatic over the chance for a fresh start with an expansion team in sunny Florida. Lana Skrudland wasn't quite so thrilled; Rudi-Tate, their first daughter, had been born two weeks earlier and Lana could think of better things to do than pack up, sell the house, and move 3,000 miles to a strange city. Typically, her husband looked at the bright side.

"I just viewed it as another breath of fresh air," Skrudland said.

By draft day, Thursday afternoon, Tom Fitzgerald's mixed feelings about being exposed in the expansion draft for the second straight year were now decidedly in favor of moving on. A first-round draft pick by the Islanders in 1986, he spent four seasons bouncing between the minors and the NHL, before Butch Goring, the coach of the Islanders' minor league affiliate, switched him from right wing to center, his original position. The move got Fitzgerald more involved in the game and allowed him to show off his defensive proficiency. In 1992-93, Fitzgerald spent his first full season in the NHL, scoring 27 points in 77 games and starring for the Islanders in their second-round upset of the defending Cup champion Penguins.

With his career on the rise, Fitzgerald, 24, was sure the Islanders would protect him in the expansion draft. They told him they would. But on the Sunday before the expansion draft, his agent called to say he was left unprotected and Fitzgerald began to wonder where he was going. Then the phone rang again at five to five and Fitzgerald braced for the worst: Islanders General Manager Don Maloney was on the line.

Oh my God, Fitzgerald thought. *Where am I going?*

"Hello, Fitz, how're you doing? How's your summer?" Maloney said.

"It's going pretty good, Donnie." Fitzgerald was in no mood for small talk.

"We made a move today."

"Yeah." Now he was really getting anxious.

"Would you happen to have Jeff Norton's phone number in Boston? We just traded him to San Jose and we can't get ahold of him."

"Okay."

"By the way, we left you unprotected."

"I know that."

Temporarily relieved, Fitzgerald hung up the phone and passed the rest of the week nervously anticipating what would happen Thursday. He was hoping he wouldn't get picked by Anaheim because he didn't want to be a Mighty Duck, but praying to get a fresh start with somebody. Beggars couldn't be choosers. He was, after all, a fourth-line forward who was thought to be of little value by the team he was still playing for, and the Islanders, though Stanley Cup semifinalists, weren't exactly loaded.

Fitzgerald and his wife Kerry spent the day of the expansion draft at her parents' house in Melrose, Massachusetts, preparing for his brother-in-law's wedding rehearsal dinner. His father was watching the draft off the satellite dish at the home of his cousin, Keith Tkachuk of the Winnipeg Jets, but Fitzgerald didn't feel like joining them. He didn't want to be around if he wasn't picked.

"My father called me that day and told me," Fitzgerald said. "Then all of my teammates from the Islanders started calling, Steve Thomas, Flats [Patrick Flatley]. Al Arbour called to wish me the best. Then I started talking to the media. That whole night, my brother-in-law's rehearsal dinner was going on, but I took the spotlight away from them because the phone was ringing off the hook.

"But it was really exciting to know that we were coming to a new place where nobody knew each other. It was just a great day for me."

Ironically, if Torrey had still been with the Islanders, he would've protected Fitzgerald. The Islanders exposed him to the man most likely to take him.

"I knew what kind of competitor he was," Torrey said.

The Panthers thought just as highly of Scott Mellanby, the most talented forward they selected. Mellanby, 27, had scored 20 or more goals four times in the NHL, but was considered a third-line winger, at best, since injuring his left hand during a barroom fight in Canada in 1989. As Mellanby told it, he was coming to the aid of a friend and found himself in the mix. He underwent surgery, missed the first 20 games of the 1989-90 season, and later successfully sued the bar owners and the instigator of the fight, claiming it damaged his career. Clarke, acknowledging the difference between Mellanby then and now, hoped the damage wasn't total.

"We see him as a big, strong NHL winger," Clarke said. "We don't expect him to score 40 goals, but he can do corner work and front-of-the-net work. We like him as a player and as a person. We think he's quality in the locker room, as well."

Jesse Belanger easily controlled his excitement when he found out he was leaving Montreal. Belanger, a 24-year-old Quebecois center, had broken into the Canadiens' lineup that spring and played in nine playoff games for the Stanley Cup champions. The Canadiens envisioned Belanger as their next Guy Carbonneau, a checking center who could defend the opposing team's best players, and that was fine with a kid who had spent most of the past three seasons in the minors. But the Canadiens had no room for him on their protected list and General Manager Serge Savard would spend most of the next two days talking the Panthers into trading him back. They resisted.

Although John Vanbiesbrouck suspected Vancouver was merely a rest stop on the way to his new home, he didn't stick around to find out his destination.

"I'm not home right now," announced the message on his answering machine. "I think I'm somewhere between Miami and Anaheim."

That was about right, because even though the Panthers selected him, Vanbiesbrouck's final stopping point remained in limbo. The Panthers now had players and were in the trade market, and Vanbiesbrouck was their most valuable commodity. Many teams made offers but, finally, the Panthers bet on Vanbiesbrouck's value increasing.

"We figured if they wanted him then, they might want him even more later on," Torrey said.

For the first time, the Panthers were dealing from a position of strength.

▲ ▲ ▲

Quebec City was in a festive mood that night. It was St. Jean Baptiste Day, the equivalent of the Fourth of July in the United States, and the Grand Allée, an old boulevard lined with fashionable cafés, hotels, and bars, was overflowing with revelers. Back in their hotel suite, the Panthers' executive staff was in a festive mood, too. Having successfully completed the first half of their job in Quebec, and before moving on to the second half, they took time to reflect on their accomplishments.

What started with meetings on the New Jersey shore at the start of June culminated with the selection of the first 24 players in franchise history. They had a team — a team of outcasts, at that — and reason to celebrate.

"A lot of the players we had identified, we got," Fletcher recalled. "Whether or not we were right in our assessments, time would only tell, but from the homework and preparation we had done, we had rated the players we had wanted to get, and we felt really happy."

South Floridians weren't equally giddy over this historic day. The Sheffield trade was the top sports story on the news that night and the lead story in the local papers the next morning. The expansion draft wasn't televised or covered on radio, so the only people who witnessed it live were the few hundred or so that gathered for a draft party at Don Shula's All-Star Café in Miami Lakes. Even that was a coup for Bouris, who sent up his own cameraman, hired an interviewer, and paid a Canadian company for an uplink truck so the signal could be sent to one location in Florida and another in Anaheim. Then the audio feed didn't work and only lip-readers knew what was happening.

Partying aside, there was work to do: Phase II of the expansion draft would be held the following day and the Panthers had to decide which goaltender to protect. That was easy: They protected Vanbiesbrouck and exposed Fitzpatrick and Puppa, knowing they could lose only one. The next morning, behind closed doors, the Panthers lost only Puppa to Tampa Bay, while Anaheim lost goaltender Glenn Healy and defenseman Dennis Vial.

With most of Friday off, Clarke, Torrey, Fletcher, Patterson, and Harris, spent the day inside, calling their expansion draft selections, going over their final plans for the next day's amateur draft, and interviewing prospects. They knew Thursday's expansion draft was likely nothing more than a temporary fix that would affect the first three or four years of the franchise. What happened Saturday could decide the team's long-term future.

▲ ▲ ▲

The amateur draft was held Saturday morning at Le Colisée, an old, dusty hockey barn located behind the backstretch of a racetrack. Outside on this dreary morning, fans lined up early to get a good seat for arguably the third most important sporting event in Canada, after the Stanley Cup and junior hockey's Memorial Cup.

It is the most exciting day in the life of a young hockey player and hundreds of them, along with their families and friends, took seats in the lower level and nervously awaited the draft's start. All eyes, all hopes, centered on the men sitting at the 26 tables set up on what, during the hockey season, was the home ice of the Quebec Nordiques. Hundreds of media representatives from all over the United States, Canada, and Europe were present to cover an event that not only affects the lives of the boys selected, but had made or broken the careers of the men making the selections. On the ground level of the Colisée, photographers from all of the major trading card companies prepared to take the first pictures of these hopefuls. Each team brought runners whose sole job was locating the newly drafted players, handing them their first NHL jerseys, and walking them to the podium.

Clarke and Torrey walked down an aisle toward a scene with which they were both very familiar. As they reached the draft floor, Clarke turned to Torrey and warned, "Don't screw up the coin toss!"

Moments before the draft began, Bettman summoned Torrey and Tavares to the main stage. The coin went up, the coin came down. Torrey glanced at the floor. The Panthers had won the toss.

The choice now for Torrey and Clarke was picking fourth in this draft and second in 1994, or fifth in this draft and first the following year. Whatever the Panthers chose, the Mighty Ducks would get the opposite. The decision could not be taken lightly.

In many draft years, there is a steep drop in talent after the first pick. Superstars are not abundant and the difference between No. 1 and No. 2 is sometimes the difference between a team going to the Stanley Cup finals or being an also-ran for the next 10 years. In 1973, the year the Islanders took Denis Potvin first overall, Tom Lysiak, a very good player who didn't compare to Potvin, went second. In 1984, the year Mario Lemieux went first, Kirk Muller, another good player who is by no means a superstar, went second. Nobody knew the difference between one and two better than Torrey, who picked Dave Chyzowski second overall in 1989 after the Nordiques took Mats Sundin. Sundin's an all-star; Chyzowski is still playing in the minors.

The depth and quality of the 1993 draft crop made the Panthers' decision easier. While scouts and experts agreed that Alexandre Daigle was a franchise player who would go first overall to the Senators, the next six players were all potential stars: Chris Pronger, the big defenseman from Peterborough, Ontario; Chris Gratton, the power forward from Brantford, Ontario; Paul Kariya, the college superstar from Vancouver who had been compared to Wayne Gretzky; Rob Niedermayer, a speedy center from Cassiar, British Columbia; Viktor Kozlov, a hulking winger from Russia; and Jason Arnott, a possibly underrated center from Collingwood, Ontario.

There really wasn't much difference between picking fourth or fifth in this draft, but the difference between picking first and second in the 1994 draft could be huge.

"Any time you have the first pick in the draft, you have a major chip to play," Torrey explained. "We would know for a whole year that we had the first pick in the draft. It's a chip you don't get very often."

Never, unless you're an incoming expansion team. By choosing fifth now and first later, the Panthers would have an entire year to scout the top prospects or use the No. 1 pick as trade bait. The Panthers felt they had the upper hand on their opponents for the second time in three days and, making matters better, they wouldn't have to disclose their decision until after Tampa Bay made the third pick.

With no chance of getting Daigle, the Panthers wouldn't have minded getting Pronger or Gratton. San Jose, which picked second, wanted Kozlov, Anaheim wanted Kariya and, if no trades were made, getting Pronger or Gratton at No. 5 wasn't a longshot.

"We didn't know whether Gratton or Pronger would slip," Patterson said. "And Niedermayer was right there with those kids. Four or five kids could've gone second or third. There were other kids, too, like Arnott, who we saw as a pretty good player, and [Todd] Harvey."

The Senators went first and surprised nobody by picking Daigle. The Sharks, up next, were working a deal on the draft floor. They liked Kozlov and figured the enigmatic Russian might still be around at No. 6. Hartford, which picked sixth, coveted Pronger, and General Manager Brian Burke offered his second- and third-round draft picks to the Sharks for an exchange in positions. The Sharks accepted with the catch that if Kozlov wasn't around at No. 6, they would receive the Whalers' first- and second-round picks in the 1994 Draft as compensation.

Clarke got word of this and moved into action. He knew if the Whalers took Pronger at No. 2, the Lightning would take Gratton at No. 3, Anaheim would take Kariya at No. 4, and the Panthers would be the only remaining obstacle to the deal. When Dean Lombardi, San Jose's Director of Operations walked past the Panthers' draft table, Clarke circled Kozlov's name on his draft sheet and said out loud, "Dean, I'm going to take Kozlov."

He was bluffing.

"We weren't going to pick Kozlov," Patterson said.

But the deal was already made and the Whalers couldn't take a chance of losing their first two picks in 1994. Clarke phoned the Whalers' table and told Burke he was going to take Kozlov and trade him to Edmonton.

"You can't," Burke said. "It will cost me a first and second round pick next year."

An apprehensive Burke offered his second-round pick in the 1994 draft in exchange for the Panthers not taking Kozlov. Clarke, still showing his poker face, accepted. The Lightning took Gratton, Anaheim took Kariya, and the Panthers, by now having opted for the fifth pick, selected Niedermayer.

The Panthers by no means considered Niedermayer a consolation prize. Harris, Patterson, and Fletcher had seen him play 50 times and liked what they saw: He was faster than any other player in the draft and big at 6'2",

200 pounds. His brother, Scott, was a top rookie defenseman with the New Jersey Devils and an instinct for smart defensive play seemingly ran in the family. Rob's numbers weren't flashy — 43 goals and 34 assists in 52 games for Medicine Hat of the Western League — but the Panthers knew he was comfortable playing in the offensive and defensive ends, a rare trait for an 18-year-old, and could make the team out of training camp.

"He's probably as close to being ready to play in the National Hockey League as anybody," Torrey said. "He has had three years in juniors, so he's physically stronger and his skating is extraordinary."

The only minor concern about Niedermayer, a right knee injury which forced him to miss the Western Hockey League playoffs, was assuaged when the Sharks' team physician performed minor surgery to repair the torn cartilage and gave him a clean bill of health. Then the Sharks gave Niedermayer a speed test and the results were so stunning that everybody assumed he was on his way to San Jose: According to the scouts' stopwatches, Niedermayer was as fast as Mike Gartner, the fastest player in the NHL.

Clarke had pulled the fastest one of all: He gave up nothing and landed a second-round draft pick. No one could believe what the Whalers had done. Everybody in the Colisée knew there was no way Bob Clarke was going to make a Russian the first pick in his team's history. Everybody except Burke.

▲ ▲ ▲

The Panthers' satisfaction with their successful three days in Quebec was tempered by the news that the Senators signed Daigle to a five-year, $12.25 million contract. Clarke was outraged, as were the other general managers.

"If that's true, I'll eat my hat," said Phil Esposito, who has a taste for black, wide-brimmed, Borcelenos.

Clarke was more blunt after the rumor was confirmed.

"It's asinine," he said.

The general managers recognized the business repercussions of what they saw as an irresponsible act by the Senators. Roman Hamrlik, the previous year's No. 1, had signed with the Lightning for $800,000. By signing Daigle for an inflated number, the Senators increased the market value of first-round picks and just about every other player in the League. *If Daigle was worth $2 million a year, then what was Jeremy Roenick worth? What's Mike Modano worth? What's John Vanbiesbrouck worth?*

In 1995-96, Daigle would be the 20th highest paid forward in the NHL, but only the ninth leading scorer on the pitiful Senators with 17 points in 50 games. He was paid more than established stars such as Theo Fleury, Teemu Selanne, Luc Robitaille, Gary Roberts, Cam Neely, and Adam Graves.

The Daigle signing would have long-term consequences for the League; 18 months later, with Daigle's salary in mind, management demanded a rookie salary cap during the damaging 1994-95 season lockout.

As for the Panthers, time would be the judge of how much Clarke accomplished with his 13 selections that day. Three years later, Niedermayer was the only one who had made it to the NHL while several others, goaltenders Kevin Weekes and Todd MacDonald, and center Steve Washburn, were still considered prospects. The Niedermayer selection was a no-brainer; the Kozlov selection, so far, a bust for San Jose. Other 1993 first-rounders, such as Arnott, Niklas Sundstrom, Jocelyn Thibault, Adam Deadmarsh, and Saku Koivu are developing into solid NHLers, and all of them were picked after Niedermayer and Kozlov. Kariya is the only budding superstar from the Magnificent Seven.

But when Clarke woke up in Quebec the following morning, his personal scoreboard was looking pretty good. He had landed two draft picks for the price of none, a former Vezina Trophy-winning goaltender in Vanbiesbrouck, and just about every character player in the expansion draft. He had gone head-to-head with Burke, an established, respected general manager, and won.

And the Panthers were no longer merely a logo and empty uniforms. They had 36 players. Finally, South Florida really did have a hockey team.

CHAPTER 6

Feels Like
the First Time

First love … It's August 3, vacation time for professional hockey players with training camp still weeks away, and Brian Skrudland, Dave Lowry, Scott Mellanby, John Vanbiesbrouck, Andrei Lomakin, Joe Cirella, and Rob Niedermayer are in Florida for what will turn out to be one of the most grueling weeks of their careers: A six-day public relations caravan during which they'll go from mall-to-mall, chamber-of-commerce lunch-to-chamber-of-commerce lunch, autograph-signing-to-autograph-signing, and street hockey-clinic-to-street hockey-clinic.

If you're going to build interest in a hockey team, the public relations staff realizes, you have to do it with the hockey players. And it all starts among the mechanical dinosaurs and screaming children at the Discovery Center, a museum in downtown Fort Lauderdale.

"Here, sir," the woman at the check-in table says to Brian Skrudland. "Please wear this name tag."

A familiar voice wanders through Skrudland's head. It's his own and it's saying, *Screwy, I believe we're not in Canada anymore.*

Every morning for the next five days, a van picks up the players at 8:00 and drops them off at 4 p.m. Then there's time for a quick nap or dinner before the van fetches them again at 5 or 6. By 10 p.m., their day finally over, they have signed hundreds of autographs, met thousands of people, and had their patience tested dozens of times.

"Nobody knows anything about hockey down here," a public relations staffer tells them. "Nobody knows anything about who you are."

And if nobody knows who you are, the thinking goes, nobody's going to buy tickets to watch you play. As it turns out, plenty of people want to know who these people are. One night, the players sit for an hour signing autographs for 650 fans prior to a Marlins baseball game. They marvel at the unlikeliness of this scene. The weather is typical of South Florida in August: hot and sticky, sometimes unbearable.

"It beats Winnipeg," Vanbiesbrouck decides, perhaps still wondering if it beats New York, too.

One night, Mellanby's patience wears out during another autograph signing at another mall. The players arrived early to find long lines of fans and, not wanting to turn anybody away, stay until after closing time. Mellanby corners Greg Bouris in the parking lot and gives him an earful.

"Hey, listen!" Mellanby screams. "We're down here, we're giving you our time for free! When you tell us we're going to be here from four to six, make sure it's four to six! Our wives are waiting for us!"

"If I have to explain what we're doing," Bouris responds, "I'm not even going to bother."

What can he tell him? That the real reason for the holdup is Skrudland, who insists on having a personal conversation with every person on line? Skrudland's in a hurry, too. He has his family waiting and some house shopping to do, but this is all too much fun. He feels like a pioneer, making inroads in virgin hockey territory and meeting all of these new fans who are so excited about hockey coming to South Florida. And who could've known that every appearance would be packed? Forget that over six days, Skrudland will meet only one person born in Florida; the rest are transplanted northerners. What's important is that hockey fans are already here and waiting.

"Hey, I can't wait to see you guys play the Rangers!" one person tells Skrudland.

As the week moves along, the obscure names the Panthers drafted are becoming congenial, real live human beings to South Florida's sports fans. People are starting to realize, "Hey, hockey players are different from football, baseball, and basketball players. They'll actually speak with us!"

And something else is happening. These seven players, members of a hockey team that hasn't even been picked, are getting to like each other. They've already chosen a target for practical jokes: Lomakin, a 29-year-old Russian.

"Hey, Andrei, you're gonna have to do some translating for us today," Skrudland says.

"What do you mean?" Lomakin responds in his thick Eastern European accent.

"Well, we're going to a Cuban area and none of us guys know Spanish. Would you help us out?"

"I don't know Spanish."

"Well, shit, you sure sound like you know one of those languages!"

Lomakin's a long way from a place where he's easily understood. Four years ago, he was playing hockey in cold, gray Moscow. Now he's creating hockey fans in South Florida. Moscow on the Intracoastal it's not.

▲ ▲ ▲

First takes.

Miami Arena looks like a movie studio today. There are cameramen and microphones everywhere and some strange things happening down on the ice. A man in running shorts is standing next to a hockey player. A gun goes off. The runner falls flat; the hockey player wins the race by default as the runner slides slowly across the ice. Then an actor dressed like a banker — pin-striped suit, briefcase, horn-rimmed glasses — walks onto the ice. *Splat!* A hockey player comes out of nowhere and checks him into the boards.

The Crispen and Porter advertising agency is filming the Panthers' first set of TV commercials and humor is the main theme.

A hockey player can beat a world-class sprinter in a test of speed... on ice.

The banker is advocating one of the benefits of ice hockey: Free checking.

Another benefit of watching the Panthers is illustrated by close-up shots of an air conditioning duct: "Good hockey, great air conditioning."

In one spot, the no-no's of hockey — slashing, tripping, spearing, and hooking — are painfully demonstrated on a live dummy.

Hockey is being sold to South Floridians in the most offbeat way possible.

Drivers traveling on the local roads can't miss the Panthers' billboards. There's the one with a picture of the hockey mask worn by Jason in the movie *Friday the 13th*: "Just in time for Halloween," the billboard reads.

All this is new to Dean Jordan. Offbeat, humorous advertising wasn't necessary a year ago, when the Marlins staff was selling baseball to South Florida. Their work was done for them. A two-year civic battle for the franchise was all the promotion they needed and the team is now on its way to drawing three million fans. Everybody wants to be a part of the Marlins. But hockey? The Panthers? They have two months to convert the detractors and making those detractors laugh seems like the best way to transform them.

The effort is monumental. Nearly 250,000 copies of the *Florida Panthers Pocket Hockey Guide*, a basic beginner's guide to the NHL, are printed in English and Spanish and distributed to banks and Blockbuster Video stores. In an area with four million people, ignoring the Hispanic community means ignoring half the market, and that's just not good business sense. So they sell hockey in explainable terms: It's just like soccer, but faster. There's a goalie and a net, but a puck instead of a ball, and the players are allowed to hit each other.

The pocket schedules are also printed in Spanish. The Panthers conduct street hockey clinics in Little Havana.

Hockey is new in South Florida, and its language is foreign to everyone.

▲ ▲ ▲

First star.

Meet Professor Beezer, Instructor of Hockey 101. He's teaching all of South Florida about ice hockey in *The Florida Panthers Video Hockey Guide*. The 14-minute video will be available in Blockbuster stores for 50 cents a day with all proceeds going to the National Fish and Wildlife Foundation.

Vanbiesbrouck is not only the most famous name on the Panthers, he also has the most unusual name, and he's been asked to teach a class he never had to give in New York.

"It was kind of an odd thing," Vanbiesbrouck explains. "I was flattered they wanted me to do it. They wanted to do an instructional thing and get it into stores really quick. We did the shooting of the video in one day and it took form right away."

Vanbiesbrouck narrates the video, in which he uses simply terminology — nothing advanced like "pinching" or "taking the man" or "headmanning" on this tape — in order to make hockey easy to understand for a novice audience. All of the equipment is described and the purpose of the video is obvious: Fans are more likely to attend and enjoy a game if they know what's going on.

It has been a busy summer for Vanbiesbrouck, and that's fine with him. Moving on was just what he needed.

His older brother, Frank, had been going through a period of deteriorating mental health which worsened because of a divorce and surgery. The change in Frank's condition happened so suddenly that John barely had a chance to notice it, and when he did, there wasn't much he could do. On April 7, Frank turned a gun to his head and ended his life. He left behind a four-year-old daughter and a brother he idolized and who idolized him in return.

This tragic compounding of the tumult in John Vanbiesbrouck's life struck at a time when he was going through professional turmoil. The irony of the Panthers selecting him in the expansion draft was that while it gave him the opportunity to move on, he was — unlike his new teammates — a star in the city he was leaving.

Vanbiesbrouck was an 18-year-old rookie from Detroit when he made his first NHL start for the Rangers on December 5, 1981. He returned to juniors for another season, played a year in the minors, and struggled though his NHL rookie season in 1984-85 before becoming a hero of the Madison Square

Garden faithful. Vanbiesbrouck won the Vezina Trophy in 1985-86 as the League's top goalie and led the Rangers to the conference finals. A crowd which hadn't loved a goalie this way since Eddie Giacomin in the early 1970s sang "Bee-zer! Bee-zer!" after every save and anointed him the team's messiah, the man who would carry the Rangers to the Stanley Cup.

But the Rangers already had their eyes on Mike Richter, a second-round draft pick in 1985, as their goalie of the future. Vanbiesbrouck was merely minding the store. In 1989, with the Rangers on the verge of an embarrassing first-round sweep by the Penguins, General Manager/Coach Phil Esposito benched Vanbiesbrouck, and Mike Richter became the first goaltender to make his NHL debut in the playoffs. The Rangers were swept, anyway.

Esposito's firing might have saved Vanbiesbrouck's career in New York, but the situation didn't improve much when Roger Neilson took over for the 1989-90 season. Neil Smith, the new GM, was suspicious of Vanbiesbrouck's playoff record — he had won only one game since the 1986 run — and wanted Richter to be the man. But neither goaltender established himself as better than the other and, for four seasons, Richter and Vanbiesbrouck split playing time in a platoon system that pleased and benefited neither.

"It was a difficult situation," Neilson said. "We had pretty good goalkeeping, but at no time did one guy just jump out. If he had, we would've stayed with him, because we didn't like it that way. We wanted one of them to jump out and neither did."

Several times the Rangers handed the No. 1 job to Richter, who couldn't hold on. Although Vanbiesbrouck held his share of the job with occasionally brilliant play and remained the crowd favorite, annoying lapses and bad goals prevented him from changing the Rangers' minds about Richter. And he was by no means a favorite in the locker room; Vanbiesbrouck had a reputation for never footing his share of the blame. A goal was always a defenseman's fault, rarely his.

No season was worse than Vanbiesbrouck's last in New York. Both goalies suffered under the platoon system and Richter was sent to the minors. But that didn't mean the No. 1 job was Vanbiesbrouck's. When the time came to pick between the goalies for the expansion draft, General Manager Neil Smith chose the younger guy and traded Vanbiesbrouck to Vancouver.

"Once the evaluation was done, they backed themselves into a corner, so they had to do something," Vanbiesbrouck says. "They knew they were going to lose a goalie. Neil said that all along. Right or wrong, there was a choice that had to be made. They said they wanted to go with young goalies, which was fine."

That sent Vanbiesbrouck on an odyssey which took him from New York to Vancouver to South Florida without ever actually moving his body. Virtual travel. Finally, in early August, Vanbiesbrouck and his wife Rosalinde packed up their beautiful home in Westchester, New York, and moved to Florida. He brought with him 200 career wins, the Vezina Trophy, and the reputation as a goalie who couldn't perform in the playoffs. But that's OK. The Panthers don't expect to make the playoffs.

"Each game as a Panther, we're going to enter thinking we're going to win it, but the expectation level is different because we have to be a lot more short-term with our goals," Vanbiesbrouck says. "We're not building to the playoffs and making a run at the Stanley Cup."

Now, with the season approaching, Vanbiesbrouck is thinking about this change in his life and the next stage in his relationship with Neilson. The player and the coach are together again, but this time looking forward to the challenge. All indications are that Vanbiesbrouck will be the No. 1 goalie and Mark Fitzpatrick, who only recently recovered from serious health complications that almost ended his career, will be the backup. Neilson knows that will make for one unhappy goalie, but he also knows from experience it's better to have one unhappy goalie than two. And Vanbiesbrouck knows that although he's already South Florida's hockey star, the pressures here will be somewhat different. Recently, he spoke to Chico Resch, the goalie who played for several bad teams in his career, about what he could expect, and Resch wasn't exactly optimistic.

"Your team's probably not going to be able to come up with the goals in a 2-1 game," Resch told him. "You're not going to be able to tie it."

But he'll deal with that when it happens because a new chapter in his life is beginning. He likes the teammates he met during the caravan. The fans at the clinics and "Meet the Panthers" functions have treated him well. The weather is beautiful. There are worse places to be. Winnipeg, for instance. Sometimes, even New York.

"Sometimes the grass isn't greener on the other side," Vanbiesbrouck philosophizes. "I don't know what's ahead. We're looking at a pretty difficult task here in Florida, but I'm really enjoying it. I didn't think it would be this good."

▲ ▲ ▲

First training camp. First day. First hotel. First team meeting.

A roomful of 52 players are gathered at a hotel in Deerfield Beach, about 15 miles north of Fort Lauderdale. Most of them are outcasts from other teams, some are career minor leaguers, a few are rookies, and they are all happy just to be attending an NHL training camp. The hockey experts are expecting the Panthers will be no better than the previous season's Tampa Bay Lightning and possibly as bad as the Ottawa Senators.

But that doesn't sit well with Bob Clarke, who walks in and tells the players that other peoples' expectations are irrelevant. Only his count and here's what he expects.

The room is silent. All eyes are on Clarke, who is standing in front of the players he drafted, acquired, and traded for. Every last one of them.

"Our expectations are that we're going to be competitive every night," Clarke starts.

"Just because we're an expansion team doesn't mean we don't have as much of a right to win as everyone else.

"If anybody came here expecting this to be a weak team and we're not going to be competitive, then you shouldn't be associated with this group.

"We're not going to use the word expansion. We're not an expansion team. We're a first year team, but we're not an expansion team and we're not going to use that phrase this year.

"Our goal is to make the playoffs, like every team in the NHL."

And, by the way, he adds, anybody who thinks they have a job nailed down has another think coming.

Clarke steps back and Bill Torrey says a few words. Then Roger Neilson. The theme is set, just as it probably was across the country in Anaheim, and one year earlier in Tampa Bay and Ottawa. A general manager doesn't tell his expansion team that it's expected to lose. The question is, do the players believe him? Call them crazy, but this team does.

▲ ▲ ▲

First impressions.

Tom Fitzgerald is counting on his fingers. Randy Gilhen. *That's one.* Brian Skrudland. *That's two.* Me. *That's three.*

Three checking centers? It's a good thing I can play right wing.

Bill Lindsay looks around and does the same thing. *Mike Hough. Dave Lowry. Me. Three checking left wings. Uh-oh. No wonder I'm on a two-way.*

Scott Mellanby doesn't have the same problem when he arrives. He looks around the room and can't find another player who's scored over 20 goals in a season, no less four times.

As players arrive at Gold Coast Ice Arena in Pompano on September 9 for the first day of training camp, they realize they're all in similar situations. None of them are superstars. Take Lindsay. He's only 5'11", 185 pounds, but doesn't have the skills to be a big scorer in the NHL. He's a defensive forward and defensive forwards tend to be big because of the nature of their jobs: Stopping people. He started the 1992-93 season, his second as a pro, with the Quebec Nordiques, but finished it in the minors. Not a good sign. He's come to camp with no guarantee of making the team and if he ever gets overly confident, all he has to do is look at his contract: It's a two-way, meaning he makes $200,000 a season to play in the NHL, about a quarter of that if he's sent to the minors. It's an insurance policy for teams who don't know if a player can make it.

Lindsay, like all of these players, is here because somebody else didn't want him. This could be his last chance. He's going to have to find a way to stand out.

Which isn't going to be easy. When Neilson, Clarke, and Dennis Patterson watch an informal scrimmage later that day, they don't know at least half of the players on the ice. Including Lindsay.

Neilson, wearing shorts, a T-shirt, and an old baseball hat, walks around the training center, unable to believe his eyes. He checks out the locker room, which wasn't there two months earlier, and then his office, which wasn't there two months earlier, and finally the video room, which wasn't there two months earlier.

The last time he was here, in mid-July, the building attached to Gold Coast Arena was a bingo hall. The Panthers were late in choosing Gold Coast as their training facility after negotiations broke off with the rink in North Miami, one of only three in the Fort Lauderdale-Miami area. Only Miami had a regulation 85-feet-by-200-feet rink, and none of the facilities were NHL-ready: The Panthers were going to have to install their own locker rooms, showers, training and exercise rooms, and offices.

Back then, Neilson offered his recommendations on what should go where and how, but couldn't imagine the conversion being completed in time for training camp. Today, nobody would ever guess that just a few months earlier, old couples were shouting, "Bingo!" in the same place that hockey players are now riding exercise bikes, watching hockey fight videos, trying on equipment, and getting to know new teammates.

But after today, the team won't return to Gold Coast for another 10 days. Training camp officially opens two days later at Miami Arena under conditions Neilson wouldn't have designed if he had his way. Most teams go out of town for the first few weeks of camp, but Torrey and Clarke thought it would be advantageous from a marketing standpoint to keep the team in town and open practices to the public. Neilson, although realizing there was no way his players were going to do their running in the slum-ridden area surrounding the Arena, reluctantly agreed. He has to create a hockey team. The marketing staff has to create a fan base. At this point, both are equally important.

Neilson is joined by three assistants. Craig Ramsay, the associate coach, was a long-time player and the assistant general manager in Buffalo since 1986. Lindy Ruff had just completed a 14-year professional career, four years of which were spent playing for Neilson in Buffalo and New York. And goaltending coach Bill Smith, the former New York Islanders great, was Mark Fitzpatrick's friend and teacher on Long Island. Prior to the expansion draft, Clarke and Torrey had asked him which two goalies they should take. He chose Vanbiesbrouck and Fitzpatrick.

Their job is taking these 52 players and reducing them to a playing roster of 18 skaters and two goaltenders by opening night, October 6 against the Blackhawks at Chicago Stadium. Neilson has done this a dozen times before, but this is different: He's starting from scratch.

As a first step, the coaches divide the players into four teams for a series of intra-squad scrimmages, two a day for five days. And fans actually come to watch! Miami Arena has a carnival atmosphere these first few days. While players are fighting for jobs on the ice — literally fighting, in the case of defensemen Paul Laus and Rick Hayward, who can't keep their gloves on — the marketing staff is working the aisles selling dasher board advertising, showing prospective season ticket buyers their prospective seats, and introducing people to the game. Another 2,000 fans sit and just watch the action on the ice. In one corner of the Arena, Clarke, Torrey, and Fletcher try to ignore the distractions and keep their minds on business. They're trying to evaluate players while all of these side shows are going on around them.

It's like we're in the middle of a field trip, Fletcher thinks.

The distractions don't end when the players leave the rink. While training in Miami, the players are staying at the Doral Resort Country Club and living in paradise. There are swimming pools, the beach, a golf course, and palm trees. This is the most unlikely setting for hockey camp they have ever seen. Fitzgerald thinks he's dreaming; he spent the past five years of his life living at the Long Island Marriott, a hotel located in the middle of a parking lot near Nassau Coliseum. A tropical oasis, it wasn't.

Mark Fitzpatrick wishes he's dreaming when he sees a car coming at him one night outside the Doral. He jumps and almost gets his entire body out of the way: Everything except his right foot, which he finds out later isn't broken. Not bad. He made a kick save on a car and lived to tell about it. Pucks would be the least of his problems.

▲ ▲ ▲

First kiss.

Bob Clarke is speaking to a bunch of reporters in the locker room area of the Lakeland Center on September 16. Phil Esposito sneaks up from behind and plants a mushy one on Clarke's cheek.

"Love ya, Clarkie!" Esposito says, then slinks away, smiling and laughing as if he just got the girl.

Clearly disgusted, Clarke wipes away Esposito's affection.

"Jesus!" Clarke says. "He's a fool."

The scene is captured by television cameras and replayed dozens of times over the following days. Clarke will spend the rest of the season on the lookout for Esposito whenever Tampa Bay is the opponent, and whenever Espo is in the vicinity spitting in disgust, "Get that fool away from me!"

Foolishness is running deep in Tampa. Terry Crisp, the Lightning coach, referred to the Panthers as "kitty cats" in a sophomoric attempt to get on their nerves. Esposito said he couldn't wait to play the Panthers. "We're going to beat the hell out of them," he promised. "We're going to kick their asses." To which Clarke responded, "Phil never kicked anyone's ass when he played." Of course, neither had Clarke.

Back in the Panthers' locker room, the players are a little more businesslike. They are about to become a minor part of history because this is the franchise's first exhibition game. Players are pulling on the Panthers' game jersey for the first time and thinking, *This is really exciting*. Fitzgerald looks at the No. 21 on the back of his jersey and feels proud. He doesn't know why, but this just feels right.

Outside, the 5,600-seat building is a little more than half full, mostly with Lightning fans wearing blue and silver, but also with the Panthers' office staff, which Huizenga flew up for the game. And what they're about to see ... well, it isn't pretty, and it isn't exactly hockey.

There's a lot of hitting, a lot of fighting (Hayward vs. Tampa's Brantt Myhres in the main events), and not much offense. The Lightning play most of their regulars. The Panthers, lacking any kind of breakout play and penalty killing, power play, or defensive systems, hold together pretty well for a bunch of guys who had never before played together. They are outshot, 17-3, in the first period, and fall behind 3-0, but rally to lose respectably, 4-3. Scott Levins scores the Panthers' first goal at 15:07 of the first period. Lindsay opens his best training camp with a late score.

All in all, not bad for openers. The teams meet again two nights later in Jacksonville and this time the Panthers win, 5-1. The cross-state rivals are already getting a little tired of each other, but they still have two pre-season meetings remaining. The first is on September 19, the Panthers' exhibition opener at Miami Arena.

Those hoping for a gala first night came to the wrong place. Although the last remaining tickets for the regular season opener against Pittsburgh were sold two weeks earlier, the Panthers are still 1,000 short of their 9,500 goal for season tickets and have reason to wonder if they'll reach their projected average crowd of 11,500. Exhibition games generally draw small crowds in any city, but the combination of the Dolphins having a rare football Sunday off and the novelty of the Panthers' first home game, pre-season or not, figures to attract a decent audience.

No such luck. Nearly 5,000 of the 14,702 seats are empty and those who don't show up can consider themselves fortunate. The Lightning are awarded eight power plays to the Panthers' three. The parade of Panthers to the penalty box begins in the opening minutes and doesn't end. The Panthers lose, 4–2, and blame it on the overbearing officiating and lack of familiarity with each other. After spending most of the first week scrimmaging, they practiced only once before beginning the exhibition schedule.

"We really haven't practiced as a team," Clarke says. "We don't have set lines or anything. We've just thrown guys onto the ice."

He has reason to worry. The games start counting in only 17 days.

▲ ▲ ▲

First team.

Brian Skrudland suspected from Day 1 that there was something right about the Panthers. He had never before played for an expansion team, so he didn't know how expansion teams were supposed to behave, but he saw players who didn't know each other getting along, even though they were fighting for each other's jobs. Better yet, a lot of the other players have his attitude: *If you're going to take my job, you're gonna have to play awfully good to do it.*

As the exhibition schedule moves along and the season approaches, Neilson likes his players' commitment to working hard and playing team defense. He and Clarke think this is a competitive team that might not win a lot, but won't get blown out, either.

The team is taking shape. With two sets of cuts, Neilson reduces the roster to 26 players by September 27. The second cut is especially crushing to forwards Len Barrie and Patrick Lebeau, who had strong camps and were leading the team in pre-season scoring. Both figured they'd have a place on a team with so few offensive players, but their scoring couldn't make up for their defensive deficiencies.

With only three or four cuts remaining, Clarke uses the media to send a message to the remaining players: Slack off, and you'll be the next to go. Three days later, he reinforces the hard working personality of the team by acquiring defenseman Keith Brown from the Blackhawks in exchange for Daren Kimble, who the Panthers brought in as a free agent.

Brown, 33, a defensive defenseman with 812 games of NHL experience, is known as a good man to have around the locker room but, in recent years, that's about the only place he's been. He missed the first 47 games of the 1992-93 season after undergoing surgery on his left shoulder, and his luck wouldn't change upon arriving in Florida.

Clarke also makes a bid to add scoring to the lineup, acquiring Russian forward Evgeny Davydov from the Winnipeg Jets for a draft pick.

Final cuts are made on October 2, the morning of the Panthers' final pre-season game against Hartford in Cincinnati, and the roster is now down to the 23 players Neilson will carry (20 players for games, plus a couple of extras just in case). The roster remains at 23 one day later, when Clarke sends Tichy, the first defenseman he took in the expansion draft, to Winnipeg in exchange for defenseman Brent Severyn. At 27, Severyn is a career minor leaguer who plays his position well and works hard, but can't overcome his lack of natural talent. This is his third team in five days, having been traded from the Devils on September 30.

"We felt Severyn was the best defenseman in the American League last year," Clarke says.

The survivors have familiar names. Of the 23 players selected by the Panthers in the expansion draft, 16 make the team: Godynuk, Mellanby, Skrudland, Lindsay, Fitzgerald, Scott Levins, Gord Murphy, Andrei Lomakin, Jesse Belanger, Brian Benning, Mike Hough, Randy Gilhen, Joe Cirella, Dave Lowry, and goaltenders Vanbiesbrouck and Fitzpatrick. Five others were acquired in trades and another, defenseman Greg Smyth, was signed as a free agent.

The status of the 23rd, rookie Rob Niedermayer, remains in doubt.

The Panthers conclude the pre-season with a record of three wins and five losses after losing their final three games by a total of 16-4. The good news is their record will be reset at 0-0 in just a few days. The bad news is they are starting to look like a first-year team.

Neilson suspects otherwise. For one, the team is surprisingly fast. A little small up front, but fast. The coaching staff, which has already implemented a conservative defensive system based on the 1-4 — one forechecker, four defensemen back, dump-and-chase after forcing the turnover — recently realized that instead of sitting back and waiting for opportunities, the Panthers have the skating ability to become a solid counterattacking team.

"We're fast," Neilson tells the players, and then begins teaching them the system that will earn them notoriety around the League: the neutral zone trap.

Another realization comes when the coaching staff sits down to choose a team captain. Unlike most NHL coaches, Neilson likes picking his own captain, but at least six players are qualified for the job. Skrudland and Hough were captains. Mellanby, Gilhen, Murphy, and Cirella might be good captains. He could simply pick a name out of a hat, but that doesn't seem fair. For the first time in his coaching career, Neilson leaves the vote to the team. They can pick anyone they want.

All six players Neilson considered receive votes and Skrudland wins the "C." He calls this the biggest honor of his career.

▲ ▲ ▲

First blink.

Rob Niedermayer didn't know he'd be affected when the Ottawa Senators signed Alexandre Daigle to a five-year, $12.25 million contract in June.

But sitting in his agent's office in Los Angeles, just two days before the start of the regular season, he realizes Daigle is going to help make him a very well paid teenager. But when? And at what cost to his career?

Nearly 3,000 miles away, Bob Clarke and Chuck Fletcher are sitting in the Panthers' office, staring at the fax machine. The time is 9 p.m. and the deadline for signing 1993 draft picks is just three hours and five minutes away. After that, Niedermayer's only options for the 1993-94 season will be returning to Medicine Hat for a fourth year of juniors or joining the Canadian National Team for the 1994 Olympics.

Neither side finds either option appealing. Mike Barnett, Niedermayer's agent, knows Niedermayer has made the team because Clarke told him so early in training camp; the Panthers had decided returning Niedermayer to juniors would be a waste of time. He is big, strong, and mature enough to play in the NHL and, although he might not have much impact on the team, just being around guys like Skrudland, Mellanby, and Brown can't help but make him a more dedicated player.

Another factor has nothing to do with hockey: South Florida is a football area. First round picks almost always make their NFL teams right away and it's a bad sign when they don't. Although that's not the case in hockey, where first rounders are routinely returned to juniors for a few more years of seasoning, Clarke knows the Florida public will perceive Niedermayer as a bust if he's not on the team. Signing Niedermayer is necessary from a public relations standpoint, but not at any price.

Although the two sides are far from an agreement, they've made progress since the summer. Barnett originally demanded $1 million a year for four years; Clarke offered $400,000 a year. As training camp approached, Barnett reduced the asking price to $900,000. The Panthers moved to $550,000 a year; Barnett dropped to $850,000 a year. With the clock ticking on deadline night, the Panthers raise their offer to $2.8 million over four years, $600,000 below Barnett's latest demand. The gap remains huge and Clarke is getting angry because Barnett hasn't faxed back a counteroffer.

"He's obviously playing games," Clarke says. Doesn't he know it. The games began the night before, when Niedermayer left camp without notice, and caught a redeye to Los Angeles.

Hockey was the only game on Niedermayer's mind when he arrived for training camp nearly a month earlier. Although his older brother, Scott, told him about the business side of hockey, Rob was basically an easy-going, small town kid from Cassiar, British Columbia who liked playing hockey and salmon fishing, not necessarily in that order. Scouts agreed Rob's on-ice intensity was a problem — his focus seemed to drift in games — but were so dazzled by his speed they were willing to overlook his minor faults.

Quiet, unassuming, almost startlingly polite, Niedermayer walked into

Gold Coast that first day feeling all the nervousness a rookie is supposed to feel but realized there was no cause for concern. The other veterans in the room had never been here or played for this team before. They were, in a sense, all rookies, too. Niedermayer felt fortunate to be playing for a first-year team and he kind of liked the idea of not being in Alexandre Daigle's shoes. Sure, the money would've been great, but the Senators expected Daigle to be an instant star. The Panthers put no such pressure on Niedermayer; Clarke and Neilson told him to relax, develop at his own pace, and work hard in training camp. Niedermayer could deal with that.

As weeks passed, however, Barnett and Clarke were barely closer to reaching an agreement and, on October 3, Clarke seemed resigned to not signing Niedermayer.

"It's frustrating," Niedermayer said. "I'd love to play this year."

Barnett rejected the Panthers' offer of $550,000, totaling $2.4 million over four years, and told Niedermayer to come to Los Angeles. Having reached the critical point in the negotiations, he wanted this 18-year-old away from the influences of management. He had seen other teams negotiate directly with a player, circumventing the agent, and wanted to make sure that didn't happen, especially with an impressionable kid who could be presented with a choice: playing in the NHL for $550,000, or playing in the Olympics for nothing. But the consequences of leaving camp were clear: Clarke could get angry and stop talking.

Barnett was willing to take the chance and so was Niedermayer, who that evening said good-bye to some teammates at the team hotel and boarded a plane, thinking he had seen the last of South Florida for another year. Convinced the deal wasn't going to get done, he was planning to spend the upcoming season playing for the Canadian Olympic Team and postponing his NHL debut. Time was running out in this waiting game and both sides were losing.

Daigle's signing had truly changed everything. Hartford still hadn't signed Chris Pronger, the No. 2 pick. The Lightning hadn't signed Chris Gratton, the No. 4, and the Mighty Ducks hadn't signed Paul Kariya, who went third. The general managers were dealing with the old market, in which No. 1 picks weren't paid over $2 million a year; the agents were dealing with the new market, with the salary scale sliding from Daigle's starting point.

Who would budge first? Would the GMs be forced to accept Daigle as the new standard? Or would they hold firm? Barnett is waiting for the market to fall into place, but nothing is happening.

"If one guy jumps off a bridge, does everyone jump?" Torrey asks.

Clarke doesn't think he's pushing Niedermayer off a bridge. Far from it. After all, Darius Kasparitus went fifth overall in 1992 and signed for $470,000 a season the year before. This fifth pick is being offered an average of $600,000 a year, a pretty healthy raise by anyone's standards, and yet the negotiations have reached the critical point: Push or shove.

Barnett is more interested in Gratton than Pronger as his point of negotiation and maintains constant communication with Don Meehan, Gratton's agent, knowing what each does affects the other's bargaining position. Before Barnett flew Niedermayer to Los Angeles, Meehan told him that Tampa Bay was offering $800,000 a year. Barnett and Meehan suspect Clarke and Esposito of the Lightning are talking, too, when the signing bonuses offered to both players are nearly identical.

Clarke is using Arnott's contract as the market-setter. Arnott, who went seventh overall, signed for $700,000 a year Canadian, the equivalent of about $525,000 U.S. This doesn't sit well with Barnett, who thinks using the conversion rate is unfair.

Now, with both sides getting nervous and waiting for something to happen — Niedermayer tries watching TV, but is having a hard time sitting still — Barnett gets a break. Shortly after 10 p.m. on the east coast, the Whalers sign Pronger for $7 million over four years. As angry as Clarke was over the Daigle signing, he is even madder about this because it validates Ottawa's ridiculous act as reasonable. Gratton signs for $3.45 million over four years, more in line with what Clarke figured, but higher than he was hoping for. The market is established.

At 11:50, Barnett accepts the Panthers' final written proposal of $3.3 million over four years: Niedermayer will receive $700,000 in 1993-94, $800,000 for the second season, and $900,000 for each of the third and fourth years.

But there's no time to relax. Fletcher has 15 minutes to change the terms on the contract, make a computer printout, have Clarke sign it, fax the contract to Barnett for him to sign, and then fax the completed contract to the League. When he finishes, he looks at the time on the fax machine: It says 12:01, four minutes short of the deadline.

Clarke and Fletcher realize the same deal could've been done a week ago, but this is how the process works: Both sides haggle, hoping they'll win out and, finally, a compromise is reached. In this case, Barnett gambled and won. Maybe his price was too high, but when Pronger and Gratton signed, both sides' work was done for them. For the Panthers, it was a matter of pay him now or pay him later; wait a year and he might sign for even more. Sign the contract today and he's yours.

With the contract signed, Barnett rushes Niedermayer to the airport for another redeye across the country. Niedermayer arrives the next morning at Miami Airport, catches a commuter flight to Fort Lauderdale and, by mid-morning, is driving to Gold Coast and feeling a little unsure of himself. He doesn't know how the players will react to his walking out of camp and returning as the second-highest paid player on the team. *Will they resent me for what I did?* On top of that, he's late for practice and sneaking in is out of the question. He walks into an empty locker room. The players are already out on the ice. He nervously gets dressed as quickly as possible, grabs his stick, and skates out onto the rink.

Skrudland is the first to notice him and starts tapping his stick on the ice. The whole team follows and, before long, they're joking around and taking good-hearted shots at the kid with all the money. The team is happy he's back. So is Niedermayer after the longest and most lucrative two days of his life. The round-trip flight to Los Angeles was worth $900,000. He showed the Panthers he was firm in his convictions. The gamble paid off.

▲ ▲ ▲

Later that day, Niedermayer is sitting in a Miami Air charter at Fort Lauderdale Airport for his third flight in less than 36 hours. This is the one he has been waiting for all his life: The plane will take the Panthers to Chicago for opening night of the 1993-94 season.

As the rest of the players settle into their seats, two Hispanic men wearing suits and carrying cases board the plane. They look lost.

Who are those guys? Greg Bouris wonders. *Maybe they got on the wrong plane.*

Bouris is trying to place the faces. Then he figures it out: They're Arley Londono and Felix DeJesus, the Panthers' Spanish radio broadcasters. *Heck, doesn't every hockey team broadcast its games in Spanish?* Bouris directs Londono and DeJesus to their seats.

The players are quiet, almost businesslike, and settle into their routines: Playing cards, sleeping, reading, watching movies, listening to music. In less than four hours, the plane will land at O'Hare Airport. Tomorrow's the day.

First game.

CHAPTER 7

Where No Team
Has Gone Before

John Vanbiesbrouck woke up the next morning in Chicago feeling neither anxious nor nervous, but, instead, filled with unfamiliar anticipation. He never felt this way before, not 12 years earlier, when he made his first NHL start, or even on nine previous opening nights. At 30 years old, it was weird, but not entirely unwelcome, for him to experience a new emotion and it stayed with him all day, intensifying as game time approached.

"I felt a sensation of starting toward a destination, like we were astronauts," Vanbiesbrouck said. "Like we were getting ready to blast off in a space ship, not knowing where we were going, and we were waiting for the countdown: Five-four-three-two-one, and blastoff! We all felt that we were going to destinations unknown."

Going someplace and ready for the journey, the Panthers were willing passengers on what they hoped would be a fantastic voyage.

▲ ▲ ▲

The Starship Enterprise could have landed in Chicago on October 6 and not a living soul would have noticed. One journey was beginning, but another was ending, and Chicagoans, as well as the rest of the sports world, cared more about Michael Jordan's retirement from the NBA than an expansion team's debut.

Jordan wasn't thinking about the Panthers when he announced his retirement on this day, just as Gary Sheffield didn't intend to be traded to the Marlins on the day of the expansion draft. But when the Panthers took the ice for the first game day morning skate in team history, only one reporter was sitting in the stands at Chicago Stadium: Karie Ross from a TV station in Miami. Everybody else — the TV and radio news crews who made a special trip to Chicago for the opener and the newspaper beat writers — was listening to Mr. Jordan.

Media Relations Director Greg Bouris had little media to relate to and the players had no distractions. They looked up into the seats and saw Bouris, Ross, TV play-by-play man Jeff Rimer and commentator Denis Potvin, and four college students wearing University of Illinois T-shirts. That was all.

Welcome to the NHL.

"It was like there was a black cloud following the organization," Bouris said. "It was a great coup for the South Florida broadcast media because they got to cover Jordan's retirement, but it wasn't great for us. I remember getting into the hotel the night before and there was all the speculation that Michael Jordan was going to announce his retirement. I thought, *So much for the media splash at our morning skate*. It was deserted. It was a very eerie, weird feeling."

The players didn't care who was watching them because they had other things on their minds.

Tom Fitzgerald. He still couldn't get over the team flying charter to Chicago instead of on a commercial airline.

Brian Skrudland, the captain. He was excited about staying at the five-star Drake, the best hotel in Chicago, in rooms overlooking Lake Michigan. Heck, that was something to remember.

Keith Brown. Coming back to Chicago for opening night meant getting to pick the restaurant.

Concentrating on minutia was more appealing than thinking about the task they faced that night: Playing the Blackhawks in one of the most intimidating settings in professional sports. The Hawks were tough enough. They had the best record in the Campbell Conference the previous season with 106 points and were picked to contend for the Stanley Cup. Chicago Stadium, a 64-year-old hockey barn in which the fans seem to be sitting on top of the ice, made the challenge of playing them even more imposing.

This was no place for an expansion team to make its debut, so instead of worrying about what they faced, the Panthers considered what they could offer.

"We knew we could play with Chicago because of the Lowrys and Houghs and Skrudlands and Mellanbys," Fitzgerald said. "We knew with Beezer in the net that night we'd definitely have a chance to win. We knew we could play defense. It was the offensive part we were worried about."

The excitement of their moment overshadowed the challenge of playing the Chicago Blackhawks at Chicago Stadium. For some of these players, their careers were starting all over and for others, such as Lindsay and the rookie Niedermayer, their careers were just beginning. With game time approaching, goaltender John Vanbiesbrouck led his team up the stairway from the visiting locker room and, at 8:29 p.m. Florida time, became the first Panther to step onto the ice for a regular season game. Center Randy Gilhen was next, followed by defenseman Gord Murphy.

The Panthers' lineup for the first game was Brown, Murphy, Joe Cirella, Greg Smyth, Brian Benning, and Alexander Godynuk on defense; Dave Lowry, Evgeny Davydov, Mike Hough, and Bill Lindsay at left wing; Andrei Lomakin, Scott Mellanby, and Fitzgerald at right wing; and Gilhen, Skrudland, Scott Levins, Jesse Belanger, and Rob Niedermayer at center.

At 8:31, both teams lined up at the blue line for the opening ceremonies, the last at Chicago Stadium; the Blackhawks would move into a new building across the street for the 1994-95 season, making this the Panthers' first and only visit to the Stadium. Frank Pellico cranked up the Stadium's ancient pipe organ and Wayne Messmer, famous for his rendition at the 1991 All-Star Game, sang the national anthem. The old building shook. The Panthers saw Wayne Huizenga, who grew up near Chicago, standing at the glass behind the bench with his wife, Marti. When the anthem ended — the crowd drowned out every note — Roger Neilson sent out his first line: Skrudland centering for Mellanby and Lowry with Brown and Cirella on defense.

There were good omens from the beginning. At 8:41, Skrudland won the opening face-off against Brent Sutter and got the puck back to Lowry. Less than a minute later, he also took the first shot in Panthers history, a wrister from the left face-off circle that was stopped by Blackhawks goalie Ed Belfour. Lindsay took the first penalty in Panthers history, for hooking at 1:44 of the first period, but all the Blackhawks could muster was a shot by Chris Chelios that Vanbiesbrouck stopped for the Panthers' first save. The Panthers got into deep trouble for the first time when Niedermayer and Brown went to the penalty box, giving the Blackhawks a two-man advantage, and Vanbiesbrouck got them through. With 8:02 remaining in the first period, a penalty to Chicago's Joe Murphy set up the Panthers' first goal.

No one could have known it at the time, but the goal was representative of the 233 they would score that season: a garbage goal scored off a scrum or a lucky bounce, created by hard work. Niedermayer went into the right corner for a loose puck, took out defenseman Bryan Marchment with a hard check, and slid it back to Davydov low in the circle. Davydov skated diagonally toward the net with Marchment now in pursuit. Chelios, the All-Star defenseman, made a critical mistake, leaving his position in front of the net to meet Davydov. Niedermayer was free for the return pass and drove to the net. Belfour, an aggressive goalie, came out to make the save and went down. Marchment, Chelios, and Brent Sutter collapsed in a heap near the right post, Belfour and Niedermayer were on the ice near the left post, and Sutter made the Hawks' next mistake, pushing the puck out of the crease instead of under Belfour's body. Niedermayer got up. Belfour was still down. Mellanby went to the net like a goal scorer and got tangled up with Niedermayer. Bodies were all over the ice. Mellanby shoved the puck into the net.

At 12:31 on the game clock and 9:07 Florida time, the Panthers not only had a 1-0 lead, they had silenced the Stadium crowd.

That messy first goal was typical of the game, too. There were two fights — Levins vs. Neil Wilkinson and Mellanby vs. Marchment — and 18 power plays, 11 for the Blackhawks, who scored all of their goals while a man up. Pretty it wasn't, a spectacle it was. The Panthers, though out-sized by the Hawks, never stopped hitting and did everything they could to contain Chicago's speed. They twice recovered from one-goal deficits, went ahead with 6:20 remaining in regulation when Skrudland roofed a close-range shot past an out-of-position Belfour, and settled for a 4-4 tie and their first point after Jeremy Roenick scored for Chicago with 3:53 remaining.

The Panthers could have only been happier if they had won the game. An excited Huizenga burst into the locker room and patted each player on the back.

"What a way to start the season!" Huizenga exulted.

Niedermayer, thrilled about scoring his first career point, momentarily forgot the final score.

"The important thing is we won, I mean, we tied," he said.

The players, overcome with energy and emotion, tried to control themselves — after all, they didn't win the game and blew a late lead — but couldn't stop smiling and congratulating each other.

"We knew from that day that we had a competitive hockey team," Lowry said.

The journey was off to a smooth start.

▲ ▲ ▲

The Panthers had no time to rest on their accomplishment. Hours later, they boarded a plane for the short flight to St. Louis, a game the next night against the Blues, and more opening night festivities: the Panthers would start the season with three consecutive home openers before their own.

Although the Panthers lost to the Blues, 5-3, their reaction to losing established their attitude for the remainder of the season. They were expected to lose, just as they were expected to lose the game in Chicago, but losing wasn't acceptable to the Panthers. Clarke's pre-camp message about not being a typical expansion team had made an impact, and when the Panthers returned to the locker room after the game, they threw off their equipment in disgust and sat quietly in front of their stalls as if they were a veteran team that just lost to a patsy. They knew they didn't play as hard as they had in Chicago and, once again, penalties were their downfall; in two games, seven of the nine goals scored against the Panthers came on the power play and another was into an empty net.

"I was so pissed off after that game," Fitzgerald said. "Guys were livid. Nobody was saying, 'Where are you going to eat after the game?' We knew we didn't play the same way we did in Chicago."

The environment the Panthers walked into two nights later in St. Petersburg, Florida, was a far cry from what they faced in Chicago: a converted domed baseball stadium that was the Lightning's new home for the 1993-94 season. An NHL record crowd of 27,227 attended the first regular season meeting between the cross-state rivals but, sitting far, far away from the ice, they were hardly as intimidating a bunch as the Chicago crazies. On the Gulf Coast, intimidation meant putting MIAMI on the scoreboard instead of FLORIDA. The Panthers protested the intentional misidentification and the Lightning backed down, just as they would for the rest of the evening.

Vanbiesbrouck's value to the Panthers was unveiled for the first time. After going ahead on Levins' tip-in with 2:19 gone in the first period, Vanbiesbrouck took over, making 35 saves, 17 in the first 20 minutes, and stopping a 3-on-0 with five minutes remaining and the Panthers clinging to a 1-0 lead. When Fitzgerald scored an empty-netter with 27 seconds to go, the Panthers had their first victory, 2-0, their first shutout, and were coming home with a record of 1-1-1, having surprised even themselves.

"It was great to start on the road because we had a couple of games to get together as a team," Lowry said. "We didn't have the pressure of playing our first game at home. It gave us an opportunity to go out and settle down and concentrate on what we'd have to do to be successful."

The Panthers, who couldn't have asked for a more difficult schedule than opening with three games on the road, prospered from the experience: The tie in Chicago proved they could overcome a hostile environment; the game in St. Louis made them realize they wouldn't take losing for granted; the win in Tampa Bay made them believe in their goaltender and themselves.

"A lot of guys came in with a chip on their shoulders," Skrudland said. "It was more of the idea that *I'm going to show that I deserve to be on a winning team and I'm going to make this a winning team,* and that sort of attitude made the coaching staff's jobs easier. We didn't really have to rely on one guy or two guys or three guys to get it moving."

Three nights later, 14,372 new friends would lend them a helping hand.

▲ ▲ ▲

Was it opening night of "Cats on Ice," or the home opener of a hockey team? Was the main attraction of the evening a hockey game, or a hat sale? Fans who came to the game in shorts and polo shirts left wearing Panthers jerseys, caps, pins, T-shirts, sweatshirts, and just about anything else they could shovel into outstretched arms. An opening night bash for season ticket holders was billed on the invitations as "a party for people who like ice with their drinks." The Panthers didn't set any on-ice records in their home opener, but 14,372 fans did for conspicuous consumption.

October, 12, 1993. Hockey Night is Souvenir Night in South Florida.

Fans arrived at Miami Arena carrying the opening night tickets that came by Federal Express the day before. No conventional tickets these; they wouldn't fit in a wallet or the average pocketbook. They were a cutout of a ferocious panther biting into a hockey stick, the same design — at about the same size — that was on the cover of the special limited edition opening night program. There were also limited edition opening night hats, limited edition opening night T-shirts and banners and pins, and limited edition just about everything else. Never mind that in some cases, limited edition meant tens of thousands and some of the stuff was still on sale at the end of the season. Because the Panthers were so late designing their logo and uniform, most of their merchandise wasn't available until the first night and fans reacted as if the chance to buy this stuff was a privilege they'd never again receive.

"We set all kinds of indoor arena records," said Dean Jordan. "The average sale to each fan in the building was $40, and that's unheard of. On a regular season night, it might be three or four bucks. The Sharks didn't come anywhere close to what we did."

If New Year's Eve is amateur night for drunks, then opening night is amateur night for sports fans. And this was the mother of all amateur nights, from the overpriced souvenirs to NHL Commissioner Gary Bettman speaking into a dead microphone, to the dancing showgirls, laser light show, and real live panther, to the game itself. Jaromir Jagr and the powerful Penguins were in town, so that should have meant plenty of passing, skating, and open-ice artistry, but it didn't. One of the drawbacks of the Panthers' work-your-butts-off, check-their-butts-off, style was revealed: Not only wouldn't the Panthers generate much creative offense, but neither would their opponents, who quickly grew tired of futilely fighting through the Panthers' seaweed defense. Patience would be the only worthwhile virtue in playing or watching the Panthers.

The Panthers, their patience tested by three opening night rituals on the road, were in the mood for a celebration of their own. Many of the players had their wives, children, and parents at the game, and they were looking forward to the extravagant festivities. The Panthers were the center of attention, and that made them feel special.

"It was just very emotional to realize that hockey in South Florida was for real," Fitzgerald said. "It was the first game and the people were jacked up, and we were able to channel all that enthusiasm and adrenaline in the right direction."

The Panthers arrived at the Arena well-rested, having that afternoon inaugurated what would become their home game day ritual: Skating in the late morning at Gold Coast, driving to a hotel near the Arena, checking in, eating a pre-game meal, and then taking a mid-afternoon nap. On the road at home. Expensive, but worth the price, and a good way to avoid late afternoon traffic, a serious problem in Miami.

"It was something I had done in New York and the team liked it," Neilson said. "Considering the distance we had to go, it was a good setup. Our team wanted team meals, and the club was quite willing. It wasn't like we were going to be making money the first couple of years, but management was really good about it. There was great spirit on the team. They felt like management was right behind them."

Management was, indeed, right behind them on opening night. After the opening pageantry ended, Huizenga took his turn in the spotlight at center ice and was cheered, a sound he should have taped so he could replay it during his frequent lulls in popularity.

"We are very excited this evening, not only because this is the first opening night of the Panthers," Huizenga told the crowd, "but because we are one of only nine cities in this country that has all four professional sports."

He didn't bother adding, "And I own three of them." Huizenga did, however, introduce Bill Torrey as "President of the Marlins" and Jordan as "Vice President in Charge of Microphones."

The game went smoother and the Panthers put on a pretty good show. Facing a team equipped with the offensive talent and speed to run over them, the Panthers put on their most disciplined performance of the early season. The Penguins had the better opportunities and finally scored with 2:20 remaining in the second period when Martin Straka scored on a wrist shot that hopped over Vanbiesbrouck's glove. Joe Mullen's fluke shorthanded goal 3:51 into the third period gave Pittsburgh a 2-0 lead, but the Panthers reserved their one offensive surge for the final 10 minutes.

The Panthers' first home goal was beautifully created by Davydov, who led the rush down the right wing on what appeared to be a harmless three-on-three. Then he skated diagonally to the left wing while moving the puck across the blue line, confusing the Penguins defense and giving an opening to Mellanby, who drove down the slot for a pass. Mellanby beat Ken Wregget with a wrist shot over the glove with 8:28 remaining, completing his sweep of team firsts: First goal in Panthers history, first home goal in Panthers history.

The crowd, now fashionably dressed in Panthers red, celebrated with a wave of noise that made the Panthers, somewhat startled by the reaction, realize, "This place is loud."

"We didn't know what to expect," Lindsay said. "The game had kind of a fun atmosphere. It wasn't like going into Chicago Stadium, that's for sure. Everybody was just watching the game to have fun. They didn't know when to cheer all the time."

The fans knew a good effort when they saw one and cheered the Panthers when the game ended in a 2-1 loss. The Penguins, in an offensive drought with injured superstar Mario Lemieux out of the lineup, were also impressed. They saw a typical Roger Neilson team playing typical Roger Neilson hockey, and that meant forcing the other team to fight for a win.

"If you think you're going to come in here and steal points, you're not going to," Penguins coach Ed Johnston said.

Once the microphone malfunction was straightened out, the only drawbacks were the pounding Levins took from Pittsburgh's Marty McSorley and Miami's usual hockey problem: the ice. Both teams agreed the ice was choppy and slowed the game. Preston Williams, the director of operations for the Arena, said he thought everything went well; Jagr said, "It was like skating on snow." Jagr clearly had the better credentials in this debate, but the Panthers were in no hurry to turn Miami Arena into a speed skating rink.

The ice was fine.

▲ ▲ ▲

Of the three major skills — skating, passing, and shooting — that go into making a hockey player, the Panthers had skating down pat. With most of their players lacking elite-level skills in the other two departments, the Panthers had no use for a fast sheet of ice because that only played into the hands of teams boasting two or all three talents. Neilson, realizing the closest he came to having a puck-rushing defenseman was Gord Murphy, and the nearest anyone came to being a goal scorer was Mellanby, found another way to use his team's speed: The neutral zone trap, a defensive system that requires team speed for its effectiveness and enables teams without full-ice offensive capabilities to generate instant offense off turnovers in the neutral zone.

"We wanted to play an airtight system when the other team had the puck, but we wanted to be able to counter quickly," Neilson said. "We felt our goal scoring would come from counterattacking, and you can't do that unless you have speed. The trap is a system where you don't let the other team get into your zone. You must attack them before center, and in order to do that, you must be able to skate and angle them properly, jump at the right time, and counter quickly. So a lot of drills were done with that in mind."

Neilson was not the father of the trap and the Panthers were not the first team to use it. The trap was invented in the 1970s by the coach of the Swedish national team, who needed a way of neutralizing the Soviet Union's powerful attack. Aggressive forechecking on the huge European ice surfaces was too risky, but sitting back at the far blue line and waiting for the Soviet attack was like inviting them to set up camp in their offensive zone.

The answer to the problem: Rather than sending in two men on the forecheck, the Swedes sent in one while the two defensemen and the other two forwards dropped back to the neutral zone. The forechecker's job was to force the puck carrier away from the middle and up either the left or right wing, while his defensive teammates read the play: left or right. As the defensive team shifted to the puck side of the ice, the forechecker backchecked to the neutral zone, where he was joined by one of the other forwards. The two trapping forwards then forced the puck carrier into giving up the puck or sending a pass through the only seemingly open avenue, inhabited by defenders.

The problem with the trap is that as much as teams hate playing against it, they hate playing it even more. Hockey players like being aggressive and forcing turnovers in the offensive zone. Reading plays is difficult and implementing the trap is tiring because of the constant skating and switching from side to side. The more talented a team, the less likely it is to trap, because it can generate offense in other ways. The Panthers accepted Neilson's system because they knew it was the best way for them to be successful.

"We wanted to be an aggressive forechecking team, but there are times you have to play smart, and if the forecheck isn't there, there's no point in giving yourself up and allowing the odd-man rushes," Lowry said. "We knew we weren't going to win 6-5, but we knew if we kept the games 2-1 or 3-2, we could win."

When the Panthers started winning and opponents realized what they were doing, they became both the talk and the scourge of the League. Rivals patted them on the back for their hard work, then swatted them across the face for being boring. The Panthers would go weeks without allowing more than two goals in a game and, seemingly, the same amount of time between quality shots on goal. Frustrated teams accused the Panthers of being a bunch of clutch-and-grabbers and called upon the League to ban the trap, saying the Panthers were ruining the game.

"There was a lot of criticism because we were playing better than an expansion team was supposed to play," Neilson said. "Teams were saying the trap is bad for hockey, but that was a lot of baloney and our guys all knew that. But there wasn't much we could do about it and it didn't matter what anybody thought, as long as we were doing well."

So the Panthers succeeded in being boring and, as a result, successful. No matter how much time remained in a game, they'd immediately switch to the trap once they took the lead, boring the fans in visiting rinks (mindful of turning off their fans, the Panthers were less disciplined and less successful at home). Falling behind early meant trouble for the Panthers because they'd have to forecheck aggressively. When the trap didn't work, clutching and grabbing did.

"We weren't the first team to bring in the trap, but we were the team that took all the heat for it," Lowry said. "We were the guys that were responsible for the downfall of the game."

The accusation made them angry.

▲ ▲ ▲

The Panthers, taking motivation from anywhere they could, began their favorite We're Outcasts, Us Against the World ritual when the Islanders came to town for the first time on October 28.

Fitzgerald and Mark Fitzpatrick, badly wanting to beat their former team, each offered $100 for the game-winning goal. Torrey, the former Islanders general manager who wanted the win more than anyone, added $1,000 to the pot. Niedermayer scored the game-winner, his second in 11 games, and won the cash. The ritual built upon itself. Mellanby and Bob Clarke put up money for Philadelphia, Murphy for Philadelphia and Boston. Neilson offered a thousand for the Rangers games, while Vanbiesbrouck and Hull chipped in another hundred each.

The pool built crazily upon itself. Poor Mike Foligno, the well-traveled right wing whom the Panthers picked up in a cash transaction on November 5, had played in Detroit, Buffalo, and Toronto. He wasn't going to offer game-winning bonuses for all three! The Panthers went into Boston for the first time on November 26 and somehow convinced Fitzgerald that because he was born there, he was a Bruins outcast. So Fitzgerald put up a hundred bucks for the Boston games. Even Bouris got into the act when the players reminded him the Islanders did him wrong.

The game-winning goal pool served two purposes, reminding the players they were outcasts who would be out of jobs if they didn't work hard and making them care for each other.

"We were playing for one another," Skrudland said. "Every time we went into another building and somebody used to play for that team, you wanted to do the best so that guy could walk out of the rink with his chest held high, hopefully with a win or at least showing we have a pretty good, hard working team. We certainly wanted to command respect, and that meant a lot of hard work."

No extra motivation was needed when the Panthers skated into the fabled Montreal Forum for the first time on November 10 and faced the defending Stanley Cup champions. Although the Panthers were 5-7-3 and showing signs they wouldn't be just another expansion team, history was a mighty obstacle: No first-season expansion team had ever beaten the Canadiens at the Forum.

History meant nothing. The Forum crowd of 16,195 went dead silent when Niedermayer opened the scoring late in the first period by beating Patrick Roy off a spin move. Jesse Belanger, exposed by the Canadiens in the expansion draft, scored a power play goal midway through the second period for a 2-0 lead. Vanbiesbrouck was brilliant, Roy was ordinary, and Randy Gilhen clinched the 3-1 victory with a typically ugly Panthers' goal: from behind the net and off the back of Roy's left skate.

The Panthers were a happy, smiling bunch when they skated off the ice. In a single road trip, they had won in Toronto and Montreal, the two hockey meccas of North America, and earned the right to be taken seriously. Vanbiesbrouck captured the significance of the victory when he stood in the visitors locker room and told his teammates, "Take a lot of pride in this, because it doesn't matter what hockey team you're on, a lot of teams don't come in here and win."

Skrudland knew. During his eight seasons in Montreal, he had imagined what it felt like to be a visiting player skating into the Forum, realizing the history associated with the building, and looking up and seeing the 24 Stanley Cup banners hanging from the rafters.

"A lot of guys played their entire careers and never won in the Montreal Forum," Skrudland said, "so it was a real thrill for a lot of us."

Motivation the next night was provided with a simple glance at the standings. A 5-4 win over the Senators on Jody Hull's goal with 51 seconds remaining in regulation gave the Panthers a .500 record after 17 games.

Sometimes, motivation was financial. Like many teams, management offered the players performance bonuses based on segments of the season. Most teams use 10-game segments. Torrey, Clarke, and Neilson, realizing a losing streak could mean a long time between payoffs, used five-game segments with two points for a home win, three points for a road win, one point for a home tie, two points for a road tie, and bonus points for the power play, the penalty kill, and goals-against. Bonuses were awarded based on points accumulated during the five-game segments and, by the end of the season, each player had earned an extra $15,000.

The bonuses, awarded uniformly regardless of contract size, kept the players focused on team goals and let them get something from nothing. If they were losing by 5-1 in the final minutes, they worked hard to prevent another goal because every goal-against meant $100 out of each of their pockets.

Another idea gave the players a say in everything done by the team. Neilson formed a committee consisting of four veteran players: Skrudland, Brown, Cirella, and Mellanby. They'd meet with Neilson and assistant coaches Lindy Ruff and Craig Ramsay every two weeks to discuss problems within the team and plan road trips, team meals, and the off-day schedule.

"Often, a general manager or coach will go into a town and say, 'We're all going out to dinner,' but four guys might have already made arrangements," Neilson explained. "Those are the kinds of things you want to avoid. With this team, in particular, we always made sure to ask, 'Is this a good time for this? Do you think we should have a day off?' We kept them more informed than most teams."

The line between winning and losing was wafer thin, and could be easily crossed in the wrong direction because of a disgruntled or tired player. There was no room for error and by allowing player input, Neilson maintained control in the most effective way possible.

▲ ▲ ▲

Eighteen-year-old Rob Niedermayer had been given a huge responsibility when Neilson assigned him to room on the road with 30-year-old Brian Skrudland.

"Well, first of all, he had to make sure that I got home on time," Skrudland said.

Then there was the matter of Skrudland's strange sleeping ritual. The man slept like a Polar bear and Niedermayer's job was making sure the shades were shut tight and the air conditioning was on high for Skrudland's pre-game nap in his artificial cave.

Of course, Niedermayer was actually Skrudland's responsibility, just as most teams have a veteran player room with, and look after, a rookie on the road. Skrudland took this responsibility as seriously as he took anything that happened off the ice. His running comedy act kept Niedermayer upbeat and laughing, even when things weren't going well.

"We did everything together," Skrudland said, "starting with getting up in the morning and going to practice and grabbing a bite to eat after games."

Niedermayer didn't need much help during the first 20 games of the season and was worth every penny of the $8,333 per game the Panthers were paying him. He was not only their fastest skater but one of their hardest hitters and scored the game-winner in two of the Panthers' first three wins. Just as importantly, he felt he belonged in the NHL, a difficult realization for a teenager playing against grown men.

"I was playing very consistently," Niedermayer said. "I had the ice time and I was gaining more and more confidence every time out there. I needed for people to know I could fit in and play at this level."

There was no doubt until November 18 in Miami. Niedermayer was having his best game of the season against Chicago. He had a goal and an assist to take over the Panthers' scoring lead, hit the crossbar on another chance, and delivered the team's three best checks. Then, while skating along the boards, Niedermayer lost his balance and was hit by Blackhawks defenseman Cam Russell. As his body crashed against the boards, Niedermayer felt his right shoulder pop out of joint and knew he was in trouble. The diagnosis was a separated right shoulder that sidelined him for 17 games and changed his fortunes for the remainder of that season and the next.

"This was a major blow," Skrudland said. "He was starting to hit his stride."

Niedermayer wouldn't regain his stride for two years. The only positive aspect of getting injured was seeing firsthand how hard Keith Brown, another injured player, worked to get back into the lineup. He realized that as diligently as he had been working, it wasn't enough if he wanted to stay in the NHL. The drawbacks were far more overwhelming and long-lasting. When Niedermayer finally was ready to return on January 3 against the Rangers, the Panthers were riding a 6-1-3 streak and Neilson said he'd have to play his way back into the lineup.

"When a team is playing too well, I don't think you can bring someone back and make him your No. 1 center and No. 1 power play guy," Clarke agreed. "The other side of the coin is, Robbie is important to the franchise and has to play."

Niedermayer returned to his spot on the first line, centering for Lowry and Mellanby, but he was reluctant to go hard into the corners and possibly re-injure his shoulder. The tentativeness which scouts noticed occasionally in juniors became a regular problem, and compounding matters was his dwindling playing time.

"It was frustrating," Niedermayer said. "I'd play one good game, then I wouldn't play good for a while, and then it reached the point where I wasn't getting the ice time I was before. My confidence was shot. It was kind of like, *I can't handle the puck anymore. I can't shoot.* The goalie would make a good save on me and I'd be thinking, *I can't shoot anymore.*"

Skrudland tried nursing Niedermayer through the bad times, and there were plenty of them. At the time of his injury, Niedermayer had five goals, nine assists, and a minus-3 plus/minus rating in 20 games. He had four goals, eight assists, and was minus-8 in 43 games the rest of the season.

"Rob was on such a roll, and then he hurt his shoulder and it changed the way he played when he came back," Skrudland said. "But when he was gone that three and a half, four weeks, it also changed the momentum of our hockey team. We had to readjust because we didn't have that big, strong skater in the lineup anymore. Even though he was a rookie, he was an integral part of our team, and all the guys were making him feel that way, too."

Everyone except Neilson, who couldn't ignore the Panthers' success during Niedermayer's absence. The Rangers were the hottest team in the League when they skated into a raucous Miami Arena on December 22, but Vanbiesbrouck, riding on the emotion of facing his former teammates and Mike Richter, the guy who had his old job, made 33 saves in a 3-2 win. That started a five-game unbeaten streak that lifted the Panthers over .500 for the first time at 16-15-3 before Niedermayer returned in a 3-2 loss to the Rangers on January 3. The Panthers were in a playoff race and Neilson had no patience for rookie mistakes.

"Every shift could've made the difference," Neilson said.

No one felt the difference more than Niedermayer, whose career was suddenly going nowhere.

▲ ▲ ▲

Stu Barnes was sleeping peacefully when the telephone in his rented apartment roused him at 7 a.m. on November 26. He had played well two nights earlier in the Winnipeg Jets' loss to Anaheim and wasn't expecting the messenger or the message: Jets General Manager Mike Smith with the news Barnes had been traded to the Florida Panthers.

Like most of the players selected in the first round of the 1989 NHL Entry Draft, Barnes was having a hard time breaking into the NHL. He spent two seasons shuttling back and forth between the minor leagues and Winnipeg, and played in only 18 of the Jets' first 24 games to start the 1993-94 season. Barnes was a healthy scratch when the Jets made their only visit of the season to Miami a month earlier, and was well on his way to becoming a first-round bust.

"I was playing on the third and fourth line in Winnipeg, and they were only playing two and a half and three lines, at the most," Barnes said. "Some games we wouldn't play at all. A lot of players were seeing a lot of ice in a lot of different situations and a lot of us weren't getting that much ice."

The 22-year-old center from Spruce Grove, Alberta, knew he had come a short way in a long time since the Jets chose him with the fourth pick overall in 1989. Long on offensive skills, but deficient in his own end, Barnes was told to work on defense when he reported to his first training camp in 1990. He spent a year with the Canadian National Team, made the Jets out of training camp in 1991, and thought he was there for good until the Jets surprised him with a quick demotion to the American League.

"One day they're picking you and patting you on the back, and the next day they're kicking you in the butt," Barnes said, reflecting on his post-draft treatment. "It's different after the draft. Guys have to learn that. It's a whole different ball of wax playing in the NHL."

Being a first round pick has its advantages and drawbacks. On the one hand, more pressure is placed on first-rounders than on late round picks. On the other hand, teams tend to give first-round picks more time to develop and every opportunity to succeed. General managers don't like admitting their first-round picks are failures, because that means their decisions are flawed. That's why Barnes thought it was a good sign when the Jets didn't expose him in the 1993 Expansion Draft.

Maybe next year I'm going to go back to Winnipeg and this is going to be a turning point, Barnes hoped.

No such luck. He began the 1993-94 season as the third center behind emerging star Alexei Zhamnov and veteran Thomas Steen when what he needed was the chance to handle the puck and get time on the power play. Not in Winnipeg, but maybe in Florida. From afar, the Panthers saw a possible bargain and, with Niedermayer out of the lineup until January, they were short on centers.

"He had two good offensive centers ahead of him, he was playing with Kris King and Tie Domi, he was up and down like a yo-yo, so we figured it was a no-brainer," Chuck Fletcher said. "He was in the last year of his contract and they were paying him a pittance, so it was basically a one-year situation where if you get the guy and he can play, you have a player, and if he can't, his contract is up at the end of the year. We felt there was no risk."

The Panthers, desperate for offense, had scored more than two goals in a game only once during the two weeks prior to the trade and knew the only way to improve their situation was by taking a chance: Teams demand a high price for established goal scorers, and the Panthers lacked the players to pay that price, so when the possibility of acquiring Barnes became realistic, Clarke put his mini-scouting operation into motion. Neilson called several scouts in Winnipeg to ask about Barnes. Ramsay and Ruff called around for opinions. Clarke didn't mind tipping off other teams that he was about to make a trade, because he wanted to make sure every deal was thoroughly researched. Besides, there wasn't exactly a bidding war going on for Barnes, whose only drawback was the price: center Randy Gilhen, who played for Neilson in New York.

"We had a chance to get a young player, and even though you hated to let Gilly go — he's a heart and soul guy — we didn't hear any bad things about Barnes," Neilson said. "It really was a big deal for us."

And an even bigger deal for Barnes, who kissed his wife, Julie, good-bye, caught a flight to Hartford, and arrived as the team was sitting down to dinner. His career was about to change and the Panthers were about to become a changed team.

Barnes fit in with the Panthers' forwards because he was small and could skate. Unlike most of them, he could also find the net with his shot or feed an open teammate through traffic. Neilson, knowing he wasn't getting just another defensive forward, greeted Barnes in a way only one other forward, Jesse Belanger, had heard.

"Hi, how're you doing?" he said. "We'd just like you to score for us."

That was fine with Barnes, whose only job with the Jets was to not mess up. After playing five or 10 minutes a game on the fourth line in Winnipeg, Barnes played 20-25 minutes a game on the first line and flourished. He scored his first goal with the Panthers on December 15 in a 2-2 tie against the Canadiens, the game-tying goal with six seconds remaining against Boston four days later, and the game-winner in a 5-3 win over the Whalers on December 29.

The pressure was off. The expectations were lifted. Neilson had given Barnes what every young player needs: Confidence and playing time. In 59 games for the Panthers, Barnes would score 18 goals and 20 assists and become one of their most valuable players. No moment was sweeter for Barnes than on February 22, when he skated into Winnipeg for the first time and scored the game-winner in a 3-2 victory over the fading Jets. *Touché!* One day, Neilson walked up to Barnes and said, "Barney, I didn't know you were this good!"

As for Julie Barnes, who had nervously watched her husband struggle with the Jets, the situation couldn't have been better. He played, she warmed up. The day she left Winnipeg, the temperature was 25 degrees below zero. She arrived in South Florida and 80 above.

▲ ▲ ▲

On-ice successes. Bottom line failures. The theme of the Panthers' first three seasons was set early. The schedule called for too many home games in October and November, before the snow birds arrived in South Florida, and not enough games in December and January, at the height of tourist season. The NHL, still operating in the dark ages, had offered little help to its South Florida franchise. The Panthers operated in the red.

Huizenga stared at the ledger, shook his head, and hoped the crowds would pick up once the tourists arrived and football season ended. On the positive side, the Panthers had based their budget on a projected average attendance of 11,500 per game, and were well above that on all but the worst nights, despite selling out only two of their first 14 home games. On the bad side, the team was going to lose at least $4 million for the season no matter how many fans showed up.

Meanwhile, the Blockbuster Park project, revealed back in May, was getting larger by the week with the original projection of a 500-acre project having grown to over 2,500 acres on the edge of the Everglades. Where most people would have seen only wide expanses of sawgrass, Huizenga saw a 20,000-seat hockey arena that would open for the 1996-97 season and finally make his team profitable. Blockbuster spent $50 million buying large parcels of property to the southwest of Fort Lauderdale and, as Huizenga pored over site plans, lawmakers nervously bickered over whether it was a good idea to turn this piece of the Everglades into Disney South.

Although the planning and politicking would continue deep into 1994, the long, slow death of Blockbuster Park began on January 7, 1994, during a meeting in New York City between Huizenga and Sumner Redstone, chairman of Viacom Inc. They agreed to merge Blockbuster into Viacom, and when the deal was finally concluded in September, Huizenga had given up control over Blockbuster's future.

"I was pretty sure it was going to happen until we sold the company in January 1994," Huizenga said. "It was getting bigger and bigger every day, and that was the problem, it just got bigger and bigger."

Until the project actually died, the prospect of Blockbuster Park, with its state-of-the-art hockey rink, infused the franchise with excitement. Torrey, who came to Florida to help build a hockey arena, didn't have much to do with the Park because Blockbuster was handling everything and the actual construction stages were far away. His role in the project would come later. Until then, Torrey spent his days watching practice or scouting, and game nights with Clarke and Fletcher in the Panthers' sky box at the Arena, knowing there was nothing he could do about the team's bottom line. It was getting redder by the day with no hope of a turnabout until they moved into a new building.

And it was from this same vantage point, high above the ice, that Torrey saw the Panthers growing together and South Floridians slowly, but surely, growing fond of the team. The Panthers came home from a 3-1-1 road trip in mid-December and played to three straight sellout houses against the Canadiens, Bruins, and Rangers. Building momentum was difficult because the Panthers would play a game or two at home, then go on the road for two weeks, but as the Panthers kept winning, word quickly spread that there was a team in South Florida that worked harder than anyone else, over-achieved where the Dolphins and Heat had been notorious underachiev-ers, and had a goaltender with the funny name Vanbiesbrouck who, by him-self, was worth the price of admission.

They were a team only a fan could love. Boring to outsiders because they were so uncreative and did little more than muck and grind for 60 min-utes, they were precious to someone who paid $40 for a ticket because they never stopped working and the outcome of almost every game came down to the final few minutes.

Before long, they became a priority to their fans. Management had cir-cled January 1 as an important test of whether hockey would work in South Florida. It was an afternoon home game against the Anaheim Mighty Ducks, hardly a marquee draw, the day after most of the area had partied in the new year and hours before the Orange Bowl football game would be played just a few miles away.

In an area crazy about football, this hockey game figured to draw a sparse crowd.

The place was packed. Hockey was a hit. The Panthers won, 4-2. Their successful journey was gaining attention.

▲ ▲ ▲

The biggest shock was that Paul Laus was at center ice to take the pass. Since Laus is usually crossing his own blue line when the attack is building up, there was only one reasonable explanation for his good fortune: He got lost.

Suddenly, Laus had the puck on his stick with only one man to beat, which is akin to telling a mountain climber he has only one mountain to climb and it's Everest. So Laus did what any defensive defenseman would do: He tried his best Jaromir Jagr imitation.

Laus skated across the blue line and faked a shot. He pulled the puck around Anaheim defenseman Sean Hill and had him beat with one step. Now he was really motoring. Then Laus skated a few more strides and took — "fired" would be an exaggeration — a wrist shot that fluttered toward goalie Guy Hebert.

The puck caught the inside of Hebert's pads. It slowed, but kept going

... and going ... and going. Finally, what seemed like seconds later, the puck was in the net and the red light was on.

"I was standing there exhaling, trying to make it go faster," Laus joked.

Neilson called it "a Gordie Howe move." The goal was the game-winner in the New Year's Day victory.

The better-known side of Laus was on display two nights later at Madison Square Garden against the Rangers, when he fought Joey Kocur, the hardest puncher in the NHL. Kocur had landed so many punches with such ferocity during his career that his hands were mangled; he soaked them in a bucket of ice water after each game, a ritual that reduced the swelling but didn't fix the deformity.

Kocur and Laus dropped the gloves and immediately tangled. Kocur tried getting his right arm loose. Laus held on. Finally, Kocur broke free and Laus nearly landed with a roundhouse right. Kocur scored from underneath, knocking Laus to the ice. The rookie was undaunted. This was his first NHL season and his moment of proof.

Laus still had one shot remaining. Kocur's jersey came off during the fight, so Laus picked it up, wiped his nose on the sleeve, and dropped it back on the ice. Then he skated away.

"I don't think I'm a dirty player, but I just have that fire in my eyes," Laus said. "It's almost like part animal. You're hungry for it. It's a really weird feeling. The contact just feels good. It's something that's unexplainable. Something just snaps."

This penchant for sticking up for his teammates hadn't impressed the Penguins, who exposed Laus in the expansion draft and didn't expect him to get picked. Neither did Laus, who spent draft day planning a Las Vegas wedding and honeymoon with his fiancée, Jeannie. Having played out his option with the Penguins, Laus planned on trying to make Anaheim or Florida as a walk-on the following fall. Then the Panthers took him with their second pick in the defensemen phase — Laus heard about it from his mother, who was watching the draft — and was surprised to find out that anyone held him in such high regard. Or in any regard at all.

Laus had to fight, literally, for his spot on the team against Rick Hayward, another career goon who spent the summer painting the upstate New York mansion of his former team's owner. Laus and Hayward knew they'd have a hard time proving themselves after Neilson banned fighting in intrasquad scrimmages, so they fought anyway. Not until Hayward went down with an injury did Laus know he had made the team.

But Laus spent most of the first two months of the season wearing a jacket and tie in the stands instead of a Panthers jersey on the ice. He sat out 15 of the first 20 games, barely played in the other five, and depended upon assistant coach Lindy Ruff to keep him in shape. Ruff, a defenseman who spent 12 years in the NHL, put Laus through the paces with exhausting skating drills and long rides on the exercise bikes.

He finally got some ice time when Cirella and Keith Brown were injured and ended up playing sparingly in 39 games, scoring two goals with 109 penalty minutes while taking the first steps toward establishing himself as an NHL tough guy: He fought Rudy Poeschek of Tampa Bay to a draw in his first NHL fight, beat Ottawa's Bill Huard, and narrowly decisioned Buffalo's Rob Ray. Laus knew his only ticket to the NHL was as a fighter, because former coach Bill Laforge had told him so during his junior hockey days.

"What you see on the highlights are always big hits or fights, and that's the role I was put into with Bill Laforge," Laus recalled. "He showed me that if there was going to be a way to get to the NHL, this was going to be the way. That's how bluntly he put it to me. I wasn't going to score 50 points a year."

Although they didn't back their words with action, and usually counted on defenseman Brent Severyn as their enforcer, the Panthers thought much more highly of Laus then he thought of himself. They saw a tough, defensive defenseman who could someday become a valuable regular in their lineup.

"I think he's pretty modest about his playing abilities," Clarke said. "He's improved a long way since training camp. Sometimes when players acquire a lot of penalty minutes, you overlook that they're really pretty good players."

The time would arrive when Laus no longer had to pick his spots.

▲ ▲ ▲

For Neilson, Clarke was the gift that kept on giving. On January 6, Clarke parlayed two more expansion draft picks, Levins and Davydov, into right wing Bob Kudelski, a five-time 20-goal scorer with a superb slapshot.

The trade was great news for Kudelski, who was leading the Ottawa Senators, the worst team in the League, in scoring with 26 goals and 15 assists. His off-season home was in Bonita Springs, a 90-minute drive from Miami, and his wife, Marie-France, was in Florida expecting their first child in less than a week. The Senators, needing Levins' size and toughness, were happy to rid themselves of a 29-year-old defensive liability who was in the option year of his contract. The Panthers, holding tight to .500, grabbed the opportunity to acquire their first pure scorer.

Notice was served to the rest of the League: The Panthers planned on making a run at the playoffs right away.

They were no mirage. With 42 points in their first 42 games, they had already passed five first-year expansion teams' full-season point totals. On January 15, the Panthers skated into the Forum and beat the Canadiens for the second time. Eight days later, the Canadiens visited Miami and got thoroughly spanked, 8-3. The sellout crowd, showing no respect for tradition, chanted, "We want eight! We want eight!" The win was the first in a nine-game unbeaten streak that broke the expansion record. On January 30, the Panthers were 21-17-10 and in third place in the Atlantic Division. Two weeks later, they reached their high point of the season at five games over .500.

"The Panthers are the talk of the NHL," said Canadiens coach Jacques Demers.

The talk of the town, too. A caller to a local radio sports show asked host John Moynihan, in a thick New York City accent, "Hey, do you think the Panthers can win the Stanley Cup?" Moynihan advised the caller to not get ahead of himself. Getting ahead of each other was the problem one morning at a TicketMaster outlet, when fans fought over places in line for the low-priced Panther Pack tickets.

Respect for the Panthers was growing. Vanbiesbrouck returned to New York for the first time on January 3, made 51 saves in a loss, and was honored with chants of "Bee-zer!" from the crowd that still adored him. Now South Floridians loved him, too, and they adopted the chant as Vanbiesbrouck was named First Star of the Game seven times within a month. Brilliant on a nightly basis, Vanbiesbrouck became the Panthers' first star and came back to Madison Square Garden, along with Kudelski, for the All-Star Game on January 21.

"The team really started to believe in itself and believe in the system and each other," Neilson said. "It was a happy team. We went into rinks and people looked at us like we were a pretty good team, and that was great for us. We honestly felt we were going to make the playoffs. I don't think we were ever overconfident, but we felt it could be done. We were telling each other we can do it, and here it looked like we were really going to do it."

Being outcasts brought them together. Skrudland had played on teams that went to the Stanley Cup finals, but never on a team in which the players cared so much about each other. If a player saw that a teammate was down or worried about playing time, he'd mention it to the other players so they could lift his spirits, or maybe drop a hint to the coaches. With some teams, the players went on the road and scattered into groups, each clique going its own way. Skrudland made sure they stayed together.

"If we went into a city and 20 guys wanted steak, nobody said, 'Hey, I don't want to hang out with him,' " Skrudland said. "Just 20 guys would go out together. It seems like we had a lot of those situations. Dave Lowry would take us to his favorite restaurant in St. Louis. We'd get into

Philadelphia and Scott Mellanby would take us to his favorite. It was like that all season long. I never ate so many good meals in my life."

The team that ate together never got full of itself, and fans liked that. With each win and each sellout, Miami Arena became the fashionable place to be seen on hockey nights. The promenade between periods was packed with beautiful people, models and others who could be, business people speaking into cellular phones, more fans wearing Panthers jerseys, and fewer wearing the crest of the opposing team. Season ticket holders were treated like royalty with player luncheons at Pier 66 and other fashionable hotels and, before one game, a party with Huizenga in front of the Arena.

"If you came to our arena, you were going to see a show no matter what," Jordan said. "We set the standards for the NHL. We just wanted to give people their money's worth. If you didn't know anything about hockey, we still wanted you to come. We started the Panther Patrol, which nobody else was doing. We came up with creative, innovative intermission games."

Typical was a nightly promotion called the "Ryder Move of the Game," in which a fan in the cheaper seats won a move-down to the front row, right next to the visitor's bench. This was the contest Pyrrhic victory to end all; the upper level seats at the Arena were fine, while the front row had the worst view of the action. Winners were actually getting a worse seat than the one they originally bought, but none of them said, "Thanks but no thanks."

In the most untraditional hockey atmosphere anyone outside St. Petersburg or Anaheim ever could have created, Jesse Belanger, the Quebec kid labeled for a checking role in Montreal, became a scorer, Mellanby got the 30-goal season expected of him for the previous seven years, and Murphy played as if it was 1990 and Philadelphia all over again. None of them thought any of this was boring.

▲ ▲ ▲

Kevin Dessart of the media relations department was biking along the ocean on A1A at 6:30 one morning when he pulled up at a traffic light, looked over his shoulder, and spotted a kinky-haired man on a bike.

"Hey, Roger!" Dessart yelled out.

Roger Neilson was so frightened he nearly fell off his bike. He stared at Dessart as if he had never seen him before. The light turned green and they rode on separately.

Later in the day at Gold Coast Ice Arena, Dessart reminded Neilson of their chance meeting.

"Man, I didn't know that was you!" Neilson said. "You scared the crap out of me!"

Typical Neilson: He had been alone in his world, probably mapping out a variation of the neutral zone trap or trying to figure out a way to hold up the Pittsburgh forecheck. His mind was always working, but seemingly on one thing at a time. Intrusions were not welcome.

Neilson's days started by getting up with the sun, pulling on a pair of shorts, a T-shirt, and a dusty old baseball cap, and riding to the rink. He'd stay there until 2 p.m., bike home for a quick nap or a swim, then return to the rink to make some phone calls, plan the next day, and watch games off the satellite. Sometimes he wouldn't get home until 2:30 in the morning and plenty of nights he slept in his office. Although he always looked tired, Neilson was somehow full of energy when he was near the rink. Hockey was his life.

"He didn't sleep at night," said Bouris, who spent as much time with Neilson as anybody. "He was like a cat, focused. He would nap here and there. He'd be on a plane, planning lines and match-ups, and then he'd put his head down for 20 minutes and sleep. Then he'd get up, do some more work, then put his head down and sleep for another half hour.

"You could always see the wheels spinning. The wheels just kept spinning, and spinning, and spinning."

These Panthers had Neilson's signature all over them. They rarely took chances or attacked with more than one man on the forecheck, and played dump-and-chase even off the counterattack. The checking line of Hough, Skrudland, and Hull, none of whom ever scored more than 16 goals in an NHL season, played more than any other line, because Neilson's system was about stopping, not instigating, and never about taking chances. In his perfect world, the hockey rink would be like a table hockey game in which he could control every player by moving the metal rods back and forth.

"I would much rather have been a baseball manager than a hockey manager," he said. "In baseball, the coach is way more involved in the game. You're right there, you run the game, control the action, make all the moves, whereas in hockey, you just set the lines, open the gate, and hope the players play well."

That hope, that uncertainty, was something he had trouble dealing with, so if the Panthers was ahead by a goal going into the third period, it was a sure bet they'd sit back and try to hold on. Going for a two-goal lead wasn't even considered. If the chance to score came, fine. If it didn't, hang on for the ride.

The irony of Neilson is that this man who takes so few chances in his professional life is such an offbeat, laid back person. During games, he'd bark out the names, "Skrudland!" "Fitzgerald!" "Lindsay!", then use Screwy, Fitzy, or Billy if he passed them in the hallways at Gold Coast. Seemingly oblivious to being a famous sports celebrity, Neilson went about his daily life as if he was just some guy on the street. One morning, Neilson complained to a reporter that he was getting dozens of phone calls from venetian blind dealers, appliance stores, and general contractors.

"It's just a headache when you buy a home," Neilson said. "All these people call you."

"Wait a second, Roger. Is your number listed?" the reporter asked.

"Of course."

Chances are he was the only head coach in professional sports who could be dialed up just by calling information.

The door of his Peterborough, Ontario, home is never locked and friends constantly wander in and out during the summer. Sometimes a friend will stay for days and Neilson won't even know he's there. He was even more at ease in Florida. He loved the climate and the situation: Coaching a group of hungry, checking forwards, most of whom were good skaters, defensemen who didn't care about joining an offensive play, and a goaltender who withstood a nightly barrage of shots. The surroundings were perfect. His backyard was the beach. He enjoyed walking barefoot in the sand or even through the corridors of Gold Coast. Drop by the rink and you might've found him outside the side door, sitting in a ray of sun with his feet up on a chair and a clipboard in hand, doodling with the lineup.

Fitzgerald remembered the first time Neilson called him into his office at the start of training camp.

"I didn't know how to react to him," Fitzgerald said. "He was very straightforward, but then he'd throw in a quick little joke, but I wasn't really sure if it was a joke. Then he'd make some kind of offbeat comment. Like, that summer he was at Tie Domi's wedding, and he was sitting at the same table with Keith Tkachuk, my cousin. And he's saying things like, 'Geez, that boy can drink. He's a partier. He's a funny kid.' Just comments, and I didn't know how to grasp them."

Bill Lindsay came from the Quebec Nordiques and a coach, Pierre Page, who believed in motivational techniques such as screaming at his players. Neilson was just the opposite: a quiet strategist who rarely screamed. The difference was refreshing.

The players quickly found out that Neilson is a patient man who loves teaching and coaching, and cares about his players. At Christmas, he mails out hundreds of cards to former players and associates. He is intense, but low-key. Some coaches like working closely with the general manager; others like barricading themselves with the team and avoiding contact with perceived outsiders. Neilson liked a little of both. His inner group consisted of the players, assistant coaches Ruff and Ramsay, and Clarke.

Goaltending coach Bill Smith, the former Islanders great, felt as if his input wasn't wanted.

"With Roger, I never had a lot to do with the hockey team," Smith said. "Roger never let me voice my opinion. I'd come in and work with Mark and talk with Johnny, but I really didn't have any input. He asked me for my opinion, but I didn't think it was going anywhere, so I didn't bother giving it."

But Neilson was, as Clarke suspected, the perfect coach for a first-year team in a new hockey area. He came in with a reputation for making mediocre players better and that's what he did; he taught the team a system that fit the individuals' playing styles and instilled confidence in veteran players who had never been shown any confidence in the NHL. They appreciated this and reciprocated with loyalty and hard work.

"When I made a mistake in New York, I wasn't going back on the ice," Fitzgerald said. "I'd sit there and sit there and sit there, because they didn't have confidence in me. I knew if I made a mistake, I wasn't going to get a second chance. And a lot of the guys were in the same situation I was in, confidence-wise, but you were going to get put back out there, and they trusted you."

Neilson, a religious man who read his Bible on plane trips, always preached positive thoughts. One of his favorite rituals was having video coordinator Jon Christiano compile a tape of five positive clips from the previous game, win or lose. Neilson didn't care if the team allowed seven goals; he'd start practice the next day with the tape of positives.

"He did his practice plans like a teacher doing a school plan," Fletcher said. "Roger was the most organized and disciplined man I've ever met and he was a tremendous positive influence on the players. We did everything together. We were a team from Day 1."

Neilson put thought and effort into even the most seemingly insignificant actions. In early March, the Panthers opened a three-game western swing in Vancouver by snapping a five-game losing streak with a 2-1 victory over the Canucks. The next day, they had three hours to kill before their flight to Edmonton, so Neilson loaded the team on the bus and took them to an old fish and chips restaurant on a beautiful, quiet bay in North Vancouver. The vistas were breathtaking, the restaurant was framed with snow-covered mountains and, after eating, the team gathered for a photo. Neilson knew of this beautiful place from the time he spent coaching in Vancouver, and wanted to share it with his players.

"It was the closest team I've ever been with," Neilson said. "We were together almost all the time."

This same man who the players considered so unusual, laid back, and down-to-earth, could be frighteningly intense. On November 26, the Panthers lost to the Bruins, 3-2, on a goal by Glen Wesley with 21 seconds remaining. The Panthers were incensed, claiming Boston had too many men, and Neilson, in a fit of rage, threw water bottles and sticks onto the ice. He was fined $5,000.

Regardless of how he acted during the game, Neilson always looked the same after a loss. Brow furrowed, he'd stride back to the dressing room as if he was trying to knock down a wall with his bowed head. Whatever the result, no matter the time of day, he always looked worried, as if he was waiting for the world to end. Yet, as much as he tried to control his players' actions on the ice, he had few team rules and no curfews. He didn't treat these players as if they were outcasts. He treated them as if they had every right to play in the NHL. They believed in him and the system. With Neilson, the system was everything.

▲ ▲ ▲

The play was coming his way and Vanbiesbrouck knew Rick Tocchet would have a scoring chance unless he did something about it. Tocchet was skating down the right wing with a step on Panthers' defenseman Greg Hawgood, but his only route to the net was by turning inside and moving the puck to his backhand. Vanbiesbrouck gambled. As Tocchet skated across the slot with his head down, Vanbiesbrouck instinctively lunged to knock away the puck with his stick hand.

The gamble worked, but as the puck bounced into the far corner, Tocchet's skate kicked away Vanbiesbrouck's stick and sliced into his right hand. Vanbiesbrouck, his hand suddenly feeling warm and wet, knew he was hurt, but had to concentrate on the play. Tocchet retrieved the puck out of the corner and sent a pass to Markus Naslund in front of the net. Blood was pouring down Vanbiesbrouck's hand and into his blocker. Naslund moved the puck to his backhand. Vanbiesbrouck went for the fake and flopped to the ice. Naslund faked again, then sent a backhander toward the goal. Desperate, Vanbiesbrouck snatched the puck out of the air with his glove.

When the whistle blew, Vanbiesbrouck threw off his blocker and examined the deep gash on the webbing between his thumb and index finger, knowing he had made his last save of the night and, perhaps, for a long time. The first thing that came to mind was the nerve and tendon damage he had suffered in his left hand a few years ago — he still hadn't completely regained his motion — and the fear that he'd lost some function in his right hand, too. *Did I cut a nerve or a tendon?* Intense worry overshadowed his pain.

The prognosis was not as bad as Vanbiesbrouck feared. A surgeon who happened to be attending the game in Pittsburgh checked out the injury and said there was no nerve or tendon damage, only a deep gash that would leave Vanbiesbrouck scarred for life. He could deal with that. What he couldn't deal with was the prospect of missing an entire month, at the height of the playoff race, because of an injury.

Vanbiesbrouck, who narrowly escaped having his hand sliced off and instead received only seven stitches, wasn't feeling very lucky.

▲ ▲ ▲

A nine-game unbeaten streak. A goalie that couldn't be beaten. Their leading scorer. The Panthers lost all three on that bloody February 1 night in Pittsburgh.

Mellanby was the first to go when a clearing pass by Pittsburgh's Larry Murphy struck him in the face, breaking his nose and the orbital bone below his left eye. He would miss four games.

The unbeaten streak ended with a 2-1 loss to the Penguins.

With their No. 1 goalie injured, the Panthers asked Mark Fitzpatrick to do what Vanbiesbrouck had done for the past four months. He very nearly succeeded.

Fitzpatrick, 25, knew this was the only way of getting the chance he'd been waiting for since 1990. That's when he came down with Eosinophilia Myalgia Syndrome, a rare blood and muscle disorder that threatened his career and very nearly his life. He allegedly got the disease from a bad dose of L-tryptophan, a vitamin supplement, and struggled through the Islanders training camp in September 1990, not knowing why his arms and legs were always swollen. With his future in doubt, Fitzpatrick returned home to Kitimat, British Columbia, and missed the first four months of the regular season. Nothing could have been more painful for Fitzpatrick, who had become the Islanders' No. 1 goalie the previous season.

He battled the disease for three seasons, contemplated retirement, and treated himself with daily dosages of prednisone, a cortisone-type medication used to reduce muscle and joint swelling. The risks were great. Prednisone, though effective, has potential side effects, including lung, kidney, and liver damage. Fitzpatrick took the risk.

"I came to the crossroads where I had to make a final decision to continue or throw in the towel and not put my body through the stress and physical exertion of playing hockey," Fitzpatrick said. "It wasn't an easy thing to do, and people gave me all kinds of advice, but the final decision was what I had to live with."

Fitzpatrick, unprotected by the Islanders in the 1993 Expansion Draft, accepted the move to Florida, hoping he'd get the chance to prove himself and play on a regular basis. He didn't know that Neilson was still gun-shy from the failed rotation in New York and favored Vanbiesbrouck, while Bill Smith, Fitzpatrick's friend and goaltending coach with the Islanders, didn't have Neilson's ear.

"Roger and I had some meetings," Fitzpatrick said. "He explained to me how John was a former all-star and how the team was just starting out and John would be playing a lot of games. It didn't seem to matter how well I played, things weren't really going to change."

Fitzpatrick made 26 saves in a 5-3 win over Hartford on December 29, but Vanbiesbrouck played the next three games. He made 36 saves in a 2-2 tie against the Bruins, and Vanbiesbrouck played the next three games. Thirty-four saves against the Islanders. Vanbiesbrouck was in goal two nights later.

This seemed unfair and unproductive to Smith. Vanbiesbrouck playing three games in four nights didn't make sense when the Panthers had a capable backup.

"If you can't trust every guy you have, then you go with one guy for 70 games," Smith said. "But if you have somebody that's good, why burn out the guy, because if you do burn him out, sooner or later he's going to get tired and make mistakes."

The Panthers discovered they could trust Fitzpatrick. He was named first star the night after Vanbiesbrouck's injury in a 2-1 victory over the Senators, and rebounded from a 7-2 shellacking by the Sabres — one of the few times all season the Panthers were booed at home — to record the Panthers' first home shutout, a 3-0 gem against the Bruins in which he made 38 saves. Fitzpatrick wasn't perfect, and Vanbiesbrouck's quicker reflexes might have prevented the overtime goal in a 4-3 loss to the Flyers on February 10, but he was better than any other backup in the League.

Not that the Panthers didn't notice Vanbiesbrouck's absence, because the two goalies are different in almost every way. Vanbiesbrouck is an outgoing dressing room leader; Fitzpatrick is quiet and reserved. Vanbiesbrouck plays an aggressive style based on reflexes and a superb glove hand. Fitzpatrick uses all of his 6'2", 190 pounds to play the angles and make every save look easy. His style inspires confidence, rather than excitement, although he looks horrible when he misplays an angle.

Ironically, an out-of-control Fitzpatrick forced Vanbiesbrouck back into action sooner than planned. After defeating the Canucks, 2-1, on February 13, Fitzpatrick learned he had been suspended for two games for a high-sticking incident in the previous game against the Islanders. When minor leaguer Pokey Reddick got shelled in a 7-3 loss to the Red Wings, Vanbiesbrouck realized he had to play.

"I don't think I have a choice," Vanbiesbrouck said. "It's an important game for us."

Vanbiesbrouck's comeback expedited Fitzpatrick's inevitable return to the bench. After serving the suspension, Fitzpatrick waited another two games before getting a start and played in only seven of the Panthers' final 27 games. This time, he wasn't a happy backup.

"As soon as John came back, I was back to the same situation as before I got injured," Fitzpatrick said. "After playing a lot of games over a short period, that should've shown to staff and management that I was capable of carrying a load."

Neilson didn't care. Vanbiesbrouck was his man and an injury wasn't going to change that, no matter how well Fitzpatrick played.

"We liked the way Mark played," Neilson said. "If he was outstanding, there was a good chance he'd be back the next game, but there was no question Beezer was going to be No. 1 and we felt that was how we were going to get the most out of him."

Neilson didn't know it at the time, but he had already squeezed all he could out of Vanbiesbrouck. Before the injury, Vanbiesbrouck led the League in save percentage, was second in goals-against average, and had a record of 16-12-8. He went 5-13-3 the rest of the way and finished second in save percentage and fourth in goals-against average.

Vanbiesbrouck knew why he slipped from great to good: He tried too hard to speed up his return from the injury and made it worse. The day the stitches were removed from his hand, he sneaked in a little practice, against the doctor's orders, until trainer "Sudsy" Settlemeyer caught him in the act.

"Having missed seven games, I should've come back stronger with my play on the ice, but I was so intent on coming back quickly that I lost focus on what I had to do to return," Vanbiesbrouck said. "I tried to come back earlier and it just didn't work out. The cut was really wide, and it was deep, and it kept opening up."

The Panthers' playoff hopes were irreversibly wounded.

▲ ▲ ▲

On March 21, the Panthers tied the Devils, 3-3, to set the record for most points by an expansion team with 74. Their 32nd victory of the season, 3-1 over the Islanders on March 26, also set an expansion record. They were 18-16-8 on the road, a remarkable accomplishment for an expansion team with a long-distance travel schedule; other than Tampa Bay, the nearest team in their division was over 1,200 miles away.

Playoff tickets went on sale April 2, with seven games remaining and the

Panthers in eighth place in the Eastern Conference, three points ahead of the Islanders for the final spot. In a season of highlights, that might've been the biggest of all.

Perhaps their biggest mistake was letting themselves think they were going to make the playoffs. They started losing close games and the goal scorers stopped scoring. Kudelski scored his 40th goal in the 70th game and was shut out the rest of the way. Making matters worse, Kudelski's poor skating skills made it difficult for him to play the trap, and Neilson cut his ice time. Clarke didn't like the idea of his $400,000-a-year acquisition sitting on the bench, but Neilson couldn't justify playing an ice-cold scorer who wasn't contributing in any other way.

Key players suffered injuries, first Vanbiesbrouck and Mellanby, then Belanger for 12 games with a broken hand, and, most crushingly, Skrudland, their captain and leader, for the final five games of the season. The Panthers went 8-14-7 over the last 29 games and wasted an eight-point lead over the Islanders.

"We were in every game," Neilson said. "We had a really tough schedule, we had five games in seven nights, including one where we went all the way up to Hamilton and back. Then we had a real tough tie in Quebec. We were outplaying them completely, and then they just happened to score a fluke goal with the goalie out. The one prior to that, too, was a heartbreaker. We outshot Philly 40 to something, and we only got the tie. There were a whole bunch of those right in a row where we couldn't quite do it. We just weren't getting the breaks."

Although they cursed a schedule that had them playing four games in five nights at the most important part of the season, their inability to convert scoring chances did them in: Playoff bound at 32-30-13 after beating the Islanders, the Panthers won only one of their final nine games.

"Things were going so well," Belanger said. "Maybe they were going too well."

▲ ▲ ▲

Living and working in Florida had no drawbacks for the Panthers players, most of whom had spent their careers playing in some of the coldest and snowiest regions of North America. Going to work in the morning was a pleasure. After practicing in frigid Gold Coast Arena, they'd shower, pull on shorts, T-shirts, and flip-flops, and walk out into 80-degree weather in the dead of winter. Arriving early in the morning at Fort Lauderdale Airport after a long road trip, they'd step out of the terminal and feel a comforting gush of warm, tropical air. Then they'd drive home with their car windows rolled down.

Visiting teams loved coming to Florida, too, especially now that a southern road trip included two stops, one in Tampa and the other in Miami, and often with a day off in between. The NHL schedule-maker must have been acting in the dual role of travel agent when he gave the Rangers two days off after a game against the Panthers in mid-November. The Rangers arrived the day before the game, checked into Don Shula's Resort, beat the Panthers, 4-2, and spent the next day golfing, swimming, and going to the beach.

No wonder the Rangers played so well in that game: If they had lost, Coach Mike Keenan was going to make them practice the next morning, forcing them to cancel their tee times! The promise of fun in the sun became part of the incentive for visiting teams and made the task of winning at home a little more difficult for the Panthers.

Quebec Nordiques Coach Pierre Page was having a hard time motivating his injury-riddled team when it arrived in Miami on April 12. The Nordiques, one of the best teams in the league the previous season, were out of the playoff race and Page's job was on the line. Losing the final two games against the Panthers and Lightning would merely hasten his departure, and the players had no desire to win one for a coach they disliked.

Page was no fool. Knowing the Nordiques wouldn't play their best for him, he offered them incentive to win for themselves: The following day off before traveling to Tampa for the final game of the season. If they lost, they'd practice.

The Nordiques players, enraged by Page's motivational tactics, couldn't believe he would use such a threat for a game that meant nothing to them. But playing the role of spoiler was all the Nordiques had left, and a season-ending mini-vacation was an enticing reward for a team that had endured a long, cold Canadian winter. Lying down and purposely losing to get a hated coach fired was one thing; not giving full effort with a day off on the line was unthinkable.

The Panthers, who could clinch a playoff spot by winning their final two games, expected to face a team with nothing to gain. But they were unaware of the power and pull of a golf course.

▲ ▲ ▲

Brian Skrudland sat in the stands and watched. He felt like he was with his teammates down on the ice, but he wasn't, and that's what made it so painful. The rutty Madison Square Garden ice had caught Skrudland's skate in the 79th game, twisting his right ankle and ending his season.

Even though the injury happened a week ago, he could still remember returning to the visitor's locker room that night and thinking, *Oh, man, the season is over!* Just this morning, he had asked the team doctors whether they could freeze the ankle, so he could get on the ice for one more game, the most important of the season, but he expected their answer: If you freeze it and you break it, your career could be over. And that was the bottom line.

But he wanted to be with the team, so he showed up at the Arena at 5:30 along with the rest of the players, hung out in the locker room, and hoped some of his spirit would rub off. *That's the least I could do,* he thought, enduring a captain's guilt over not being able to play. Unfortunately, spirit and hard work was the least of the Panthers' problems, even with Skrudland sitting upstairs.

In the game that meant everything, April 12 against Quebec at Miami Arena, the Panthers came up with their worst performance. Vanbiesbrouck couldn't save them because he was just as bad. The 5-2 loss kept the Panthers one point behind the Islanders with one game remaining, and gave the Islanders the opportunity to clinch the final playoff spot the next night against Tampa Bay.

So, as the clock ticked down, Skrudland tried to not feel sorry for himself and failed miserably. There was nothing he could do, and he hated that.

▲ ▲ ▲

The players sat in Pete Rose's restaurant in Boca Raton, prayed for a miracle, and watched their playoff hopes die 300 miles away. The Islanders were hot, Tampa Bay had nothing to play for, and although the Panthers hoped professional pride would motivate the Lightning, they knew the neediest team usually wins.

Clarke watched at home with several members of the front-office staff. Neilson and Torrey watched in person in St. Petersburg. In the middle of a crowded restaurant, the Panthers ate, drank, and ended the night feeling empty. The Islanders' 2-0 victory clinched a playoff spot in the 83rd game and meant tomorrow's 84th, a showdown between the Panthers and Islanders at Miami Arena, would be meaningless.

"We thought Tampa Bay was playing well, they had done very well against the Islanders," Fitzgerald said. "Seeing them celebrate, knowing they made the playoffs, it was very disappointing."

The Panthers had established high goals for themselves. They weren't trying to be a .500 team or set the record for most points by an expansion team. Their goal was making the playoffs and, at this point, the best first-year team ever felt like failures.

"The guys were sitting there that night saying, 'We would've had the Rangers in the first round,' " Skrudland recalled. "We wanted them."

The Islanders didn't get what they wanted, either. Their playoff exit was quick and painful, a four game sweep by the eventual Stanley Cup champion Rangers, who humiliated them from the get-go. The victory over Tampa Bay was the last good night of the season for the Islanders. The Panthers still had one glorious evening remaining.

▲ ▲ ▲

The ovation started with three minutes remaining and didn't end for another half hour. The game meant nothing in the standings, but every seat was filled, and as the Panthers counted down toward a 4-1 victory that ended their season one point short of a playoff spot, they realized something special was happening. At the final buzzer, the fans were still standing and thanking them in an outpouring of emotion the players never expected.

Confetti and balloons floated down from the rafters. The noise had never been louder inside Miami Arena. The players stayed on the ice, waved to the fans, and threw T-shirts, sticks, pucks, and hats into the stands. Huizenga, the businessman, wiped a tear from his eye. Skrudland, dressed in jacket and tie, walked out to center ice, and addressed the crowd.

"We didn't know what to expect when we came down to Florida," he told them, "and we certainly didn't expect to have the greatest fans in the National Hockey League."

Until now, the players hadn't realized how much the team meant to the fans and the importance of this final game. All of an expansion team's games are supposed to be meaningless, but not until Game 84 did the Panthers play one that meant nothing in the standings.

"I had some trouble holding back tears," Skrudland said. "What happened after the game was something I'd never seen before in my life. 14,703 people were still cheering a hockey team that didn't make the playoffs, but they were just showing their appreciation for what we had done all year. There are moments in my hockey career that are as big as any moments I've had in my life, and that night will always remain the most positive."

With a record of 33-34-17 for 83 points, the Panthers were the best NHL expansion team ever and far more competitive than even Clarke could have foreseen. The journey that started 190 days earlier in Chicago was finally over and, although they didn't arrive at their intended destination, the Panthers knew they really went where no first-year team had gone before.

CHAPTER 8

Taking a Bruising

When Sandy Clarke said her husband was like an extra piece of furniture in Minnesota, she might have guessed that same piece of furniture would have an equally hard time finding its place in South Florida. Moving it around changed nothing.

For Bob Clarke, the difference between Minnesota and Florida was that he was successful in Florida and building a new fan base. Credited for making shrewd selections at the expansion draft, setting the tone for the season before training camp began, and stealing Stu Barnes from Winnipeg, Clarke was finally establishing himself as a capable general manager. But try as he might, Clarke couldn't separate himself from Philadelphia, the city in which he was a hero.

The season had barely started when Flyers President Jay Snider announced he was leaving the team indefinitely, although not giving up his post; rumors of Clarke's return followed shortly afterward. On October 22, an off-day for the Panthers, a Philadelphia reporter spotted Clarke at the Spectrum watching the Flyers play the Islanders.

"Just a simple scouting trip," Clarke explained with a nervous laugh. "I don't have any idea what's going on at all."

Clarke's refusal to rule out an eventual return to Philadelphia was translated by many as meaning, "I'm coming back." The rumors persisted. The Philadelphia question came up again before a November 3 game in Toronto, as Clarke and a reporter sat in the media dining room.

"What the heck do they want?" Clarke growled. "I just bought a house in Florida!"

Indeed, from all indications, Clarke had every intention of staying in Florida for the duration of his three-year contract. He bought a new home and sold his old one in Moorestown, New Jersey, certainly not the acts of a man on temporary leave from an organization. Yet his ties to the Philadelphia area hadn't been entirely cut. He kept his beach house in Ocean City, New Jersey and stayed in touch all season with Eric Lindros, the Flyers' superstar center he tutored the year before.

When the Flyers hosted the Panthers for the first time on February 10, they were in fifth place in the Atlantic Division and their fans were howling for a change. A reporter asked Clarke how he might respond to the fans' pleas to return home.

"I don't know," Clarke answered. "I have no idea. I was the guy who was managing when we didn't make the playoffs."

Asked whether he intended to return, Clarke said, "That would be unfair to discuss. I don't think that there's any reason to start rumors."

Maybe there wasn't. The Flyers didn't have any job openings. Russ Farwell, the general manager, was given a vote of confidence by Ed Snider, the Flyers' owner, and Jay Snider, though spending most of his time in the Far East, retained his title. But the Flyers were a bad team and bad teams always have potential job openings.

"The first time I heard about it was from a newspaper guy during the season," Bill Torrey recalled. "It was January or February, the Flyers were playing that night in New York, and one of the Philadelphia writers came up to me and asked if I had discussions with Bob about returning to Philadelphia. I said it was news to me. I was pretty surprised to hear about it. Then I heard it again a couple of weeks later, after I came back off the road, so I said 'Bob, there's rumors going around, and Wayne called me and said he had a call from one of the other owners, who had heard through the grapevine that Snider wanted you to come back.'

"Bob said there was no truth to it."

Although Clarke and Torrey got along, their working relationship was never perfect, as least from Clarke's standpoint. He accepted the job in Florida for the opportunity to build a team, but it turned out he wasn't even second in command, he was third in command after Huizenga and Torrey. Torrey was the governor and attended all League meetings; Clarke attended only the general managers meetings. Torrey watched practices, joined Clarke for post-game meetings with Roger Neilson, had input on trades, and carried out many of a general manager's duties, including scouting prospects. He attended the Winter Olympics. Clarke stayed home. When a reporter needed a comment on a trade, he was just as likely to call Torrey as Clarke.

Torrey's seeming ever-presence made sense, considering he had spent most of his career as a general manager. Not offering his input would have been counterproductive. And Torrey had another reason for remaining active in scouting: Despite the denials, he suspected Clarke wouldn't be around for long.

"I had to be prepared because in the back of my mind, there was a possibility he could be going back to Philadelphia," Torrey said.

Huizenga, on the other hand, had no idea. He liked Clarke, whose work habits and desire to win at any price fit his model of the perfect employee. Wayne and Marti Huizenga had Bob and Sandy Clarke to their home for dinner and became, if not friends, friendly acquaintances.

The rumors became impossible to ignore on March 2, when Jay Snider officially resigned. Asked whether Clarke might return, Snider said: "I wouldn't rule anything out. That relationship between Ed Snider and Clarke is still strong and anything is possible. I didn't rule it out when he went to Florida, either."

Clarke insisted he was happy in Florida. On March 7, before a game in Vancouver against the Canucks, Clarke got testy when a reporter questioned him about the stories coming out of Philadelphia.

"I don't know anything about that," Clarke said, then walked away in a huff.

Later in the month, Ed Snider angered the Panthers by saying, "Bobby Clarke can always come back here." Hearing this, Torrey discussed possible tampering charges with NHL Commissioner Gary Bettman.

No one knew what to believe. Clarke, described by some as a "bad liar" — meaning it's obvious when he isn't tell the truth — clearly still had his heart in Philadelphia, but he was doing such a great job in Florida that people figured, "Why would he want to build this and leave?"

To which there was only one answer: You can take Bob Clarke out of Philadelphia, but you can't take Philadelphia out of Bob Clarke.

▲ ▲ ▲

One week after the Flyers' season ended, on April 14, Ed Snider confirmed Farwell's return as general manager for the 1994-95 season and said there were three candidates for team president. Although he wouldn't name names, Snider said Clarke would be one of them "if he came knocking on our door."

"I wanted Bob and thought he was the best guy out there," Snider said. "He learned a lot in Florida and Minnesota and did fabulous jobs. I thought he had a feeling for every element. Us not making the playoffs didn't have anything to do with that. I wanted to make him president."

By now, Clarke was willing to listen and notified Snider through a third party. Less than two weeks after the end of the regular season, he approached Torrey and requested permission to speak with Snider. Torrey granted permission ... to a point.

"I told him if he wanted to have lunch with Ed Snider and talk to him, fine, but he can't talk to him about employment," Torrey said.

Clarke interpreted this as permission to speak with Snider about anything he wished. But by the time Clarke arrived in Philadelphia for a lunch meeting with his former boss, Snider had received a fax from Huizenga's lawyers forbidding the two from discussing employment.

"Bob and I didn't talk about anything," Snider said. "We hugged each other, had lunch, and were upset that we couldn't talk. We had a conversation about why we couldn't talk and we were sorry we couldn't get anything done."

Clarke returned to Florida, told Torrey he was staying with the Panthers, and publicly denied he was thinking about returning to Philadelphia.

"I'm staying in Florida," Clarke said. "I don't know why I have to say that, but I will. I'm staying."

But 24 hours after Clarke said he wasn't going back, he phoned Torrey and again asked for permission to speak with the Flyers. Torrey suggested they discuss the situation with Huizenga.

"Philadelphia's my home," Clarke told Huizenga, "and I want to talk to Mr. Snider."

Huizenga reiterated what Torrey told him earlier: Clarke was free to speak with Snider, but not about employment. If he considered Philadelphia home, he could pack his things, move back north, and stop working for the Panthers, but he couldn't work for any other team.

Clarke interpreted this as a release from his contract.

Said Clarke: "He gave me permission. I told Mr. Snider I had no intention of coming back as club president. I wanted to manage."

Snider made Clarke a dream offer that included the dual roles of general manager and president, and equity in the team. Now, with no doubt of his desire to return to Philadelphia, Clarke told Torrey of his intentions.

"I said, 'Bob, after your public statements, and after telling me that you're definitely staying, you're reversing yourself,' " Torrey recalled. " 'The first person you'd better tell is Wayne.' "

Clarke walked a few blocks across town to the Blockbuster building and broke the news to Huizenga.

"He told me to clear out my desk and leave," Clarke recalled. "It was pretty chilling."

When the meeting ended and Clarke left, Huizenga wasted no time getting on the phone with Torrey. He was upset, wanted to take legal action, and planned on enforcing the contract. Torrey sent off a letter to the Flyers accusing them of tampering with Clarke. Snider, hoping to settle the mess owner-to-owner, phoned Huizenga.

"He told me to go fuck myself," Snider said. "He acted like a goddamn spoiled child ... I know the problem was Wayne Huizenga. I don't think he thought that Bob Clarke would ever leave. He felt jilted or something ... I started to deal with Torrey because I wanted to get it done."

Torrey felt Huizenga had every right to be so passionately displeased.

"If Ed Snider had called Wayne Huizenga and said, 'Here's my circumstance. There's only one guy for the job. He's Mr. Hockey in Philadelphia. I want permission to bring Bob Clarke back here, whatever it takes,' I think he could've saved a lot of people a lot of problems. You don't go through the denials we went through and then at the last minute change your mind and create a lot of problems for a lot of people in the organization. Not the least of whom was Wayne Huizenga, who treated Bob pretty damn well."

Clarke didn't think that was a fair view of the situation because he never intended to return to the Flyers until he spoke with Snider after the season.

"Bill wants to make it seem like I was plotting all winter long, and that's not true," Clarke said. "Mr. Torrey gave me permission and then it was taken away."

On May 20, Snider fired Coach Terry Simpson, a friend of Farwell's, publicly intensifying the rumors of Clarke's return. With his power diminished, Farwell was clearly on his way out. During the Memorial Cup — the championship of Canadian junior hockey — Clarke canceled an appointment with Jesse Belanger's agent, adding to speculation that he wasn't planning on remaining with the Panthers.

"I can't say anything about anything," Clarke said. "Bill knows what's going on. Until it all gets sorted out, it's better I say nothing."

By then, Bettman had discussed the situation with both sides. Torrey, claiming he had evidence that Snider and Clarke spoke by phone during the season, demanded $1 million and a first-round draft pick as compensation for tampering. The Flyers, who had traded their No. 1 pick in the Lindros deal, were reluctant to give any compensation at all.

"I didn't feel there should be any," Snider said. "Bob and I are very close and we talked on a regular basis while he was general manager of the Florida Panthers, but as friends. We're extremely close, and I just didn't want to get into all that. I didn't have any clear records of anything. I don't like tampering. I've never been accused of tampering by anyone else. Sure, I was angry."

In early June, with the draft less than three weeks away, Bettman stepped in to arbitrate the dispute. Snider was off on a fishing trip in Alaska and Clarke, trying to settle the matter on his own, offered a second-round draft pick and some monetary compensation. After conferring with his scouts,

Torrey decided the Flyers' second-round pick in the 1994 draft would be nearly as valuable as their first-round pick in 1995, projected to be a shallow draft year.

"We had to consider it to the satisfaction of the League and to Wayne and, for a long while, Wayne was not easily satisfied," Torrey said. "At one point, Wayne said that if we hadn't gotten some form of compensation, he'd fight him legally. But we felt at a certain time we had to cut the cord and move on.

"The reason we filed tampering charges was because after telling us all through the season that he wasn't going, he all of a sudden reversed himself 30 days before the draft. Obviously, there was damage being done to this franchise by a competitor in our division. All the knowledge we paid for all year, they were getting for nothing. To say there wasn't damage was ludicrous."

The Panthers settled for the second-rounder, $500,000, and the Flyers' share of the gate receipts for a 1996 exhibition game at Miami Arena. On June 15, two months and a day after the end of the regular season, the Flyers called a press conference to announce Clarke's second return.

For Clarke, his dream of running the show in Philadelphia was realized.

"I'm just glad it's over," he said.

Torrey's work had just begun. With the draft less than two weeks away, the Panthers didn't have a general manager.

▲ ▲ ▲

Radek Bonk's coach had no doubt about who should go first in the 1994 NHL Entry Draft. As Butch Goring, coach of the International Hockey League's Las Vegas Thunder, entertained a media contingent outside the Hartford Civic Center, he challenged Torrey and the Panthers.

"If they don't take Radek, they're going to have a lot of explaining to do," Goring said.

Goring was understandably proud of his project. Bonk, a 6'3", 215-pound native of the Czech Republic, was reminding many people of Pittsburgh Penguins star Jaromir Jagr, and not just because of his long, curly hair. At the start of the season, the 17-year-old Bonk had shocked the Canadian junior hockey establishment by signing with the Thunder and becoming the youngest European to ever play pro hockey in North America.

Although many people, including Bob Clarke, debated the decision and argued it wasn't in his best interests, Bonk became a regular in the Thunder lineup, scored 42 goals and 45 assists, and was named the IHL's Rookie of the Year. Scouts were calling him a big-time NHL scorer.

The Panthers, not quite so impressed, were further put off by the public statements of Bonk's agent, who said signing his client wouldn't come cheaply. They didn't think Bonk was worth breaking the bank over.

"Bob [Clarke] went to see Bonk play and didn't like him," scout Dennis Patterson recalled. "And he wasn't going to take a Russian No. 1."

The Russian was Oleg Tverdovsky, an offensive defenseman with Paul Coffey-like speed and skating ability who was moving up on teams' lists. Although Clarke was no longer with the Panthers, his scouts were and all of them agreed Tverdovsky wasn't the man.

For the Panthers, No. 1 meant only one. They knew by January who they would select with the first pick in the draft and it wasn't even a contest: Ed Jovanovski.

The son of Konstadin and Liljana Jovanovski is hardly an intimidating sight off the ice, despite his substantial 6'2", 205 pounds. His face seems to be in a perpetual state of smirk, as if he finds everything around him humorous, and he doesn't mind a bit that people don't consider him a worldly character. Teammates call him "Special" Ed, in reference to the special education classes they good-naturedly rib fit Jovanovski's intelligence level. He was born in Windsor, Ontario, grew up in Windsor, Ontario, and played junior hockey in Windsor, Ontario. Never, however, did he leave any doubt that he was going places.

From the instant he stepped onto the ice for a game, Jovanovski zeroed in on opponents with a ferocity that struck fear into their hearts.

"This was a kid who had played relatively little hockey, but he had a presence. Eddie bothered people," Torrey recalled. "He's fearless. There were some games in juniors when he made all kinds of mistakes, but that fearlessness, you don't see that very often. Then, obviously, the kid had good hands and did certain things naturally, so as the kid gets bigger and stronger, you knew those things would get better."

He was an impact player in every sense of the word, and although the Panthers realized he was deficient in his defensive skills and needed to exercise a little more control, they figured that could come later. The natural skills combined with the physical package were irresistible and Jovanovski reminded Torrey of the defenseman he drafted No. 1 in the 1973 Draft: Denis Potvin, who had a Hall of Fame career with the Islanders.

"There weren't any doubts," Chuck Fletcher said. "But if I had any, they were erased when I went to see him practice one day."

Jovanovski was hardly winded the day after an Ontario Hockey League game in Windsor and, even if he was, rejuvenation would have come with one look up in the stands at the man wearing the trench coat. Jovanovski was undergoing another audition, this time for the Panthers, and he welcomed the opportunity to show off for the team picking first.

"They had a three-on-three practice, 10 players on one bench, 10 on the other, and they just rotated three players at a time for one minute," Fletcher recalled. "Eddie went out with the same threesome every time, three defensemen, and they kept getting matched against the three top forwards on the team.

"Eddie's team beat them about 12-2 because Eddie wouldn't quit. He was competing. He hit guys. He had skill, but he was out there smiling and having fun. He was having more fun than any other kid out there, and he was the best player out there."

At lunch after practice, Jovanovski gave Fletcher all the right answers to all of his questions: "Do you like to fight? Do you like to hit? Do you like to play the way you do? Who's the toughest player you've ever played against? Are you ever intimidated? Do you see yourself playing in the NHL next year? What's your family like?"

Jovanovski told Fletcher how he loved to check and fight, and stopped playing soccer, his father's sport in Yugoslavia, because there wasn't enough contact. He was close to his parents and, unlike many junior players who leave home, he was still living with them. Jovanovski said his parents were supportive and willing to help him through the early years of his NHL career.

One mind was made up for good: Jovanovski would be a Florida Panther.

Jovanovski didn't merely love hitting people; he genuinely frightened opposing players. Ontario Hockey League opponents didn't want to be on the ice, or anywhere near the puck, when Jovanovski was around, or angry, as he was after not being invited to try out for the 1994 Canadian junior national team. He took out his frustrations on Alexei Lojkin, a junior team member, at the Canadian Hockey League All-Star Game, by pulverizing poor Lojkin with three memorable checks.

"He kept coming into our zone with his head down," Jovanovski recalled. "I had a great time. It was a night I'll never forget. I felt I had something to prove. I knew a bunch of scouts were there. It was a showcase. It was my night."

Every night was Jovanovski's night. Although he made more than his share of defensive mistakes, such as skating halfway across the ice and out of position to make a hit, he always played with anger and intensity, as if he had been slighted. The Panthers' scouts who saw Jovanovski and Bonk play dozens of games couldn't say the same thing about Bonk, whose concentration and intensity wavered from night to night.

"Eddie was the best player on the ice every game I saw, but not only the best, but to the point where 17- and 18-year-olds were scared to death of him," Fletcher said. "The rank and file of the OHL were scared to death of Ed Jovanovski."

Those who weren't afraid of Jovanovski got high marks from the Panthers' scouts. One night, Jovanovski and Matt O'Dette of Kitchener went toe-to-toe at center ice. Jovanovski won the fight, but O'Dette stood in and cut him over the eye.

Jovanovski, blood pouring from his forehead, waved to the cheering crowd as he left the ice. "Ed-die! Ed-die!" they chanted.

The Panthers liked that, too. Here was a 17-year-old basher with real charisma. Even their fans could tell from 2,000 miles away. About 4,000 of them, packed into the Omni Hotel in Miami for a draft party, chanted "Ed-die! Ed-die!" when Torrey stepped to the podium and made Jovanovski the first pick in the 1994 Draft.

As for O'Dette, well, 156 picks after the Panthers selected Jovanovski, they took him, too.

Torrey, handling the draft in the dual role of president/interim general manager, was joined at the Panthers' draft table by the scouting staff Clarke had assembled: Patterson, who would join Clarke in Philadelphia after the draft, Ron Harris, John Chapman, Fletcher, and European scout Matti Vaisanen, as well as Neilson. Clarke's departure wasn't a great loss because the scouts had all the information Torrey needed to make his decisions. Any lingering resentment Torrey felt over Clarke's presence at the Flyers' table was tempered by Philadelphia's inactivity. The Flyers didn't have any picks in the first two rounds and Clarke wouldn't make a selection until the third round was held the next day.

By that time, Torrey had already gone to the podium four times. After resisting several offers to trade the top pick, and taking Jovanovski (Anaheim would take Tverdovsky with the second pick while Bonk fell to Ottawa at No. 3), the Panthers made three selections in the second round. The first was defensive defenseman Rhett Warrener of Saskatchewan, who impressed the scouts with his ability to read the opposition attack, make the right decision, and play the man.

"Warrener was an interesting kid," Patterson said. "When we went out west, we liked him. We plugged along following him, but we didn't think he would get to the second round."

Warrener, once projected as a first-rounder, had lost some of his draft appeal the previous fall when he reported to his junior team 25 pounds overweight. After taking Warrener, the Panthers made other teams' selections for them. They took Jason Podollan at 31st overall with the pick Clarke conned out of Hartford at the 1993 Draft. Center Ryan Johnson went 36th overall with the pick the Panthers received from the Flyers as compensation.

"Overall, it was a strong draft for us," Torrey said. "To be in that position at that time was very positive for us."

It was literally huge for the Panthers. None of the 10 players they selected over the two days of the draft were under six feet tall. In back-to-back rounds, they selected 6'5", 221-pound defenseman David Geris and O'Dette, Jovanovski's 6'4", 205-pound sparring partner. The small, speedy Panthers were getting bigger and stronger, and with new friends like these, they had absolutely no explaining to do.

▲ ▲ ▲

Bryan Murray walked into owner Mike Ilitch's office on June 3 and suspected why he was there. Just four years earlier, Ilitch had handed him the power to run the Detroit Red Wings as he saw fit, and Murray told Ilitch that with patience and an infusion of young players, the Wings would be a League power for the next decade. Well, now the Red Wings were good but not powerful, and Ilitch's tenuous patience had worn out.

"Bryan, we're going to have to let you go," Ilitch said.

"Can we talk about it?" Murray asked.

"No," Ilitch responded. "I don't think there's any sense in rehashing it."

Maybe there wasn't. Murray, like almost every coach and general manager before him, was hired to be fired, and the situation in Detroit was anything but the exception to that rule.

This wasn't his first dream job that turned into a nightmare. Murray, 51, had worked his way up from the frozen ponds of Shawville, Quebec, where he played alongside his younger brother, Terry, and shared visions of playing in the NHL. Terry made it, Bryan didn't, but Bryan's success would come in a different area: coaching. He worked his way up, through Regina, Saskatchewan, where he turned a last place team into Western Hockey League champions, and then through Hershey, Pennsylvania, where he guided the Washington Capitals' American League affiliate to its best season in 40 years. In 1981-82, with the Capitals off to a 1-12 start, Murray was promoted to take over a team that hadn't made the playoffs in its first seven NHL seasons.

There were good times in Washington. The players liked him and so did the fans and the media. Along the way, he both coached his brother, Terry, and made him his assistant coach. In 1988, when Terry moved over to coach the Capitals' AHL affiliate in Baltimore, Murray found not only a new assistant, but a friend: Doug MacLean. The Capitals made the playoffs seven straight seasons under Murray's watch and became one of the strongest teams in the NHL.

But Murray's success was also his downfall. Having transformed the Capitals into regular season winners, he was expected to win in the post-season, too, and that just didn't happen. The Capitals were always missing something — a top-flight goaltender or a scorer — and when May 1 rolled around, they were always on the golf course.

Even the most popular coaches don't last long under such circumstances and, after the Capitals won the Patrick Division in 1988-1989 and lost to the Flyers in the first round, General Manager David Poile handed Murray a message: a one-year contract that made him a lame duck. Win or else. To get a second contract, the Capitals would have to make it past the second round, something they had never done.

Murray didn't get a chance to win even one round. On January 15, 1990, with the Capitals riding an eight-game losing streak and some of their top players out of the lineup, he was fired.

And replaced by his brother.

"I went to practice that morning and phoned David [Poile]," Murray recalled. "At the end, he said, 'Are you going to drop by the office?', so I did and then he told me. I said to him, 'So, who's going to replace me?' and he said he was offering the job to Terry. I remember thinking, *At least he made one right decision today.*"

The Murray brothers handled this awkward situation as best they could, but Terry's wife, Linda, and Bryan's wife, Geri, had several run-ins, and the brothers were caught in the middle. On the night of Terry's coaching debut with Washington, a banner in the Capital Centre read, "Hi, mom, it's Terry. I've got some good news and some bad news."

Bryan's bad news was replaced shortly thereafter by good news. On July 13, 1990, he landed his second NHL job as coach and general manager of the Detroit Red Wings, an original six team that hadn't won the Cup since 1955. Murray then hired MacLean, who also had been fired by Washington, as his assistant coach, and embarked on what he considered the job of a lifetime.

Ilitch was driven to win and willing to pay the price with cash. He had built Little Caesars into one of the largest pizza chains in the country after discovering, using simple mathematics, that he could provide two tasteless pizzas for the price of one. This irresistible bargain turned Ilitch into a multi-millionaire and, in 1982, enabled him to purchase the Red Wings and later baseball's Detroit Tigers. But Ilitch's instant success in the pizza business didn't carry over to hockey. Four coaches had been shown the door since his arrival and the latest to go, Jacques Demers, had been hand-picked by Ilitch himself. Even Jim Devellano, Ilitch's trusted general manager since he bought the team, was demoted to vice-president after the Wings missed the playoffs in 1990.

Murray wasn't thinking about the past when he preached to Ilitch about being patient and building through youth and the draft. Ilitch nodded his head and Murray implemented his plan. The seeds for success had been planted by Devellano, the former Islanders scout who drafted Sergei Fedorov, Keith Primeau, Slava Kozlov, and Nicklas Lidstrom. Murray supplemented these developing youngsters with the acquisitions of Dino Ciccarelli, Paul Coffey, and Ray Sheppard. Two years after his arrival, the Red Wings won the division championship and Murray prepared for the next step of the building process.

Murray wanted to concentrate on his duties as GM and, when the 1991-92 season ended, he told Ilitch the following season would be his last behind the bench. Barry Melrose, the bright, young, and unconventional coach of the Wings' American League affiliate in Glens Falls, New York, would replace him, and Murray would remain as general manager. That was fine with Ilitch, who loved Melrose and his colorful motivational style, fashioned after self-help guru Anthony Robbins.

But Melrose became a hot prospect after coaching Adirondack to the 1992 Calder Cup championship, the minor league equivalent of the Stanley Cup. Although he wanted nothing more than to coach the Red Wings, that job was at least a year away, and the $25,000 raise he'd receive for staying in Glens Falls was nothing compared to one offer: The Los Angeles Kings wanted to make him the highest paid rookie coach in NHL history at a salary of $1.2 million over four years. Just as importantly, they wanted to do it right away.

Murray knew there was no way Detroit could match the Kings' offer. Jim Lites, working in the untitled role of team president, discussed it with Ilitch, who agreed the matching price was too high. Ilitch appealed to Melrose and begged him to wait a year, but Melrose knew what a difference a year might make.

"I could've had a bad year," Melrose said. "Detroit could've won the Stanley Cup. If my team doesn't make the playoffs, all of a sudden I'm out."

At 10 the next night, Melrose received the official offer from the Kings and told Murray they wanted an answer right away. Murray offered Melrose the head coaching job in Detroit, but said he couldn't match the Kings' offer. Melrose was gone.

"It was a bit of a blow," Devellano said. "We groomed him. We were disappointed because when you groom somebody, you want to retain him."

So began the erosion of Murray's power in Detroit. He didn't think losing Melrose was a major blow — after all, another talented young coach, Doug MacLean, was as qualified for the job — but Ilitch thought otherwise. Devellano, aware of Murray's fondness for MacLean, later suggested Murray was happy about Melrose's departure.

"You could surmise," Devellano said, "that he was happy to see him go."

Absolutely untrue, said Murray, who knew MacLean had no chance of coaching the Red Wings.

Devellano's opinion and power should have been a major concern to Murray. Jimmy D had become the owner's eyes and ears of the team — even more so than Lites, Ilitch's son-in-law — and was a frequent visitor to the owner's box at Tiger Stadium. Murray wasn't capable of playing such games and found himself at a severe disadvantage in the arena of team politics, but there was nothing he could have done to prevent the autocratic Ilitch from contemplating his next move.

Ilitch, impatient with Murray's youth plan, had set his sights on a more impulsive, fiery, make-things-happen-now coach: Mike Keenan, who had just been fired as general manager of the Chicago Blackhawks. Three months into the 1992-93 season, Jay Bielfield, Ilitch's chief legal counsel, and Rob Campbell, Keenan's attorney, secretly worked out an agreement under which Keenan would become general manager and coach after the season ended. Murray learned of the plan prior to a game at Joe Louis Arena and angrily confronted Lites.

"What's going on?" he demanded. "Is Mike Keenan coming here? I don't want to be strung along. Mike Ilitch can come and coach the game tonight. I don't give a shit."

Lites didn't know what was going on, either, but wasted no time finding out. He marched up to the Olympic Club in Joe Louis Arena, where Ilitch was hosting a dinner honoring former Red Wings great Gordie Howe, pulled aside a stunned and perturbed Ilitch, and asked him, point blank, "What's going on with Keenan?"

None of the guests could hear what Ilitch and Lites were saying, but it was clear they weren't discussing the next family outing. Ilitch, who's not used to being confronted by his employees, didn't take well to this and exchanged some fervid words with Lites.

"It's my call," Ilitch reminded him.

Over the next few days, Lites and Devellano used all their powers of persuasion to talk Ilitch out of the idea and eventually prevailed. Lites, who liked Murray and his game plan of building a winner with young players, reminded Ilitch of his commitment. Devellano, realizing that if Keenan came in, his job would be gone, too, used another tack: the possibility of hiring Islanders Coach Al Arbour or Penguins Coach Scotty Bowman, who had worn out his welcome in Pittsburgh.

"Had I not recommended to ownership that they bring in Al Arbour or Scotty Bowman, Mike Keenan would've come in and had both jobs," Devellano said.

Having temporarily survived this turmoil and unaware of Devellano's suggestion to Ilitch, Murray realized his own foundation was crumbling. The Red Wings' organization resembled nothing so much as one of the octopi fans traditionally threw onto the ice during the playoffs: Many tentacles, each reaching directly to the head, Ilitch, but with no discernible chain of command. As for Murray, his tentacle was breaking off.

"He was angry," Lites recalled. "Detroit was playing well at the time and Bryan was upset that the rumors existed. He thought it hurt his credibility in the locker room. I thought he was the right man for the job."

Ilitch no longer agreed, especially when the 1992-93 season ended in bitter disappointment for the Wings with a loss to Toronto in the first round after compiling 103 points during the regular season. Two story lines that had plagued Murray in Washington were back with him in Detroit: Weak goaltending and playoff failure.

On May 26, three weeks after the Wings' playoff exit, Ilitch met with Murray and told him he would be allowed to retain only the general manager's half of his job.

"We need a coach who isn't afraid to lay down the hammer," Ilitch told Murray.

That was no surprise. What shocked Murray was being told he wouldn't be allowed to pick the replacement, a duty which usually falls under the GM's job description. Meanwhile, on the west coast, Melrose, the coach who got away, was leading the Kings to the Stanley Cup finals.

This time, Murray had no backers. Lites, his most ardent supporter, had flown the coop to Dallas after being denied the official team presidency by his father-in-law. Devellano had Ilitch's ear and he wasn't whispering sweet nothings about Murray. He was pushing for Bowman.

On June 15, 1993, Murray held the press conference that wasn't his idea and announced the hiring of a coach he didn't want. This was the ultimate act of a manager no longer being allowed to manage, castrated at the desktop. Murray had been given an ultimatum: Off with your nose, even if it spites your face, or off with your head.

Murray wanted his job and chose his nose. The neck would come later, as was assured by his action on this very day: Naming William Scott "Scotty" Bowman as the new coach of the Red Wings.

"Fans should look at this as getting the greatest bench coach in the history of the game," Murray said, putting on his company face. "If you talk to anybody in our game, they regard him as a winner. He's won Stanley Cups. He's had top, top players perform at the highest possible level. They should be excited."

Murray sure as hell wasn't. Bowman's résumé showed six Stanley

Cups, but what it didn't show was just as important. He had won with great teams, but lost with great teams, too, and had never won with a bunch of underachievers. His coaching style was out of touch, a throwback to the 1960s, and players detested his confrontational style. The situation got so out of hand in Pittsburgh that Bowman was forbidden from running practices.

Murray's fears were soon realized. Bowman had his own agenda and it was different from Murray's. The situation quickly deteriorated as it became clear there were two factions within the Red Wings: Bowman, Assistant Coach Barry Smith, and Devellano on one side, Murray and MacLean, now the assistant general manager, on the other. Murray was on the losing side.

"In October, I talked to Mr. Ilitch and told him I needed to know where I stood," Murray recalled. "I said, 'Scotty and you talk and do all the decision making.' He said, 'Bryan, I'm so happy with the way you've built this team. You'll be a manager here for the next seven years.' "

Convinced of Ilitch's sincerity, Murray began renovating his Detroit home and prepared to settle down. That was his next-to-last mistake.

While differing over everything else, Murray and Bowman agreed that their goaltending tandem of Tim Cheveldae and rookie Chris Osgood was ill-suited for the playoffs. Although Murray thought Osgood could one day develop into a top goaltender, his job rested on winning in the playoffs. There was no time to wait, so he went shopping for goalies in a seller's market.

The Panthers wouldn't part with John Vanbiesbrouck or Mark Fitzpatrick. The Calgary Flames offered Mike Vernon, but demanded defenseman Steve Chiasson and prospect Mike Sillinger in return. The Buffalo Sabres offered Grant Fuhr, who had led the Edmonton Oilers to four Stanley Cups in the 1980s, but wanted Osgood and Primeau, considered one of the top young power forwards in the League. According to Murray, Bowman agreed the price was too high. On March 8, 1994, two weeks prior to the trading deadline, the Red Wings sent Cheveldae and Dallas Drake to the Winnipeg Jets in exchange for goalie Bob Essensa.

This was one of the rare times when Murray's assessment of talent failed him. Essensa was no more suited to playoff pressure than Cheveldae, and the Wings, despite having the best regular season record in the Western Conference, suffered a shocking first-round loss to the third-year San Jose Sharks.

If Murray's job wasn't history by then, Bowman and Sabres General Manager John Muckler didn't help matters. Muckler, denying he demanded Primeau, said of the aborted Fuhr deal, "I offered him the Stanley Cup and he didn't take it." Bowman told a Buffalo newspaper that Murray had been impatient in his dealings for a goalie and should have waited.

Murray was undergoing a public burial. Muckler and Bowman were shoveling on the dirt.

About a month later, Murray received a call from New York Rangers General Manager Neil Smith, who'd heard that Keenan's agent was talking to Detroit about becoming general manager and coach. This concerned Smith as much as Murray because Keenan was coaching the Rangers in the Stanley Cup semifinals.

On June 3, amid rumors that Keenan was again in the running for Murray's job, Ilitch called Murray into his office and told him that he and MacLean were fired. Later, Ilitch told the media that he and Murray agreed it was time for a change, but Murray didn't recall agreeing to any such thing.

"What had happened, and I think this is where Mr. Devellano became a part of it, was that he made a point that Murray and MacLean can't work together with Bowman and Smith, and one pair will have to go," Murray said. "He was Scotty's friend, not mine."

Devellano phoned Murray and denied having any input in the firing. To this day, he staunchly denies influencing Ilitch. Bowman also called, swore he had nothing to do with the decision, and told Murray, "I'm not going to be coaching next year, anyway." Bowman fully expected Keenan to come in and take his job.

Keenan ended up leaving New York, but not for Detroit. On July 18, he broke his contract with the Rangers and became general manager/coach of the St. Louis Blues. In Detroit, Bowman took over the dual roles of coach/director of player personnel.

By that time, Murray didn't care. He already knew where he was going.

▲ ▲ ▲

Torrey had no shortage of candidates for general manager when Clarke returned to Philadelphia. The question was, did he need one? Huizenga had asked Torrey to handle both jobs, GM and president.

"I told him I'd give it a lot of thought," Torrey said. "It's not that I don't love being general manager. I love it. It was a question of whether it was in the best interests of the franchise."

Among the candidates was Russ Farwell, the Flyers general manager whom Clarke replaced, and Mike Milbury, the former Boston Bruins GM. Torrey also discussed the opening with Denis Potvin, the Panthers' radio and television commentator. Torrey ended up speaking to 20 candidates, most by phone, but few were established and only one stood out as a clear choice.

On June 14, the day before Clarke's departure was officially announced,

Murray phoned Torrey and asked for an interview. They met two days later in Toronto, and Torrey could have hired Murray right away; he had Detroit's draft list and was ready to move forward.

"He said he had an inkling Mr. Huizenga might want him to do both jobs, but said let's wait until after the draft," Murray said. "We talked a little about the players in the draft, and he said he'd call me right after it was over."

A few days after the draft, Murray flew to Fort Lauderdale, met again with Torrey, and had dinner with Huizenga. After his experience with Ilitch, Murray was particularly interested in Huizenga's attitude toward running a hockey team.

"He certainly appeared to be ambitious in the hockey area, but he was also willing to let the hockey people run the show," Murray said. "That's all I was looking for, the chance to be in an organization where you were treated with respect. I knew Bill was a guy who had been in hockey for a long time and understood that if you're the manager of a team, you have to be allowed to do your job. He was certainly willing to do that and more."

Torrey and Murray agreed to talk again in two weeks, after Torrey returned from a vacation in Ireland. With the franchise losing money and the Blockbuster Park deal coming together, Torrey knew he'd have to devote his energies full-time to the business side of the Panthers and hand the hockey reigns to an experienced man.

"Bryan has an extraordinarily good eye for talent and that's not something you can dismiss lightly," Torrey said. "I personally interviewed five or six people, then I came back to talk to Wayne. We had talks about where the franchise was going down the road and, in studying the situation, I thought Bryan and his ability to access talent early on would be important for this franchise."

Torrey was reluctant, but willing, to continue as general manager and president. Neilson and the rest of his coaching staff were concerned about having somebody come in from the outside. Although the franchise was young and even the insiders were outsiders a year ago, Neilson feared that a new general manager might not approve of his style. In what turned out to be an attempt at self-preservation, Neilson offered to shoulder the dual role of assistant general manager and coach, allowing Torrey more time for the business side of the team.

Torrey might have agreed to Neilson's suggestion had Murray not been available. After returning from Ireland, he offered the job to Murray, who promptly accepted.

But Detroit was not yet in his past. Murray was getting nowhere in his demand that Ilitch pay him for the final, guaranteed year of his contract.

Devellano, having heard the Panthers were about to hire Murray, phoned Torrey, his former boss.

"He called me and tried to talk me out of it," Torrey said. "Obviously, Bryan's contract matter hadn't been settled, so Jimmy was probably speaking as much on behalf of Mike Ilitch. He said Bryan doesn't like to do this, that, and the other thing, and didn't fit in, but I knew that what one person does for one organization is different from what he does for another."

Torrey wouldn't be swayed. On August 1, Murray was named general manager of the Panthers. In less than two months, he had gone from a team on the verge of contending for the Stanley Cup to one that would be lucky to make the playoffs. Murray could live with that.

"I wasn't really unhappy when I was let go in Detroit," Murray said. "When you can't hire your own coach and you have two other guys going to the owner all the time, you'd better not be there. I survived that final year. Really, when I left, I was frustrated, I was disappointed, but I was kind of relieved."

Murray would have plenty of time to make the transition from Detroit to Florida. Training camp in Peterborough, Ontario, was less than a month away, but Murray's first season with the Panthers was a long way off.

CHAPTER 9

The Season
That Almost Wasn't

Roger Neilson looked around and saw nothing but perfection: Wide open spaces in which to run, weight rooms, places to ride bikes, a short walking distance from the hotel to the rink, computerized fitness equipment, and a small hockey town enthusiastic about hosting an NHL team for 10 days.

A year earlier, the Panthers had opened their first training camp in Miami Arena under conditions only a salesman could love. Now, here in Peterborough, Ontario, Neilson was looking forward to opening the Panthers' second training camp with no distractions and all the amenities he desired. A coach's paradise.

Not even close. When camp began on September 4 with a six-mile run through Peterborough, the players saw a sign that read, "Heartbreak Hill." Heartbreak, as it turned out, was just around the corner. The NHL was on the verge of its worst ever labor dispute and many of the 59 players who reported to camp knew they might not play a meaningful game for a long time.

A month earlier, NHL Commissioner Gary Bettman sent a memorandum to the NHL Players' Association clamping sanctions on all players if progress wasn't made on a new collective bargaining agreement. Canada's labor laws exempted the Panthers from two of the cutbacks: Paying their own way to camp and expenses once they got there.

But Bettman had fired the first shot in this battle and the players planned on fighting back. What the owners called a link between salaries and revenues, they viewed as a salary cap, and there was no way they were going to let any artificial restraints on salaries curb their rights in a free market.

"I don't mind paying star players," said Edmonton Oilers owner Peter Pocklington, whose statement sounded like a warning. "But that doesn't mean the journeymen should share in the abundance."

141

The Panthers, a team with only one star, John Vanbiesbrouck, and journey-men filling out their roster, had much at stake. Under the current free market system, a player's value was determined by a scale sliding from the highest paid player in the League. After decades of a management-controlled system, the players were finally getting their fair share and salaries had uniformly risen from an average of $220,000 in 1990 to $532,000 for the 1993-94 season.

Under a salary cap or a luxury tax — both equally repugnant to the NHLPA — the big money would be reserved for the best players, and the journey-men would get the leftovers. The owners wanted to maintain competitive balance among big- and small-market teams and control spending. The players suggested self-control.

"As a third- or fourth-line guy who works hard every night, if there was some sort of structured salary, it would hurt guys like me," said Tom Fitzgerald. "And I feel the higher percentage of guys in the League are like me. Mario Lemieux and Wayne Gretzky are not the norm. There are stars that carry our League, who promote it because of their talent, but you have to fill it in with guys like me, and that's who it would hurt."

The unsettled labor situation worsened as training camp continued. Bettman and the owners wouldn't budge from their hard line and accused the players of not negotiating in good faith. NHLPA President Bob Goodenow, who thought the union made a good faith gesture by playing the previous season under an expired contract and not walking out during the playoffs, pointed out that the players were willing to negotiate, but not on a salary cap. When Bettman responded, "It's not a salary cap," the players were enraged by his arrogance and doublespeak. He had become Players Enemy No. 1.

Under these volatile conditions, the Panthers had a hard time preparing for a season that might not be played. The first weeks of camp were competitive because players were fighting for jobs, but the exhibition games were farcical displays of river hockey with almost no hitting. The Panthers didn't consider opposing players enemies; they were union brothers.

The Whalers and Panthers shook hands after a pre-season game in Hartford, Connecticut. General Manager Bryan Murray, who heard so much about the Panthers' work ethic, was seeing none of it in the exhibition games. An exasperated Bill Torrey pulled aside player representative John Vanbiesbrouck and explained, in an animated discussion, that management was trying to make decisions about players and needed them to play hard.

Four days later, fans at Miami Arena booed both teams after the Panthers finished their exhibition schedule with their seventh consecutive loss, 2-0 to the Tampa Bay Lightning.

"The whole focus was not on the team, it was on the outside stuff," Bryan Murray said. "We're hockey people, we want to be in the games and tend to be loyal to each other, but we had the players going one way and management and owners going the other. This team only survives with belief in each other and a great work ethic."

The Panthers believed in each other. It was management they didn't believe in. Somehow, they had trouble feeling sorry for an owner, Wayne Huizenga, who had recently added full ownership of the Miami Dolphins to his sports portfolio and was first on the *Forbes* list of the wealthiest men in South Florida with a net worth of $700 million.

On September 27, the union rejected a proposal from the owners that included a luxury tax, a rookie salary cap, and an end to salary arbitration. Three days later, Bettman rejected the players' offer to play throughout the negotiations in exchange for a no-lockout pledge.

"I'm preparing myself for a long vacation," Brian Skrudland said.

An early vacation. It started on October 1, when Bettman locked out the players.

▲ ▲ ▲

Wayne Huizenga and Bill Torrey were hard-liners of a small-market team and strongly believed in a salary cap and greater control on free-agency. If achieving that meant scrapping the momentum the Panthers had gained in their first season and the public good will that went along with it, they were willing to take that risk. The Panthers had lost nearly $4 million in their first season, despite playing to 97 percent of capacity, and the bottom line was worsening because of escalating salaries.

"First year teams don't necessarily lose money," Torrey said. "We lost money because our lease is bad but, with an expansion team, you have to remember, your payroll is not high, but compared to your revenue streams, it's high. Our percentage of money spent on salaries compared to revenue is as high as anybody. And then you have to take into account the $50 million Wayne paid to get in the League, which you never get back. The only way you get that back is when you sell the team, but if you continue to lose money, it doesn't appreciate."

The owners begged the players to consider the future of the game and think of the fans, who were paying inflated ticket prices. But the players viewed the owners as an historically stingy group that thought only of themselves.

"They locked us out," Vanbiesbrouck said, "and people have to know that there's a real fine line to management taking that stand of locking out. Even though there's a disagreement, the players' willingness to play is a key focus and the key issue there. Management not wanting to play, I would think, says volumes to the fans. How can they want to provide a product, and then say they don't want to provide this product anymore because they don't want you to see it?"

The Panthers players were united in their misery. Unlike most teams, whose players returned home during the lockout or played in one of several exhibition tournaments, nearly every player remained in South Florida. The exception was Rob Niedermayer, who returned to his junior team in Medicine Hat, Alberta.

There are worse places than Florida to spend an unplanned vacation. They played golf, worked out, and rented the ice to skate on their own four or five times a week at Gold Coast Ice Arena. Jeremy Roenick of the Chicago Blackhawks and several other NHLers joined the Panthers for the workouts, and Associate Equipment Manager Tim LeRoy lived out every hockey fan's fantasy by playing goal in several scrimmages.

The players were like all other customers at Gold Coast: paying $200 an hour for ice and using the public changing areas because, for most of the lockout, they didn't want to use team facilities. Eventually, they succumbed to comfort and convenience.

Neilson, forbidden by the League from participating in these informal skates and scrimmages, used Skrudland as his liaison. He felt tighter to the players than to management and knew the Panthers could take advantage of the lockout; while other teams were scattered, they were together and skating. Adversity brought them closer.

Nothing prevented Neilson from socializing with the players away from the rink and, one day, he invited Fitzgerald, Bill Lindsay, Stu Barnes, LeRoy, assistant equipment manager Scott Tinkler, and training facility assistant Andre Szucko out on his boat for an afternoon of inner tubing. They departed from Lindsay's place on the Intracoastal Waterway, cruised through the Deerfield Beach Inlet, and spent a fun, lazy day, lying around on the warm, tropical waters of the Atlantic Ocean.

"For some reason," Fitzgerald told Neilson, "I can't picture myself boating with Al Arbour."

Neilson couldn't help but laugh.

Lindsay, one of the few bachelors on the team, spent his mornings golfing and reading the newspapers, and his evenings dining at the home of one of the married players or trying to figure out the cookbook his fiancée had sent him. For two weeks, players and coaches held nightly chalk talks for season ticket holders at Gold Coast Arena. The subject: What Went Wrong At The End of the 1993-94 Season. The attraction: Lectures from Neilson, Lindy Ruff, and the players, and food from a local chicken outlet.

"We were so sick of chicken," Neilson said.

As the lockout dragged on through November, the players were getting tired of meaningless skates, redundant newspaper reports about the dispute, and the sporadic, failing, bargaining sessions.

"I've become bored because I realize I'm not doing what I should," Skrudland said. "I feel so distant, too, because the meetings go on a thousand miles away. It's too bad. I've found a job I love and enjoy, and I get paid a great deal of money to play it. I'm proud to play it, but I'm not proud of what's happening right now. We have to get this thing settled."

John Vanbiesbrouck's feelings, exactly. Although not involved in the front-line negotiations, Vanbiesbrouck was in the middle of the action. Instead of stopping pucks, he was sending and receiving faxes, answering telephone calls from union reps, and updating his increasingly anxious teammates.

"I got into it with a few players," Vanbiesbrouck said. "There were a lot of guys who were concerned. They wanted to play, and they wanted to make their point known that they were concerned. There's bills to pay, there's things to do. And speaking with management was real tough, too, because they didn't see eye-to-eye with what we wanted. We weren't looking to gain anything. We were looking to keep what we had."

Which is exactly what the Panthers' marketing and ticket staff was trying to do: Keep what it had. Season ticket holders demanded refunds and the Panthers' ticket base dropped from 9,800 to 7,800. Advertisers and sponsors pulled out and TV revenue was lost with each canceled game. After an inaugural season filled with good will and positive press, the Panthers were in danger of fading off the South Florida sports map they had just inhabited.

"We kept intensifying our youth hockey efforts," Dean Jordan said. "We did clinics for season ticket holders, we did everything we could. Our staff stayed busy, but as time wore on, it became more difficult and we couldn't answer the question: Will the season start? We told them to keep the faith. That worked for a couple of months, but then the lockout dragged into December."

By that time, the Panthers had more than their share of bad news.

▲ ▲ ▲

At the beginning of December, talks between the union and the owners broke off and prospects of starting the season looked grimmer than ever. Negotiations had reached the basest level with Bettman insulting Goodenow across the bargaining table.

On December 9, in a meeting room at Blockbuster Plaza, Wayne Huizenga's dream of building a sports and entertainment complex died when Steve Berrard, the new CEO of Blockbuster Entertainment since the Viacom merger, killed Blockbuster Park. He considered the $2 billion price tag too expensive, and Paramount Parks, another new sector of Viacom, decided South Florida wasn't right for expansion. Huizenga was disappointed, but powerless.

"Viacom was buying Paramount, and Paramount had theme parks, and it was a natural to build a theme park out here," Huizenga said. "But Viacom started squeezing for cash and they had this big amount of debt, so they didn't want to build any more theme parks. They wanted to conserve their cash and sell the land instead.

"It would've been great for South Florida," Huizenga said. "That place would've been packed out there, but I wasn't the boss anymore."

He was, however, still the owner of a hockey team, and the death of Blockbuster Park meant two wasted years of arena planning. The Panthers would have to stay at Miami Arena for longer than planned and lose even more money than anticipated. The lockout was no longer Huizenga's most pressing hockey problem.

▲ ▲ ▲

The cash register starts ringing from the time you buy your ticket to a sporting event and doesn't stop until the game is over and you leave the building. For fans, the goal is getting out with some money remaining. For the Panthers, that ringing sound was their bottom line getting redder and redder.

Sure, it doesn't make sense. Huizenga's a multi-millionaire and he wouldn't buy a business to lose money. But by going to a game and following the money trail, it's easy to see why Miami Arena was the Panthers' money pit and the closing of the Blockbuster Park escape route deepened the hole.

So let's go!

Traveling to Miami Arena, you leave the traffic off I-95 and drive east on I-395 because there's never any traffic. Off at the first exit, you deftly steer around a stopped car, in which an illegal ticket transaction is taking place, then hang the first right. About a mile down, you take another right onto NW Sixth Street. The Arena is the big pink thing up ahead on the right, a few blocks past the scraggly prostitute and the old men playing cards in front of the Congress Hotel.

Resist the temptation to pay $3 for parking five blocks from the arena and splurge for the $10 lot adjacent to the arena or, if you're with a hot date, the $15 valet parking. Doesn't matter to the Heat or the Panthers. They're not getting a red cent.

Now that you've parked, proceed to the Arena, go to the box office, and pick up your tickets at will call. If it's a Heat game, a person paid by the

Arena will hand you your tickets. If it's a Panthers game, the employee was paid by the hockey team.

With seats in hand, round the corner, climb the steep steps, and find an open door. The Panthers pay $9,000 a game in rent to open those doors. The Heat pays $13,954. That sounds like a bargain for hockey, but it isn't. The Panthers aren't finished paying until the night is over: 75 cents a ticket and another 7.5 percent of gross ticket sales over $200,000. The total: over $30,000 per game.

You hand your ticket to the ticket-taker and pass a security guard. If this is a basketball night, they're being paid by the Arena. If it's a hockey night, they're being paid by the team. So are the building engineers, maintenance workers, cleaners, ushers, and security guards. It adds up to over $13,000 a game. The Heat pays for excess staff only when there's a big crowd.

At your next stop, you visit a souvenir stand to buy a program and a hat. Whether it's a hockey or basketball game, the team and the concessionaire share the proceeds, about $30,000 per game. The Arena gets nothing.

Suited up, informed, and ready to root, you have an usher show you to your seat. Because this is your first visit to Miami Arena, you take a look around and the first thing you notice is all of the advertising. The building looks like a high-tech Little League field.

Companies paid the Heat for the permanent ads on the scoreboard, end zone matrix boards, and the mini-billboards throughout the Arena. The Panthers don't get a dime. The Heat pays the Miami Sports and Exhibition Authority over $350,000 a year for exclusive advertising rights within the building, including the promenade area.

But if there's a hockey game on this night, you see advertising on the dasherboards and the ice, and flickering on the matrix boards. Once in a while, the P.A. announcer plugs the J.J. Kelly Panthers Express or the Ryder Move of the Day. The Panthers pay MSEA $50,000 a year for the rights to these limited sources of advertising revenue. And you can bet your life — because it says so right there in the lease — that the Panthers' advertisers aren't competing with the Heat's advertisers. If there's a conflict, the Heat's client stays, the other one goes.

Sick of staring at ads, you redirect your attention downward, to the playing surface. If that's a basketball court you see, it was paid for by the Arena. The guys mopping and dusting the court? Arena employees. If it's a hockey night, the rink belongs to the Arena, too, but the Zamboni drivers were paid for by the Panthers. One of those Zambonis is owned by the Arena. The Panthers paid for the other one because two are required by the League. The four additional full-time employees the Arena hired to work hockey games are also paid for by the Panthers.

Rent doesn't buy much these days, does it?

With 15 minutes remaining until game time, your stomach is growling and you decide to get something to eat. You stand on line at the concession stand, settle upon the soggy hamburger, the salty fries, and the ice with coke, then hand $8 to the cashier. About 96 cents of that purchase will end up in the home team's pocket on a hockey night, a little more on a basketball night.

Now it's almost game time, so you rush back to your seat and get ready for an evening of excitement. But, boy, wouldn't it be more fun to watch from one of those plush luxury boxes hanging from the Arena ceiling? Waiter service, TV sets, and comfortable seats. The good life!

It would be the good life for the Panthers, too, if they ever saw a dime from the sale of those boxes. Fact is, the Heat are paying around $300,000 a year for the exclusive rights to every suite for every event at the Arena. If there's a concert, the Heat get free tickets for their suiteholders. If there's a circus, the Heat get free tickets for their suiteholders. If there's a hockey game ... you guessed it: Twenty tickets for each of the 16 suites, 320 tickets in all, free of charge, sent directly to the Heat.

Ah, who cares about luxury, especially when it's at the expense of seeing the game! You're with the crowd, sitting close to the action ... close enough to freeze if there's a hockey game going on. The air conditioning is on high because the building has to be kept cold on hockey nights, and air conditioning costs money. The Panthers pay all utility bills, a total of $160,000 a year. The Heat doesn't. Every time the ice is removed and redone, another $12,500 is charged to the Panthers' account.

Doesn't sound fair? Sounds like somebody played hard ball and won? Well, go ahead and complain. Complain to the Heat. Their rent-free executive offices are located on the main floor of Miami Arena, convenient to their complimentary executive parking spaces.

As for the Panthers' staff, those tired looking people running around with walkie-talkies and media guides, they drove all the way from downtown Fort Lauderdale this afternoon and had to bring their offices with them. If they forgot something, it's a long trip back to Broward Boulevard with all of that night construction on I-95. Chances are they made a list, checked it twice, and are scurrying back and forth between the press room and the home team locker room ... built and paid for by the Panthers.

Now it should be pretty clear: Attend a Heat game and you're supporting the Heat, attend a hockey game and you're supporting the Heat.

The Panthers pay $2.5 million a year to use Miami Arena. The Heat pays $1.3 million a year. Add in the advertising and suite revenue and there's a $6.4 million difference in value between the leases.

Disney CEO Michael Eisner, wearing a Mighty Ducks jersey from the movie, and Wayne Huizenga were major components in the NHL's plan to increase its visibility and compete for a larger share of the sports market in the United States. On December 10, 1992, Disney and Huizenga were awarded NHL franchises.

(Photo: Bruce Bennett/Bruce Bennett Studios)

Few established teams could field a more impressive — or famous — management team than the Panthers, who had President Bill Torrey, General Manager Bob Clarke, and Coach Roger Neilson doing their bidding at the 1993 Expansion Draft. The result: 10 players who would compete in the 1996 Stanley Cup finals.

(Photo: J. Giamundo/Bruce Bennett Studios)

Rob Niedermayer, the Panthers' first-ever draft pick, had Bill Torrey behind him at the 1993 Entry Draft, but didn't feel he received quite the same support from Coach Roger Neilson.

(Photo: Bruce Bennett/
Bruce Bennett Studios)

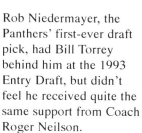

Scott Mellanby was left unprotected by the Edmonton Oilers in the 1993 Expansion Draft, but twice he scored 30 goals for the Panthers and proved he hadn't lost his touch by one-timing a rat against the locker room wall.

(Photo: J. Giamundo/Bruce Bennett Studios)

Coach Doug MacLean thought he faced a long building project with the Panthers until Captain Brian Skrudland assured him that the players wouldn't accept a step backwards. MacLean was the brain of the Panthers, Skrudland the heart.

(Photo: R. Lewis/Bruce Bennett Studios)

Defenseman Ed Jovanovski, a finalist for 1996 Rookie of the Year, was a feared checker who became an offensive force in the second half of the season. He took on big Eric Lindros in the playoffs and won the battle.

(Photo: R. Lewis/
Bruce Bennett Studios)

After four tumultuous seasons in Detroit, Bryan Murray didn't mind moving on to Florida as General Manager of the Panthers. He inherited a hard-working team and supplemented it with acquisitions such as Ray Sheppard, Robert Svehla, Martin Straka, and Johan Garpenlov.

(Photo: Bruce Bennett/
Bruce Bennett Studios)

Forward Tom Fitzgerald, preparing for a defensive zone face-off with Terry
Carkner, is a defensive specialist who played right wing and center ... and for a
while thought he might be a left wing, too, during the 1995-96 season. He
scored the biggest goal of the season in the Eastern Conference finals.

(Photo: Bruce Bennett/Bruce Bennett Studios)

"The 'Rat's Nest' is not an easy place to play," Coach Doug MacLean said, and here's one of the reasons: Loud, loyal fans gave the Panthers a decided home-ice advantage throughout the 1996 playoffs.

(Photo: R. Lewis/Bruce Bennett Studios)

"Pinch me!" John Vanbiesbrouck outplayed goalie Ron Hextall, shaking hands with Brian Skrudland, in the Eastern Conference semifinals, and the Panthers defeated the heavily favored Philadelphia Flyers.

(Photo: R. Lewis/
Bruce Bennett Studios)

The Panthers' final post-goal rat storm: The Orkin Rat Patrol scurries to clear the ice after Rob Niedermayer's goal gave the Panthers a 2-1 lead in Game 3 of the 1996 Stanley Cup finals.

(Photo: Bruce Bennett/Bruce Bennett Studios)

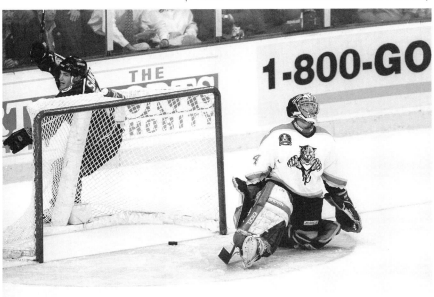

The goal that won the Cup: John Vanbiesbrouck can't see Joe Sakic celebrating behind him, but he knows the season is over. Uwe Krupp's goal in the third overtime of Game 4 gave the Avalanche a 1-0 victory.

(Photo: Bruce Bennett/Bruce Bennett Studios)

But don't worry about that. You're here to have fun. Sit back. Enjoy the game. And watch your step when exiting the building. The liability insurance was paid for by the teams and only one of them can afford it if the premium goes up.

Got the picture? Other NHL teams might have been exaggerating their losses, but not the Panthers.

▲ ▲ ▲

The lockout couldn't have come at a better time for Bryan Murray. With little more than a month on the job from the time he was hired to the start of training camp, Murray underwent a crash course on the Florida Panthers. The lockout gave him extra time to learn more about the organization.

Torrey and Huizenga were busy with the lockout, so there wasn't any need for Murray to stay in Florida. He, Fletcher, Neilson, and Ruff scouted prospects, watched the minor leaguers, and kept tabs on Ed Jovanovski, who still hadn't been signed and couldn't be until after the lockout because of a League-ordered moratorium on contract negotiations. Murray attended the World Junior Championships in Canada which, because of the lockout, included many first- and second-year NHL players, including Jovanovski.

"He wasn't used as much as we wanted him to, but he played pretty well," Fletcher said. "Eddie was a kid who had a lot to learn about how to play."

Then, with Bettman authorized to end the season if a modified 50-game schedule couldn't be played, both sides finally started bargaining as if the world was about to end. Goodenow was feeling pressure from the player agents, whose clients wanted to start collecting paychecks. The big market owners, especially those who owned the arenas in which their teams played, pushed Bettman to end the lockout.

On January 11, an agreement was reached that called for unrestricted free agency for players over 32, restricted free agency for players after three years, and a rookie salary cap. Bettman, perceived as the villain all along, was the savior of the season when he convinced several reluctant governors to vote in favor of the proposal. But not everyone was swayed. As he did throughout the lockout, Torrey, on behalf of Huizenga, voted against the agreement because it didn't include a salary cap or luxury tax.

"Obviously, for us, the [lockout] didn't come at a very good time and it hurt us," Torrey said. "We lost season ticket holders, we lost business. On the other hand, we were one of the teams that held out until the very end. Wayne was not satisfied, because he thought there was no way this would restrain salaries. But even though we voted no on the deal, I was still not convinced the season would be canceled. Wayne voted no because he didn't feel the deal was what it should be. He wanted a full cap. Wayne is a believer in the cap."

Nobody had to convince Vanbiesbrouck, who noted Huizenga's hawkish position during the lockout.

"I don't know what was told to him before he went into this, and I don't know what was told to him after, and I'll never know, but maybe he was sold something that he didn't quite get," Vanbiesbrouck said. "So if you go to the store, and buy something that isn't exactly right, you usually take it back, right?"

Vanbiesbrouck's suspicion was shared by many: Maybe Huizenga was promised a salary cap when he bought the franchise. Although, in reality, nobody made any such promises to Huizenga, in December 1992 the governors were discussing the need for restraint on salaries in the next collective bargaining agreement. Never anticipating the owners wouldn't get what they wanted, Huizenga was willing to sacrifice the season and wait for the players to give in to the owners' demands.

▲ ▲ ▲

Training Camp II began on January 13 at Gold Coast Arena with none of the amenities of Peterborough, but at least the assurance of a season: 48 games, reduced from 84, shoehorned into 102 days, with teams playing only within their conference. For the Panthers and the other Eastern Conference teams, that meant no trips to the west coast, one meaningful game after another, and every team undefeated and in the playoff race when the season opened on January 21.

The Panthers had one week to get back into playing shape, but with only 23 players on the roster, they didn't have to worry about who was going to make the team; those decisions had been made in Training Camp I. The only question was Ed Jovanovski, who had a surprisingly strong camp in September until late in the pre-season, when he started overplaying his position and making rookie mistakes on defensive reads.

Anton Thun, Jovanovski's agent, and Murray had progressed from being $2 million apart to $1 million apart on a four-year deal, a realistic gap that could've been narrowed with serious bargaining. Serious or not, negotiations were put on hold by the lockout and Jovanovski returned to juniors.

The lockout provided the Panthers a second chance to evaluate and sign Jovanovski, but because he was playing 40 minutes a night in the Ontario League, Murray thought it best to take the contract negotiations at a slower pace and keep Jovanovski in Windsor. At least that was the official line.

In reality, Murray and Neilson already had their first private conflict: Murray wanted Jovanovski on the team, Neilson didn't.

"We never thought Jovanovski was even close to making the team," Neilson said, speaking for the coaching staff. "He didn't have the maturity to play professional hockey the first year, and it was tough with a team like ours for him to step in and play that style. But never mind that. You can live with a guy's mistakes if he's going to be good. It wasn't that. It was off-ice. We didn't think he had the maturity. We thought he'd get into a situation where he'd have trouble being with the team. We just felt he was very young and immature in that first year, and it would've been a mistake to put him in that social situation."

Murray didn't agree with Neilson's assessment of Jovanovski's readiness and could've tried harder to sign him. Jovanovski had initially demanded $6.5 million for four years and rejected an offer of $5.75 million just before the original signing deadline. With No. 2 pick Oleg Tverdovsky having signed with Anaheim for $1.4 million per year and No. 3 pick Radek Bonk having signed with Ottawa for $1.2 million per year, Thun thought the market had been set: Jovanovski deserved at least $1.6 million.

When contract talks resumed in January, the sticking point was the 1994-95 season; the Panthers didn't want it to count as a full year against the contract. But Murray didn't force the issue and Jovanovski remained in juniors.

"It just seemed we could never get the negotiations to exactly where we wanted to get to or where they wanted to get to," Murray said. "We'd get close, and it would look like something was going to happen, but for some reason there'd be a bailout on the deal. It took a little bit of the fun out of it at the time, but I guess he wouldn't have been able to play, the way Roger was talking. He's a first-round pick that should've had a chance to come here and learn that first year."

As it turned out, Jovanovski, who signed a four-year, $5.7 million contract six months later, could've avoided a lot of trouble if the deal had been completed in January and he had played the season in Florida.

The Panthers thought they were in better shape than most teams for the shortened season because so many players had stayed in Florida during the lockout. They didn't mind having only a week to prepare for their season opener on January 21 against the Islanders.

"We felt this was a chance for us, and I know Roger felt the same way, to get off to a good start because the teams that were really loaded, the Rangers, the Flyers, and the Devils, hadn't been skating together," Fitzgerald said. "He told us, 'This is where you guys have to work hard in the off-season, work hard when you're scrimmaging three days a week or running,' because the start of the season was very important."

151

Duly noted, the Panthers flopped.

The Panthers opened with a lineup not much different from their first-night roster of more than 15 months earlier: Joe Cirella, Paul Laus, Keith Brown, Gord Murphy, Brian Benning, Geoff Smith, Randy Moller, and Brent Severyn on defense; Dave Lowry, Bill Lindsay, Mike Hough, and Jeff Daniels on left wing; Jody Hull, Stu Barnes, Andrei Lomakin, and Scott Mellanby at right wing; and Brian Skrudland, Tom Fitzgerald, Bob Kudelski, Jesse Belanger, and Rob Niedermayer at center. All but Laus, Hull, Barnes, Kudelski, Smith, Moller, Daniels, and Severyn, had played on opening night in Chicago.

The major difference was in goal, where Mark Fitzpatrick, who went undefeated against the Islanders in 1993-94, got the start at Nassau Coliseum. Neilson, having spoken of the importance of having two No. 1 goaltenders in a tight, busy schedule, saved Vanbiesbrouck for the home opener two nights later against Pittsburgh.

Not much went right on Opening Night II, from the NHL's obnoxious Game On! promotion — which conveniently overlooked the reason for nearly four months of Game Off! — to the Panthers' lack of offense. Despite being outshot by a wide margin, the Panthers took a 1-0 lead on Skrudland's first-period goal and had history on their side: They were 30-0-5 in 1993-94 when leading after two periods.

So much for perfection. Ziggy Palffy scored twice in the third period and the Islanders won, 2-1.

A forgiving and exuberant sellout crowd of 14,703 packed Miami Arena for the home opener — Game On! again, laser light shows again — and witnessed another unfortunate Panthers first: five goals, no victory.

"You score five goals in your own building, you should win the hockey game," Lowry said.

That's the way it usually worked, especially for the Panthers, who were 9-0 in 1993-94 when they scored five goals. But this time, they blew two leads in the first period and, despite Vanbiesbrouck's heroics, lost to the Penguins, 6-5. In two games, the Panthers had been outshot, 77-39, and the neutral zone trap wasn't looking very effective.

After going 3-0-2 against their cross-state rivals the previous season, the Panthers pulled off another franchise first two nights later in St. Petersburg when they lost to the Lightning, 3-2. Enrico Ciccone, the Lightning's head-smashing, penalty-box-door-slamming, on-ice madman, enticed the Panthers into several penalties in a game that featured four fights and three game misconducts. Neilson, momentarily forgetting his unclean past, complained about the Lightning's goons.

The Panthers were 0-3.

But in this weird season that almost wasn't and maybe shouldn't have been, order and disorder were quickly restored. Five days and three wins later, the Panthers were at .500 and in first place in the Atlantic Division for the first time in their short history. The League was off to a crazy start. The Rangers and Devils, the previous season's Stanley Cup champions and Eastern Conference finalists respectively, had four wins between them. The Panthers, Islanders, and Lightning, all of whom had missed the playoffs the previous season, were on top of the Atlantic Division.

Order and disorder. The Panthers won only three of their next 12 games. More alarmingly, a team that prided itself on hard work and defense was regularly allowing well over 30 shots a game. Neilson called the second period of a 7-3 loss to the Penguins on February 7 "maybe the worst in our history" and responded by sending a message. Right winger Jamie Linden and defenseman Dallas Eakins were recalled from the International League and Cirella, Benning, and Kudelski were benched for the next game. The Panthers won, 3-0, over the Flyers but it was a quick, ineffective fix. When February ended, the Panthers were in 12th place in the Eastern Conference and, although they trailed the eighth-place Islanders by only two points, their playoff hopes were fading.

▲ ▲ ▲

Brian Skrudland was feeling very warm where he didn't want to feel warm. The warmth was followed by a burning sensation and Skrudland knew what happened: Some joker had rubbed Flex-All, a hot ointment, in his underwear!

Skrudland threw off his shorts and stood in front of a giant fan, desperately trying to relieve his pain. Then he turned around and saw Keith Brown.

Although Brown, a deeply religious man, was one of the least likely people to pull such a stunt, Skrudland enjoyed getting on his case.

"I owe you," Skrudland warned.

"I don't know what you're talking about," Brown responded.

"I owe you," Skrudland repeated.

"I don't know what you're talking about, Brian."

"You know what you did," Skrudland said, then pointed to the sky. "And so does He."

Every player in the locker room, except Brown, was in stitches.

"I still don't know what you're talking about, Brian," he said.

"You know something, Brownie," Skrudland said. "You're an asshole. And you're not just an asshole. You're a sinner."

Even Brown laughed at that.

Skrudland never figured out who really put the Flex-All in his underwear that day, and he never found out who placed one of his dress shoes in the laundry bin so it would get washed. With the team leaving on a road trip and no time to go home for a new pair of shoes, Skrudland spent the weekend wearing a sport jacket, dress pants, and flip-flops.

Not that he had any right to complain. Skrudland was the one always pulling pranks on Rob Niedermayer, like rubbing Vaseline all over the phone receiver and saying, "Neids, it's for you," or removing the batteries from the remote control and leaving Niedermayer staring at a blank TV screen, pushing frantically at the remote buttons while "Screwy" laughed at his young teammate.

Equipment managers and trainers were the preferred target for pranks. After playing in Ottawa in late February, the Panthers had a few days off before their next game against the Rangers and accepted an invitation to train at the U.S. Military Academy in upstate New York. They stayed on the base, skated in the morning, and had lunch with the cadets.

Assistant Equipment Manager Scott Tinkler, an enlisted Marine in the Persian Gulf War, was sitting at a table with several players and cadets when Vanbiesbrouck motioned at him to look under the table. The other players were tapping their forks against their water glasses and calling out, "Shoe check!"

Not here. Not now, Tinkler thought, knowing exactly what was going on. He looked down and saw mustard smeared all over his dress shoes.

Tinkler, who'd been victimized by the same trick several times before, didn't think this was very funny, but the cadets did. The room was roaring with laughter.

"They thought it was the funniest thing they'd ever seen," Tinkler said. "For all I know, it's a new tradition at West Point."

The Saga of the Missing Shirts and Clipped Socks confounded the Panthers for most of their first two seasons and, although there were numerous suspects, the culprit was never caught. Assistant Coach Lindy Ruff was victimized every time the team went to Pittsburgh. He'd return to the locker room after the morning skate, only to find that somebody had absconded with his shirt. So Ruff, wearing only a sport jacket over his bare chest, would return to the hotel for a new one.

Ruff wasn't the only victim. Just about every player eventually lost a shirt. Again in Pittsburgh, during the first season, defenseman Greg Hawgood pulled on his socks and watched, less than amused, as his toes shot right through! Andrei Lomakin, a frequent victim of the clipped socks trick, accused trainer Dave "Sudsy" Settlemyre, figuring Settlemyre was tired of Lomakin demanding a pair of thin socks every second day.

Because the missing shirts and clipped socks were always discovered after practice, the trainers, equipment managers, and any players or coaches who came off the ice during the skate, became suspects. This would have been a harmless stunt, but whoever was stealing the shirts never returned them. Players and coaches got angry, especially when a shirt turned up missing on the day of their twice-monthly team golf outings.

"Enough's enough," Neilson demanded during a team meeting.

Whether the shirt thief/sock clipper was traded, left the organization, or merely decided to put an end to his capers, was never known. But in his own way, he belonged in some kind of Stall of Fame.

"I've been around for 15 years," an amazed Keith Brown said, "and this guy's the best I've ever seen."

Or had never seen.

Fortunately for the Panthers, a losing streak or missing golf shirts wasn't enough to pull them apart. They were a strong group, on and off the ice, and Skrudland was their emotional center. On many teams, the captain is the best player. Not so on the Panthers. Despite being a finalist for the 1993-94 Selke Trophy as the League's best defensive forward, Skrudland trailed several teammates in terms of raw talent.

He was, however, perfect for the job of captain. Skrudland would play practical jokes, break up the room with his humorous banter, and chatter non-stop during practice, but the players realized they could depend upon him in a pinch. To Skrudland, the best example he could set as a captain was working hard and keeping positive through the bad times. And these were bad times.

▲ ▲ ▲

Murray wasn't dismayed when Brian Benning and Joe Cirella complained about their playing time. He'd been around long enough to know that every team has a few unhappy players. Besides, he wasn't exactly enamored with these two slow, veteran defensemen who didn't fit into his long-term plans.

He was more concerned when Niedermayer, the team's first draft pick and a mentally fragile 20-year-old, made the same complaint. Although Niedermayer was dressing for every game, he was on the fourth line with Lindsay and Fitzgerald and getting very little playing time. Neilson, aiming for the playoffs, had no room in his plans for a second-year player's mistakes.

"Roger felt he would maybe someday replace Brian Skrudland, not be a goal scorer, but be a defensive type of guy," Murray said. "And player evaluation, to me, is what makes or breaks general managers or coaches. I felt we had Jovanovski, and Roger had a question about him, and there was a question about Niedermayer. Well, there was our future."

The problem became more serious when Neilson promised Niedermayer time on the penalty killing unit and asked Assistant Coach Craig Ramsay to work with him in practice, then never followed through on his intentions.

"They were looking at using me as a penalty killer, and I didn't do any penalty killing," Niedermayer said. "In that way, it was tough, but the only reason I needed more ice time was to get my confidence back and to get playing the way I was capable of playing."

Niedermayer voiced his frustration to some teammates, such as roommate Brian Skrudland, and relayed the penalty killing promise to Murray.

"I told Rob, 'If they made these comments to you, you have an obligation to the coaches, but they have one to you, too,' " Murray recalled. " 'If they tell you something, they have to give you a chance by doing what they tell you.' I went to Roger a few times and said, basically, 'I don't care who else you play, or how much they play, but I really believe that Rob Niedermayer has to play a more important role on our hockey team if we're going to have any future.' "

Murray had to look hard to find the Panthers' future: rookies would collectively play in a total of nine games all season.

On nights when Niedermayer barely played at all, Chuck Fletcher would sarcastically say to Neilson, "Hey, I see Niedermayer got his three minutes tonight."

One day, Neilson suggested to Murray that Niedermayer could get more ice time in a checking role.

"We shouldn't think of him that way at all," Murray replied.

Neilson wasn't entirely closed to experimentation. Niedermayer had gone more than two months without a goal when Neilson moved him to right wing and switched Fitzgerald to center for a game on April 12 against the Islanders. Although Niedermayer scored in a 3-1 victory, his playing time didn't increase and he continued losing faith in Neilson. He was working hard in practice, but not playing, and that didn't seem fair; everywhere else he had been, hard work had been rewarded by playing time.

"Some coaches have different philosophies," Niedermayer said. "We were successful, but I didn't feel I got as much ice time as I needed to develop. I was just sitting at one point and it wasn't very good."

Niedermayer scored only one goal in the final 38 games of what turned out to be a wasted second season. Forget the sophomore jinx, which supposedly affects standouts in their second season; Niedermayer would've loved the chance to experience some bad luck.

By the end of the season, Neilson was openly wondering whether Niedermayer would develop into a top NHL player. Prior to the final regular season game in Pittsburgh, he sat down with Ramsay, Ruff, and Torrey, to discuss individual players and their progress during the season. Neilson was down on Niedermayer and disappointed with the way he had played.

Ruff disagreed. He thought Niedermayer was a young player who was growing up and learning what it took to play in the NHL. He was even more sure of it when Niedermayer went out and fought Penguins enforcer Chris Tamer, a 6'2", 185-pounder who knows how to fight.

"That's a pretty good sign that the kid is going to show up and play the game," Ruff said. "It's the last game of the year, a nothing game, and he didn't back down. I thought that was a pretty good sign of courage and determination."

Maybe, but it wasn't good enough for Neilson. He wasn't sold on the Panthers' first-ever draft pick.

▲ ▲ ▲

Had Stu Barnes heard correctly? Did somebody really compare him to the great Mario Lemieux? Sure enough, Chris Moore, the radio voice of the Panthers, had done just that.

"The Panthers losing Stu Barnes," Moore said on the air, "is like the Pittsburgh Penguins losing Mario Lemieux."

Fair enough. Moore wasn't comparing Barnes to Lemieux in terms of talent, but in how much he meant to the team. Barnes not only played on the top scoring line, centering for Bob Kudelski and Dave Lowry, but was depended upon for the power play, penalty kill, four-on-four situations, and important faceoffs. But according to the evidence, the Panthers losing Barnes was far worse than the Penguins losing Lemieux.

The Panthers were 1-5-1 in his absence.

With Lemieux sitting out the season because of chronic back problems and the effects of cancer radiation therapy, the Penguins were 28-16-4.

"I should call him up and thank him for putting those two names in the same sentence," Barnes said of Moore's comment. "That was nice of him, but I think this team has never depended on one player, outside of Beezer."

Barnes was sidelined at the worst possible time, riding the hot streak of his career with 14 points in 14 games. He was the team's only dependable source of offense and scored another goal in a 2-0 win over Ottawa on February 15, before a high stick by Pat Elynuik caught him in the left eye. Although Barnes' eye was swollen shut, the injury wasn't as serious as it looked and far better than doctors originally thought when they examined him after the game.

The Panthers, winners of three of their last four games, sank into a deeper offensive slump, scoring only 14 goals in the seven games Barnes missed. If Mellanby hadn't hit a minor goal-scoring streak during that period, the Panthers' offense would have disappeared entirely.

Neilson knew he couldn't depend on Kudelski for offense. Kudelski, who didn't score in the final 14 games of the 1993-94 season, had only two goals in the first 18 games of the 1994-95 season and twice was a healthy scratch. And when Barnes, his linemate, went down, Kudelski's playing time decreased even more because Neilson used only three lines. Eventually, Kudelski was being used only on the power play and wondering why Neilson wasted a lineup spot on him.

Murray, on the other hand, was wondering why he bothered signing Kudelski to a contract that paid his supposed sniper $700,000 a year. When Murray became GM in August, Torrey was negotiating Kudelski's new contract with agent Steve Reich. Kudelski had made $400,000 the year before and, coming off his first 40-goal season and All-Star Game appearance, wouldn't accept the Panthers' offer of $600,000 a year.

Murray, who didn't know much about Kudelski, asked Neilson, "Do we need this guy?"

Neilson's response made perfect sense: "We don't have very much offense," he said. "We need a guy who can score some goals."

With the two sides far apart, Kudelski became the Panthers' first holdout when training camp began in Peterborough. He signed five days later to a contract for two years and an option year, and reported to camp. When the season finally started, however, Murray wished he hadn't wasted his time or the team's money. Kudelski was no more capable of playing the trap than he had been the year before.

"He couldn't counterattack, and that's what we needed," Neilson said. "He wanted to do the job defensively, but we just felt he couldn't get the job done. His lack of skating just really hurt in our system."

Kudelski's insistence that he had played a checking role when with the Los Angeles Kings was meaningless, because Neilson didn't want him to check; he wanted him to play the trap. Kudelski needed open ice to crank up his big slapshot, but the Panthers' system wasn't about creating room, it was about quick changes from offense to defense and back again. When Neilson started keeping Kudelski out of the lineup, Murray shopped him around to other teams and found no takers.

"I tried the whole second half of the year after I signed him," Murray said. "Roger wouldn't play him very much, he didn't like him, and Bob wasn't doing very much, and nobody was interested. Bob found out he was going to be put in a particular role here, and only that role, and if he didn't do it on the power play, it affected his play. But he never showed by my way of thinking that he should've gotten more ice time, because he wasn't the type of guy that would go out and do it."

Kudelski played in only 26 games and finished with six goals and three assists, meaning he made $45,500 per point scored. The numbers made Murray wince.

Murray did more than wince on February 19, when the Panthers learned that Ed Jovanovski had been brought in for questioning by police in Windsor, Ontario, in connection with an alleged sexual assault of a 24-year-old woman. One week later, Jovanovski, along with two teammates, was arrested and charged with two counts of sexual assault. The Panthers were so concerned over Jovanovski's future that a clause protecting the team in the event of a conviction was written into the contract they eventually agreed upon. The prosecutor would drop the charges in August after deciding the alleged victim wasn't credible but, until then, Jovanovski's career was in danger.

Between Niedermayer's lack of playing time, injuries to Barnes and Keith Brown, Kudelski's wasted salary, and the Panthers' inability to win, everything was going wrong. Even the victories were accompanied by grief. After a 4-1 victory in Ottawa on February 25, the Panthers were taken to task by the Canadian press for playing the trap.

The Ottawa Citizen wrote, "With the Panthers never certain when they would be called for their customary interference, they were briefly forced to play a game unfamiliar to them: hockey."

Neilson, not caring how his team won, tried to figure out a way to make things right. That's exactly what he was doing early on a Sunday morning, while biking along U.S. 1 in Pompano to Gold Coast Arena. Neilson ran a red light, was struck by a car, flew over the handlebars, and broke his left elbow. Coaching the Panthers had become hazardous duty.

▲ ▲ ▲

Here comes Wayne Huizenga, John Vanbiesbrouck thought, *and here comes the same old question.*

"Hello, John," Huizenga said. "How's the house going?"

Huizenga knew very well how the house was going. The house was being built, in upscale Boca Raton, and Vanbiesbrouck's only concern was whether he would live in it or sell it. The implication behind Huizenga's question couldn't have been clearer: If you want to live in that house, maybe you'd better come down on your contract demands.

They're playing games, Vanbiesbrouck knew. He and his wife, Rosalinde, had optimistically started building their new house during the lockout, but now they weren't sure what the future held.

Vanbiesbrouck wasn't getting any answers. Playing in the option year of a four-year contract signed with the Rangers, he was scheduled to make $1.1 million for the season, prorated at 58.5 percent for time missed because of the lockout. But under the terms of the previous collective bargaining agree-

159

ment, he had the right to have an arbitrator determine his option year salary. That's what his agent, Lloyd Friedland, and the Panthers were trying to avoid.

At least Vanbiesbrouck hoped they were. The Panthers made their most attractive offer of $6 million for three years shortly after the lockout ended; Vanbiesbrouck wanted a long-term deal of five years at $10 million. With Blockbuster Park dead and the Panthers uncertain over where they'd be playing after the 1995-96 season, Torrey asked Friedland to postpone the negotiations.

But Vanbiesbrouck, whose suspicions about management's motives intensified during the lockout, thought the Panthers had no intention of making a serious offer and preferred getting rid of his contract, perhaps by trading him.

"They don't want to sign you, and everything's leading toward arbitration," Vanbiesbrouck said. "They don't make a legitimate offer, ever, they don't communicate with you. What are you supposed to think? I'm just thinking, *Hey, if that's the way they're thinking, get yourself prepared for the reality, not the bullshit. Don't think that you're bigger than the game, or bigger than the team, or the fans won't let you be traded. Deal in reality. You're a player, you can be traded any time, any place, for anything.*"

Vanbiesbrouck wanted to stay in South Florida and hoped management saw him as a franchise player — valuable to the team, extremely popular with the fans — who had an important role in the birth of the franchise. He thought loyalty and respect mattered. But he wondered about that every time Huizenga asked him about the house.

"They know what plays on your chords," Vanbiesbrouck said. "And I've played in this game long enough to know, but the reason it didn't affect me and it didn't affect my play was because the group was so strong. I didn't want to let anybody down."

He didn't. After a 3-7-1 start that was no fault of Vanbiesbrouck's, he played brilliantly on February 28 in a 0-0 tie with the Rangers at Madison Square Garden. The final score was deceiving; the Rangers dominated with 44 shots while the Panthers' offense consisted of dumping the puck into the Rangers' end and dropping back on defense. Vanbiesbrouck, named first star, could've been second and third star, too.

Two nights later, the Flyers thoroughly outplayed the Panthers, with the newly-formed Legion of Doom line of Eric Lindros, John LeClair, and Mikael Renberg dominating from the opening faceoff. But Vanbiesbrouck made 35 saves and received the first star in a 2-2 tie. He went 4-1-2 during a seven-game stretch between February 28 and March 16, stopping 201 of 209 shots.

Almost single-handedly, Vanbiesbrouck pulled the Panthers out of their slump and got them back into the playoff race. A 35-save performance and another victory in Montreal on March 22 lifted them into a tie with Buffalo for the final playoff spot with 18 games remaining. Having lost three overtime games in six nights, the victory was like medicine for the Panthers' declining morale. Yet, as Torrey spoke to reporters outside the visitor's dressing room at The Forum and proclaimed, "Every player on our team is available," he meant Vanbiesbrouck, too.

As the April 7 trade deadline neared, rumors intensified that Vanbiesbrouck was being shopped around the League. He was, but not in such a direct manner. Murray's conversations with fellow general managers went along the lines of: "We have two goalies, Vanbiesbrouck and Fitzpatrick. Are you interested in one of them?"

In most cases, teams weren't interested. The closest Murray came to making a trade was with the Quebec Nordiques, a young team that led the League in points, but had two young goalies, Jocelyn Thibault and Stephane Fiset, who hadn't proven themselves in the playoffs. Murray asked Nordiques General Manager Pierre Lacroix for rookie center Adam Deadmarsh and rugged prospect Landon Wilson, a Toronto second-rounder in 1993, in exchange for Vanbiesbrouck. Lacroix thought it over for a day and a half and decided not to pull the trigger.

Murray had an idea why Vanbiesbrouck wasn't in demand. Teams not in contention for the Stanley Cup had no need for a big-money goaltender whose actual contract hadn't been determined. And teams in the Cup hunt had no interest in a goaltender who had a career playoff record of 13-20 and faded down the stretch the year before.

"History's a major thing, and guys are labeled fairly early on in this business," Murray said. "We talked to Quebec a little bit and it was just a matter of them thinking, *Well, are we going to be better at the end of the year if we make this trade?* And there's never any assurance until a guy does it [in the playoffs]."

Because the Panthers were a team of outcasts, Murray fielded few serious trade offers. Kudelski was untradeable. Vanbiesbrouck wasn't attracting fair value. He considered parlaying Vanbiesbrouck, Skrudland, Mellanby, and Lowry, players other teams were asking about, into first- and second-rounders or young players, but the offers were never attractive enough. The Rangers offered a fourth-round pick for Skrudland. On the other hand, teams rejected the Panthers' offers of prospects or draft picks and a veteran player in exchange for goal scorers.

Murray was learning one of the drawbacks of running the Panthers: Players who work well within a system lose some of their value when they leave the system. Skrudland, Mellanby, Lowry, Lindsay, Hough, and the others, were more valuable to the Panthers than they were to any other team.

▲ ▲ ▲

Back in September, Murray had asked himself a question key to the Panthers' future: Did they need a complete overhaul to become a top team, or could they get there simply by adding some skill to the current base of hard-working veterans? In his first attempt to answer the question, Murray phoned Calgary Flames General Manager Doug Risebrough.

Risebrough was having trouble signing Robert Svehla, a 25-year-old defenseman from Slovakia who starred in several World Championships and the 1994 Olympics. Svehla was putting up big scoring and penalty-minute numbers in the defense-oriented Swedish Elite League, and now his high-powered agent, Rich Winter, was demanding big money from Calgary: $1 million Canadian a year guaranteed.

"I thought Svehla had the potential to be a real good player," Murray said. "He was smart, he moved the puck, he was strong, and I thought he could come in and play in the NHL. I knew he could play on our team, because we needed some puck skill back there."

Murray recognized that although the Panthers had speedy forwards, their best defensemen were Murphy and the injury-prone Brown, while Brian Benning, Joe Cirella, and Randy Moller, were too old and immobile to play the high-tempo style he preferred. Svehla could fit right in and make some of those slow defensemen expendable.

Murray calculated. *$1 million Canadian was the equivalent of $750,000 U.S. Winter might lower his price to get the deal done with a team eager to put his client in the lineup.*

"I told him I'll make a deal, but we have to do a contract," Murray said. "I told him if you're representing a player, and you don't want to make a proper deal with me, I'm not going to trade for him."

Careful to structure the deal so the Panthers wouldn't have to pay signing bonuses if Svehla was a bust, Murray and Winter agreed on a contract that paid Svehla $600,000 a year. Risebrough eventually accepted Murray's offer of a third-round pick in the 1996 Entry Draft and a fourth-round pick in 1997, conditional on Svehla's performance.

Then, in a well-planned afterthought, Murray asked Risebrough about Magnus Svensson, a 31-year-old defenseman who had spent his entire career in the Swedish and Swiss elite leagues. The Flames obviously had no intention of doing anything with Svensson, despite his performance on Sweden's Gold Medal-winning 1994 Olympic team, and Murray wanted his rights as part of the deal. Risebrough agreed.

Svensson wouldn't make his NHL debut until March 20. In the final 19 games of the season, he logged more ice time than any Panthers defenseman except Murphy. Svehla arrived in Florida on April 20 after missing his plane two days earlier. No sooner had he skated onto the ice at Gold Coast than he declared himself ready for the NHL. Even Murray didn't realize just how ready.

A fast, tireless defenseman with wonderful offensive instincts and superb defensive skills, Svehla answered Murray's question: Only a jump-start, not a complete overhaul, was necessary.

The mid-season acquisitions of Swedish left wing Johan Garpenlov from the San Jose Sharks and minor league defenseman Jason Woolley from the Detroit Vipers reinforced this estimation. Garpenlov had played for Murray in Detroit and scored 18 goals while playing a defensive role on a line with rookie Sergei Fedorov. Woolley was starring in the IHL with 36 points in 48 games. At the bargain price of $275,000 a year, the Panthers acquired a fast-skating, left-shooting defenseman who could play the point on the power play.

"A guy like Woolley was something we didn't have the first year," Fletcher said. "He could quarterback the power play. Then Svehla could quarterback the power play. We brought in Svensson and drafted Eddie Jovanovski, so even though Eddie didn't play, we knew we were going to have Jovanovski, Svensson, Svehla, and Woolley as possible additions to our blueline the next year."

At Neilson's request, Murray made one more deal, acquiring defensive forward Gaetan Duchesne from the Sharks for a sixth-round draft pick. But that trade was more in line with the Panthers' past; Woolley, Svehla, Svensson, and Garpenlov symbolized the future. The Panthers were becoming less Neilson's team, and more Murray's.

▲ ▲ ▲

In the lockout-shortened 1994-95 season, the Panthers never had an unbeaten streak of more than three games and never went above .500. They never controlled their playoff destiny and, with 17 days and 10 games remaining in the season, had a record of 14-19-5. Andrei Lomakin and Kudelski, two of their top scorers from the first season, had played their way out of the lineup. Their leading scorers, Barnes and Belanger, would finish 41 points behind NHL leader Jaromir Jagr.

Yet, on April 14, they trailed the Hartford Whalers by four points for the final playoff spot and the defending Stanley Cup champion Rangers by only two points. The Panthers were going nowhere and getting somewhere at the same time.

"We spent the last 25 games trying to erase the first 18," Neilson said.

"I don't know if there was any particular thing that got us going, we just kept working away and gradually cut it down."

The Panthers shared a treadmill with the rest of the League. After Quebec and Pittsburgh, which were battling by themselves for the Eastern Conference title, and Ottawa, dismal for the third consecutive season, not much separated the other 11 teams.

The playoff drive didn't begin in earnest until a 3-0 loss to the Capitals left the Panthers five games under .500 and five points behind Buffalo for the final spot. With so many teams in playoff contention, the Panthers figured they needed to go 7-3 the rest of the way to have a chance. Neilson laid out the challenge: Win three of the next four games at home, or kiss the season goodbye.

The Panthers tried being optimistic, but they knew Miami Arena had never been their safe haven. The lockout hadn't affected the Panthers' popularity and the Arena was regularly sold out with increasingly enthusiastic fans whose support wasn't rewarded: The Panthers played to four consecutive sellouts in February and lost all four games. They had lost their two most recent home games, both in front of sellout crowds.

In 1993-94, the Panthers' situation was win and they're in. This time, it was win or else.

But in the way most important to Mark Fitzpatrick, the 1994-95 season was just like the first: Vanbiesbrouck was the No. 1 goalie, he was the backup, and whatever Neilson said at the start of the season about the importance of having two quality goaltenders was meaningless. One was going to waste.

"After going through the first season, it wasn't a shock," Fitzpatrick said. "Even though I think I played well enough to earn some more starts, it was like déjà vu all over again. It was the same exact situation, the season was the only thing that changed."

Three times, Vanbiesbrouck played three games in four nights and twice he played four games in seven nights. During a nine-game stretch from February 28 through March 18, Vanbiesbrouck played all but 40 minutes. Neilson saw no reason to use Fitzpatrick because Vanbiesbrouck was playing so well; on many nights, he was the only reason they got away with a win or a tie.

"We wanted to be fair to both John and to Fitzy," Neilson said. "And it was a tough thing for Mark, who felt he had the capabilities, and I think he was right, to be a first-stringer. I tried to be up front with him. I said as long as Beezer's playing well, he's going to be No. 1."

Although he didn't have a vote, overplaying Vanbiesbrouck didn't make much sense to goaltending coach Bill Smith, who thought giving Fitzpatrick more playing time would've made both goaltenders more effective.

"Mark would come in and stand on his head, and he wouldn't play for another two weeks," Smith said. "That's mentally and physically very tough on you, and he didn't understand why he'd play real well, then Johnny would come in and have a bad game, but Johnny would stay in. Then Mark would have a real good game, but then if he played the next game and had a bad game, he'd sit forever. You have to take your chances. You have to use them both. And we all know who the No. 1 is."

That was uncertain in April, when Vanbiesbrouck was showing signs of wear and Fitzpatrick shut out the Devils, 1-0, on April 20 for the franchise's first win over New Jersey. The victory moved the Panthers two points behind in the playoff race with seven games remaining. Two nights later, Fitzpatrick started a crucial home game against the Eastern Conference-leading Quebec Nordiques. If Fitzpatrick played well and the Panthers won, Neilson might have had no choice but to keep using him down the stretch.

"I was feeling really good and felt as close to the top of my game as I could be, and really looking forward to the challenge of answering the bell if I was called upon," Fitzpatrick said. "Unfortunately, that didn't happen."

The Panthers scored three goals, including Svehla's first in the NHL, to take a 3-0 lead after only 11 minutes, but, with seven minutes remaining in the period, Nordiques tough guy Chris Simon bore down on a clean break-away. Simon went one way. Fitzpatrick followed the move. Simon went the other way. Fitzpatrick did a split to the left, twisting his body in the opposite direction. Simon scored. Fitzpatrick felt a pain in his back like he had never known before.

Although Fitzpatrick finished the period, he couldn't bend into his crouch for a face-off in the final minute. Standing up, with pain shooting down his back, Fitzpatrick prayed the Nordiques wouldn't get a good scoring chance. They didn't and, with the pain now unbearable, Fitzpatrick returned to the locker room, didn't bother removing his leg pads, and spent the second period chest-down on the training table with an ice pack on his back. Vanbiesbrouck finished the game while Fitzpatrick agonized.

Why did this have to happen now, when I'm playing so well? Fitzpatrick asked himself. *Is my career over?*

Fitzpatrick's concerns were alleviated when X-rays taken that night revealed he merely sprained his back and sustained no permanent damage. But his season was over and the painful back spasms he suffered over the remaining two weeks were a constant reminder why.

Otherwise, hopes were high for the Panthers. With consecutive victories over the Devils and Nordiques, teams who had humbled them over the first two seasons, the Panthers harbored realistic playoff chances. A

165

5-1 victory over the Senators on April 24 put them two points behind the Rangers.

But with their season on the line, the Panthers and Vanbiesbrouck saved their worst for a dismal night in Buffalo. Trailing 1-0 after the first period, the Panthers allowed three goals in a 1:41 span of the second period. Jason Dawe scored into an empty net after a bad bounce off the ancient Memorial Auditorium boards. Garry Galley scored a power play goal at 9:56. Scott Pearson beat Vanbiesbrouck to the short side at 11:04. The Sabres finished the game with only 19 shots, but won, 5-0, leaving the Panthers four points behind the Rangers with four games remaining.

Two nights later, while the Rangers were losing to the Islanders, the Panthers wasted a good effort in New Jersey and lost to the Devils, 3-1. Bobby Holik broke a 1-1 tie with 7:11 remaining and, with the Panthers pressing for the equalizer, Claude Lemieux scored a breakaway goal, reducing Florida's playoff hopes to a glimmer.

Needing to win their last three games, time ran out on the Panthers in their final home game of the season. Kudelski, dressing for the first time in 11 games, scored in the second period to give the Panthers a 1-0 lead before the Capitals rallied with two goals. Belanger tied the game with under eight minutes remaining in the third period and, when Lindsay drew a penalty with 2:53 left, the Panthers had a chance to win the game. But they generated nothing on the power play, couldn't score in overtime, and settled for last year's consolation prize: A standing ovation from the sellout crowd.

Almost making the playoffs didn't feel any better the second year than it did the first.

"The teams sort of came back to us," Lindsay said. "We were behind all year. We were in front the first year and lost it at the end. This year, we were behind most of the way, then teams started to lose and come back to us and let us in the door. We just could never get there."

The sense of lost opportunity was the same as the year before and, this time, the Panthers couldn't even call themselves the best first-year team ever. They were simply another second-year team that didn't make the playoffs.

Even worse, thought Skrudland, there was the possibility this group of players would never again be together. Murray figured to make more changes. The labor situation, which hadn't been resolved to Huizenga's liking, left the players uncertain about their futures.

Hearing the fans cheering, Skrudland couldn't let the moment pass. After receiving the fans' award for best sportsman, he returned to center ice and thanked Vanbiesbrouck for carrying the team. As the crowd chanted "Beezer!", Skrudland skated over to his goaltender for what he knew might be a parting embrace. His teammates followed. The cheering got louder. Vanbiesbrouck fought back tears.

Was this his farewell to Florida?

"My blood pressure went up," Vanbiesbrouck said. "If I were a meter with mercury in my body, the mercury would have shot up to 100. I don't think I've ever been that proud in my career. I'll never, ever forget it."

Desperate for recognition from his bosses, Vanbiesbrouck discovered recognition from his teammates and the fans was the most meaningful gift he had ever received.

▲ ▲ ▲

With two meaningless victories over the Rangers and Penguins, the Panthers finished their second season with a record of 20-22-6 and, once again, out of the playoffs by a point. They scored fewer goals than any team in the League and the team-leading 29 points scored by Barnes and Belanger extrapolated to a horrendously low 51 points over a full season. Even the League's sixth-best defense and standout goaltending couldn't make up for that.

After the last game, Neilson and his assistants gathered the players at Gold Coast for a final meeting. Murray was there, too, and Neilson realized that he hadn't invited him to speak.

"Geez, Bryan, I should've asked you earlier, but you should say a few words," Neilson said.

"I will," Murray answered.

Murray stood in the back of the locker room and listened as Neilson told the players how satisfied he was with their season: They had missed the playoffs by one point, finished two games under .500, and, for the second year in a row, were over .500 on the road. Not bad for a second-year team. But Murray thought, *Listen to these guys. It's going to be the same next year. We're not going anywhere. They're satisfied with missing the play-offs.* By the time Neilson, Ramsay, and Ruff finished speaking, Murray knew exactly what he wanted to say, and it wasn't, "Great job, guys!"

"I have to tell you, I'm not happy," Murray told the players. "I don't think we should be satisfied with this. I want to play in the playoffs for a while. At least if you get there and don't win, that's OK, but I want us to be serious contenders in a series."

Neilson didn't think much about what Murray said until Dave Lowry approached him after the meeting.

"Roger, what was that all about?" Lowry asked.

"What do you mean?" Neilson said.

"He didn't seem very happy."

"I think he just wants us to do better."

Neilson had no idea that he had just met with his team for the final time.

CHAPTER 10

The Summer
of Our Discontent

Roger Neilson was thinking about the future when he returned to his summer home in Bridgenorth, Ontario. Though disappointed over missing the playoffs, he thought he had done the best he could with the talent he had and was looking forward to a third season in Florida.

The end-of-season coaches meeting with Murray had gone well. Neilson asked Murray about Jovanovski's status and Murray said Jovanovski would have to play next season if his legal problems were settled. "Fine," Neilson said. Murray said Niedermayer would have to get more playing time. Neilson agreed.

"We were pretty happy with the team," Neilson said. "We thought the team was playing solid hockey all along and all we needed was a little more scoring. We thought some of our young players would come along. We just thought we were a little short."

He couldn't know, and wouldn't know until later, that Murray was stewing over the Panthers' victories in the final two games. Neilson thought beating two playoff teams on the road was a pretty good feat, but Murray wasn't impressed: the two meaningless victories cost the Panthers three spots in the draft. Instead of picking seventh overall, they would pick 10th overall. He saw this as classic Neilson, always thinking about the present, never concerned about the future.

Neilson didn't even suspect there was a problem when his agent, Rob Campbell, phoned him in early June. They had been discussing a contract extension with the Panthers — Neilson didn't want to go into his final year as a lame duck — and Campbell expected to meet with Murray in Toronto. When Neilson found out that Torrey, not Murray, had requested his presence for a meeting at Campbell's office in Toronto, he didn't know what was going on.

"You're the one who looks after the contract, Rob," Neilson said.

"He wants you there," Campbell responded. "Maybe you'd better come."

Neilson agreed to be there, totally unprepared for what was about to happen.

▲ ▲ ▲

Bryan Murray didn't wake up one night and decide, "I'm going to fire Roger Neilson." This was a cumulative canning with one little, nagging problem after another adding up until Murray decided it was time for a change.

Although he got along with Neilson, they didn't have the kind of working relationship he considered necessary between a coach and a general manager. He'd attend practice and feel like an outsider. They spoke, but not on a daily basis, and his input didn't seem welcome. He thought Neilson didn't trust his judgment. They'd decide to pick up a player on waivers, or go after one in a trade, and Neilson would check around on his own, tipping off the other teams. In two cases, once with Winnipeg and the other time with Calgary, they didn't get the waived player they wanted.

Most telling, Murray thought, was Neilson's reluctance to play Neidermayer and his resistance to Jovanovski making the team. Here was a second-year team, one not expected to make the playoffs, with a free opportunity — a few years of no pressure, no expectations — for its kids to play. This wasn't New York, or Detroit, where everybody was demanding a Stanley Cup. This was Florida. He couldn't forget the time when they were negotiating with Jovanovski and Neilson said, "If you do sign him, do we have to play him?" Murray couldn't believe what he was hearing.

To make matters worse, there were nights he couldn't stand what he was watching. He understood Neilson's goal was making the team competitive and doing so meant being conservative, but he didn't like it. How many nights did he have to watch the Panthers play that horribly boring defensive style with no creativity or attempt to do something with the puck, no forechecking, faceoff after faceoff in the defensive zone, and only John Vanbiesbrouck saving them from a loss?

"I used the year to watch our players, to educate myself with what this team had to have if we were going to start playing with better teams," Murray said. "We had to work awfully hard and play unbelievably good defense and get great goaltending to survive every night. There were nights we'd get outshot 50-20 and John would make a big stop and we'd get the point, but you shouldn't have to be holding on for your life all the time."

Back when Murray coached against Neilson, he knew that if he could get into the third period tied or down by a goal, his team would win because he'd be using his stars while Neilson would be playing his checkers until their legs

169

fell off. And how about Brian Skrudland, Mike Hough, and Jody Hull? Their legs *were* going to fall off while Niedermayer was rotting on the bench!

The relationship simply couldn't work. Murray knew the worst possible situation was for a general manager and his coach to have different philosophies about running a team. Detroit wasn't that long ago, and, in this case, the chain of command would prevail: The coach would go. But he also knew firing Neilson wasn't going to be easy: The media, players, and the fans liked him, and for good reason. The Panthers were the most successful expansion team in NHL history and he was a major part of their success. Firing Neilson would be a public relations problem for a team that had been getting pretty good press.

He couldn't let that affect his thinking. He thought Neilson's style was going to grow old in a hurry to these fans, especially if the team never improved, and was convinced the Panthers had the makings of a successful team. The veterans were willing to accept and help develop the younger players. Robert Svehla and Magnus Svensson added an offensive dimension to the defense. Niedermayer and Jovanovski could become stars if given the chance. A more aggressive forecheck would not only mean more goals, it might even excite the fans.

"Roger did a heckuva job and nobody should say anything negative about the way the team performed," Murray said. "But all I could do was watch our team. We played a very negative style. Roger didn't think that there was anything but this year or next year. I think differently than that. If you're ever going to make the turn, and you have the talent, in today's hockey you have to allow the players to play up to their talent level. You have to put some talent into your lineup and you have to play some kids.

"The way we coached and with our style of play, making the playoffs by one point instead of being out by one point didn't matter. We'd be knocked out in the first round anyway. Our objective here is to play big teams, not just the little guys, and barely squeak in and get wiped out. Don't be satisfied to survive a game. Once in a while try to win, not try not to lose."

His mind was made up by early June. Torrey agreed with the decision. If Huizenga went along, Neilson would be gone.

"I hired you to do the hockey," Huizenga told Murray.

Now came the hard part: Telling Neilson and then standing in front of the media.

▲ ▲ ▲

The knifing was quick, but certainly not painless. On June 6, Neilson sat in his lawyer's office in Toronto, feeling like his head was spinning and trying to decipher the words coming out of Torrey's mouth. He thought he was asked here to discuss a new contract and now he was being fired? After missing the playoffs by a point two straight years with an expansion team? Surely he was hearing wrong.

"There are going to be a lot of changes," Torrey said, "and I'm not sure you would be agreeable to them. We're going to make a coaching change."

"Why don't you at least try us?" Campbell asked. "Maybe we'd be willing to make the changes."

Neilson couldn't believe he was getting fired for not playing the young players. Wasn't Paul Laus a rookie when he joined the team? Bill Lindsay had improved beyond all expectations. Stu Barnes, a fourth-line guy in Winnipeg, was a first-line scorer. Hadn't he already agreed to give Niedermayer more playing time next season? And this thing about Jovanovski: Maybe playing rookies into the lineup works in some cases, but this didn't seem like one of them. The kid was immature and not ready to hang around adult, professional hockey players. Hadn't his arrest proven that? And where was Murray? Didn't he have the guts to be here and fire his own coach?

But Torrey wasn't here to negotiate. He was here to deliver a message. The meeting was short and Neilson walked out confused. His confusion hadn't abated when he spoke with Murray that night. The conversation was going nowhere when Murray cut it off by saying, "I don't see what's so confusing. You're fired." Then Neilson called Ruff.

"They fired me," Neilson told his former assistant coach.

"C'mon, you're joking," Ruff said.

"No, they fired me," Neilson said.

"Wow. Where does this leave me?"

"It's the ninth time for me and the first for you," Neilson said. "The first is always the toughest."

The ninth wasn't much easier for Neilson, who agonized over what had happened, knowing his career could be over: He was a 61-year-old coach who had just lost his sixth head coaching job and, for the first time, he didn't understand why.

Although the Panthers hadn't yet officially announced the firing, word was out and Neilson spent a good part of the next day on the phone talking to reporters, friends, and players, trying to sort out the situation. Usually, coaches get fired when their teams underachieve. Nobody, except Murray and Torrey, understood how the coach of one of the most overachieving teams in history had lost his job.

"I would've thought that since we had a pretty good record, we would have had a chance, they would have given us an opportunity to at least listen to the new directions," Neilson said. "We're as adaptable as any coaches and, whatever they had in mind, we would have liked the opportunity to try to do it. I thought we had earned that."

Neilson combed his memory. He remembered hearing rumors during the season that Murray was criticizing him behind his back. At the time, he assumed people had heard wrong. Maybe they hadn't. He thought he had a good relationship with Torrey. Now he was hearing that he was Clarke's man, not Torrey's. None of the possible explanations fit until several respected friends in the NHL called and offered Neilson their take on the matter.

"He's going to hire Doug MacLean," they all said. "That's his guy."

▲ ▲ ▲

Torrey broke the news to Neilson because he thought it was the right thing to do. He had finalized Neilson's contract back in 1993 and, having hired him, thought it was right to be the one who fired him.

"In retrospect," Murray said, "Maybe I should've gone."

The day after, Murray was flying to Greensboro, North Carolina, to announce the Panthers' new American Hockey League affiliate, the Carolina Monarchs. He and Greg Bouris were going over a list of head coaches who had recently been fired, assistant coaches who might be looking to move up, and junior hockey coaches.

"Who do you think would be good?" Murray asked.

"What we need," Bouris said, "is a young coach, a young guy who's going to let the kids play, who knows the game. Maybe he'll be a bit of a risk taker, but the biggest risk offers the biggest rewards."

They talked about it some more and tossed around ideas. *Why recycle an NHL coach who's already lost in half a dozen places? Why go for the obvious big name? If you want to go with youth, start with the coach.*

"I think I have a guy like that," Murray said. "I know the perfect guy."

By the time the plane touched down in Greensboro, Bouris thought he knew exactly who it was.

As for Murray, he was wondering if this was the perfect situation to hire Doug MacLean.

The next day, June 8, Murray faced the press at the Panthers' office in Fort Lauderdale. In addition to Neilson, Murray also fired Ramsay and retained Ruff.

"I kept Lindy because he was the one guy who objected at times, who had a bigger picture in mind," Murray said.

The only picture the media saw was of Murray stabbing Neilson in the back. Their questioning of Murray at the press conference was overtly hostile. Mercy was reserved for Neilson, whom they felt had been treated unfairly by a new boss who obviously wanted to bring in his own person.

"I just felt for this organization at this time, we've reached a certain level and I want to go beyond that," Murray explained. "I want to emphasize Roger is not being released because of his past performance with the Panthers. Roger's record is a good one. He helped establish a solid foundation for this franchise."

Murray said he wanted to bring in young players and play a more wide-open style which, he felt, wasn't consistent with Neilson's coaching philosophy.

"I want someone who is open-minded," he said. "Someone who is willing to play young players, someone who is willing to give players a chance."

The press wasted no time choosing sides. Greg Cote of *The Miami Herald* wrote: "There is no sane way to justify it, no adequate rationale to explain away the blood on the ice. Ruthlessly, suddenly, and without class, the Panthers indulged the power play of General Manager Bryan Murray. It is, in every sense of the word, a shame. It is unseemly. It stinks." The blood, Cote decided, was on Murray's hands.

Murray didn't try wiping off the blood or defending his decision until a few days later, when for the first time he publicly discussed his disagreements with Neilson over playing Niedermayer and Jovanovski. He knew he had done the right thing, but he also knew time would tell if he was right. In firing Neilson, he had, in effect, announced, "This is my team," and by doing so, he was putting his neck on the line. If this new direction didn't work, he'd be the next to go.

Time for a change. Hadn't he heard that somewhere before?

▲ ▲ ▲

Neilson knew he shouldn't have bought the house. He had made the same mistake in Buffalo, buying a house after he got the job, then having to sell it once he got fired. But Florida seemed like a place where he'd want to live even after his coaching years were over, and he was convinced this would be his last job. He'd coach the Panthers for three or four more years, then retire, do some scouting, and live in his beach house. Now he'd have to sell this house, too.

Looking back, he realized these were the two most enjoyable years of his coaching career. The team was so close, the environment perfect. He loved going home in the afternoon and taking a swim, then sunbathing on the beach. Everything was so good, and then this happened. He was still angry that Murray hadn't fired him in person.

173

"I found it upsetting," Neilson said. "I thought he should've come and told me himself. If I were a general manager and I was firing somebody, I'd do it myself. You would expect that."

Neilson sent a letter to Huizenga. He wrote that he still wasn't over the shock of being fired and that Craig Ramsay and his family were devastated. He reminded Huizenga how he had helped draft the team, shaped its early existence, and set the path for its future. He had appeared on radio and TV shows, spoken at luncheons, given chalk talks and coaching clinics, and helped market the team. He talked about the pride he felt in being associated with the Panthers and how the original plan under Clarke was to be as competitive as possible until the prospects could be inserted into the lineup.

And then — surprise! — the team nearly made the playoffs two years in a row and was on the verge of being a legitimate contender. He felt he had contributed to the team's character, spirit, and work ethic. Then, at the end-of-season meeting with Murray, the coaching staff had given its opinions about the team and addressed the need for two scorers to supplement the improved defense. Opinions were offered, none were returned; now he knew why.

"I gave everything possible to the organization and got terminated without one reason being given," Neilson wrote. "Just some vague reference about wanting to go in another direction."

Neilson wasn't surprised when Torrey, not Huizenga, wrote back with the same comments about going with youth and a more offensive style. The discussion was going nowhere, Neilson realized. He'd have to live with what happened. The only choice was moving on, which he did. After getting turned down for the open head coaching positions with the Flames and Islanders, Neilson was hired in September as Mike Keenan's assistant in St. Louis. Later that winter, Keenan bought Neilson's Florida beach house, sight unseen.

▲ ▲ ▲

In July 1994, Doug MacLean walked along a beach near his cottage in Summerside, Prince Edward Island, and tormented his best friend and wife. He had been out of work since June 3, the day he and Murray had been fired by the Red Wings, and the prospects of finding a job for the upcoming season weren't promising.

"I was scared," MacLean recalled. "I was a month looking for a job and I was scared. I was wondering if I was ever going to get the chance to work in the League again."

Shortly after being fired, MacLean was interviewed by Boston Bruins General Manager Harry Sinden for the job as his assistant. MacLean heard through the grapevine that he was close to getting the job, but Sinden ended up giving it to Mike O'Connell, the head coach of Boston's American League affiliate. Then Maple Leafs General Manager Cliff Fletcher interviewed him for a position as head scout and director of player personnel. Nick Beverley got that job and MacLean was so panicked, he considered getting back into teaching.

The only bright point for MacLean was that his friend Bryan Murray was about to be hired as general manager of the Panthers and would probably offer him a job. But even that had its downside. MacLean, aware of the perception people had of him as "Bryan's boy," thought it might be best to go out on his own.

"I was hoping I would've gotten something else," MacLean said.

He didn't, but Murray didn't have any job openings, either, when he was named GM of the Panthers on August 1. Chuck Fletcher was assistant general manager. Neilson had two assistant coaches. All of the scouting positions were filled. John Chapman was director of player personnel. And with the Panthers' budget bleeding red, Murray had no room for extraneous hires.

But Murray wasn't merely MacLean's friend, he liked working with him. Their relationship went all the way back to the early 1970s, when Murray was coaching an amateur team in Ontario and MacLean was a player. Murray had recommended him for a college scholarship and, after a failed tryout with the St. Louis Blues, MacLean attended the University of Prince Edward Island.

They didn't meet up again for another 15 years. By that time, MacLean had his Masters in educational psychology from the University of Western Ontario and two seasons as an NHL assistant coach under Jacques Martin in St. Louis. Martin was fired after the 1987-88 season and MacLean figured he was on the chopping block, too, when he heard about a job opening with the Washington Capitals: Bryan Murray, the head coach, needed a new assistant after Terry Murray had moved on to become the head coach of the Baltimore Skipjacks.

"I remember, my oldest daughter, Heide, was sitting on the porch when I was talking to Doug," Murray recalled. "I showed him around the area and when he left, I said to Heide, 'What do you think of this guy?' and she said, 'Pretty nice guy, Dad.' He was young, but he was an open guy, willing to converse and have fun. I was looking for a guy who had the ability to be a coach and also deal with the players."

Once hired, MacLean was exactly the kind of assistant coach Murray wanted. Often, Murray would walk past the training room and see MacLean sitting on a table, casually talking to the players, exchanging stories and small talk, or listening to their complaints about playing time.

Their working relationship, good from the beginning, quickly developed into a dedicated friendship. After Murray was fired by Washington during the 1989-90 season and MacLean moved over to Baltimore, Skipjacks owner Tom Ebright offered MacLean some friendly advice: Stay away from Murray if you want to stay with the Capitals.

"I told him I wasn't planning on doing that," MacLean said. "I said, 'He's a friend and I'm not going to do that.' "

Not that it mattered. The only reason the Capitals kept MacLean around was so they wouldn't have to pay another contract; he was fired after finishing the last half of the season with the Skipjacks. Murray hired him again in Detroit and, after two years as assistant coach and another two as assistant general manager, MacLean was fired along with Murray in 1994.

Murray wasn't concerned about a pattern developing. He really didn't care how people perceived his relationship with MacLean. Their theories on developing young players, judging talent, and playing an offensive system were similar, and, besides, the entire Panthers staff was comprised of people he hadn't hired. He wanted MacLean.

In mid-August, with all of the good hockey jobs taken, MacLean did the only thing he could do: He accepted the position Murray created as director of player development and head scout.

"I was thrilled at the time," MacLean said, "but I really would've liked to go on my own, to be quite honest."

He needn't have worried about public perception. MacLean's new job, scouting minor league and junior players, kept him far away from Florida. Although he spoke daily by telephone with Murray, he held onto his house in Detroit, spent the season living in hotels, and saw only a handful of Panthers games. His major contribution was talking Murray into signing Jason Woolley, who he thought was the best offensive defenseman in the minor leagues.

MacLean, however, was getting itchy for a change in career direction. Having spent three years watching young players for Detroit and Florida, he realized what he really wanted was to get back into coaching. In March, MacLean phoned Murray and told him he'd like the chance to coach the Panthers' new American League affiliate in North Carolina.

"He was pretty well prepared to give me that job," MacLean said. "And then, all of a sudden, after we got through talking about that, Roger got fired."

MacLean immediately set his sights on the Panthers vacancy, but thought it was a long shot. Giving him the job would open Murray to criticism that he was merely hiring his friend. MacLean hadn't coached in three years and had only a half year of head coaching experience in the minor leagues. Other candidates were far more famous: Larry Robinson, the former Canadiens great, was an assistant coach for the New Jersey Devils and would receive a great deal of credit for the Devils' run to the Stanley Cup. Robbie

Ftorek had just coached Albany to the American League championship. Pierre Page, the former Quebec coach, was scouting in Toronto. Craig Hartsburg had just been named Coach of the Year in the Ontario League.

And what did MacLean have on his résumé? Two seasons under Jacques Martin in St. Louis, two seasons under Murray in Washington, another two seasons under Murray in Detroit, and a measly half year as a head coach in Baltimore. This didn't seem like much until he added it all up.

"I had been in the NHL for nine years as an assistant coach, associate coach, I coached in the minors a bit, I was an assistant GM," MacLean figured. "I looked at everybody else being considered and I didn't see any other unbelievable backgrounds, either. I saw fair backgrounds."

A little less than a month after Neilson's firing, MacLean phoned Murray and asked, "Aren't you going to give me a chance?"

"Doug, do you know what it's going to be like?" Murray responded. "There's the label that you're my buddy and that's why you're getting the chance. There's the pressure, and coaches don't last forever."

"I want the job," MacLean said.

"Are you serious?" Murray pressed. "Do you really want to get out of what you're doing? I want you to really think about it before we sit down and talk."

"Yeah, I want the job," MacLean repeated, knowing he didn't have to hash out anything. He simply wanted the job. He needed the job. He knew if he didn't get this job — especially with one of his best friends making the hire — he might never again get the chance to coach in the NHL.

They agreed to sit down and talk two days later. Although Murray and MacLean lived 20 minutes apart near Detroit, they didn't want to meet at either's home with wives and families around. They settled on a Bob's Big Boy restaurant.

"I wanted him to tell me, 'I'll play young guys. I'll teach and take some chances with my career, and if I have to get rid of veteran guys, I'm willing to do that. I'll play an aggressive style,'" Murray said. "I wanted to hear how he felt the game should be played."

For MacLean, it was a matter of showing his friend how much he wanted the job. For Murray, it was a matter of showing his friend what they were getting themselves into. General managers generally don't fire their assistant GMs. Head coaches generally don't fire their assistant coaches. Coaches, however, are hired to be fired — only a select few leave before they're tossed out — and Murray knew there was a fair chance he'd one day have to fire his friend. They argued over whether this new working relationship would change their personal relationship.

Finally, MacLean said to Murray, "You will not be happy unless you hire a guy that allows you to have a fair amount of input. You know I'll do that, but how many other people will?"

Their conversation was intense and lasted three hours. The diners sitting at adjoining tables and the waitress refilling their cups would never have guessed that these two men arguing with each other were friends, and one was trying to convince the other to give him the job of his life. They talked about everything that could possibly go wrong, and how they would deal with problems. When the meeting was nearly over, MacLean made a final attempt at impressing upon Murray that giving him the job was the right thing to do.

"Bryan," he said, "you'd be an idiot if you don't hire me."

▲ ▲ ▲

Murray's doubts were waning as he left the restaurant and drove home. He had wanted to give MacLean the head coaching job in Detroit two years earlier, after Barry Melrose went to Los Angeles, but Ilitch wanted Keenan or Arbour or Bowman or any of the big name coaches. Certainly not Doug MacLean. Here was another chance to hire the young coach who he knew was perfect for the job and fit all of the qualifications he outlined at the Neilson hanging.

Someone who is open-minded. *Check.*

Someone who is willing to play young players and give them a chance. *Check.*

A younger guy who's getting into the business or has been in the business a short time. *Check.*

Someone who believes a coach and general manager should work together and exchange ideas, rather than keeping out of each other's way. *Check.*

And someone he could trust. *Check.*

"That's the biggest item," Murray said. "Trust is the whole word in this business. You're not going to burn me, I'm not going to burn you. And I could trust Doug. I knew he was going to support me and he knew I was going to support him. We're not buddy buddy all the time, but we're good friends."

Maybe he *would* be an idiot if he didn't give the job to MacLean, but there was that one obstacle: He knew by hiring MacLean, he'd be open to criticism. And there was another question: Would Torrey and Huizenga allow him to do what Ilitch wouldn't? He had been guaranteed the freedom to run the hockey team in the manner he saw fit, but how long was his rope, and would he be using that same rope to hang himself?

Besides, there was another candidate for the job who was even more qualified than MacLean, a man just as willing to play young players, open up the offense, and work with the general manager: Bryan Murray. After all, hadn't the press written that Murray fired Neilson to hire himself?

"Bill Torrey asked me to coach," Murray said. "Mr. Huizenga and Bill both asked me. They said, 'There are all these candidates you're talking about, why don't you do it?' Wayne said, 'Aren't you a good coach? Why don't you coach?' I told them I'd think about it overnight."

Murray decided that an expansion team needed a separate coach and general manager. He had no shortage of candidates from which to choose. He interviewed Hartsburg in Windsor, Ontario, and was impressed. He had a productive conversation with Robinson in Ottawa. Robinson, the hot candidate with the media, had a home in Florida and dearly wanted the job, but Murray didn't think he was right for the team at the time. Besides, he was still under contract to the Devils, who would likely demand compensation. Ftorek was anxious to get back into the NHL and proved in Albany he could coach young players. Butch Goring had just won the IHL championship in Denver and came to his interview well-prepared. Murray also interviewed Page, Jacques Martin, and Paul Baxter, but never seriously considered hiring any of them. From the time he left the meeting at the Bob's Big Boy, Murray was merely confirming that MacLean was the best man for the job.

Of course, MacLean didn't know what Murray was thinking. He read newspaper reports about Robinson being offered the position, and knew they were untrue from his conversations with Murray. (Robinson, who ended up coaching the Kings, later said he was disappointed about not getting the job.) He thought, but wasn't sure, he was the leading candidate.

"I was nervous," MacLean said. "I was hearing a lot of names. I knew I had a chance. I didn't know I had it."

Murray interviewed 10 candidates, including MacLean, during the first week of July at the NHL Draft in St. Louis. Torrey spoke with MacLean for two hours in St. Louis and approved his hiring. A few days later, Murray received a phone call from Hartsburg's agent, who said Chicago was ready to make them an offer.

"Go ahead," Murray said.

Robinson's agent also called to reconfirm their interest. Murray said he already had his man. MacLean could have relaxed on July 20, when Murray named Rich Kromm head coach of the Panthers' new AHL affiliate in Greensboro, North Carolina. This was the position Murray all but guaranteed to MacLean four months earlier; clearly, Murray had another job in mind for him.

A day later, Murray phoned MacLean and offered him the job, pending final approval from Huizenga. An anxious MacLean didn't need reminding about what had happened in Detroit. The only thing standing between him and the coaching job he so coveted was another intrusive owner.

"I didn't know what the response would be," MacLean said. "I really didn't have a clue and I didn't count on anything until it happened."

Huizenga told Murray to hire whomever he wished. At 5:00 that afternoon, Murray phoned MacLean in Summerside and told him to fly down immediately for a press conference. The job was his.

Doug MacLean was introduced as the second coach of the Panthers on Monday, July 24, at the Pier 66 Hotel in Fort Lauderdale. Before the press conference, Torrey pulled MacLean aside and warned him about the press' possible take on the hiring: That he was hired to be controlled by Murray. MacLean wasn't concerned; he considered dealing with the media the least of his problems. Murray was equally confident, knowing it wouldn't take long for the media to be charmed by MacLean's personality and sense of humor. He was right.

After being introduced, MacLean stepped to the podium and spoke his first words as an NHL head coach: "I could cook cheeseburgers in here right now it's so hot."

Asked if he could work young players into the lineup and seamlessly blend them with the veterans, MacLean cracked, "I'd better."

He called being hired "the big-time thrill of a lifetime" and told how his parents and his children were flipping out over the news.

"When you come from a town of 8,500 and every single resident has given you advice, it's a big-time achievement," MacLean said. Meanwhile, the Mayor of Summerside, Prince Edward Island, was proclaiming August 1 Doug MacLean Day.

Inevitably, he was asked whether he'd set the Panthers' agenda, or follow Murray's marching orders.

"I say what I believe," he said. "I give my opinion. I'm not a pushover. I'm my own man. But Bryan Murray was one of the top coaches in the NHL. If I'm not going to take advice from Bryan Murray, I'm an idiot."

Having already advised Murray on how to avoid being an idiot, MacLean wasn't going to fall into the same trap. Had he been looking for an ambush, however, MacLean might have refused an interview with Vic Rauter from TSN in Canada. Rauter had an agenda: MacLean was hired because of his friendship with Murray and would be the GM's puppet. He attacked Murray for hiring cheap and not going after a big name. Rauter's televised bashing was big news all over Canada and the basis for the story line everywhere MacLean went for the next three months.

"I had never met the guy in my life, and it sort of caught me off guard that on the biggest day of your life, somebody has to carve you up that bad,"

MacLean said. "What shocked me was that they were making it sound like I had been a Junior B coach. It was like I was the first guy in the world who got a job because I worked with a guy.

"But I couldn't care less about it. I was so excited about the fact I got the job that I couldn't care less about anything. And the next day, I picked up the Florida papers and the Florida media was fair. That's all I asked for."

▲ ▲ ▲

All John Vanbiesbrouck wanted was for one of them to look him in the eye, just to let him know this was business and they really didn't mean what they were saying. Torrey, Murray, Fletcher, any one of them. They never had any trouble looking at him when they were asking him to speak at another luncheon or conduct another clinic, did they? Or how about that night this past season, when the Rangers outshot the Panthers 44-23 and he was the only reason they escaped Madison Square Garden with a 0-0 tie. The nerve of them to argue he was only so good because of the team's defense! Anybody who watched this team play for two seasons knew that was untrue.

Well, they weren't going to look him in the eye and he knew that when this awful day ended, his relationship with the team would be forever changed. He really had no choice but to sit there and listen to Larry Bertuzzi, the Panthers' high-paid independent counsel, explain to an arbitrator why he didn't deserve a salary among the elite goalies in the NHL.

The truth was, it shouldn't have come to this. As recently as January, the only sticking point was the length of the contract; the Panthers offered three years at $6 million, Vanbiesbrouck wanted five years at $10 million. But after Vanbiesbrouck turned down the three-year deal, the two sides never came closer than the $1.5 million a year offered by the Panthers the night before the arbitration. Lloyd Friedland, Vanbiesbrouck's agent, turned them down.

"Sometime toward the latter part of that season, something happened where that offer of $6 million seemed to have been withdrawn or evaporated," Friedland said. "There was no more discussion about it. They came back to me with other proposals, but they were nowhere near the three-year deal at six million, and we didn't believe that was market value."

Under normal circumstances, Vanbiesbrouck's contract would have gone to arbitration during the 1994-95 season. Because of the lockout, all hearings were put off until after the season, meaning Vanbiesbrouck played without knowing how much he was making (although he couldn't earn less than the $1.1 million called for in his contract, minus 40 percent for games lost during the lockout).

The arbitration hearing, held on June 14 at the Miami Airport Hilton, concerned Vanbiesbrouck's 1994-95 salary, so only his performance through the 1993-94 season could be discussed. Richard McLaren, the independent arbitrator, could award Vanbiesbrouck the $2.3 million he demanded, the $1.2 million offered by the Panthers, or any amount in between.

Vanbiesbrouck wanted a salary placing him among the League's elite goalies, such as Patrick Roy, Bill Ranford, and Mike Richter. The Panthers slotted him a notch below the elite along with Sean Burke, Kelly Hrudey, Kirk McLean, Andy Moog, Mike Vernon, and Curtis Joseph.

Vanbiesbrouck's lawyers argued that he was a finalist for the Vezina and Hart Trophies in 1994 and finished fourth in the League in goals-against average — below Roy, above Richter — on a team that allowed the fourth most shots in the League.

The Panthers' case hit Vanbiesbrouck where it hurt most: His reputation as a goaltender who folded down the stretch and couldn't be counted upon in the playoffs.

"I don't think the term clutch was ever used," Fletcher said. "What we pointed out was that John's regular season numbers spoke for themselves, but for a goalie who had been in the League as long as he played, he had 13 career playoff wins. John used a lot of guys, Belfour, Roy, who had won 50 or 60 playoff games and been to the finals or won the Stanley Cup. We pointed out that five of the models he was using had at least three times as many playoff wins as he did."

Bertuzzi came armed with numbers. Vanbiesbrouck had won only five playoff games since 1987. In 1993-94, he was 16-12-8 until January 31 and 5-13-3 down the stretch. Mark Fitzpatrick was 7-3-3 during the same period. Of course, he didn't point out that in those 21 games, the Panthers scored only 49 goals for Vanbiesbrouck while he was allowing less than three a game. Then Bertuzzi mentioned Mike Richter, and Vanbiesbrouck felt like he had been kicked again.

"We used the point that he was made available in the expansion draft and the Rangers determined that Richter was better than Vanbiesbrouck or they wouldn't have let Vanbiesbrouck go," Fletcher said. "That was a very sore point because obviously there was a rivalry but, you have to remember, the Rangers had just won the Cup. All the data and evidence was based on some kind of objective criteria. We weren't going in there and slandering John Vanbiesbrouck."

Vanbiesbrouck felt slandered and mortally wounded. Afterward, he said he had been scarred and suggested that even if the Panthers won the arbitration, they had possibly lost the loyalty of their most valuable player. "Is that worth it?" he asked.

Vindictiveness and loyalty weren't the point. Vanbiesbrouck was naïve in thinking the opposing side would praise him in an arbitration hearing. As the Panthers' player representative during the lockout, he knew better than anyone that hockey is a business — a business once controlled by the owners that the players were now getting a piece of — and personal feelings were not an issue. Did he expect the Panthers to state their case by saying how great he was?

The Panthers' point was well taken: Roy had won two Stanley Cups and 70 playoff games; Ranford had won a Stanley Cup and 45 playoff games; even Ed Belfour, who had a well-worn reputation as a playoff choke artist, had 20 playoff wins and a trip to the finals; Richter had just won the Cup with Vanbiesbrouck's old team. They were right: The Rangers had chosen Richter over Vanbiesbrouck, and there wasn't a general manager in the League — Murray included — who wouldn't have traded Vanbiesbrouck even-up for Roy, Ranford, or Richter in a heartbeat. Indeed, Vanbiesbrouck had gone belly-up down the stretch of the 1993-94 season, going 0-5-2 and coming up with his worst performance of the year in the biggest game of the year, the 5-2 loss to the Nordiques on April 12 that effectively knocked the Panthers out of the playoff race. And what did he do for an encore? He came up big in the meaningless final game of the season.

But the Panthers conveniently ignored a mitigating factor: Vanbiesbrouck, though no Roy or Ranford, was worth more to the Panthers than to any other team. That's why they'd had so much trouble trading him in March: Playoff teams didn't want him because of his reputation; non-playoff teams didn't want him because of his uncertain salary. To the Panthers, Vanbiesbrouck meant the difference between respectability and being a typical expansion team. The Panthers were unfairly blaming Vanbiesbrouck for a demise that wouldn't have been possible if he hadn't lifted them high enough to fall.

The arbitrator leaned toward Vanbiesbrouck, awarding $1.9 million; $400,000 lower than Vanbiesbrouck's request, $600,000 higher than the Panthers' offer. Ironically — or maybe not — his award struck smack in the middle of Vanbiesbrouck's demand and the Panthers' final pre-arbitration offer of $1.5 million.

"Weighing and judging everything, I find the player to be properly at the top of the range of the middle-tier group and just below the elite group," McLaren ruled.

Though boosted by the arbitrator's decision, Vanbiesbrouck was more concerned with what the Panthers thought about him. He wanted their confidence and a commitment, too. Without both, he wasn't going to be happy playing in South Florida.

Contentment was a long way off, and Vanbiesbrouck's ordeal had just begun. He was now a Group II free agent, meaning any team that signed him would have to give the Panthers three first-round draft picks. The Panthers had until July 3 to make a qualifying offer of $2.185 million for the 1995-96 season — representing 115 percent of his arbitrated 1994-95 salary — and immediately did so, retaining their right to match other teams' offers; if they hadn't, Vanbiesbrouck would have become an unrestricted free agent and they could have lost him for nothing. Vanbiesbrouck had to decide whether to accept the offer or go elsewhere.

"We were exploring other options," Friedland said, "but there really weren't many options available."

Vanbiesbrouck accepted. Having done that, both sides faced decisions.

For Vanbiesbrouck: Do I want to stay in South Florida for the rest of my career, or do I want to become an unrestricted free agent and move to another team after next season?

For the Panthers: Do we want to pay Vanbiesbrouck the long-term elite-level salary he's demanding or are we willing to lose him for nothing after next season?

"My response to the team was, if you don't want to pay him, then trade him," Friedland said. "Not in a pejorative way and not in an adversarial way but, I said, unless you're prepared to pay him value, then trade him."

Vanbiesbrouck wanted a commitment and that meant a three-year deal for $7.5 million. The Panthers, still not convinced Vanbiesbrouck was a $2-million-a-year man, offered $5.5 million. By now, Murray had taken over the contract negotiations from Torrey and began shopping Vanbiesbrouck around the League. In August, Vanbiesbrouck was offered to the Islanders in exchange for left wing Steve Thomas, whom the Panthers coveted, and prospect Todd Bertuzzi, the Islanders' first round pick in the 1993 Draft. Islanders General Manager Don Maloney, put off by the price and Vanbiesbrouck's contract, decided he wasn't interested. Vanbiesbrouck's playoff history had kept Murray from making a trade back in March and now the contract was an additional obstacle. Vanbiesbrouck watched in dismay.

"What else is there for me here?" he said. "They made it clear to me they don't think I'm worth the money they're going to pay me. They're paying me what they have to, not what they want to. The guys in the organization who evaluate talent don't feel I'm worth what they're paying me."

Vanbiesbrouck's future remained in doubt through the rest of the summer, and he reported to training camp convinced it would be his last with the Panthers. The two sides were far apart and Vanbiesbrouck refused to sweet talk an organization that wouldn't sweet talk him back.

▲ ▲ ▲

The view of the Atlantic Ocean out the east window of Dean Jordan's office is the one visitors first notice, but it's the view to the south that stirs his imagination. Most people can see only a crane in the middle of an empty lot off Las Olas Boulevard, the main thoroughfare in downtown Fort Lauderdale, but Jordan sees a hockey arena that's never going to be built.

When Blockbuster Park died and the Panthers went searching for possible arena sites, their first instinct was to build in Fort Lauderdale's vibrant, fashionable downtown. They envisioned trolleys carrying fans back and forth from restaurants and hotels before and after games, and fans who arrived by car parking in one of the 10,000 spaces already available within 1,500 feet of the site. As opposed to Miami's attempt to revitalize a downtown area by building a sports arena, this arena would enrich an already bustling area.

But by the start of training camp for the 1995-96 season, plans to build an arena for the Panthers in downtown Fort Lauderdale or anywhere else in the area were dead. Huizenga wanted a city or county to build him an arena and hand over the keys — including all luxury suite and advertising revenue — and the response of the citizenry was blunt.

"Politicians said right from the start that if Wayne wants to build an arena, great, but we're not going to put any money into it," Huizenga said. "The *Sun-Sentinel* would write a great editorial about how forward thinking this would be for Broward County, and if Miami could build a facility a long time ago, we can do it, too. Then on the front page of the sports section or the business section, some columnist would write, 'Why should we do this for this fat, bald-headed rich guy?' "

Huizenga had an answer for them: He had already spent $50 million to buy the Panthers, lost $4 million the first year, and was losing $1 million a month, mostly because he received little revenue from Miami Arena and the team's payroll had increased by $12 million. At the current rate, the Panthers, despite playing to 97 percent of capacity, would cost him over $110 million by the time a new arena was built. And, he figured, if Miami or Fort Lauderdale were trying to lure a team, instead of keep one, they would've rolled out the red carpet. Instead, the public sentiment seemed to be: If you want to stay, stay; if you want to leave, leave.

"You didn't have a public outcry for a hockey team," County Commissioner Scott Cowan said after Broward's original effort to fund an Arena through a hotel and restaurant tax died. "We weren't going to pay for the whole thing ourselves. The more we expected a private contribution from Huizenga, the less attractive it became to him."

The majority of the public viewed a new arena as a $165 million gift to Huizenga. He saw it, however, as an incentive to keep the team in town.

The Broward County effort had collapsed when the hoteliers said they'd agree to a tax as long as the restaurateurs were also taxed. That was akin to killing the project; residents don't mind a hotel tax because out-of-towners are paying it, not them. But locals patronize restaurants as frequently as tourists and view a restaurant tax as a tax increase.

"As soon as we did it, the restaurants came after us and the newspapers said it's another tax," Huizenga said. "We said we're just doing what the hoteliers asked us to do, and we had the shit kicked out of us. No wonder the hoteliers asked us to do it! They knew what was going to happen!"

Huizenga didn't make any friends when the Panthers announced a 21-percent hike in ticket prices, making them South Florida's most expensive ticket behind the Dolphins. Although the Panthers were still paying to nearly-full houses, they had lost 2,000 season tickets during the lockout, and their TV rating had dropped by 42-percent. From all indications, the area had 14,703 hockey fans and they were all at Miami Arena on hockey nights.

On July 19, Huizenga called a press conference to announce he had given up on Broward County, his first preference, as a site for the new arena, and was allowing the rest of South Florida three months to offer a new facility. If nothing happened, he'd move the team or sell it for the 1996-97 season.

West Palm Beach, which had been considering proposals for a 10,000-seat building, was the first to enter and drop out of the bidding.

"They didn't have the tools to work with to make it happen. The dollars," Huizenga said. "They couldn't get it done."

Huizenga and Miami Heat owner Micky Arison briefly looked for a location together, then realized they weren't looking in the same place: Arison in downtown Miami, Huizenga further north and closer to South Florida's population center. Then Dade County stepped up with a plan to fund an arena in northern Dade, possibly on a site adjacent to Joe Robbie Stadium. Local opposition — area residents didn't want Joe Robbie Stadium in the first place — shot down that deal. Metro Dade Commissioner Art Teale then came up with a plan to build an arena in downtown Miami; that wasn't the location Huizenga was looking for, but it was better than nothing. It turned out to be nothing when county commissioners and other politicians opposed a bed tax.

"Nobody really gave a damn if the Panthers stayed or not," Huizenga said. "Hockey was a newcomer and a lot of people figured, 'We didn't have it before, we don't need it now.' Now, if you talked about moving the Dolphins, that would've been a different story."

As the 1995-96 season approached, Huizenga was publicly questioning his original decision to buy the team. He acted hastily, he said, and if he had it to do all over again, he wouldn't have bought the franchise. This wasn't a sudden brainstorm; Huizenga didn't need until 1995 to realize his mistake. He knew almost right away he had committed the worst business faux pas of all: Boxing himself into a bad bargaining position and giving the other side, the Miami Sports and Exhibition Authority, all the power.

"If we were a team from out of town, they would've said, 'You can play for nothing,' but if you go in with a team in hand, they say, 'Sure, you can play here. Here's the deal,' " Huizenga said. "If you were going to get an expansion team, they would've opened the doggone gate."

The public thought Huizenga was bluffing in an attempt to get his way. But one critical action by Huizenga proved he meant business: On July 26, the Panthers sent a letter to the Miami Sports and Exhibition Authority saying they were not exercising their Miami Arena lease option for the 1996-97 season.

"We said we were willing to sit down and negotiate with them on terms that were more favorable," Torrey said. "If we extended our lease, we were talking about another $13-14 million a year in debt. Locking ourselves in didn't make any sense whatsoever."

MSEA wasn't interested in negotiating, and now John Vanbiesbrouck wasn't the only one who didn't know where he'd be playing in a year. The Panthers didn't know where they'd be playing, either.

CHAPTER 11

The Year
of the Rat

Doug MacLean felt right at home when training camp opened on September 11 in Greensboro, North Carolina. This was his 10th NHL training camp, so he had a pretty good idea what he wanted to do from watching others, but it was his first as a head coach and he didn't know the players.

He was nervous, not with fear but with excitement that came from being so anxious to get something started, and then finally doing it and being so comfortable, so sure you're doing the right thing. After being out of coaching for two years, that was a comforting reassurance.

The players did their best to make him feel at home. Brian Skrudland, who had never played for a bad team, told MacLean during their first telephone conversation that he and the other 10 remaining expansion draftees didn't plan on handing their jobs to the rookies.

"When you walk into our dressing room and see the leadership and the type of people we have, you're going to be surprised," Skrudland told MacLean. "I think we're going to have a better year."

MacLean felt pretty good about that, because he, too, had no intention of giving away anything, and established his philosophy from Day 1: Rookies were rookies, veterans would get a little leeway.

One of those veterans was third-year man Rob Niedermayer, who struggled through two seasons of limited playing time under Roger Neilson. MacLean phoned Niedermayer and assured him he would have the chance to play regularly. Other players were unsure of their status.

"So you played a lot at center last year, but you prefer right wing, right?" MacLean asked Tom Fitzgerald.

"It doesn't really matter," Fitzgerald answered.

"You like right wing, right?" MacLean asked again.

When the conversation ended, Fitzgerald hung up the phone and said to his wife, "I have a feeling I'm gonna play right wing this year."

Then camp opened and Fitzgerald didn't know where he was going to play. He played center in the intrasquad tournament and left wing in the first few pre-season games. Fitzgerald had never played left wing in his life, but with veterans Jody Hull, Bob Kudelski, Scott Mellanby, and Brett Harkins and rookie Dave Nemirovsky, MacLean had more right wings than he needed.

Fitzgerald, who had signed a new three-year contract during the summer after scoring only three goals the previous season, didn't know what to think later in the month when MacLean called him into his office.

Oh my God! Doug wants me, Fitzgerald thought. *I've been traded. I'm going to be left unprotected in the waiver draft.*

"Don't be discouraged by the numbers on that line," MacLean said. "You're going to play right wing for me. I'm just looking at other guys and I wanted to tell you that to ease your mind."

Fitzgerald's mind needed a little easing. Like many of the players, he was saddened over Neilson's firing, and realized the former coach had been a major part of the team's success. But they had to move on. Neilson had given many of them the best opportunity of their hockey careers, but change — getting fired or being traded — is part of the business. Players have to adjust. Stu Barnes, knowing the Panthers would be playing a more wide-open style, was looking forward to something new.

Despite the talk about change and giving young players a chance, MacLean wasn't planning a complete overhaul. General Manager Bryan Murray had bought out the contracts of defensemen Brian Benning and Joe Cirella and forward Andrei Lomakin during the off-season, leaving MacLean three open spots with which to work. They were filling up smoothly.

Ed Jovanovski, who had signed a four-year, $5.7-million deal in June, then had the criminal charges against him dropped in mid-August, was assured of a spot on the team. Defensemen Magnus Svensson, Robert Svehla, Jason Woolley, and Gord Murphy were secure. So was Paul Laus, who had won the enforcer's job from Brent Severyn last season and was becoming a dependable defensive defenseman.

"During the lockout year, Roger had a lot of confidence in me," Laus said. "I met Doug once during the year, and I had no idea who he was. Then Doug came in and said, 'We're going to get you in the lineup a lot. You're going to be a big part of the team,' and that gave me so much confidence going into training camp."

Murray also signed Terry Carkner, a big, strong defenseman who had played for him in Detroit. The Red Wings had shopped Carkner during the 1994-

95 season, but Scotty Bowman and Jim Devellano wouldn't deal with their former colleague. Murray waited for Carkner to become a free agent, signed him for $700,000, and didn't lose any draft picks or players in the bargain.

MacLean scrapped his plan of utilizing Keith Brown, 35, as the eighth defenseman and Jovanovski's on- and off-ice mentor, when Brown's chronically injured left knee forced him into retirement. That left Geoff Smith, 26, and Randy Moller, 33, fighting for a job with rookie defenseman Rhett Warrener, a second-round pick in 1994.

The battle among the forwards looked more contentious, with Harkins, Steve Washburn, and Nemirovsky, a fourth-round pick in 1994, battling for spots, and Kudelski trying to hold on. A few others, such as Brad Smyth and Jamie Linden, were borderline minor leaguers who'd have a tough time winning a job. The biggest threat to the veterans was Radek Dvorak, the Panthers' first-round pick in the July draft.

Dvorak didn't know where he stood because nobody could tell him. The 18-year-old right wing from the Czech Republic didn't speak a word of English and had become fluent in the sign language of pointing.

"Cup," Assistant Equipment Manager Scott Tinkler said, pointing to a protective cup in the storage room.

"Cup?" Dvorak asked, completely confused.

"You know," Tinkler said. "Pee-pee."

"Ah, pee-pee," an enlightened Dvorak acknowledged.

Fortunately for Dvorak, he had a translator: Svehla, who also didn't speak English when he joined the team the previous spring, but learned a bit of the native tongue over the summer. Otherwise, all Dvorak heard from his coach and teammates was a cacophony of "blah-blah-blah."

One word Dvorak apparently had no trouble understanding was, "Go!" On the opening day of training camp in Greensboro, Dvorak won the annual five-mile run, proving speed on ice translates well to speed on pavement. Coaches and management liked what they saw from a player they never expected to get.

Born in Tabor, a town in the picturesque Southern Bohemian region of the Czech Republic, Dvorak was a goaltender until his parents convinced him it was better to score goals than prevent them. The metamorphosis from goaltender to left wing came easily and, at age 16, Dvorak signed a contract with Ceske Budejovice.

"It was my first year in juniors and I realized I could do something in hockey," Dvorak said through a translator.

Dvorak was one of the highest-rated European draft prospects when the 1994-95 season began, but in the second game of the Czech elite league season, he collided with an opponent and suffered a broken wrist. The injury sidelined him for three and a half months and caused him to miss the 1995 World Junior Championships, a major showcase for prospects and draftees.

After recovering from his injury, Dvorak was projected to go as high as fourth in the 1995 Draft. Matti Vaisanen, the Panthers' European scout, compared Dvorak to Teemu Selanne, the Finnish goal-scoring phenomenon, and amateur scout Paul Henry, who had seem him play several times during the 1993-94 season, had no doubt Dvorak was the player the Panthers wanted.

"But you'll never get him," Henry told Murray.

The Panthers were drafting 10th and Dvorak, ranked second among Europeans behind Aki-Petteri Berg of Finland, figured to get taken much earlier. Dvorak was fourth on most of the Panthers' scouts' lists, behind defensemen Bryan Berard, Wade Redden, and Aki-Petteri Berg, who went one-two-three as expected. But the draft was a toss-up after the top three and when the Panthers' turn arrived, Dvorak was still available.

The discussion at the Panthers' table didn't last long. John Chapman, the director of player personnel who would rejoin Bob Clarke in Philadelphia after the draft, was the only one who wanted hard-hitting defenseman Jay McKee. For everyone else, the choice was between Dvorak and Petr Sykora, another highly-regarded Czech center whose stock had declined because of an early-season injury.

"We saw a big upside in Radek," Murray said. "He missed a big part of the year, and that was the only reason he slipped. We had a little discussion at the table, a couple of guys didn't want him, but we were strong on him. There was no hesitation. We picked Dvorak because he had size and we thought he could be a real top pro."

Unlike some of the GMs picking before him, Murray wasn't worried about dealing with Dvorak's agent, Rich Winter. Dvorak later signed a three-year deal worth $2.1 million, perfectly in line with his draft position, and the Panthers brought him to the United States for training camp. The only question was whether he'd start the season in Greensboro or Florida.

The good news for Dvorak and the other rookies was that MacLean gave them the chance to show their stuff in exhibition games. Dvorak was impressive, not just offensively but also in the defensive end, and clearly belonged in the NHL.

MacLean's first decisions would be easy. If only everything else was going so smoothly.

▲ ▲ ▲

John Vanbiesbrouck celebrated the one-year anniversary of his contract dispute with the Panthers by coming to camp, doing his job, and keeping his mind on business. He wasn't in a very talkative mood. Unless something changed soon, the 1995-96 season was going to be his last with the Panthers, and Vanbiesbrouck wasn't happy about being a lame duck goaltender.

In Greensboro and two weeks later when the Panthers returned to Florida, Vanbiesbrouck wasn't the locker room leader he had been for the past two seasons. How could he lead the team, he figured, if he had no idea where he was going? He didn't even know if he'd still be a member of the Panthers when the season started on October 7.

"It's a tough situation for Doug to be in, too," Vanbiesbrouck said. "He came in, and I wasn't very talkative to anybody. I came in and did my work. He wanted me to communicate better but, by the same token, they weren't making any offers. It was just going to be a one-year deal and there was big talk of a trade, and I thought they were going to trade me. I didn't know what to think, other than I knew I had to get myself ready to play and be very business-like."

Vanbiesbrouck separated his commitment to management from commitment to his teammates and the fans. He continued his charitable work because that was a personal activity unrelated to the Panthers. But Vanbiesbrouck and agent Lloyd Friedland were not going to be shortchanged. Bill Ranford had just signed a one-year deal for $2.3 million, and Mike Richter was making over $3 million. The Panthers' bumped-up offer of $6 million over three years represented a pay cut over the $2.185 million Vanbiesbrouck was going to make for this season.

"We couldn't get them to the point we wanted to get them to," Friedland said. "Frankly, we never got to that point. We believed we were entitled to something similar to Richter and we were looking for a three-year deal averaging $2.5 million a year. We would've settled for $7 million."

The talks between Murray and Friedland were neither acrimonious nor intense. They were, however, a distraction. MacLean was counting on a goaltending tandem of Vanbiesbrouck and Mark Fitzpatrick, and Vanbiesbrouck didn't want his situation hanging over the team all season. Fortunately for both sides, they were never so far apart that a deal was out of the question.

"We talked fairly well at that time," Murray said. "We were going to get it done. It was a matter of the numbers being right."

Signing Vanbiesbrouck was in the best interests of both sides. Murray couldn't get value for Vanbiesbrouck and didn't want to lose him to free-agency after the season. Vanbiesbrouck could've tested the free-agent market, but he and his family wanted to stay in Florida.

Vanbiesbrouck opened the season without a new contract but, five days later, on October 12, he signed a three-year deal worth $6.5 million plus bonuses. The only thing not guaranteed was security. Now that the Panthers had signed Vanbiesbrouck, trading him would be easier.

"I really had to focus on playing for the Panthers and being a Panther every day," Vanbiesbrouck said. "And that took a lot, because you never knew when they would pull the trigger."

But Vanbiesbrouck's trade value hadn't increased and Murray eventually gave up trying to move him. John and Rosalinde Vanbiesbrouck could finally decorate their new house, knowing they were in it for the long haul.

▲ ▲ ▲

The crowd at Miami Arena for the pre-season game stood and roared its approval. They had just seen a preview of what they hoped would become a Panthers tradition: Jovanovski taking on one of the toughest men in the NHL and standing in like a heavyweight.

The Panthers' young players had been getting tossed around by the Hartford Whalers and the team's lack of size was alarmingly obvious to everyone, including Jovanovski. Having decided there was no way he was going to let his teammates get pushed around, Jovanovski got in the face of Brendan Shanahan, a 6'3", 215-pound power forward with a solid reputation as a fierce fighter. Many players were afraid to fight him.

Not Jovanovski. He caught Shanahan with a big right hand. Shanahan fought back by landing a few punches of his own. Jovanovski, who had been stripped of his sweater, counter-punched and scored. So did Shanahan. The fight lasted a minute and a half, and its impact would linger far longer. That big right had crashed into Shanahan's helmet, fracturing Jovanovski's right index finger. The next day he was on an operating table at the Cleveland Clinic, undergoing surgery that would sideline him for the first 11 games of the season.

There went the Panthers' hopes of getting Jovanovski into the lineup right away. And so much for any remaining questions MacLean had about trimming the roster. The Panthers opened the season with defensemen Laus, Murphy, Woolley, Svehla, Geoff Smith, Warrener, Carkner, and Svensson; left wings Dvorak, Dave Lowry, Bill Lindsay, Mike Hough, and Johan Garpenlov; right wings Jody Hull, Scott Mellanby, Bob Kudelski, and Dave Nemirovsky; centers Barnes, Skrudland, Fitzgerald, Jesse Belanger, and Niedermayer; and goaltenders Fitzpatrick and Vanbiesbrouck. The only newcomers were Dvorak, Warrener, Carkner, and Nemirovsky. Eleven players chosen in the 1993 Expansion Draft remained on the team.

Because Murray and MacLean scrapped the defensive system that got the Panthers to within a point of the playoffs, the outlook for the Panthers was bleak. *The Hockey News* ranked them 22nd out of 26 teams. Las Vegas oddsmakers made the Panthers 60-1 underdogs to win the Stanley Cup. They had their reasons.

▲ ▲ ▲

Was Bryan Murray crazy, overconfident, or merely a masochist presiding over the Panthers' imminent demise? The NHL's Committee on Obstruction was heading in a direction that couldn't help a defensive team and Murray, silver-haired and crazy like a fox, was one of the ringleaders.

This group of coaches, general managers, and on-ice officials had gathered during the summer with the sole purpose of speeding up the game and allowing talent to win out. How could that help a team whose leading scorer had 29 points?

"I thought our speed, our positional ability, our willingness to be responsible, would really help, and give us a tremendous advantage over other teams," Murray said. "I was fortunate. I was around the Panthers all year and knew what we did and didn't do. What the committee tried to do was make the game more interesting, but allow the teams to play."

The Committee recommended stricter enforcement of a minor penalty for players who restrain an opponent without the puck and the 26 general managers unanimously approved the recommendation. As if they had a choice: They were merely enforcing rules already on the books.

As for Murray, he was neither crazy nor pushing his team over a cliff. The Panthers had a plan. Rather than trapping, the Panthers were going to let their speedy forwards forecheck aggressively. Two of their top young players, Niedermayer and Jovanovski, and the defense of Robert Svehla, Magnus Svensson, Gord Murphy, and Jason Woolley, would be comfortable in a more offense-oriented system.

The anti-obstruction rules would hurt poor-skating teams, and help teams, like the Panthers, who skated well. Publicly, Murray and MacLean spoke about being patient with young players and building for the future. Privately, they didn't believe that at all. The Panthers' goal hadn't changed: They wanted to make the playoffs.

▲ ▲ ▲

The thrill of the moment overshadowed the ominous challenge facing MacLean when he stepped behind the bench at Meadowlands Arena in New Jersey for the season-opener against the defending Stanley Cup champion Devils: He was finally in the big time.

And this was some way to start a coaching career! The building was packed with 19,040 fans to watch the raising of the Stanley Cup banner. The Panthers, the team that abandoned the trap, were up against the team that perfected the trap. The mismatch was overwhelming, the Devils' dominance complete. While the Devils played their typical disciplined game, the Panthers ran around and made mistakes. Their new two-man forechecking system didn't look systematic at all and the Devils won, 4-0, outshooting the Panthers, 32-17.

"It seemed like we were going to have to play at a much higher level in order to make the playoffs and compete with New Jersey," Vanbiesbrouck said.

MacLean, the loser of his first NHL game, considered his team capable of competing at a higher level. Losing the first game of the season to the Stanley Cup champions in their building didn't seem like such an ominous foreboding. The Panthers hadn't really been that bad, he decided.

"A lot of people were hoping we would collapse," MacLean said. "And we left that game feeling good. It was a 2-0 game in the third period. Then they have a five-on-three to make it 3-0, so instead of us pressing to get back in the game, we're down, and then they score an empty net goal. I didn't leave that game disappointed. I felt pretty good."

That was typical of MacLean, who's pessimistic when things look best, and optimistic when things look worst. He had no reason to worry.

▲ ▲ ▲

October 8. Miami Arena. A few minutes before the home opener at Miami Arena. Hull, Fitzgerald, Lindsay, and assistant equipment managers Scott Tinkler and Tim LeRoy are standing outside the locker room. Players are lining up for the introductions. And here comes the rat!

"Hey, Tink!" Hull yells out. "A rat just ran in!"

As Tinkler and LeRoy give chase, the rat scampers through the door, stops, and looks to his right into the skate sharpening room. Then he decides to continue down the hallway toward the main area. Through another door, he makes a left turn and runs around the room. Jovanovski sees him and jumps out of the way. Laus tries to kick him and misses. The rat ends up near Mellanby's stall. It's the worst mistake he's ever made. He's about to become famous.

Mellanby, who's standing and waiting to go on the ice, looks down and sees the rat coming at him. He grabs his hockey stick and, with the rat still on the run — *Splat!* — one-times it against the wall in self-defense.

"Oh my God!" a few stunned players say. Mellanby's killed a rat!

The rat is Dead On Wall Arrival and bleeding all over the floor. Tinkler, realizing they can't have a dead rat in the middle of the locker room, grabs Magnus Svensson's stick, which was just freshly wrapped in white tape. Tinkler shovels up the rat and carries it outside to a garbage bin. Then he returns to the locker room and hands the stick back to Svensson, who's not happy about it being covered in rat blood. Mellanby shows his teammates the little rat hairs stuck to the tape on his stick.

The rat is gone, but not forgotten. Svensson sprains his left knee in the game and half-jokingly says to Tinkler, "Hey, Tink, why'd you use my stick? The rat cursed me." Mellanby, not jinxed by the same rat, scores two goals in a 4-3 victory over the Calgary Flames, and misses his first career hat trick by one.

"Yeah," quips Vanbiesbrouck, "but he scored a rat trick. Two goals and a rat."

Somebody suggests to Tinkler that he should have the rat stuffed as an appropriate memorial. Tinkler's already tossed it, so he grabs a magic marker, circles the spot on the wall where the beast met its death, and writes, "R.I.P. Rat 1. 10-8-96."

The next day, Tinkler's in a shopping mall when he sees a giant toy rat in a costume store. He buys the rat and, before the next home game against the Montreal Canadiens, places it underneath the memorial. A photographer snaps a picture of this strange scene and a tradition is born.

▲ ▲ ▲

The entire rat spectacle would've been perfect for one of those between-periods personality pieces on *Hockey Night in Canada*, the kind Ralph Mellanby produced when his son, Scott, was growing up.

Perfect hockey theater.

It had symbolism: Cat kills rat.

It had heroism: Man saves teammates from killer rat.

It had irony: If Mellanby had scored one goal instead of two, Vanbiesbrouck never would've come up with the rat trick line.

There was even a bit of mystery: Why did Tinkler use Svensson's perfectly good stick when Mellanby's already had rat all over it? Even Tinkler didn't know for sure.

Then there could've been a flashback. Toronto, 1974. Eight-year-old Scott Mellanby plays hockey for the first time. Most of his friends have been playing for years, their fathers having thrown skates on their feet when they were old enough to walk, but that's not the way things happened in the Mellanby household.

"Maybe that's because my father wasn't a player, although he was involved with hockey," Scott said. "But my mother wanted me to learn how to skate before I started playing in leagues, so I took a couple of years of power skating to learn how to skate."

Ralph Mellanby was a former basketball and baseball player, not a hockey player, who made his living in hockey as the executive producer of *Hockey Night in Canada* and was influential in its development as the most important television program in the country. He never intended to turn his son into one of the stars of his Saturday night show.

"It never crossed my mind that he'd be a hockey player," Ralph Mellanby said. "He was skinny and scrawny as a kid. *He* said he was going to be a hockey player, not me. His mother used to say to me, 'Don't spoil his dream.' "

The dream, though meaningful to young Scott Mellanby, was pursued without parental pressure. Since he had no brothers and only one younger sister, Laura, he never felt the need to prove himself or perform for anyone. He'd see his friends' parents arguing with a youth hockey coach or screaming at their sons from the stands, and think how lucky he was to have supportive parents who let him do what he wanted, without expecting a child's fun and games to turn into a career. His father couldn't even skate.

"I was beating him skating backwards when I was about six," Scott recalled.

His hopes of one day playing in the NHL grew on their own, with a little helpful, unintentional nurturing from his father. Ralph took Scott to work a couple of times a year and, one night in the late 1970s, brought him down to the Montreal Canadiens dressing room to meet Guy Lafleur. This was a big deal for Scott, who loved the Canadiens and idolized Lafleur, but envisioning himself pulling on the Canadiens jersey and playing in the NHL was another matter. He had never been more than an average player on his youth teams.

"Every kid goes out in the driveway and pretends he's scored the game-winning goal in the Stanley Cup, but I never really had in mind what I wanted to do," Mellanby said. "I know some kids say, 'Oh, I want to be a policeman,' but I was never like that. I just played and things just developed. I put on a little size when I was 16 and got a chance to play on a good team and got some exposure then, all of a sudden they were saying, 'Oh, you're going to be drafted into Junior A,' and I was like, 'Oh, sure.'"

Mellanby still didn't think playing professional hockey was going to be a career option when he accepted a scholarship to the University of Wisconsin. Then Bob Clarke, at that time the general manager of the Philadelphia Flyers, selected him in the second round of the 1984 Entry Draft.

Two years later, after scoring 82 points in his first two seasons at Wisconsin, Mellanby faced a career decision: Should he sign with the Flyers, stay in college, or join the Canadian Olympic program for the 1988 Games in Calgary? The decision ate at Mellanby because, although the financial pull of the NHL was strong, he didn't want to sit in the minors when he could be playing in the Olympics. Then again, Clarke was strongly hinting that he might fit into the Flyers' immediate plans.

Mellanby chose the NHL and played his first game on March 22, 1986, against the Rangers. He never spent a day in the minors. Clarke saw him as a potential impact player who could play tough and score 30 or 40 goals a season and Mellanby did nothing to temper those expectations when he scored 25 goals in his second NHL season.

But in August 1989, Mellanby came to the aid of a friend during a brawl at Steamer Jakes' bar in Toronto. During the fight, Mellanby's left hand and arm were cut by glass from a broken beer bottle. He suffered nerve and tendon damage that sidelined him for the first 20 games of the 1989-90 season, and later successfully sued the owners of the bar and the instigator of the fight, claiming the injuries hurt his career.

"He became just another player," Clarke testified. "He couldn't handle the puck. He couldn't be confrontational."

No longer thinking of Mellanby as a potential impact player, the Flyers traded him to the Edmonton Oilers after the 1990-91 season. Two years later, after scoring only 32 points in 69 games and missing 15 games with an injured shoulder, Mellanby was exposed by the Oilers in the 1993 Expansion Draft. Once again, Clarke figured he'd take his chances but, at 27, Mellanby wasn't at all excited about being drafted by an expansion team.

"At first, I was dismayed," he said. "Most of the expansion teams weren't doing very well, and I saw it as a step backwards. But after a few days, I saw some of the players the team picked up and started to realize the opportunity that might present itself to me. Any time you're let go by a team, it's a blow to your ego, to feel unwanted but, after a couple of days, you realize someone wants you. It's the best thing that ever happened to me."

In the Panthers' first season, Mellanby, the alternate captain, finally came through on Clarke's projection as somebody who could play tough and score 30 goals. Indeed, he scored 30 and was second on the team in penalty minutes in what he considers the best season of his career. Mellanby was finally coming through on his potential and, although he slumped to 25 points in the lockout-shortened 1994-95 season, his precision shot on the rat was a portent of good tidings. For the first two months of the season, Mellanby was better than he had ever been.

He scored two more goals in a 6-1 victory over the Canadiens and another goal in a 6-2 rout of the Senators. Mellanby was hot; the power play was clicking. Another two-goal game in a 3-0 win over the Whalers gave him seven goals in seven games, and he scored again three nights later in Toronto as the Panthers won and moved into first place in the Atlantic Division.

"I've never had a stretch like this, definitely not from the start," Mellanby said.

Mellanby didn't cool off until the New Year, and his 21 goals and 20 assists earned him his first selection to the All-Star Game.

"At that time in my career, after hurting my arm so seriously, I never thought an All-Star Game would lie ahead," said Mellanby, who uses only four fingers of his left hand to grip the stick. "When I got hurt, a few years went by and I lost an opportunity and was used in a certain way, but I came to Florida and got the chance to show I could play at a good level again. I certainly would've liked to have had this opportunity with 100 percent of my arm instead of 75-80 percent of my arm, because it never healed correctly."

The Panthers' new aggressive forechecking system contributed to Mellanby's success because it allowed for quick chances off of turnovers in the offensive zone. The Panthers kept winning, even when Lowry was sidelined for 18 games with a sprained knee. With Mellanby hot, Barnes scoring more than ever, Fitzgerald piling up shorthanded goals at an unprecedented clip, and Svehla alternately exciting and exasperating MacLean and the fans with his daring offensive zone forays and long, cross-ice passes, the Panthers were not only winning, they were exciting.

"People were starting to gain a little respect for us," Vanbiesbrouck noted.

With each win, respect for their coach was growing, too. MacLean was no longer perceived as Murray's puppet, but as a capable coach who had energized the team. He had wanted to prove he was his own man, and he did.

The differences between their old coach and their new one couldn't have been more obvious to the players. Of course, there were the practices, during which the Panthers no longer worked on the neutral zone trap. MacLean's drills were heavy on breakouts, forechecking, and driving to the net. Practices were intense, fast-paced, but MacLean was easy with a joke and quick to laugh at his own mistakes.

MacLean, like Neilson, was intense and hyper, a high-energy person who was demanding of his players. He believed in positive reinforcement. Although he'd never dress down a player in front of the team, he'd quickly pull that player into his office and let him know that he wasn't living up to expectations. MacLean preferred one-on-one meetings, and the players always knew where they stood with the coach.

"The most enjoyable part of the job all year was 10:30 to 12:00 every morning," MacLean said, referring to the team's daily skate. "No matter what happens, you get up in the morning and you're either high or low, based on the results of the previous night's game, but as soon as you get onto the ice, you're rejuvenated. It's a sort of high. Players look at how you handle losses as much as how you handle wins. It was really a test for me to make sure I was in the right frame of mind to handle situations properly."

Pigeonholing MacLean is no easy task. Later in the season, an out-of-town reporter would describe him as "cocky and thin-skinned," words which are as accurate as "modest and willing to accept criticism." He is, like most people, all of those things: Confident enough to believe in his methods, modest enough to pinch himself every day, just to convince himself that what was happening was real.

While Neilson often made dry remarks that passed right over his players' heads, MacLean was more direct with a joke or a comment, usually at somebody else's expense, but rarely in a mean-spirited way.

Perhaps you wouldn't find MacLean biking along the beach early in the morning, like Neilson, but you would certainly finding him jogging with an assistant coach. When his work day is over, he doesn't head to a beach house for a few hours on the sand and the surf, but home to Coral Springs, a family-oriented suburb of Fort Lauderdale, for time with his wife, Jill, and children, Clark and MacKenzie.

There was never any down time for MacLean, who thought about hockey every waking hour, whether he was sitting at home eating dinner or watching TV. That part of the job differed from being an assistant coach, he realized, but it also made it exciting.

"The kids get your mind off it and Jill's great," MacLean said. "She gives her two cents worth and she always keeps things in perspective, which is really important, especially after losses. And the kids are terrific, because they're kids, and they don't care."

The last thing MacLean wanted at this point was perspective, because the wins were piling up. Dvorak had found his scoring touch after going the first 11 games without a goal. Jovanovski's return on November 2 against the Flyers coincided with Dvorak's first NHL goal in a 2-1 victory that started a seven-game winning streak. Niedermayer scored in four of six games. Mellanby scored his 13th goal of the season in a 5-1 win over the Kings, improving the Panthers to a League-best record of 17-5-1.

They were the hottest team in hockey, and Miami Arena was the site of the newest fad: Fans were bringing rubber rats and throwing them on the ice after each Panthers goal. What started with a few rats had grown to tens, then hundreds. The Panthers renamed their locker room, "The Rat's Den," and artistic fans painted the toy rats in team colors and sent them to the players. Each home goal was followed by the amusing sight of the Orkin Rat Patrol cleaning up the ice.

And, in the most absurd irony of all, February 7, 1996, would begin the Year of the Rat on the Chinese Calendar.

▲ ▲ ▲

The rat throwers were an exclusive club. The Panthers were playing to a limited audience. South Florida sports fans, never ones to come out in droves to support their own teams, certainly weren't going to support one that was leaving town. The Panthers won and won and won. And the fans stayed away.

Nearly 3,000 seats went unoccupied at the home opener. Only 10,085, a franchise low, showed up for the October 13 game against Ottawa. Management increased the number of $9 Panther Pack tickets by 1,000, but the fans resisted the offer. The Panthers drew crowds under 11,000 four times in the first two months. With a home record of 11-2-1, the Panthers were more successful than they had ever been, and the fans who showed up lavishly praised their performance and effort, but not until Wayne Gretzky and the Kings came to town on November 26 did the Panthers have their first sellout.

Nobody could blame the fans for resisting the urge to fall in love with the Panthers. What was the purpose of giving their hearts to players who were leaving in a year?

Taxpayers, outraged by Huizenga's threat to move or sell the team if a deal for a new arena wasn't struck by Halloween, reasoned, *Why should we build an arena for a millionaire?* Having failed to get anywhere with his threat, Huizenga announced on October 20 that he was seeking a new home for the team outside South Florida.

"You don't spent $175 million on something you're losing money on," Huizenga said. "That doesn't make any sense. We weren't going to move the team, we were going to sell it, because I don't have any interest in owning a team in another city. We were going to sell it, and if somebody wanted to keep it here, let him keep it here."

Another villain was the City of Nashville, which offered $20 million and most of the revenue inside the building to lure a hockey team into its new 20,000-seat arena. Nashville had tried and failed to lure the New Jersey Devils the previous summer, and now it was enticing the Panthers. Portland, Oregon also wanted the team. So did a group in New York City, which would've relocated the Panthers to Texas.

Politicians played their part in this farce. Unwilling to assume a leadership role and investigate a project that could have long-term benefits for the community, they considered only the political backlash of supporting an arena with public funds.

"The commissioners were not about to support any kind of taxation or pay any kind of public money because they didn't want to look like they were pandering to a guy who has a lot of money," Bill Torrey said.

Slight movement was detected in late October, when Huizenga vowed to sign a 30-year lease for a new arena in Broward County and cover any losses after it was built. That won support for a two-percent hotel tax from County Administrator Jack Osterholt, who called the deal "doable." Finally, people were talking. Fort Lauderdale and the nearby suburb of Sunrise began quarreling over where the prospective arena should be located. Other cities joined the bidding. There was action.

Then inaction. Frustrated by the tortoise-like movement among government officials and fearful it would take three or four more years for an arena to be built, if it was built at all, Huizenga officially placed the team for sale on November 7. All indications had the Florida Panthers becoming the Nashville Panthers.

"Wayne probably would've moved the team himself," Torrey said. "At one point he talked about moving it to Nashville, then eventually selling it, and then down the road, if a building was ever built here, getting a franchise back. But Wayne did not ever want to leave the National Hockey League."

NHL Commissioner Gary Bettman, concerned over losing a franchise in an area where the League wanted to be, jumped into the fray and met with politicians from Broward and Dade Counties. The lack of movement had reached the critical stage; the League wanted to know by January where the team was planning on playing the 1996-97 season. So did Huizenga's employees.

"The team was going to Nashville," Dean Jordan said. "I thought we were gone four or five times. I thought we were going to get the call any day."

But Huizenga wanted to be perceived as the man who brought hockey to South Florida, not the one who drove it out of town, and had a last-ditch plan up his sleeve. Huizenga realized he was one of the obstacles to having an arena built, and finding a local buyer for a team losing $12 million a year would be impossible without the promise of a new building. On December 22, he offered $25 million toward a new arena in Broward County.

The gift came with some very important strings attached. The County had until February 1, 1996 — only 40 days — to make all commitments necessary for constructing the arena, including approving an increase in the bed tax. The County would have to turn over management, operation, and all revenues from the building to the new owner of the hockey team. And at that point, there was no prospective owner.

"This gift is given with the assumption that we will have no ownership in the team or the civic center," Huizenga said. "There is nothing in this for Wayne Huizenga. And I want to be clear that this is not a negotiating ploy. The gift is purely an effort to get the facility built so the team will play in Broward."

Finally, Huizenga issued a warning: "If this challenge is not met by February 1, 1996, I must then enter into final negotiations for the sale of the team to someone who would relocate it elsewhere."

Although the $25 million offer amounted to less than 12 percent of the cost of the building, Huizenga's challenge finally prodded the politicians into action. Broward County Commission Chairman John Rodstrom, who became a key player over the next four months, said the County would try to meet the deadline.

For the first time since Blockbuster Park had died a year earlier, Torrey had reason for optimism. Finally, it looked as if he'd have the chance to complete the job he was hired to carry out: Building a new arena for the Florida Panthers.

A few weeks later, Torrey sat in a cold arena in Boston, watching the World Junior Championships, and offered a prediction: "It's going to get done."

▲ ▲ ▲

Rob Niedermayer's season began with a lot of talking and not much scoring. Now that he was finally getting playing time, he wasn't getting positive results: Four games, no goals, no points.

"I would make a mistake and always look over my shoulder," Niedermayer said. "You're playing not to make a mistake, and nobody's going to be successful like that. So I had to refocus and if I made a mistake, I made a mistake. I just worked to improve."

Niedermayer's problem was that his mind was still working under the old coach's rules, in which making a mistake meant taking a seat on the bench. MacLean, who told Niedermayer before training camp that he didn't have to worry about getting playing time, thought this might be a good time to tell him again.

"He deserved to play," MacLean said. "Everybody makes mistakes, whether you're a third-year player or a 10-year player. You have to weigh out what the benefits are. With some guys, if they make a mistake, you know they're going to do it for you before the game's over. Others make mistakes, you know they're not going to get it done. As a coach, you decide who plays and who doesn't play."

Niedermayer, a key part of the Panthers' plans, was playing. In the next game, Niedermayer scored two goals in a 5-3 win over the Islanders, kicking off a career-turning streak during which he'd score 10 goals in 15 games, assert himself physically, and become one of the Panthers' top players.

Although MacLean deflected credit to Niedermayer for taking the incentive to become a better player, playing on a line with Mellanby and

Garpenlov didn't hurt his cause. Nor did the input of assistant coach Duane Sutter, who coached him during his final season of junior hockey.

Here was another example of the Panthers' misfortune turning out fine: MacLean originally wanted Newell Brown, his former colleague in Detroit, as the second assistant, but the Red Wings wouldn't release Brown from his contract as coach of their Adirondack farm club. He hired his second choice, Sutter, who brought along the advantage of knowing Niedermayer's personality.

"Neids is a very receptive young player who needs a sounding board and needs a little bit of a push," Sutter said. "In juniors, he was more of a laid back guy in the dressing room, and at times it might have hurt his performance on the ice. He wasn't as assertive as he could have been, and at times now you can see a little of that."

Niedermayer spent hours with Sutter watching videotape and executing drills. In the third period of games, Sutter would come down from the press box to the bench and show Niedermayer what he was doing wrong. Usually, the mistakes were simple, like not finishing a check or not driving hard to the net. He'd beat a defenseman to the inside with his great speed, then ease up just as was about to score. He didn't bear down. Sutter told Niedermayer to try and score all the time, even in practice.

"He'd get into a situation, and instead of shooting the puck from the top of the circle, he's thinking, *Well, I have to get that extra five or six feet or pass to Mellanby*," Sutter said. "But when you're playing with Mellanby, you can shoot the puck, because you know he's going to the net."

As his scoring increased and he became more assured of his spot in the lineup, Niedermayer's confidence grew. No longer did he spend every waking hour thinking about hockey or worrying about the next game. He became more relaxed off the ice, better and more intense on the ice.

"I don't like thinking about hockey all the time," Niedermayer said. "When you're not doing well, you say, 'Jeez, can I play in this League? Can I contribute?' You're always asking yourself that. Knowing that you're going to get a chance to play. That's all you want, for it to be in your hands, to fail or do well."

While Sutter worked with Niedermayer, Lindy Ruff fine-tuned Jovanovski. Size was both Jovanovski's greatest asset and worst enemy. He enjoyed using his big body to make a big hit and often wandered far out of position to find his target. Or he'd overplay an offensive rush and focus on the puck, rather than the puck-carrier. The Panthers had no problem with other aspects of Jovanovski's game, such as his skating, passing, and intensity, but sometimes he was too intense. MacLean didn't want him fighting all the time; they needed him on the ice, not in the penalty box.

"We started from Day One, doing video work with him and showing him areas where he could improve," Ruff said. "Sometimes in the heat of a game, you don't realize what you're doing. We spent a lot of time talking on the ice in practice. One of his biggest assets was Gord Murphy. Gord would say to him, 'Listen, we should've played it this way,' or 'We would've been better off if you just stayed with your man.' "

Ruff noticed when training camp opened that Jovanovski was an improved player over the previous year. At his first NHL camp in 1994, Jovanovski was immature and didn't know how to conduct himself around his teammates. He was nervous, always trying to make an impression, and at times he thought he didn't belong.

"I didn't know what I was doing," Jovanovski said. "But then I knew what to expect after going through one training camp, and I concentrated over the summer on working really hard."

Jovanovski, a teenager away from home for the first time, could concentrate on playing because his parents took care of his off-ice business. His father, Kostadin, helped him pick out a townhouse in Boca Raton and his mother, Liljana, spent the season in Florida, cooking, cleaning, and doing the laundry for her son.

But he was obviously a boy in a man's body. Big Ed's checks were the shots heard round the League. Wingers who dared skate down Jovanovski's side of the ice were punished with pummeling hits against an area on the boards about 20 feet inside the defensive blue line. Nicknamed "Jovo-Cop," he policed the open ice, flattening Keith Primeau of the Wings with a hit so hard it hushed the crowd, mauling Rod Brind'Amour's nose in a game against the Flyers, and giving Martin Gelinas of Vancouver a concussion.

Then Jovanovski mixed his hits with a little bit of offense. He took a regular spot on the power play and penalty-killing units and, on some nights, was the Panthers' best defenseman, playing over 20 minutes a game. Jovanovski became the first Panther chosen to the NHL's All-Rookie team and a finalist for Rookie of the Year.

Young players were doing as much as the veterans to carry the Panthers through their hot stretch. After not scoring in his first 11 games, Dvorak was temporarily moved to a line with Skrudland and Hough and responded with six goals in four games. Svehla, a first-year player, but technically not a rookie because of his age, scored 16 points in the first 20 games.

Offensive contributions came from the most unlikely sources. Hull, a checking forward, had 13 goals by mid-December. In a 6-1 win over Toronto on October 24, the checking line of Skrudland, Hull, and Lindsay, combined for nine points. It didn't matter that Kudelski wasn't scoring and Belanger was playing his way out of the lineup. Stone hands had turned to gold.

▲ ▲ ▲

On three priceless nights, it was reasonable for a fan or player to imagine the Panthers playing for the Stanley Cup in June. For two seasons, hard-fought, close games, defined the Panthers' personality, but in 1995-96, they won games even the players expected to lose and came up with key victories when something real was at stake.

After completing a 5-0-1 homestand on November 16, the Panthers flew coast-to-coast by commercial airline for a 3-2 loss to the Los Angeles Kings and a 4-3 victory over the Anaheim Mighty Ducks. The Panthers boarded another commercial airliner on November 20, the morning after the Anaheim win, and changed planes twice before arriving in Miami 8:00 that night. Awaiting them, relaxed and rested, were the New Jersey Devils, who hadn't played in two days.

The Panthers, faced with their fourth game in six nights against a fresh team, thought the schedule was a ridiculous joke. An angry Chuck Fletcher said, "It'll take an act of God for us to win this game."

The Panthers had an all-time record of 1-7-2 against the Devils and had been hammered in their previous meeting in the season opener. The Devils, a big, strong team, matched up well against the Panthers, and appeared to have more skill. And with a four-day Thanksgiving break coming up, the Panthers could've easily said, "We're in first place. We've lost only one of our last 10. Nobody's going to criticize us if we lose."

"Everybody talked about it," Lindsay said. "Everybody mentioned it. The coaches said, 'This is one of our toughest games.' "

The Panthers were dead tired. The Devils were ready for them.

"The schedule maker should have been impeached," Fletcher said. "It was almost like it was a challenge."

When the Devils scored twice in the first eight minutes to take a 2-0 lead, the situation looked even more hopeless. But Hull and Mellanby scored before the end of the period, and Hull's second of the night late in the second period put the Panthers ahead for good. They won, 4-3, and weren't too tired to celebrate.

MacLean called it "a heart-and-soul win." Fletcher walked into the locker room and saw exhaustion in the eyes of the euphoric players. *That was pure courage*, Fletcher thought.

"We always had that, but to combine the courage and effort to get the result is something else," said Fletcher, who realized for the first time that the team wasn't merely on a hot streak. They were good. "It was the defining moment of the year."

Few games ever meant more to the organization than a December 23 rematch with the Devils at the Arena. Because of a new rule, the head coaches of the teams in first place in their respective conferences on December 27 would coach in the All-Star Game. The Panthers needed a win over the Devils to clinch a trip to Boston for their rookie coach.

MacLean, whose coaching career consisted of a little over two months, was modest to the point of embarrassment whenever the subject came up, but the players liked him and viewed getting their coach to the All-Star Game as a matter of organizational pride.

"We knew that by a certain date, if we were in first, our coach was going to the All-Star Game, and that was a big deal," Fitzgerald said. "We knew if we had so many points, we as a group would be represented. Not just Doug, but all of us. We were all going. We were all part of it. And we all felt that way."

The game was meaningful to MacLean in a far more personal way. It was the first time his parents, Jim and Fran, saw him coach an NHL game.

The relationship between Jim and Doug MacLean was typical of Canadian father and son. Father loved hockey and passed on his passion to his son. Growing up, they'd watch games together on TV and talk hockey, and Jim MacLean would get up early on cold winter mornings to drive his two sons to their games.

It's the typical hockey story, but with an unfortunate twist. In 1955, when Doug was only two, Jim MacLean was driving home from work early in the morning when his car skidded off a bridge. He spent a year in the hospital, another year in a wheelchair, and 20 years walking with a cane. In 1975, Jim MacLean was confined to a wheelchair.

Talking about his father doesn't come easily to MacLean, who refuses to play this story as a tragedy. Jim MacLean has undergone numerous operations over the past 20 years and suffers from congestive heart failure. His ability to travel is limited to the point where, even though he winters in Daytona Beach, going to games in Miami is an ordeal.

So, in what had been a storybook season, a loss on December 23 with Jim MacLean watching would've been the rudest plot turn of all.

Then the Panthers went out and did everything possible to make sure they lost. After Mellanby scored his 20th late in the first period and Belanger added his 11th early in the second for a 2-0 lead, the Panthers began an endless parade to the penalty box. Lowry for tripping, Skrudland for hooking, Laus for high sticking, Fitzgerald for slashing, even MacLean for too many men on the ice.

The Devils had four power plays and two five-on-threes in the second. Valeri Zelepukin cut the lead to 2-1, and the Panthers kept committing penalties. Mellanby for cross checking, Jovanovski for elbowing, Skrudland again for hooking. Vanbiesbrouck was outstanding on the five-on-threes, and the Panthers held on for a 2-1 lead in a game that made Jim MacLean's heart flutter.

The rookie coach of the third-year team was going to the All-Star Game and the proud, joyous Panthers were heading into the Christmas break with a record of 25-8-2, the best in the Eastern Conference.

But the happiest man in the building wasn't in the locker room, as MacLean discovered when his eight-year-old son, Clark, ran up to him after the game and sat on his lap.

"Boy, Dad," Clark said. "Your Dad is really proud of you tonight."

That made Doug MacLean feel pretty good.

The All-Star Game deadline came just in time. The Panthers returned from Christmas and started their first losing streak with a disheartening 5-4 defeat by the Washington Capitals after leading 4-2 late in the third period.

"I don't remember a collapse like that in two and a half years here," said Mellanby, whose memory served correctly.

The Panthers began a two-week road trip by losing three straight, including a 7-2 loss to Vancouver that Murphy called the worst of the season. A horrifyingly boring 3-2 victory in Edmonton stopped the losing streak at three, but the Panthers apparently left their offense behind when they traveled to Calgary and lost to the Flames, 2-0.

Meanwhile, the Rangers were hot and had taken over first place in the Atlantic Division. A 5-2 victory over woeful San Jose temporarily righted the Panthers, but another schedule maker's trick did them dirty: Their sixth game of the trip and fifth game in eight nights was against the high-powered Colorado Avalanche, who rallied from a two-goal deficit for a 4-4 tie.

Finally, with home in sight, the Panthers dragged themselves into Dallas on January 12 for a game against the lowly Stars. Lowly was a relative term. The Panthers, on the road since December 29, had visited seven cities, all on commercial airlines. Everyone, from the players to the coaches to the media and the equipment managers and trainers, was exhausted from the long road trip, hotel beds, and restaurant food. They couldn't wait to get home.

The Panthers spent two periods playing like they felt. The Stars led, 6-2. Vanbiesbrouck was playing with a pulled muscle in his side because Fitzpatrick bruised his knee during the morning skate. Manny Fernandez, the Stars' rookie goalie, had seemingly suppressed the Panthers' last gasp by making 17 saves in the second period. A dismal road trip was going to end in appropriately dismal fashion.

Then, between periods, Skrudland stood up in the dressing room and said, "Beezer is hurt. Let's not give up any more shots. We can win this game."

The players started talking themselves into this crazy idea: *If they could sustain their pressure from the second period, Fernandez was bound to break.*

"Everyone was sitting in the dressing room saying, 'Hey, guys, we can come back,' and you don't know if it's going to happen, but we thought we could give it a shot," Lindsay said. "Then things got rolling."

As good as he had been in the second period, that's how bad Fernandez was in the third. With 3:12 gone, Belanger scored on a stoppable shot from the left boards and the Panthers felt the game changing. Thirty seconds later, Jovanovski made it 6-4. The Panthers were swarming; the Stars were generating absolutely no offense. Niedermayer scored a power play goal with 10 minutes remaining and Fernandez was yanked. With time running out on a possible miracle, Barnes tied the game with 22.3 seconds left.

The Panthers dominated the overtime and easily could have won, but gladly settled for their biggest comeback ever in the final game of their longest road trip. The entire team was elated. None of the players could remember being so excited after a regular season game.

"We were sitting around the room and everybody was just shaking their heads and saying, 'That was unbelievable that we did that,' " Barnes said. "For me, that was the definition of the team. We just battled right to the end."

From that point on, the Panthers would never consider any obstacle or deficit insurmountable. They had proven something to themselves.

▲ ▲ ▲

Mark Fitzpatrick had to admit it: He was shocked. As well as he had played two nights earlier in a 4-1 victory over the Devils, and as closely as MacLean had adhered to the hot-goalie-plays rotation, Fitzpatrick didn't expect to get the start in what was being billed as the most important game of the season. Especially against the Rangers, Vanbiesbrouck's former team.

Thanks to a quirk in the computer-generated NHL schedule, the first meeting between the top two teams in the Atlantic Division didn't take place until February 24 in Miami. The Panthers circled the date on their calendar weeks earlier and when game night arrived, the Rangers led the Panthers by only two points. A sellout crowd, generously peppered with more Rangers fans than the home team would've liked, was in a playoff mood. But Vanbiesbrouck was disconsolate.

"I thought that the coaching staff had lost confidence in me, and that bothered me," Vanbiesbrouck said. "And they had. But I didn't lose confidence in myself. I knew I had to rectify it."

Despite being selected to the All-Star Game for the second time in three years, Vanbiesbrouck had shown signs of wear at the turn of the year, when he was pulled from consecutive losses to Pittsburgh and Vancouver. Throughout January he was rarely stellar and usually ordinary. The Panthers had a real goaltending platoon for the first time in three seasons as MacLean went with the hot goaltender and switched off only when the Panthers played on consecutive nights. Much to MacLean's dismay, neither goalie was consistently outstanding and in early February, he called in goaltending coach Bill Smith from the road and told him to make things better.

"Dougie just said, 'Hey, our goaltending isn't what it should be,'" Smith said. "Johnny was trying to do too much. He started trying to help defensemen, he started trying to bring his game up a notch, when it was fine where it was. Sometimes you try to do too much and make mistakes. He was trying to help out more than he was capable of doing."

Vanbiesbrouck listened and learned, but he was so self-critical that recognizing his mistakes was just another way of getting down on himself. A key test came on February 7 and 8, when the Panthers and Red Wings met in a potential Stanley Cup finals preview. The Panthers entered the first game in Detroit third in the League, while the Red Wings were threatening the record for points in a season. In two nights, the Panthers would find out whether they were the real deal or simply first-half pretenders headed for a fall.

The first game was no contest. The Red Wings' small but high-powered offense scored three goals in the opening 11:09, chasing Vanbiesbrouck from the net in a 4-2 victory. None of the goals were Vanbiesbrouck's fault, but the contrast to Chris Osgood, the young Red Wings goalie, couldn't have been more obvious: Osgood made the big saves, Vanbiesbrouck didn't.

Riding a 10-game winning streak into Miami the next night, the Red Wings faced a team with an entirely different attitude. The Panthers were somehow more composed than they were in the first game, and Vanbiesbrouck played like he had during the first three months of the season. With the game tied, 1-1 in the second period, the Red Wings outshot the Panthers, 11-1, but couldn't beat Vanbiesbrouck. Garpenlov, a former Wing, broke the tie with 9:18 remaining in regulation and the Panthers won, 3-1.

"That was a big game for me," Vanbiesbrouck said. "I had been beating myself up pretty hard internally, because you're your own worst enemy, and I was my own worst enemy. I was drilling myself pretty hard, just trying to make myself play better."

The 29-save victory should've marked the end of Vanbiesbrouck's self-flagellation, but in his next start against Philadelphia, he got lost behind the net — trying to do too much — on one of the Flyers' goals. Then he was pulled after the second period of a 5-4 loss to Colorado. Those games, along with Fitzpatrick's 30-save performance in a 4-1 win over the Devils, led to Vanbiesbrouck's low point of his three seasons in Florida: a spot on the bench for the game against the Rangers.

MacLean didn't understand the drama in his decision. He had gone with the hot goaltender all season, and Fitzpatrick had been outstanding in the New Jersey game. The choice was easy.

"I didn't put a lot of thought into it, other than sometimes you have to reward people," MacLean said. "We had four more games coming up with the Rangers. I never really worried about being second-guessed."

But the second-guessers were out in full force when Brian Leetch scored just 25 seconds into the game, banking a shot off Terry Carkner's leg. Two minutes later, Mark Messier tossed a harmless backhander that hit Fitzpatrick's stick and bounced into the net. The Panthers, looking more tentative than they had all season, didn't have a shot on goal in the opening 14:39. Vanbiesbrouck replaced Fitzpatrick at the start of the second period with the Rangers already leading 3-0, but it was too late. The Rangers won, 4-0, and took a four-point lead in the division.

Although Vanbiesbrouck was angry about the apparent slight, he wouldn't say anything to MacLean or his teammates. The only shoulder he had to cry on was that of his wife, Rosalinde, and he conveyed to her his disappointment over not getting the start.

"I knew I hadn't been playing well, but every other player gets an opportunity and I don't," Vanbiesbrouck said. "It's different in my position, because only one guy could play. But by the same token, I knew going through this stretch was going to be good for me, one way or another. Not everything's rosy all the time and for anything to happen good, something has to be tough on you."

The game was toughest on Fitzpatrick, who knew he wasted his chance to become the No. 1 goaltender down the stretch and in the playoffs. For Vanbiesbrouck, the negative experience played a major part in his self-discovery. For reasons even he didn't quite understand, Vanbiesbrouck became more religious during the season and came to the understanding that things happen for a reason. Instead of pouting or going public with his disappointment over not starting, he became more at peace with himself.

If Fitzpatrick had won, Vanbiesbrouck might have been out of a job, and the course of his history and the Panthers' might have changed. "Maybe," he decided. "But it didn't happen that way, did it?"

"If you want to climb the highest mountain in the world, you have to train extremely hard for it, and you're going to hate your training," said Vanbiesbrouck, who a few weeks later consulted with Panthers scout Paul Henry, a part-time sports psychologist. "It's going to be tough on you. But you're going to get to the top of the mountain. You might cry some days, you might breathe hard some days, you might even bleed some days, but you're going to get to the top of the mountain."

So Vanbiesbrouck started from its base. The loss to the Rangers began a franchise-record nine-game winless streak during which injuries to Barnes, Lindsay, and Mellanby, an inability to score, and lapses by both goaltenders contributed to the Panthers' woes. Murphy was a less effective player after returning early from an ankle injury. Fitzpatrick had one more chance to win the No. 1 spot, but wasted it in an 8-4 loss in Chicago on March 11 that would mark a turning point for the Panthers. Fitzpatrick's season was all but over, and his chance to overtake Vanbiesbrouck was gone for good.

"He didn't play bad, but he didn't play great," Smith said. "That's the difference. You can have a good game, but if you lose 2-1 or 3-2, it's not a great game and, unfortunately with this hockey team in the last three years, good games are not enough to win. You have to play great. You can't have an off night and walk away with a win."

Fitzpatrick wasn't walking away with many wins. After making 23 saves in a 2-1 victory over the Penguins on January 29, he won one game the rest of the season, started consecutive games once, and played only 125 minutes from Game 68 on.

The Panthers were Vanbiesbrouck's team once again and his spectacular climb would now begin.

▲ ▲ ▲

Keeping a level head and remaining optimistic wasn't easy for MacLean during this stretch, but he had ways of staying sane. His family was always a source of support, perspective, and humor. One day, Clark MacLean was speaking on the phone with his grandfather.

"You coming to the game tonight, Grampy?" Clark asked.

"No," Jim MacLean answered.

"Good," Clark said. "I think it'll kill you if you go."

That made Doug MacLean laugh. His wife, Jill, would remind him that the Panthers were still in second place in the division. When needing self-preservation, he'd recall a conversation from several summers ago with his friends on Prince Edward Island. MacLean was complaining to them about the rigors of coaching in the NHL, and they didn't want to hear his belly-aching.

"Doug, do us a favor," one of his friends said. "Don't ever come to PEI and complain about coaching in the NHL, because we really don't want to listen to it."

So he considered himself lucky after a 6-1 hammering by the Sabres and while the Panthers were getting outscored, 14-4, in three straight road losses to the Whalers, Blues, and Jets. Sure, he was a lucky man, even after a 4-1 loss to the Bruins extended the winless streak to seven games. Lucky or not, he acknowledged there was a problem when the Panthers got tossed around like rag dolls on March 11 in an 8-4 loss to the Blackhawks at the United Center.

It wasn't merely a bad loss. The Panthers hardly competed and the Blackhawks took advantage of Florida's shortage in manpower by hitting and fighting them at every opportunity. Niedermayer was jumped by Jim Cummins and had his nose broken. The Panthers trailed 7-1 early in the third period and only a belated and meaningless rally made the final score semi-respectable.

MacLean recognized the problem: It was the same one, but on a larger scale, that had affected his goaltenders. The entire team was trying to do too much. Players who trusted each other during the first half of the season were trying to get the team out of a slump by doing everybody's job except their own. This was a significant problem for a team that relied on trust, and with only 15 games remaining in the season, MacLean was more concerned about righting this problem than missing the playoffs. Only a total collapse could ruin them now. But MacLean, on the verge of panic and losing sleep, thought the team was tired of hearing from him. When the game ended, he asked Murray to meet with the players.

"I thought there was a legitimate reason for the way we were playing," Murray said. "We didn't have any trust in each other. We were playing like a bunch of guys who were better than they were, and we didn't trust our partners. It was all very obvious. We didn't stick up for each other nearly enough in some physical confrontations."

Murray walked into the visitor's locker room at the United Center and closed the door.

"Boys, there are 15 games left and this team's going to make the playoffs, so let's get that off our backs." Murray told the players. "Let's not panic. You're good enough. We're too good to not make the playoffs."

The meeting was effective and timely, because their next opponent was the Rangers, who hadn't won in six home games. Rather than being a battle of the top two teams in the Atlantic Division — the Rangers entered the game leading the Panthers by seven points — it was a meeting of teams furiously digging themselves out of a hole. Although the Panthers didn't win, they outplayed the Rangers in a 3-3 tie that temporarily restored their confidence.

"Just tying it was a big deal for us," Fitzgerald said.

Three days later, the Panthers received the biggest boost of confidence they could've hoped for.

▲ ▲ ▲

Ray Sheppard had listened to the rumors around Detroit in October and knew they couldn't be true. There was no way Scotty Bowman was going to trade him or Dino Ciccarelli to any team run by Bryan Murray. No way.

Sheppard couldn't believe he had to ask for a trade. Despite establishing himself as one of the highest-scoring right wings in the NHL, he fell out of favor with the Red Wings after winning a 1995-96 salary of $1.55 million at arbitration, and dressed for only five of the Red Wings' first eight games.

"Their payroll was pretty high and they felt they could trade me and get a guy to play with Fedorov and Kozlov," Sheppard said. "The thing that bothered me was that I scored 52 goals two years before and 30 the year before in a 48-game schedule. I felt I did enough not to worry about coming to the rink to see whether or not I was dressing. Both myself and Dino Ciccarelli weren't dressing and we were saying, 'Why is this happening to us?'"

Sheppard had asked that question before. He scored 38 goals in his rookie season with Buffalo and 22 in his second season before the Sabres decided his goal scoring didn't offset his below-average skating and defensive skills. The Rangers came to the same conclusion after the 1990-91 season. The Red Wings were Sheppard's third team in two years when Murray signed him as a free agent in August 1991.

Unlike Sheppard's previous coaches, Murray asked him to concentrate only on scoring and setting up his linemates. He responded by producing 36, 32, and 52 goals in three seasons, but when Murray was fired, Sheppard's playing time decreased, and Bowman divided it among youngsters Darren McCarty and Martin Lapointe.

Having heard through his Detroit sources of Sheppard's possible availability, Murray called Red Wings Assistant General Manager Ken Holland and asked whether they'd be interested in making a trade.

"Holland told me they didn't know what they were doing," Murray said. "But I knew they weren't interested in trading with me."

That came as no surprise to Sheppard, who learned from one of the Detroit writers that Florida wanted him. Having witnessed firsthand the tension between Bowman and Murray during the 1993-94 season, he knew they'd never talk trade with each other.

"They thought Bryan was trying to get all of his boys out of Detroit and into Florida," Sheppard said.

Murray looked on with a combination of bitterness and annoyance when, on October 24, the Red Wings traded Sheppard to the San Jose Sharks in exchange for 34-year-old Igor Larionov. *A 50-goal scorer for an aging defensive center who scored four goals the year before? They never would've made that deal with me,* Murray knew.

Although Sheppard would've preferred a reunion with Murray and

MacLean in Florida, he liked the weather in San Jose and the lack of pressure on the Sharks to win the Stanley Cup. On the other hand, he didn't like playing for a team that was out of the playoff race, suffered through long losing streaks, and changed coaches early in the season from Kevin Constantine to Jim Wiley. And the atmosphere around the team wasn't right.

After losing to the Rangers on January 10 at Madison Square Garden, the Sharks skated the next morning for their game that night in New Jersey against the Devils. Some of the players couldn't understand why they were skating on the morning of their second game in two nights.

"Hey, Shep," goaded Owen Nolan, 25, the Sharks' only other reliable goal scorer. "Why don't you ask the coach why we're skating?"

Taking the bait, Sheppard skated over to Wiley.

"Some of the guys were wondering why we're skating this morning after playing last night," Sheppard said.

"Well, we're not in a situation to take mornings off," Wiley replied.

"Do you really think the team is going to be any better tonight because of the morning skate?" Sheppard asked.

"Maybe you're right," Wiley said.

Sheppard would've let it drop right there, but Nolan didn't. After the skate, he walked up to Wiley and said, "This is minor league."

Wiley responded by telling Nolan that he and Sheppard wouldn't dress for the game that night.

"Why not Shep?" Nolan asked.

"Sheppard asked me why we were skating."

"I was the one who told him to ask," Nolan volunteered.

"I already made my decision," Wiley replied. "You're not playing."

"Well, who's going to score for you?" Nolan shot back.

Sheppard wasn't sure what bothered him more, getting benched, or Nolan dragging him into the fray. What peeved him the most was Wiley telling the media that he and Nolan were benched because of their attitudes. Wiley had given him a bad rap.

He had nearly forgotten the incident a few months later, when he sat down for a conversation with Sharks Director of Hockey Operations Dean Lombardi. Sheppard, scheduled to become a free agent at the end of the season, wanted to know if he was in the Sharks' plans. Keeping him would cost San Jose a minimum of $1.55 million a year.

"He said the only way we'll trade our veteran players is if we get something really good in return," Sheppard recalled.

In mid-February, Murray had made his first of 20 phone calls to Lombardi inquiring about Sheppard's availability. The Panthers were losing, Mellanby and Barnes had stopped scoring, and Murray was more desperate for a sniper than ever because, unlike in October, he knew his team was headed to the playoffs. Kudelski was in the minors. Belanger was about to be traded to Vancouver. Murray asked Lombardi if Sheppard fit into his plans.

"I've always liked Ray," Murray said. "I don't think I've ever had a guy around the net do things like he can. We had some excellent defensive players, but it was fairly obvious to me that we needed some guys who could put the puck in the net."

Lombardi didn't bite at first, but after 19 phone calls from Murray, he came to a conclusion: Keeping Sheppard would be expensive, and the Sharks weren't going to the playoffs. If they weren't going to re-sign him, they might as well see what they could get in return.

"I'll trade Sheppard to the first team that offers a second-rounder," Lombardi told Murray.

Murray thought about it overnight and called back with a revised offer: Sheppard for a second-rounder and an exchange of fourth-rounders. Murray wasn't looking for a short-term fix; if he could get Sheppard, he knew he could sign him to a long-term deal.

When Lombardi agreed, on March 16, Murray hung up the phone overjoyed about acquiring the goal scorer he coveted without giving up a player. Sheppard was happy, too, when Wiley told him the news during a flight from San Jose to Philadelphia. The plane touched down and Sheppard rushed to a phone to call Murray.

"We're playing New Jersey tomorrow night," Murray said, knowing it wasn't necessary to tell Sheppard what his role would be or what he expected of him. Sheppard was supposed to score goals.

The shock of the trade wore off quickly for Sheppard, who knew he was going to a team where the coach and general manager had confidence in him. The transition was tougher for his wife, Lucie, and daughter, Lindsay, who were getting adjusted to San Jose after leaving Detroit, and now had to move and change schools for the second time in five months.

Sheppard arrived in Fort Lauderdale later that day and checked into a hotel. The room would be his home for longer than he could have ever expected.

▲ ▲ ▲

Murray looked like a genius the next night when Sheppard had an assist and Martin Straka, the little Czech winger he acquired on waivers, scored a goal and an assist in a 3-0 win over the Devils that broke the nine-game winless streak. Vanbiesbrouck returned to top form with 33 saves, by far his best performance in two months. Sheppard already felt good about his new situation. He was playing on a line with Niedermayer and former Wings teammate Garpenlov, the hottest scorer on the team until Sheppard arrived.

The victory over the Devils came at an unlikely time. The Panthers hadn't won since beating New Jersey on February 21, while the Devils were unbeaten in 10. A 5-2 victory over the Senators two nights later improved the Panthers to 37-24-9 and assured them of their first .500 finish. Sheppard just about single-handedly beat the Islanders in the next game, scoring all three goals in a 3-2 victory.

The Panthers were confident and finally looking like a playoff team, unaware that more bad times were around the corner: Another four-game losing streak before eking out a win over the Whalers. Montreal was challenging them for fourth place in the Eastern Conference and the Panthers, who six weeks earlier were fighting for first place, were in danger of not getting home ice in the opening round of the playoffs.

"The team was working hard, but they weren't really confident in what the outcome was going to be," Sheppard said. "They weren't sure they could get the big goal when they needed it, or make the big defensive play. When you go through a situation like that as a team, you sort of look around and somebody's got to really come up big. But there were no results, and that wears on a team."

The Panthers tried everything. They skipped a practice and discussed their problems. Then they blew a 2-0 lead in the third period and lost to the Senators, 3-2, in their lowest point of the season. Worse, even, than the Chicago game.

On a night of indignities, the Panthers managed only six shots over the final two periods, allowed a shorthanded goal to tie the game, and then watched, almost in resignation, as Straka missed a penalty shot with 9.6 seconds remaining.

"I don't know what to think," said Vanbiesbrouck, whose strong performances were going unrewarded.

"There's no excuse for a performance like that," MacLean said.

The short bus trip after the game from Ottawa to Montreal was an ordeal for everyone on board, even for the driver, who had to keep his eyes focused on the road while MacLean spewed out one expletive after another. Nobody else dared say a word, and the players were as upset as their coach.

As turning points of the season go, this one was disguised. The Panthers played well against Montreal, but lost, 2-1, and finished the night only two points ahead of the red-hot Bruins for seventh place in the conference. The Panthers and Rangers met two nights later at Madison Square Garden — by this time, neither team was worried about first place — and put on one of the worst defensive displays of the season. On this strange night, defen-

217

sive forward Fitzgerald contributed in another way, with two goals, and the Panthers escaped with a 5-3 win.

With so much going wrong, the Panthers took the good with the bad. They clinched their first playoff berth on April 10, despite losing to the Lightning, 2-1, at home. The Devils' loss to the Flyers put the Panthers into the playoffs and, although no one celebrated, several players smiled.

"It was a relief," Laus said. "We went two years and missed the playoffs by one point, and now we finally had a couple of games at the end to relax, not having to go into the last game and not worrying about whether we were going to make it."

The Panthers couldn't help but look at the bad side: They should've clinched the playoff spot much earlier after their great start, instead of waiting for the 80th game to do it in a loss. Home-ice advantage in the first round still wasn't assured. Making the playoffs was a worthy accomplishment, considering what the experts said about them at the start of the season, but this wasn't the most impressive way of achieving their goal.

"Kind of cheesy," Niedermayer quipped.

▲ ▲ ▲

Torrey's prediction at the World Junior Championships was correct: The arena deal did get done. Huizenga's challenge prodded the politicians into action and, for three months, the Panthers were a big story on and off the ice. An arena was going to be built in Sunrise, a western suburb of Broward County, for the 1998-99 season, and the Panthers would remain in South Florida.

Who saved the team? Was it Huizenga, who never received the $70 million offer to buy the team he might or might not have been looking for during January and February and ended up keeping the Panthers?

Or was it one of the politicians: John Rodstrom, the Broward County Commission Chairman who joined Torrey and Jordan for a tour of the Fleet Center in Boston during the All-Star break and backed the plan when it was still the politically incorrect move; or Fort Lauderdale City Manager George Hanbury and Sunrise City Manager Pat Salerno, who kept insisting that not only was it reasonable to build an arena, but that it should go in their cities; or County Administrator Jack Osterholt, who asserted the arena would be profitable to the County.

Maybe it was NHL Commissioner Gary Bettman, who patiently explained to the most skeptical County Commissioners how other cities were publicly financing arenas, and enticed them with promises to play the All-Star Game and hold the draft in Broward.

The task was overwhelming: building a $212 million arena without raising local taxes and somehow guaranteeing that the arena would remain state-of-the-art in 30 years, when the mortgage was paid off. At first a possibility, it then became reality. Suddenly, Huizenga was no longer a villain. The NHL governors and the politicians wanted him to retain ownership of the team.

How did all this happen?

Let's take the romantic view. In one scenario, the Panthers play down to expectations and win only 10 of their first 40 games. They're in last place in the Atlantic Division and Miami Arena is half-empty on game nights. The players are unpopular. They're a bunch of surly, whining, overpaid brats, who never acknowledge their fans and never take the time to sign an autograph. Nor do they acknowledge each other's efforts. It's a "me first" team that takes off nights and excuses its bad performances. Season ticket holders, who feel they've been ripped off, litter the ice with cups and paper after each loss.

Huizenga announces he's moving the team. The public advises him, "Don't let the door hit you on the way out."

But in the scenario that plays out, the Panthers surprise everyone. They're 25-8-2 at the Christmas break and sports fans who stayed away all season, in protest of Huizenga's threat to move the team, can't resist the urge to see them play. The players are hard working, supportive of each other, and underpaid compared to most major league athletes, even in the NHL. Fans who wait outside Miami Arena late at night after games are always rewarded with autographs and a few kind words. And then there's the rat craze. Each rat that's thrown onto the ice seems to represent a vote for keeping the Panthers in South Florida.

One day in February, Huizenga invites the players to his house in Stuart, Florida, for a team golf tournament. The players are personable. He enjoys being around them. His wife, Marti, becomes one of their biggest fans and most avid rat throwers.

"There's no question that it's much easier to fall in love with a beautiful girl than with an ugly girl, and this is a beautiful team," Torrey said. "This team is an easy team to like. It's a snowball effect. It's much easier to do things as this snowball started to gather momentum. The politicians read the paper and see how much media we're getting. People are saying, 'We can't lose the Panthers.'"

So the politically correct move of not building an arena for a multi-millionaire becomes the politically correct move of building an arena to house this beloved team. Huizenga, who never wanted to sell the Panthers in the first place, happily discovers that nobody's willing to make a serious offer and he might have to end up keeping them.

On March 12, the NHL announces that the Panthers will stay in South

Florida and play in Broward County. Huizenga, aware of his promise to sell the team, rejects a serious offer from Dallas businessman John Spano, and announces he's taking the Panthers public. Fans will be able to buy stock in the team. In April, the Broward County Commissioners, comically wary of the political dangers of choosing an arena site, decide they want Huizenga and the NHL to make the decision. Huizenga chooses a site in Sunrise, near one of the biggest malls in North America.

Finally, on April 23, the County Commission votes in favor of the hotel tax, but only after Huizenga agrees to cover any shortfall in revenue and assures taxpayers they'll never spend a dime on the arena.

What was improbable five months earlier becomes reality. The team is saved. Huizenga has his arena.

"I like the Panthers and I'm glad we made the decision to bring them here, but there've been lots of tough times along the way," Huizenga said. "This thing will probably never make much money, or any money, but that's OK. We've done this for South Florida, and if we sold our interest tomorrow, I'd still go to all the games and have fun, and we'd have the pride of saying, 'Hey, we did this for South Florida.' And we've taken a lot of shit along the way."

▲ ▲ ▲

After tying the Islanders, 1-1, the Panthers entered their final game with seven losses in their previous 10 games and short on confidence. Although the defense had improved and Vanbiesbrouck was on top of his game, the Panthers weren't winning. Another loss to the Rangers and they'd finish fifth in the Eastern Conference and open the playoffs on the road.

"Hockey gets harder down the stretch," Lindsay said. "We were sort of locked into a playoff spot, we needed a few points to secure home ice, and it came down to the last game. But when you get to that situation, teams are just dying to get into the playoffs and fighting every game, and maybe we were in a laid back position compared to other teams. We ran into some hockey clubs more desperate than we were."

Other factors contributed to the Panthers' second-half slump. In a 3-2 loss to the Penguins on March 28, the Panthers sat back rather than pressuring Pittsburgh, as if they were scared to death of what Jaromir Jagr and Mario Lemieux might do to them. The Penguins, whose defensive unit was among the worst in the League, pressured the Panthers into numerous turnovers.

Murphy, their steadiest defenseman for three seasons, had been making rookie mistakes since coming back from a sprained ankle. Then he broke his foot against the Rangers on April 8. Mellanby stopped scoring. Barnes got hurt. When Murray and MacLean said they wanted the Panthers to be more aggressive offensively, they didn't mean for them to dangerously mishandle the puck in traffic and make ill-advised passes that resulted in odd-man rushes the other way.

Most damaging of all, the referees stopped enforcing the new obstruction rules. Despite NHL Vice-President Brian Burke's protests to the contrary, players were getting away with the same interference away from the puck that they had been in previous seasons, and it affected the Panthers' forechecking.

"We rely on speed," Murray said. "We don't get a lot of scoring chances, so when you're held up on a scoring chance, it affects you. Our guys had to work harder when the bigger defensemen on some teams were able to put a stick on our guys, and put their arms around us."

Yet, MacLean saw reason for optimism. Despite Murphy's absence, the Panthers were relatively healthy and had allowed an average of under 2.3 goals in their last 14 games. The Panthers got blown out of games during the losing streak in late February and early March. At least now they were losing games they could've won.

"The confidence came on late in the season," MacLean said. "We played real solid. We didn't win, but Johnny was on top of his game, and defensively we were on top of our game, and in the playoffs there's less scoring. So we knew we'd be tough to beat."

But not as tough without home-ice advantage in the first round, and not so confident if they had to face the reality of finishing fifth after being in first place in February. All of the intangibles were at stake in the final game of the season against the Rangers. The playoffs were starting one game early for the Panthers.

And, suddenly, as if somebody had clicked a switch, the Panthers turned in one of their best games of the season. They came out hitting and forechecking and ran the Rangers out of the Arena. In front of a roaring mid-afternoon crowd, the Panthers took a 4-0 lead on goals by Sheppard, Niedermayer, Mellanby, and Garpenlov, got key saves from Vanbiesbrouck in the first period, and won, 5-1.

"We got that can't-lose feeling back," Lindsay said.

After all the losing they had gone through over the past two months, one game got the Panthers ready for the playoffs. They finished 41-31-10 and in fourth place in the Eastern Conference and, with their confidence restored, prepared to open the playoffs at home three nights later against the Boston Bruins.

They hoped confidence and home ice would be enough. For all the talk about the Panthers' aggressive forechecking style, their leading scorer, Scott Mellanby, had only 70 points, 91 fewer than Mario Lemieux, while the rest of the scoring was spread out among Niedermayer, Sheppard, Svehla, Garpenlov, and Barnes. The defense was generating more offense than it had the past two seasons, thanks mostly to Svehla, but Murphy was going to miss the first two weeks of the playoffs ... if the Panthers lasted that long.

For decades, teams had won the Stanley Cup by combining a great center, a great defenseman, and a great goaltender, with a good supporting cast. All the Panthers had was the goaltender, Vanbiesbrouck, and the supporting cast. Despite their optimism, it didn't look like the Panthers had any chance at all.

CHAPTER 12

The Ultimate
Warriors

John Vanbiesbrouck, the man with the bad reputation, finally had the chance to change his image. Not since 1986, when he carried the Rangers to the semifinals, had he been given the opportunity of being the No. 1 goaltender for a playoff team, but his heroics of that year were long forgotten. Vanbiesbrouck had the rap sheet of a man who couldn't get the job done in the clutch.

Many people had contributed to the bad rap. Phil Esposito, for one. When the Lightning general manager was running the Rangers in 1986, he traded for Bob Froese, the runner-up to Vanbiesbrouck in the previous season's Vezina Trophy balloting, because he didn't think Vanbiesbrouck could get the job done. Bob Clarke, the Flyers' general manager at the time, feared Vanbiesbrouck more than any other Ranger, and laughed after making the deal.

In 1989, Esposito kept Vanbiesbrouck out of the lineup for Game 4 of the first round and Mike Richter became the first goaltender to make his NHL debut in the playoffs. Vanbiesbrouck was humiliated, and he might have been run out of New York altogether if Esposito hadn't been fired after that disastrous season.

Neil Smith, the Rangers' next general manager, contributed to the reputation, too. In 1993, Smith decided that Richter was the goalie who would lead the Rangers to their first Stanley Cup since 1940, and exposed Vanbiesbrouck in the expansion draft.

Even Bryan Murray and Bill Torrey played a role in the damaging of Vanbiesbrouck's reputation. After all, they were the ones who took the whispers about Vanbiesbrouck and turned them into shouts during the previous season's salary arbitration hearing: VANBIESBROUCK ONLY HAS 13 CAREER PLAYOFF WINS! HE DIDN'T DO THE JOB DOWN THE STRETCH!

223

Part of the problem, as Vanbiesbrouck would've liked to point out, was that he shared the workload in New York for sub-par teams. Nonetheless, Vanbiesbrouck had contributed to his reputation, too, with erratic playoff performances. As Bryan Murray said, "There's never any assurance until a guy does it."

"Mark Messier once said to us in New York that the playoffs is when we all start over and everything goes back to zero," Vanbiesbrouck said. "I don't take this game personally. It's a team game and we're all responsible for the result. I try not to put too much pressure on myself."

Back to zero. That sounded fine with Vanbiesbrouck, whose strong play over the final three weeks of the season went unrewarded with two wins, seven losses, and one tie. In most of those games, he was the only player saving the Panthers from one-sided losses, but now he had reached the stage where valiant defeats weren't going to be good enough. He had to win: For his team, and for himself.

Vanbiesbrouck once called the playoffs the chance to be the ultimate warrior. Now here he was at the ultimate point in his career: Put up or shut up. Erase the reputation or live with it. The Panthers coaches and players had faith in Vanbiesbrouck because, unlike the two previous seasons, he played well down the stretch.

"The way Johnny finished the year, the way he came around in February, you had to be confident," goaltending coach Bill Smith said. "He gave you no reason to be anything but confident."

Vanbiesbrouck was in a groove, as sharp as he'd ever been, and if he could just keep playing like this for two months, he could become the ultimate warrior. He didn't want to prove anything to anybody. He just wanted to do his job and help. He didn't have to be the reason his team won; he didn't want to be the reason they lost.

"You never say, 'I showed you,' because the problem with 'I showed you' is that it ends right there, as soon as you showed them," Vanbiesbrouck said. "I'm aching to get back in there, but the emphasis is not just on getting there. We feel we can compete with every team in there, and let the chips fall."

▲ ▲ ▲

A proud history had made the Boston Bruins seem far more imposing than they really were. They reached the playoffs in 28 consecutive seasons and the finals seven of those times, winning twice. But stingy ownership, along with poor drafting, had reduced the Bruins to a team content with merely playing in the post-season.

Even that modest goal was in doubt in mid-January, when the Bruins were 16-16-2 and in danger of not making the playoffs. Then, within two weeks, General Manager Harry Sinden pulled off two season-turning deals. Goaltender Bill Ranford, reacquired from Edmonton, had beaten the Bruins in the 1990 finals and was considered one of the best goalies in the League. Two weeks after getting Ranford, ailing, aging power forward Rick Tocchet was acquired from the Los Angeles Kings in an apparently innocuous trade for ailing, aging power forward Kevin Stevens. At the time, it seemed like a typical recent Sinden deal, trading strength for strength, weakness for weakness, and merely treading water when all was said and done.

But Tocchet was reincarnated when he pulled on the black, gold, and white uniform, and the Bruins, led by Ranford and the spectacular 30-minutes-a-night play of future Hall of Fame defenseman Ray Bourque, went 13-3-3 in their final 19 games and surged to finish fifth overall in the Eastern Conference.

On the surface, this matchup was everything the Panthers didn't want. They were a third-year team that skidded into the playoffs, taking on a traditional power stocked with a great player, Bourque, a great goaltender, Ranford, and one of the League's finest, yet overlooked, playmakers, Adam Oates, who had 25 goals and 67 assists.

In reality, the matchup was everything the Panthers could have asked for, a puzzle they could solve. The Bruins' best players, Bourque and Oates, were setup men with no one to set up except Tocchet, and their most reliable goal scorer, Cam Neely, would never play another game because of hip and knee injuries.

Even if the Panthers didn't have the two or three best players, they were the better team and, with that in mind, the coaching staff designed its game plan: The Panthers' forwards would hound Bourque in the offensive zone by dumping the puck into the corners and hitting him hard when he retrieved the puck; their checking efforts would concentrate on the Oates line. After examining videotapes, Ruff, Ramsay, and Smith made presentations to the players on the Bruins' offense, defense, special teams, and goaltending. Their conclusion: Our four lines can beat their one line, as long as our goaltender can match their goaltender.

"We felt we should've been the favorite against them," Doug MacLean said. "Even though they were playing really well, we felt like we were the favorite going into the series."

With Brian Skrudland out of Game 1 with an injured hip, MacLean needed another checking center to watch over Oates. The day before the series started, MacLean called over Tom Fitzgerald, Bill Lindsay, and Jody Hull, and gave them their assignment.

"You guys are the checking line," MacLean said. "You guys have Oates. He's your responsibility."

Gulp! Playing against the Bruins, his hometown team, was pressure enough for Fitzgerald, who as the center shouldered much of the responsibility for stopping Oates.

"I knew I had a huge job to do," Fitzgerald said. "If we wanted to be successful, we needed our goal scorers to score, we needed our checkers to check against their top line, and now I knew what my role was. It was defined for me."

When the series started, Fitzgerald would look across the face-off circle at a center regularly among the lead leaguers in assists and who had played a major role in Tocchet's rejuvenation. He was being asked to succeed where many others had failed.

MacLean's other important line change was made in the 81st game of the regular season, when he placed Ray Sheppard at right wing on a line with center Stu Barnes and left wing Dave Lowry. This was a classic hockey line: Lowry, the checking winger with straight-ahead speed, would crash the corners and the front of the net; Barnes, the finesse playmaker, could set up Sheppard, the natural goal scorer whose office was confined to a 15-foot area around the net.

"Doug just said, 'You're going to be a line, and Ray, you know what you're supposed to do, Stu, you know what you're supposed to do, and Dave, you know what you're supposed to do,'" Sheppard recalled. "And he said, 'This could be a real good line.' The three of us just clicked so well and it carried on. Anything we touched turned into a scoring chance."

With a first line of Johan Garpenlov, Rob Niedermayer, and Scott Mellanby, and the second line of Lowry-Barnes-Sheppard, the Panthers thought they could score goals. Robert Svehla and Terry Carkner would help cover Oates. But then there was the Ranford problem, and the Panthers wasted no time solving that one, either.

▲ ▲ ▲

Northwest First Avenue outside Miami Arena was renamed Stanley Cup Drive after the final game of the regular season, and the crowd that gathered on the barricaded street prior to the Panthers' first playoff game was in a dreaming mood. A few fans carried aluminum foil replicas of the Stanley Cup, others had their faces painted, and the general mood was, *We're here, why not dream?*

Inside, the tense playoff atmosphere wasn't anything like supposedly laid-back South Florida; it felt like Chicago Stadium. When the fans cheered through the national anthem, it sounded like Chicago Stadium. A rat was thrown onto the ice. It looked like Miami Arena. Then Michael Buffer, the most famous boxing ring announcer in the world, came out wearing a white tuxedo and virtually beat the fans over their heads with the enormity of the moment.

"Are you ready?" Buffer asked in his baritone.

The crowd cheered.

"Are you ready, Panthers fans?" Buffer asked again.

More cheers. A few boos.

"Let's get ready to RUMMM-BULLLL!" he shouted, letting the words "let's" and "rumble" lie on his lips for a few seconds. Management needn't have wasted its money on Buffer; artificially stimulating this crowd was unnecessary.

The Panthers might have been too ready. Instead of shutting down Oates and Tocchet, they allowed the first five minutes of the game to become an open skate. Oates and Tim Sweeney fired wide on open chances from the slot. Vanbiesbrouck stacked his pads to stop Tocchet after a cross-crease pass from Oates. The Bruins were swarming and the Panthers were running around, looking very much like a rookie playoff team.

"We were way too excited," Ruff said. "We're in the playoffs, so it's let's go, go, go, but we had guys gambling, guys going for it. We were so excited to be in the playoffs, we were just careless. We had some bad breakdowns."

Vanbiesbrouck kept the game scoreless in the early minutes before the Bruins started making mistakes. With 7:37 gone in the first, Barnes forced a turnover on the forecheck and passed to Sheppard, standing in the right circle, whose quick-release snap shot beat Ranford to the glove side for a 1-0 lead.

Hundreds of rats rained down from the stands, but the delay in clearing the ice didn't slow the Panthers. Mike Hough, who had been out of the lineup with a bruised thigh, stepped off the bench with rookies Radek Dvorak and Steve Washburn. Washurn's forechecking forced another turnover, then Hough skated alone into the high slot and beat Ranford with a backhander through traffic.

More rats. Another delay. The Panthers didn't care. Carkner found Lindsay with an outlet pass. Lindsay waited. Hull went to the net and deflected the shot between Ranford's legs. The Panthers had scored three goals in 1:17.

"The biggest thing was when they had a couple of breakaways and Beezer stopped them early in the game," Sheppard said. "I think that was the turning point of the series. We started playing more like we could, we weren't tentative, because we knew John Vanbiesbrouck was going to make the save. He proved it to us in the first five minutes, and when you have a goaltender making big saves for you in the playoffs, you have to do something to help him out. Then we turned it up, we started to forecheck, and we had a three-goal lead. That gave us the confidence that we could score on Ranford."

The Panthers had a 3-0 lead and Ranford no longer seemed impervious.

Watching from the Panthers' sky box, Bill Smith knew there was something wrong with the Bruins' goaltender.

"I could see he was hurting," Smith said. "I realized he wasn't moving. I didn't really know what was wrong with him, all I knew was he was hurting, because he wasn't moving the way he could move. He was doing things he normally wouldn't do. He was falling all over the place. He couldn't get out to control the puck. He just wasn't himself."

Smith's perceptions were confirmed after the game, when Ranford revealed he was playing with an injured right ankle. Smith, who had played in enough post-seasons to know the importance of not exposing an injury during the playoffs and giving the other team a mental advantage, couldn't believe Ranford's honesty.

"He should have never said anything like that," Smith said. "He should've just played and let it fall like it falls."

Although the Bruins outshot the Panthers, 45-30, in Game 1 and got back into the game on second period goals by Tocchet, a series of bad penalties and Vanbiesbrouck kept them from drawing closer. Sheppard scored his second of the night midway through the third period to restore the three-goal lead, Bourque was hit all night to the point of distraction, and the Panthers won, 6-3.

"You can't put all your eggs in one basket for the first game, but we were starting at home, our crowd was getting into it, and it's just a matter of being very focused," Vanbiesbrouck said. "You know they have Bourque and Adam Oates and Tocchet, they have a good power play, and you have to be focused on what you're doing. As a group, we were really pumped up that people didn't think we could score goals. The first period, we scored three goals, and that's a pretty good start."

More than a pretty good start: This was a sign of things to come.

▲ ▲ ▲

Garth Brooks gave the Panthers and Bruins four days off before Game 2. Usually, the playoffs are scheduled with an off day after each game. But with the country music star previously booked into Miami Arena for concerts on Thursday, Friday, and Saturday, and a basketball game on Sunday, the Panthers rested their nagging injuries and the Bruins returned to Boston.

The break took both teams out of their playoff routines. If hockey is how a player makes his living during the regular season, then it's his life during the playoffs. The two teams that reach the finals don't see their families for most of two months, because they're either at the rink practicing, traveling, playing a game, or staying in a hotel.

The Panthers allowed the playoffs to consume them. On off days before home games, they'd check into a hotel in Fort Lauderdale, eat dinner, then have a team meeting at 9:30 p.m. The following morning, they'd drive to Gold Coast for the skate, then return to the hotel for a pre-game meal and a nap before driving to Miami.

"A lot of the players had young kids and wanted to be focused," MacLean said. "The coaching staff wanted to do it and the players said they'd like to do it as well. And it worked out, because we stayed in a beautiful resort and it was great to have everybody together."

During the four-day break, the Panthers practiced, spent time with their families, and tried keeping their minds on the series. Riding the emotion of their victory in Game 1, they would've preferred playing Game 2 two nights later, but the layoff wasn't entirely unwelcome. Several players had been banged up in Game 1 and Skrudland, his hip recovered, could assist Fitzgerald with the chore of stopping Oates.

The Bruins, unsure whether the layoff helped or hurt them, knew they'd have to play better and offer Bourque more protection. But they'd have to do it without Ranford, whose injured ankle hadn't healed. Shortly before the start of Game 2, the Bruins announced that Craig Billington, who had appeared in three playoff games in his career, would replace him in goal.

Billington didn't get much help. The Bruins' idea of increasing their intensity meant skating out of position to make hits, and the Panthers made them pay.

With 6:15 gone in the first period, Jovanovski stepped into the high slot off a turnover, took a pass from Sheppard, and whistled the puck past Billington for a 1-0 lead. Paul Laus stood up to Bruins tough guy Dean Chynoweth in a fight midway through the period, and Sheppard scored his third of the series on a power play early in the second. Bourque got the Bruins on the board with a power play goal at 7:49, but just 42 seconds later, Lowry shook off a defender and restored the Panthers' two-goal lead.

Lowry, who had 10 goals in the regular season, scored again to make it 4-1, and Vanbiesbrouck, who was even sharper than he had been in Game 1, stopped Dave Reid on a breakaway. Barnes, Sheppard, and Lowry combined for nine points in a 6-2 victory that was as decisive as the final score.

Ranford, his ankle still not 100 percent healed, returned for Game 3 two nights later at the Fleet Center in Boston. The fans stayed away; nearly 5,000 seats went unoccupied, and those who showed up were in an ugly mood, especially after Hull scored only 30 seconds into the game. Hull added another, Vanbiesbrouck made 40 saves, and the fans littered the ice with garbage in the third period of a 4-2 Panthers win that gave them a commanding three games to none lead.

The Bruins avoided the sweep by winning Game 4, 6-2, the following night. Vanbiesbrouck was pulled after the second period, MacLean was ejected for arguing a line change with referee Andy Van Hellemond, and Oates scored his only two goals of the series. The Panthers played as if they expected the Bruins to go down easily.

They didn't, setting up a Game 5 to remember at Miami Arena.

The Panthers came out hitting, Skrudland scored three minutes into the game, Laus beat Ranford on a 60-footer five minutes later, and the Saturday afternoon crowd was sensing an easy victory. But Ted Donato cut the lead to 2-1 before the period ended and Jozef Stumpel scored on a redirected shot midway through the second to tie the game.

"It became a battle then," Lindsay said. "Everybody was fighting for everything."

Lowry's third goal of the series restored the Panthers' lead, but when Sandy Moger scored a power play goal with 8:31 remaining in the third period, the game was tied and the series hung in the balance.

"There wasn't any sense of panic," Skrudland said later.

Oh no? On the bench, MacLean was trying to keep one nagging, negative thought out of his mind: *If we don't score the next goal, then the Bruins take the series back to Boston with a chance to even it up and force a Game 7.*

▲ ▲ ▲

Oates won the offensive zone face-off from Fitzgerald, and Lindsay had just about made it to his man at the left point. Out of the corner of his eye, he saw Hull sliding to block a shot by Dean Chynoweth, and then the puck was going the other way, bouncing toward center ice. Lindsay put his head down, trying to move as fast as he could, hoping to beat the defenseman.

Within an instant, the puck was on his stick, there was daylight ahead, but the defenseman to his left was just one step behind.

It's Bourque, Lindsay realized. *Just keep going!*

Hull, behind the play after getting tripped by Chynoweth, felt a surge of energy because he knew there was a chance. He saw Lindsay driving down the right wing. *But who's the defenseman?*

Now Lindsay realized he had the advantage, because Bourque was coming across, trying to keep him to the outside, and would have to pivot. So he turned back to the inside, toward the net, and Bourque couldn't get turned around fast enough. Bourque was beaten and Lindsay had a path to the net.

Yeah! Just put it in the net, Billy, Hull thought as he rushed back to join the play. *Just put it in the net!*

But Lindsay had to keep his balance after making the turn, and Bourque was still on his tail. Everything was happening so quickly that he had no time to think. Ranford squared for the play and got ready to make his move as Lindsay skated into the slot.

I'm going to score! I'm going to score! Lindsay thought. *But now what am I going to do?*

Ranford slid across. Lindsay tried to bring the puck back, but was falling as Bourque desperately slashed at his right ankle. He was in mid-air, the puck was right in front of him, and as the ice approached, he reached out and flicked the puck toward the net. Ranford, whose eyes were focused on the puck, had started going down, and his pads were slightly separated. Lindsay, sliding past the net, didn't see what happened next: the puck bouncing off of Ranford's right pad, through the opening between his legs, and into the net.

Lindsay heard nothing, then a sudden roar, so he looked back and saw the puck in the net. The red light was on and rats were pouring down, hundreds of them, it seemed like thousands! Pure excitement and joy washed over him, at the same time stunned disbelief. He looked again. Ranford was still down. The puck was still in the net. *For real!* Now his teammates were coming at him. As Hull arrived, he wanted to scream, "You just beat Ray Bourque!" and remind Lindsay of the 1993 playoffs, when the Bruins and Sabres were in overtime, and Brad May beat Bourque one-on-one to win the series. He'd save that for later.

Lindsay skated back to the bench and looked up at the clock.

There was 4:57 remaining and the Panthers had a 4-3 lead.

We can win this game, Lindsay thought. *We can really win this game.*

But that final 4:57 would last an eternity. Lindsay kept looking up at the clock, trying to will it to go faster. *C'mon, go down, go down*, he kept saying to himself. Finally, it did. Reality hit at the buzzer. The Panthers had won the game, 4-3, and the series, four games to one. And Bill Lindsay, who three years ago wondered if he could make an expansion team, was a hero.

"It was a dream goal," Lindsay said. "It'll probably be the biggest goal I ever score. Maybe there'll be a bigger one, but I don't know if there'll ever be one on a play like that. Sometimes you get a big goal and it's a rebound you put in, maybe something not so spectacular. This was one of those once in a lifetime things."

A bright, white smile that seemed to blend in with his fair skin and boyish blond hair took over Lindsay's face. This kid from Big Fork, Montana, who in the previous six seasons had played in only one playoff series, in the Western Hockey League, kept reviewing the goal in his mind and thinking about everything that could have gone wrong.

I beat Bourque, one of the greatest defensemen of all time, but what if it was a different defenseman, maybe one that hadn't been out there for 35 minutes. Wasn't I just lucky? And how about Ranford? What if he had had his head up and realized I was falling? Then he could've come at me with a poke-check. I had my head down, after all, and there was nothing I could've done about it.

But every replay ended the same way, with the puck in the net and the crowd screaming so loud the noise still rung in his ears. Then Hull walked over and together they recalled the Brad May goal.

"I didn't want to bring it up, but I remembered when Brad May put that old May Day move on him and scored," Hull said. "Ray's a great player and he's been a great player, but the guy plays 40 minutes a game. He's going to give up a bad one here and there."

Bourque's latest famous miscue couldn't have come at a better time. Lindsay looked around the locker room at his joyous teammates, realizing he was part of the reason for their delight, and that, this time, everything had gone his way. After replaying the goal again, he came to the most logical conclusion: "I wouldn't have cared if it had deflected off my bum and went in!" he said.

Lindsay still hadn't come down from his natural high when the team gathered for dinner in a private room at Gatsby's, a local restaurant. By then, he didn't have to replay the goal in his mind because it was being shown over and over again on the local news. Later that night, he drove home and went to bed, but every time he closed his eyes, he kept thinking about the biggest moment of his career. Sleep wouldn't come for hours.

▲ ▲ ▲

Having caused their minor annoyance, the Panthers were expected to go quietly. The Philadelphia Flyers, their second-round opponent, were even hotter than the Bruins during the final month of the season, going 13-3 to pass the Rangers and Panthers and win the Atlantic Division. Their fans were expecting a Stanley Cup and Al Morganti, the ESPN analyst, wrote the Flyers' game plan: Four-five-six-seven, predicting them to win the first round in four games, the second round in five, and so on, right through the finals.

The Flyers had already strayed from the plan, needing six games to eliminate the pesky and overmatched Tampa Bay Lightning, the other Florida team making its playoff debut. But that didn't make the Panthers' task any less imposing: Stop the Legion of Doom.

Eric Lindros, the Flyers' 6'4", 236-pound center, was living up to the otherworldly expectations of becoming one of the most dominant and feared players in the league. Lindros, who scored a career-high 47 goals during the regular season, didn't merely hit opponents; he skated over them. And with 6'3", 226-pound John LeClair, who owns one of the hardest slapshots in the NHL, on Lindros' left and 6'2", 218-pound Mikael Renberg on his right, the Flyers had an offensive steamroller of almost mythical proportions.

Tale of the tape: the Legion of Doom had nearly 100 pounds on either of the Panthers' checking lines. Determined and nasty, Lindros planned on carrying the Flyers to the finals and nothing was going to stop him.

Yet, the Panthers weren't buying into projections of a series mismatch.

"We felt really good," MacLean said. "We played them even all year, and we played well against them even the game we lost. We didn't know we were going to win it, but we felt that we had a chance."

The Panthers thought they had the edge in goaltending, with Vanbiesbrouck over the occasionally shaky Ron Hextall, and saw no reason they couldn't shut down the Flyers' scorers.

"I thought our defense was better, but I thought they had more firepower up front, so that gave us the nod in two of the three categories," Ruff said. "We're one of the best defensive teams in the league. Why can't we shut down Lindros, LeClair, Renberg, Hawerchuk, and Brind'Amour? We relied on four lines against any line in the League."

The assignments were clear.

Svehla and Carkner: Handle the Legion of Doom.

The checking lines: Play better against Lindros and LeClair than you did against Oates and Tocchet.

Niedermayer: Score some goals.

Vanbiesbrouck: Have the series of your life.

"We were confident in what we were capable of doing," Barnes said. "We were just confident that we had a good team and with a conscious effort from everybody, we could win."

But in this David vs. Goliath matchup, there was no questioning which team played which part. The Flyers were the best team in the conference and, to others, the idea of the Panthers stopping them was ludicrous.

▲ ▲ ▲

For once, Vanbiesbrouck wasn't needed. The sellout crowd of 17,380 was so quiet that for most of Game 1, the only sound in the Spectrum was the constant whirring of the air conditioner and the fans sighing in disbelief. Or boredom. Plenty of nothing happened for 60 minutes, and that was fine with the Panthers. Their game plan of preventing second and third chances was stunningly effective. The Flyers had only 18 first chances.

"I don't think anybody did enough to deserve to win that game," said Flyers' Coach Terry Murray, perhaps trying to will away the result.

Every time the Flyers tried dumping the puck into the Panthers' end, Svehla or Carkner or Fitzgerald or Skrudland would prevent Lindros or LeClair or Renberg from getting to the corner. Lindros didn't have a shot on goal, LeClair only one. The Panthers took only 15 shots in a 2-0 victory that was delightfully perfect and boring. The fans finally woke up at the end of the game and booed the home team. The Panthers, who hadn't lost at the Spectrum in over two years, won Game 1 in the easiest way possible.

Lindros planned on showing up two nights later.

▲ ▲ ▲

Doug MacLean couldn't take credit for starting the titanic rivalry of the 1996 playoffs. The game plan going into the series was for Carkner and Svehla to handle the Legion of Doom, and hope the other defensive pairs could take up the slack. Ed Jovanovski vs. Eric Lindros wasn't premeditated. It just happened.

MacLean didn't have the luxury of deciding whether a rookie like Jovanovski could stay with Lindros for an entire series; the Legion of Doom was on the ice too often for the Panthers to counter with only Carkner and Svehla. Besides, Jovanovski had made his NHL debut against the Flyers in November and didn't back down from a crushing Lindros check.

"It wasn't a thing we wanted right off the bat," Ruff said. "We had relied on Carkner and Svehla to play against the other teams' top lines, and that's what we were going with, but we had to come up with another pair to play against their big line. Eddie got out there, made a couple of key hits, and the emotion spilled over. Something natural was born for us."

Stopping Lindros in Game 2 turned out to be hazardous duty. Eric the Dread was playing with a chip on his shoulder, and he was taking it out on the Panthers.

Jovanovski struck first in the second period by smearing Lindros into the boards just inside the defensive blue line, then going into the corner and shouldering Lindros into a heap. Lindros rose and went face-to-face with Jovanovski.

"Hit me, hit me," Jovanovski challenged.

"You'll hear me coming," Lindros promised.

The Flyers played a lackluster first period and trailed, 1-0, on a goal by Sheppard, but Lindros used his body and stick to turn the game around. Lindros cut Barnes above the eye with a high stick and slashed Hull in the mid-section, breaking his rib. Laus took a stick to the helmet and Lindros sent Jovanovski limping to the bench with a two-handed slash beneath the knee. In the third period, Lindros looked like he was trying to decapitate Jovanovski with a high elbow.

The Panthers looked on in disbelief as referee Mark Faucette whistled Lindros for only two minor penalties. It didn't seem fair when, with the game tied, 2-2, midway through the third period, Lindros scored the game-winner.

"We were all frustrated, from management to coaching staff to players," Mellanby said. "We're working hard, and sometimes there's a perception that there are different sets of rules for different players. We thought he should've been out of the game by the time he scored the game-winning goal."

After being outshot, 47-26, and playing as undisciplined a game as they had in the playoffs, the bruised, cut, and battered Panthers considered their problem: Lindros was big and tough enough, but if he was allowed to get away with murder, stopping him or the Flyers would be impossible. MacLean and Murray complained to Supervisor of Officials Bryan Lewis, and later to NHL Vice-President Brian Burke, but Lindros got off without even a warning. Flyers General Manager Bob Clarke, who had helped build the Panthers and now wanted to ensure their elimination, ridiculed Murray for complaining, calling Lindros' actions typical for the playoffs. But the Panthers' protest achieved its intention: The refs would call a much tighter series the rest of the way.

"Eric's a physical force," Murray said. "He's a strong, great player, but we had four guys cut in that game and no penalties were called. That bothered me. Eric Lindros is going to be a physical force and if he plays within the rules, there's nothing you can do about it. We just felt he didn't."

Lindros was now Panthers Enemy No. 1 and the fans who packed Miami Arena for Game 3 came prepared to boo. Some of them held banners berating Lindros' tactics and a Lindros doll was hung in effigy over the balcony railing. "LINDROS KING OF CHEAP SHOTS" read one banner and another tried a play on his name: Lose-Idiot-Nasty-Dirty-Rotten-Obnoxious-Stinks. Fans threw plastic rats at him during the national anthem and chanted "Lindros Sucks!" all through the game.

Gord Murphy's return to the lineup was the only bright spot for the Panthers, who came out flat and were outshot, 17-2, in the first period. Lindros, aware of League scrutiny, kept his stick down and scored the game-winner late in the first period. The fans threw more rats and a bottle. With time expiring on the Flyers' 3-2 victory, Lindros wound up to fire a shot toward the empty Panthers' net. Mellanby grabbed his stick. Jovanovski skated by and punched Lindros in the face, inciting a minor riot. Lindros and Jovanovski exchanged punches. Vanbiesbrouck and Hextall met at center ice.

By that time, most of the crowd was gone, and the Panthers' chances looked grim.

▲ ▲ ▲

Mellanby was playing with a broken bone in his right hand and didn't even know it. He thought it was merely a sprain.

He had suffered the injury a few weeks prior to the end of the regular season, in a 3-0 loss to the Rangers at Madison Square Garden, when he crashed into Ulf Samuelsson in front of the net. Mellanby felt the problem right away, as his hand bent backwards into Samuelsson and a bone popped, but the injury wasn't serious enough to keep him out of the lineup.

Although Mellanby scored three goals in the final nine regular season games, the injury didn't heal on its own. By the time the playoffs started, the pain limited him to the point where he lost speed on his shots and sometimes didn't want to shoot at all. That might not have been a major problem if Mellanby was a checking forward, but he wasn't. He was the Panthers' leading scorer during the regular season, and now he had scored only one goal in the Boston series and managed only one shot in the first three games against the Flyers.

That's when Mellanby decided to find out the truth about his "sprained" hand and discovered that it was actually a small chip fracture. So Mellanby now had a bad right hand to go along with his bad left hand and forearm.

"Sometimes I just wasn't shooting because of a mental block," Mellanby said. "Your body shuts it down and you don't have the ability to shoot. It's frustrating, because I was counted upon during the season to score."

In keeping with playoff tradition — never give the other team an edge by revealing your injuries — Mellanby kept his injury under wraps, and under ice, until after the playoffs, when he underwent surgery. He wasn't the only Panther keeping a secret.

Lindros' slash had cracked Hull's rib in Game 2. Fitzgerald's back was hurting badly because of several checks-from-behind in the Boston series. Vanbiesbrouck walked around on off-days with an icepack attached to his shoulder. Just about every player suffered from some kind of nagging injury.

But creative coercion is often the only way of getting an injured player to take a day off during the playoffs. In the third period of Game 1, Ray Sheppard was flipping the puck out of the Panthers' zone when Bob Corkum of the Flyers crushed him up against the glass with a late hit. Sheppard felt the pop of his shoulder separating.

That kind of injury might have kept Sheppard out of the lineup for three weeks during the regular season, but he played and scored a goal in Game 2, and played again in Game 3, despite feeling twinges of pain. With the

Panthers trailing, two games to one, and facing their most important game of the season, Sheppard had no intention of sitting out Game 4 until MacLean reasoned with him.

"We can get through Philadelphia," MacLean told Sheppard. "Let's rest it for a game."

He was half-joking, of course, but Sheppard got the point. Beating Philadelphia wouldn't do the Panthers much good if their best goal scorer couldn't play in the Conference finals. Sheppard sat.

▲ ▲ ▲

What happened next wouldn't have been possible if not for Vanbiesbrouck. The Flyers had taken control of the series in Games 2 and 3, and Lindros, though not scoring prolifically, netted the game-winner both times. More disturbingly to the Panthers, he was dominating physically. Although the Panthers thought he was getting away with something approaching murder, they didn't want the lack of penalties called against Lindros to affect them mentally. Crying wasn't going to do them any good, especially if Lindros ran them out of the playoffs.

"We put it out of our minds," Mellanby said. "If we were so concerned about him, we weren't going to win, anyway. We said, 'This is what we have to do to win,' and we stuck to the game plan."

But the game plan wasn't working. The Panthers' perceived edge in offensive defensemen hadn't proven out. Eric Desjardins of the Flyers was the first star in Game 3, while Svehla, Murphy, and Woolley combined for one shot. The forwards were diligent in their forechecking, yet Petr Svoboda, Karl Dykhuis, and Desjardins were getting the puck to the Flyers' centers, Lindros and Dale Hawerchuk. Vanbiesbrouck had become the Panthers' only line of defense.

Not that he was the only star of Game 4 at Miami Arena. Niedermayer used his speed to score his first two goals of the playoffs early in the second period, the second on a two-man advantage, and the Panthers had a 2-0 lead. Svehla broke his nose when he fell against Lindros' skate in the first period, so Jovanovski and Laus — a rookie and a former enforcer who spent three seasons in the minors — did double-duty against the Legion of Doom. Jovanovski destroyed Lindros with a hit in the first period and kept up the pressure and the chatter all night.

Jovanovski pointed at the scoreboard to show Lindros that the score was 2-0, but that advantage couldn't last much longer, even with Vanbiesbrouck at his best.

The Flyers took 24 shots in the second period and Vanbiesbrouck stopped

Renberg, Desjardins, Joel Otto, Shjon Podein, and Lindros from close range. Renberg scored the Flyers' first goal, and Brind'Amour tied it at 17:36. The Panthers looked lost until good fortune struck with six seconds remaining. Hextall wandered from the crease, as Hextall tends to do, and Barnes deflected Laus' arcing shot into the net.

The Flyers maintained their pressure in the third period and Vanbiesbrouck kept them from tying the game. Then, with 1:07 remaining, Renberg beat Jovanovski out of the corner and scored to make it 3-3. The Flyers had out-shot the Panthers, 44-29, in regulation, and only Vanbiesbrouck prevented them from taking a three games to one lead back to Philadelphia.

"Beezer stood on his head. He was huge," Fitzgerald said. "All of a sudden, we really relied on Beezer, and we knew if he was solid, he was giving us a chance to win."

At the moment, nobody could have known that Vanbiesbrouck's performance had turned the series. Overtime would tell.

▲ ▲ ▲

Sudden death had taken on literal meaning for the Panthers, who knew no amount of perseverance, no resurfacing of character or force of will, could save them if the Flyers scored the next goal. They had been outplayed for most of three straight games and if they lost this one, their season would likely come to a painful conclusion two nights later in Philadelphia.

The crowd sensed this as overtime began. The fans were quiet, not from boredom but from being so nervous they were unable to speak or scream. Those who were superstitious went through their good luck rituals. The promenade, usually crowded when a period begins, was practically deserted. The organist played, "Let's Go Panthers!" and the fans couldn't choke out the words. On the bench, the Panthers concentrated on the immediate task, rather than the enormity of what faced them: their season.

"We were really trying to stay focused because they had tied it late," Mellanby said. "It was tough, because we thought there was a non-call on a breakaway by Niedermayer with two minutes to go. You feel there's a bad call against you, and it's tough to remain focused, but that's where our experience came in. We were just positive, trying to stick to the game plan, instead of worrying about what happened."

Others were having a hard time staying focused. Chris Moore, the Panthers' radio play-by-play man, and Denis Potvin, the color commentator, spent most of the third period telling their listeners that the Flyers' game-tying goal was inevitable and at the current rate, so was a Panthers loss. The game had turned into a sudden death watch when, with under four minutes gone, Barnes cleanly won a defensive zone face-off back to Jovanovski.

Lowry and Mellanby switched sides; Lowry skated to the right point, Mellanby to the left. Lowry looked over his shoulder and saw Jovanovski skating the puck out of the zone and gaining the red line. One stride later, Jovanovski lifted a soft dump-in behind the Flyers' net. Hextall held his ground. Kerry Huffman, the Flyers' defenseman, glided behind the net to pick up the loose puck. Mellanby and Lowry bore down hard on the forecheck and slammed into him. The puck skidded loose and ended up on Mellanby's stick. Mellanby threw the puck into the slot, hoping Barnes was skating down the middle for the pass. He wasn't. The middle was vacant and the puck kept going. Now it was on Jovanovski's stick, just inside the blue line. Suddenly, there was a play going on.

Mellanby and Huffman kept battling for position. Mellanby tried to get to the front of the net; Huffman tried to keep him from getting there. Lowry, however, was free.

Go to the net! he told himself as he skated into the mid-slot, about 15 feet from the net and to Hextall's right. He was hoping for a screen or a deflection, anything that might change the angle of the shot or block Hextall's view. They had worked on exactly this play in practice and now it was happening in a game.

But the puck wasn't there yet. Jovanovski tried to see if he had room to get his shot through to the net. Then Eric Desjardins, the Flyers' defenseman, made a critical mistake. Instead of staying with Lowry he skated a few feet toward Jovanovski to block the shot. Jovanovski, having found an opening, limited his windup.

The Flyers were in trouble. One of their defensemen was tied up behind the net; the other was going to the point. Nobody was with Lowry.

Jovanovski shot. Desjardins missed and the puck skidded past. Lowry, who had his back to the net, got a piece of the puck and Hextall didn't have a chance of reacting to the re-direction. The puck was behind him. The red light went on, but the fans didn't realize Lowry had scored. At that very instant, Huffman had rammed into the back of the cage, lifting it off its moorings. Finally, the crowd reacted. There was bedlam and a rat storm! Mellanby and Barnes were the first to get to Lowry, then Jovanovski and Woolley joined the celebration.

But Hextall was going ballistic, claiming Lowry had redirected the shot with his skate. Referee Rob Shick skated to the scorer's table and phoned the video replay judge.

Jovanovski didn't know what to think. His entire body tensed as his mind explored the possibilities. *Was the net off its moorings when the puck went in? Did Lowry redirect it with his skate?* Mellanby knew Huffman had lifted the net, but if the net came up before the puck went in, it wouldn't matter.

Schick would have to disallow the goal. Lowry skated over to Shick and asked what was happening.

"We want to see if it hit your skate or not," Shick told him.

A relieved Lowry knew it hadn't.

The longest minute in Panthers history passed as the video replay judge reviewed the goal. Finally, Shick nodded his head: the goal was good, and another celebration broke out. More rats came down, as if the Panthers had scored twice in the same overtime.

"At that point, it's just bedlam," Mellanby said. "We were just thrilled, elated that we won, and it's fun being out there when it happens. Everybody's jumping up and down and you're not thinking about much. You kind of reflect about it after."

Having escaped with a win, the Panthers could afford the luxury of looking over their shoulders at the wreckage they had avoided.

"We would've been in trouble because they were on us all game," Hough said. "They had tied it with a minute to go, and we took it back from them when we won it in overtime. They had just won the two previous games and if they won three in a row, they would've been up 3-1 going back to their building."

The series was tied, and the Panthers knew they owed their survival to Vanbiesbrouck's outstanding saves in the first three periods.

"We really took over the series from that point on," MacLean said. "Confidence is a part of it. Realizing there's a really good chance to win. Johnny was obviously on top of his game, because he was so solid positionally. He was making the tough shots looks easy."

In keeping with their history, nothing came easily to the Panthers.

▲ ▲ ▲

Lindros kept trying to take off Jovanovski's head, but Jovanovski kept coming back at him. Lindros would carry the puck through the middle of the ice and, as Jovanovski made contact, Lindros' legs would keep churning, his body fighting desperately. But the puck had been knocked off his stick, and another scoring chance had been stopped.

There were uneasy moments for the Panthers in Game 5. Laus received a five-minute major penalty for elbowing 2:27 into the first period, and the Flyers could've put the game away right there, but Svehla was incredible, stripping Lindros, LeClair, and Renberg of the puck at least four times, icing it repeatedly, and wasting time. Lindros finally scored late in the power play, but allowing only one goal was a mini-victory for the Panthers.

As the game continued, the Flyers became frustrated. They were no longer thinking about themselves, they were bothered by the Panthers' style of play. They couldn't forget that one year ago, the Devils had stopped them with a patient defensive system that forced Lindros to carry the puck through traffic in the neutral zone. Now they were facing another patient defensive system, and Lindros was no more capable of leading the charge than he had been a year earlier. The Flyers, unable to cut through the Panthers' seaweed defense, experienced one frustration after another.

"It's like playing the Devils," Desjardins said later.

The middle of the ice was never open when the Flyers gained the offensive zone, so the defensemen ended up taking as many shots as the forwards. LeClair was helpless, because Lindros couldn't get him the puck, and even when he received a pass, there was no time for him to crank up his big slapshot.

Flyers fans, impatient as ever, couldn't comprehend what they were watching. The Flyers seemed to be skating in slow motion, almost as if they weren't trying. In reality, the Panthers' forechecking was so oppressive, their backchecking pursuit so tenacious, that the Flyers didn't have room to skate.

"Bobby Clarke said to Scott Mellanby, 'Your team really knows how to play the game the way it's meant to be played,'" Vanbiesbrouck said. "I'm really confident that every player that dresses up is responsible for his own actions and, if we're not responsible, we're going to be in trouble. And that's the way our team thinks."

Conditioning and team speed had become a factor. The Flyers, who were relying too heavily on Lindros' line, were tiring, while the Panthers, who constantly churned four lines, were relatively fresh and always quicker to the puck. Vanbiesbrouck kept the game close for two periods, and Barnes tied it on a fluke goal with 2:39 gone in the third period.

In the first overtime, the Flyers were spent, the Panthers were pressuring for the winner, and Hextall had to be Philadelphia's savior. And that just couldn't last long.

▲ ▲ ▲

A little over 12 minutes remained in the second overtime and MacLean couldn't believe his team hadn't yet ended the game. Shot after shot glanced off of Hextall and the glass behind the net, but none of them found the opening the Panthers needed.

"Psychologists say you're supposed to park your negative thoughts," MacLean said. "Well, I was doing a lot of parking. I felt like a valet."

The game was far past the point where coaching had anything to do with the outcome. MacLean was just tapping players on the shoulder and sending them out for another shift, so when he finally called for his checking line, he didn't care that Lindros, LeClair, and Hawerchuk, the Flyers' top offensive players, were sitting on the opposite bench. The other three lines were tired, while Skrudland, Hull, and Hough had missed a shift.

"Let's go guys," Skrudland said to his linemates. "We're fresh. Let's finish it!"

The checking line barreled into the offensive zone at full speed as Hull dumped the puck into the corner. Skrudland went after the defenseman, Kjell Samuelsson. Hull, to the right, and Hough, to the left, stayed high in the defensive zone, hoping for Skrudland to force a turnover.

Don't give him time. Force him into making a mistake, Skrudland thought. Samuelsson had no time to waste. The puck was on his backhand and Samuelsson, realizing the best he could do was knock the puck out of the zone, tried to clear it up the left wing. Skrudland got a piece of it with his stick. Hull captured the puck in the right circle and everything was happening so quickly. He looked up and realized he had room.

Maybe I can get to the net by myself, Hull thought. But Rob DiMaio had left Hough and was charging at the puck carrier. Hull could almost see what would happen next. DiMaio had made the wrong split-second decision. Hough, left alone, was skating to the net all by himself. There was no time for DiMaio to correct his error. Samuelsson, almost in horror, knew he had to get to Hough or the game would be over.

"They had two defensemen trying to get back into the play, so I was trying to cut one of them off," Skrudland said.

Hull sent the puck toward Hough. Skrudland, tied up with Samuelsson, saw the puck bouncing and Hough standing perpendicular to the goal.

Put it in the net, end this thing now, Mike! I don't want to keep playing, rushed through Hull's mind.

Geez, thought Skrudland. *What the heck is he doing there all by himself?*

In that split second, Hough remembered the tapes he and his teammates had watched of Hextall overcommitting and going down. Like in the movies, Hextall lunged, thinking his only chance was to knock the puck off of Hough's stick. Hough protected the puck by pulling it away and taking a few steps to the left. He looked up and saw a wide open net.

Don't fall! Hough told himself. *Take your time!*

Take your time? Back on the bench, split seconds felt like hours.

"Shoot it, Mike! Shoot!" Hough's teammates pleaded. Hough couldn't hear them. There was only him and the net and nothing else.

He turned, but the puck was caught between his skates.

"Shoot it!" MacLean screamed.

Finally, Hough lifted a soft wrist shot. A desperate Hextall batted at it with his arm, but missed. The puck was in the net and Hough wasn't sure he could trust his eyes. Skrudland was charging at him with a big smile overtaking his face.

I scored! Hough realized.

For Skrudland, there was a moment of disbelief. *What just happened couldn't have happened,* but an entirely different thought was going through Hull's mind.

Thank God this is over! he said to himself.

Hough's teammates bounded over the bench and raced to him at the far boards.

I can't believe this! Skrudland thought. *We're heading home up 3-2 and now we have a chance to finish this thing off.*

Hough was happily crushed in the middle of a celebration like none he had ever experienced: Exhilaration mixed with exhaustion. The crowd was stunned. The Flyers made a quick exit from the rink. A few plastic rats hit the ice, then a metal folding chair. The Panthers couldn't wait to get back to their locker room to continue the celebration. There was more screaming and yelling, more patting Hough on the head.

"I called it! I called it!" half of his teammates said.

Then Hough turned to Skrudland and, remembering the captain's words of encouragement before the shift began, said, "You called it!" He really had!

The celebration continued in the locker room for about another minute, and then, as if somebody had pulled a switch, nobody said a word. The Panthers were sitting in front of their stalls, staring happily at each other but unable to talk. They were exhausted. Eighty-eight minutes and five seconds of the most intense hockey any of them had ever experienced was over and now they were too tired to enjoy the payoff.

And what a trifecta this was! Lindsay, Lowry, and Hough, who combined for 29 goals during the regular season, had scored the three biggest goals in team history: Lindsay against Boston, Lowry in Game 4, and Hough in Game 5. The greatest satisfaction came in knowing that the winner was a team effort: Skrudland forced the turnover, Hull was in the right spot on the forecheck, Hough, the checker, exercised a goal scorer's patience and looked like he did these things all the time. Which he had, of course. In his imagination, back when he was a kid and played street hockey with his friends. *Double overtime. Next goal wins. Hough shoots! He scores!*

"And I just happened to get it," Hough said. "It's something you dream about, no doubt about that, especially when you're a kid growing up. You more or less dream of it being the seventh game of the Stanley Cup, but double overtime? I'll take it any time."

Hough and his teammates, wrestling with the reality that the series wasn't over, that they were only up three games to two and would have a chance to end it two nights later in Miami, tried to control their emotions. It was an important goal they realized, but not yet the most important.

"We're in the driver's seat now," Jovanovski said.

A few hours later, the Panthers boarded a charter flight back to Florida and tried to focus on the job ahead. The Flyers were down, but certainly not out. Hadn't the Panthers been in a similar situation just three days earlier, down by a game and facing a must-win situation? Lindros certainly wasn't giving up. Just moments after the game, a dozen Philadelphia reporters pressed his back to the dressing room wall and demanded a prediction.

"We're coming back home," Lindros said. "We're going to win."

But by this time, Lindros didn't know how he planned on carrying out his promise. The Flyers had been outshot, 17-5, in overtime and were lucky the game hadn't ended sooner. Lindros' mission was clear: He would have to back the guarantee on his own.

Hundreds of fans greeted the Panthers when they arrived at Fort Lauderdale International Airport that evening. It was a heroes' welcome for a group of players who had never been heroes and sure as heck didn't want to start getting giddy now. But that wasn't going to be easy for Hough. When he walked through the door of his house in Boca Raton, his wife Tracy had been talking on the phone for two hours with people calling in their congratulations.

"The phone was ringing so much that I kept thinking, *Who's going to call next?*" Hough said. He was tired and wanted nothing more than quiet and maybe a bite to eat, but Hough's family and friends were going to make sure he felt like a star. Later that night, after the phone stopped ringing, Hough enjoyed quiet for the first time all day.

It finally happened, he thought. *I finally got the big goal.*

▲ ▲ ▲

Bill Lindsay had one more big goal in his system. Svoboda fanned on a clearing pass with the Panthers killing a penalty, and Lindsay swooped in for the turnover, then beat Hextall for a 1-0 lead with 6:06 gone in the first period of Game 6. The Flyers came out swarming in the second period, but Vanbiesbrouck sent them back to the their room without a goal.

Philadelphia's hopes were crushed when Kjell Samuelsson took a bad interference penalty in the neutral zone early in the third period and, with 2:55 gone, Niedermayer got free in front of the net and slipped the puck under a sliding Hextall.

The third goal was typical of the Panthers: Lowry making a great sliding block at the defensive blue line, Barnes speeding off with the puck, and Lowry hustling back into the play for the return pass and beating Hextall with a high shot.

Nonetheless, there were moments when the Panthers wondered if the game would end up going their way. In the second period, Fitzgerald had a clean breakaway and Hextall went for his move, but the puck slid off of Fitzgerald's stick and harmlessly into the corner.

"I'm thinking, I could've blown this series by not scoring," Fitzgerald said. "I have no goals, so if I put this one in, it's 2-0, and the way we're playing, it's a pretty good lead for us to sit on. And I missed it and all I could think was, *They're going to come down and score, and now we're going back to Philly.* So I had all negative things going through my head. But then my teammates said, 'Keep going, keep going,' and I never thought twice about it."

Vanbiesbrouck turned away the Legion of Doom for the final time with 8:13 remaining after Lindros setup LeClair on a two-on-one. As the clocked ticked down on the 4-1 win, a fan in Miami Arena held up a sign reading, "Pinch Me, I'm Dreaming!" and the Panthers wrestled with the almost unbelievable idea that they were headed to the Conference finals. They had beaten the best team in the east.

"People said we were boring," MacLean remarked as he was handed a victory cigar. "If this is boring, I like boring."

▲ ▲ ▲

Drop by Gold Coast Arena on a regular season morning and you'll find no more than three reporters attending Panthers practice. Now the Panthers had entered the big time, and the first evidence was the media horde gathered three days prior to Game 1 of the Eastern Conference finals: Two or three reporters from each of the local papers, hockey writers from *Newsday*, *The New York Times*, *The Boston Globe*, *The Toronto Star*, and the Montreal *Gazette*, ESPN, and local TV news crews who had recently declared themselves "cat crazy."

In Pittsburgh, the Penguins happily awaited the Panthers after easily disposing of the Rangers, four games to one. They were getting what they asked for.

"Who would you rather play, Philadelphia or Florida?" a reporter asked Penguins star Jaromir Jagr a few days earlier.

"Florida," Jagr replied. "I would rather play Florida because I get killed by the Flyers."

245

With those words, Jagr replaced Lindros as the enemy of Panthers fans.

MacLean entered a converted exercise room at Gold Coast and greeted the assembled media with an amused smile. Predictably, the questions were about home-ice advantage, the Miami Arena crowd, the rat craze, and, of course, Mario Lemieux and Jagr.

"Could you learn anything from the Rangers series?" MacLean was asked in reference to the Rangers' complete inability to stop Lemieux and Jagr.

"I really didn't get to see much of that series," he answered. "We really don't pay much attention to what the other teams do. We pay more attention to the team we're facing."

Another reporter asked MacLean what he thought about Mario Lemieux possibly retiring.

"Before the series?" MacLean asked, only half-hoping.

When MacLean was finished cracking jokes and not answering questions, the media moved on to the Panthers' locker room, where public relations director Greg Bouris observed the scene and cracked, "They must think they're at a Dolphins practice."

Amid this craziness, TV cameramen, acting with all the seriousness of tourists at the Louvre focusing in on Mona Lisa's smile, took turns shooting an object that sat to the right of John Vanbiesbrouck's stall: a rubber rat painted in Panthers colors. On one side of the room, Jovanovski spent 30 minutes answering questions, mostly about stopping Lemieux the way he had stopped Lindros. Skrudland took his turn shortly afterward. Reporters from the Pittsburgh press and others from the national media worked on stories that must have seemed like reruns to the Panthers players: the Mellanby rat story and its aftermath, the idea of hockey being popular in South Florida, the in-line hockey craze.

But not a single player gave short shrift to any questions, even though they had answered most of them hundreds of times before. These players who were ignored for their entire careers enjoyed being the center of attention.

Cinderella story? Forget the logic that said the Panthers had every right to be here. The Panthers gladly tried on the glass slippers and forced them to fit. Hard-working team that somehow overcame the much more talented Flyers? Forget that the Panthers were faster than Philadelphia and deeper on defense. They wanted to be the overlooked, underrated team that defied reason.

They were happy underdogs and if the media hadn't figured them out, well, that probably meant the opposition hadn't either. The local papers had picked them to lose each of the previous two playoff rounds. Flyers Coach Terry Murray huffed after Game 6, "I still think we're the better team." At that very moment, Murray was fending off the critics calling for his head, while Lindros was bunkered down in an Atlantic City casino.

The Panthers were Team Bandwagon and the hottest thing in the area since the 1972-73 Miami Dolphins went undefeated in an entire National Football League season and won their first Super Bowl.

Inside Gold Coast, the small bleachers were packed with fans watching practice. Outside, hundreds of others who either had nothing better to do, or did and simply didn't care, waited in the parking lot on a typically steamy, late-May South Florida day, holding banners, sticks, hats, and jerseys for the players to sign. They knew the players could, if they chose, make a right turn out the side door and head to their cars for an easy getaway, but day after day, the players kept taking the detour to the left.

Panthers flags, the hottest item of team merchandise in South Florida, adorned cars and vans. Traffic backed up on the road alongside Gold Coast. Grown men and women stuffed toy rats into their pockets and no one found any of this odd. Crazy really was the word. South Floridians were going nuts over a hockey team.

Before the playoffs started, Mellanby could go anywhere without being noticed. Now he'd go food shopping with his wife and spend most of the time signing autographs. Players were in demand for TV appearances, when in the past any Marlins or Dolphins player would have done just fine. MacLean was taking in the excitement, while at the same time wondering if all this was really happening. *Pinch me!*

"It's been a dream season," he said. "But one of my buddies phoned from Prince Edward Island and told me that a guy on the radio said, 'It looks like Doug is going to win the Stanley Cup. If he does, next year is going to be tough.'"

MacLean wasn't concerned about next year. This year was just too good, and the effects of the Panthers' success went beyond the fans and the media, or even the players. His father had been having one of the worst years of his life, undergoing one operation after another, and watching the Panthers on the satellite dish was like medicine.

"It was a real joy for him," said MacLean, who called his father after every game.

The Panthers' story had everything: A sick father and his son the coach; outcasts who became winners; and fans in the subtropics falling in love with an ice hockey team. It couldn't get any better, and then it did.

▲ ▲ ▲

Six days had passed since the Penguins completed their second-round destruction of the Rangers, but it would take far longer than that for anyone to forget the damage done by Lemieux and Jagr. In five games, Lemieux scored eight goals and two assists, Jagr scored seven goals and two assists, and both recorded hat tricks in a Game 5 performance that dazzled Rangers Coach Colin Campbell.

"They're the two best players in the world right now," he said.

Although the greatness of Lemieux and Jagr is unquestioned, Campbell and the Rangers made them look even better with an ill-conceived game plan. The Rangers, a team comprised mostly of old, slow defensemen and scoring forwards, arrogantly thought they could stop Lemieux and Jagr one-on-one and allowed them to skate up and down the middle at will. The Penguins, who love beating the Rangers, played a smart, patient, defensive series. At times, Lemieux looked like a checking forward.

But the Penguins, who finished second in the Eastern Conference behind the Flyers, had far more weaknesses than a team with 102 points should have. With the exception of Sergei Zubov, the brilliant Russian defenseman, the Penguins were slow and immobile on defense with Francois Leroux and Neil Wilkinson getting too much ice time. Ron Francis, one of the finest two-way forwards in League history and their best face-off man, broke his foot in the final game of the Rangers series, leaving Petr Nedved as Pittsburgh's only dependable scoring forward after Lemieux and Jagr.

A good team with two great players, the Penguins were so in love with their offensive firepower that they forechecked too aggressively, putting too much of a burden on a shaky defense. This was a shallow, impatient, poorly-coached team that could be beaten by a fast, intelligent, well-coached team with a good game plan. And the Panthers were all of that.

Bring on the trap! Not the neutral zone trap, which the Panthers had played to perfection during their first two seasons, but a trap nonetheless. It would start when a Penguins forward carried the puck across the offensive blue line, always wide because the Panthers wouldn't give him anything else. Two men would collapse on the puck carrier, one in direct coverage, the other as a backup — there's the trap — while the other players flooded the middle of the ice.

"If Jagr's going to beat us he's going to beat us on the outside, and he's not going to beat one guy and get a clear shot to the net," Ruff said. "If he beats one guy, he's going to have to beat another guy. We preached containing their star players instead of putting them through the boards. If you run at Jagr, you bounce off him, and there's a good chance he just spins off and makes a better move. So we tried to push him into traffic.

"We thought we'd get more chances against them, because they're looser and gamble more on offense, and maybe they wouldn't get back as quick as we did, so we'd get chances on three-on-two rushes. But we knew they were going to get a few more chances coming in."

The Panthers' forwards were urged to backcheck even after they were beat, because if Lemieux or Jagr pulled up or dipsy-doodled, as was their tendency, they could still be caught. Carkner and Svehla, who helped shut down Lindros late in the Flyers series, now had the assignment of stopping Lemieux and Jagr.

The Penguins' problems were compounded by their arrogance and lack of respect for opponents they considered inferior. They played hard and forechecked with only one man, putting less burden on the defensemen, against the Rangers because they wanted to beat them so badly. The Panthers were considered a minor obstacle on their road to the Stanley Cup finals for the third time in six years.

The joke was on Pittsburgh.

Game 1 in Pittsburgh was a walk ... for the Panthers. Vanbiesbrouck, who had allowed more goals to Lemieux than any other goalie in the League because he had faced Lemieux more than any other goalie, set the tone in the first period. Lemieux bore in on a breakaway and Vanbiesbrouck, remembering all the times Mario had shot the puck over his glove on breakaways, lunged to poke it off his stick. The save set the tone for the series and Lemieux's frustration.

The Penguins were permissive to the point of allowing the Panthers all the room they wanted in front of the net. The Panthers played playoff hockey; the Penguins were in the pre-season. Lemieux and Jagr became frustrated by the lack of room up the middle. Penguins Coach Ed Johnston later accused the Panthers of being too liberal with the use of their sticks and arms to restrain Lemieux and Jagr. Which they were. But, right or wrong, that type of obstruction on the puck carrier has been allowed for years, and the Panthers were merely seeing how much they could get away with.

"You have to be able to take the body on those guys and hold them for a second, so they can't jump back into the play," Fitzgerald said. "They're too strong and they'll go back to the net and tap in a rebound, or make a play some other way. Not holding and tackling the guy, but containing him, and I think we did that well. My job was against Lemieux and Brian Skrudland's job was against Jagr. And we knew if we could keep them off the board, we were going to give our team a chance to win."

Fitzgerald, a defensive forward who had scored two shorthanded goals on one penalty against the Penguins in the 1993 playoffs, and Lowry, surprisingly the Panthers' most dependable playoff scorer, each had two goals, while Lemieux and Jagr were held to nothing in a 5-1 win.

Lemieux's frustrations continued in Game 2. Late in the first period, with the Penguins on a power play, Vanbiesbrouck slid across the crease and stopped Lemieux's one-timer off a cross-ice pass from Jagr. At the other end, Tom Barrasso, the sullen Penguins goaltender who had replaced Ken Wregget after Game 1, was being tested more than Vanbiesbrouck, and turned back four odd-man rushes in the first period. If not for Barrasso, who had watched Wregget play the entire Rangers series, the Panthers might have put away the game in the first 30 minutes.

But even in a 3-2 defeat in which Lemieux and Jagr both scored, the Panthers had reason to feel good: They were the better team for five of six periods and going home with a split seemed like a fair consolation prize. The Penguins, wondering why their supposedly superior talent wasn't dominating, started looking for answers.

▲ ▲ ▲

Excuses, excuses. There were plenty of them when the series moved to Miami for Games 3 and 4.

Bad ice: With high heat and high humidity a fact of life of South Florida in May, the Penguins worried that slushy ice at Miami Arena would prevent them from playing their game. They suspected that was just the way the Panthers wanted it, and figured the Arena doors would be kept wide open on game days. To the contrary, the Panthers spent $40,000 to rent 10 giant dehumidifiers that dried the air and kept the ice in playable shape.

Too much rest: The Penguins contended they were rusty after getting so much time off after the Rangers series and another three days off between Games 2 and 3.

Boredom: Joe Lapointe wrote in *The New York Times* that a Panthers victory would hurt hockey. The Panthers, taking motivation where they could find it, posted the column on the bulletin board outside their locker room at Gold Coast Arena. Wrote Lapointe:

> The sport faces a crisis — the possibility that the Florida Panthers could take their sleep-inducing act into the finals. The Panthers are tied with Pittsburgh at one victory each, with Games 3 and 4 on the mushy slush of Miami Arena tomorrow night and Sunday afternoon.
>
> "The 'Rat's Nest' is not an easy place to play," Florida Coach Doug MacLean said. If the Panthers win four of seven games, the League should either demand a recount or amend its bylaws to extend this round to best of 9 or best of 11 or whatever it takes to get the Penguins in the finals.

The Panther style of play could devastate the television ratings of the Fox network and ESPN. Imagine the frightening possibility of the Stanley Cup presented in South Florida on a steamy night during the week of the summer solstice as fans litter the ice with plastic rats. At least real, flying octopuses are traditional. But not plastic rats. Is nothing sacred?

"It was just a depressed sports writer in New York," MacLean quipped. "He's had a tough year. Both of his teams are on the sidelines. My father said it's the best hockey he's ever seen in his life and he's been around the game 60 years."

Some of the players were angered, a few were amused, but all of them planned on using the column as motivation. If people thought they were boring, fine. They'd bore their way into the finals. If other teams worried more about what they weren't doing than what the Panthers were doing to them, fine, too.

"It became a rallying point," Mellanby said. "'Let's see what they're going to say about us in the paper about what they didn't do instead of giving us some credit. We found it amusing. When you underestimate an opponent and constantly think it's something you're not doing instead of respecting the other team, that can get you into trouble. A couple of teams we played thought just because they had some big-name talent, they should win."

Maybe that's what the Penguins were thinking in the third period of Game 3, when the Panthers' superiority was so vast that at times it seemed Barrasso was the only player on the ice wearing black and gold. The onslaught started innocently enough. Sheppard scored his seventh of the playoffs early in the first period after making Wilkinson look like he was standing still. The Penguins came back to take a 2-1 lead early in the second, but after Dvorak tied it with his first of the playoffs at 3:51, the Penguins turned stupid.

At times, the Penguins had three men behind the net chasing the puck carrier. They sent clearing passes up the middle of the ice and over-aggressively forechecked with two men. Occasionally their gambling paid off, but when Vanbiesbrouck made an incredible sliding save on Jagr with 1:15 remaining in the second period, the Penguins had made their last gasp of the night. The third period was a wipeout.

The Penguins were held without a shot for the first 16 minutes and, by that time, Barnes had scored twice and Martin Straka once to put the game away. Barrasso spent most of the period either making one outstanding save after another or hiding inside the goal to avoid the raining rats. The Panthers outshot the Penguins, 61-28, in a one-sided 5-2 victory.

"We just turned to garbage," said Bryan Smolinski of the Penguins.

"You don't expect Florida to get 60 shots," Lemieux said.

Despite the humiliating defeat, the Penguins didn't go quietly. As time expired, Dave Roche of the Penguins butt-ended Fitzgerald in the face, breaking Fitzgerald's nose. Barrasso skated to center ice and tried to spear Niedermayer. Vanbiesbrouck rushed to the defense and the two goaltenders squared off. Six players received penalties and Roche was suspended for Game 4. Two teams that never had any reason to dislike each other finally felt like they were at war, blood and all.

▲ ▲ ▲

For three seasons, the Panthers had never underestimated any opponent and took it as a fortunate fact of life that everyone else underestimated them. Although they didn't entirely buy into the Cinderella-story aspect of their play-off run, they realized they were considered underdogs because the opposition had the great players, while they had a bunch of above-average workers.

But when the Penguins barely competed in Game 3 and appeared unwilling to take the hard road to victory, the Panthers underestimated a team with two of the greatest players in the world.

"We thought they were going to lay down," Sheppard said. "Then they won the next two and suddenly we're down 3-2 and we're saying, 'We haven't played that well in the last two games. We better put in a better effort or the season's done.' We just talked to each other. We knew what we had to do to win, but we also knew we could do it, because we beat Philadelphia in six games. A lot of us thought the Flyers were the best team in the east."

The Panthers became complacent and lost their intensity, and it was nearly too late by the time they got it back.

Not that they entirely eased off in the two losses. Jagr took a beating in the first period of Game 4. Barnes caught him with an unintentional high stick and Hough shouldered Jagr into next year with an open-ice hit. The Panthers went into the third period with a 1-0 lead, on Lowry's 10th at 12:50 of the second period, and would have been ahead by more if not for Barrasso. For the first time in the playoffs, the opposing team's goaltender was the difference.

The Penguins scored twice in the third period for a 2-1 win, knotting the series at two games each. MacLean wasted his breath screaming for a penalty on the game-winning goal with 3:21 remaining, claiming Smolinski set an illegal pick, but he had his terminology wrong; it wasn't a pick, it was blatant interference. As Lemieux skated down the left wing and reversed direction toward the slot, Smolinski plowed over Murphy deep in the offensive zone. Murphy stayed down, Smolinski got up, Vanbiesbrouck made the save on Lemieux's first shot, and Smolinski deposited the rebound.

Two nights later in Pittsburgh, Barrasso made 28 saves in a 3-0 victory that pushed the Panthers to the brink of elimination for the first time.

"We still felt confident we could win," Mellanby said. "We were using more people and we felt they were a team we could beat. The confidence was there. We didn't panic and we felt being down 3-2 that we deserved to be in better shape than we were."

They weren't, even though Jagr and Lemieux each had only one goal, thanks in part to the outstanding defensive play of rookie Rhett Warrener. That was the worst omen of all for the Panthers: Lemieux and Jagr weren't scoring, and yet the Penguins were still winning.

▲ ▲ ▲

Martin Straka was two seasons removed from a 30-goal season in Pittsburgh and five teams away from being a real nowhere man on March 15. Mike Milbury, the general manager and coach of the New York Islanders, had placed the little 23-year-old Czech center on waivers, clearly for the purpose of getting rid of him, but so far 21 teams had passed.

The Islanders never wanted Straka in the first place. They were close to consummating a deal with the Senators that brought Bryan Berard, the No. 1 pick in the 1995 Entry Draft, to New York in exchange for Wade Redden, the No. 2 pick in 1995, when the Senators basically said to Milbury, "Here, take Straka and his $750,000 salary."

Bryan Murray was thinking, *I'll take him*, when he saw Straka's name on the waiver wire. A first-round draft choice by the Penguins in 1992, Straka was a great skater with a board-shattering slapshot and one of the most talented players Murray had ever seen on waivers. And with Barnes having sprained his knee a few days earlier, the Panthers needed some scoring up the middle.

The problem was, Murray didn't think he had any chance of getting Straka. Priority on claiming waived players is determined by the teams' reverse order of standing — from worst to first — and the Panthers were fifth in the league, 22nd on the waiver list. Surely, one of the 21 teams ahead of the Panthers would want him. Murray was even more certain of that when Penguins General Manager Craig Patrick said he gave positive reports on Straka to several other teams.

So, at five minutes to midnight on the final day of waivers, Murray put in a claim on Straka, figuring that was the last he'd hear of it. Fifteen minutes later, the league notified Murray that Straka was a Panther.

"Surprised?" Murray said. "I was pleased."

Straka had exactly the opposite reaction: He wasn't sure if he was pleased, but he certainly was surprised. He had gone from Pittsburgh to Ottawa to Long Island to Miami in less than a year without having had time to settle down in Ottawa or Long Island.

"So many things happened with the Islanders and I didn't play well," Straka said. "I was so tired every practice. After 20 seconds on the ice I was tired, I couldn't breathe. I still couldn't believe they traded me to the Islanders. I'm thinking, *Oh my God, what am I doing bad?* I didn't want to go onto the ice. I couldn't figure out what I was doing bad."

Straka had scored two goals in 22 games with the Islanders when he found out from his mother, who was listening to the radio in Ottawa, that he had been claimed by Florida. On the bright side, he was headed to a team that wanted him.

"When a young guy is traded a couple of times, you wonder whether it's his character or a personality conflict," Murray said. "Everybody I talked to was very complimentary about him as a person. Obviously, his shortfall is that he's not tall, but he's quick, he's skilled. I knew he could score some goals for us. You look at some guys and say, 'Gee, how can this guy not play on a team that likes speed and needs some talent.'"

But at $750,000 a year, Straka was by no means an automatic steal and MacLean immediately found out why the Senators and Islanders had considered him expendable. Straka didn't work as hard as his teammates on every shift and occasionally cheated on the rush by leaving the defensive zone too early. Although MacLean liked Straka's talent, he saw him as a typical European center who would rather pass than use his great shot. MacLean wasn't asking Straka to be his first-line center. He wanted him to score some goals and play like what he was: a 23-year-old whose career could be over with one more slip-up.

"If I was on my fourth team in two years, I'd be desperate," MacLean said. "I'm desperate enough now and it's my first team."

Until May 30, 1996, Straka's claim to fame in Florida was scoring the first goal against the Panthers at Miami Arena. He waited until the Panthers were on the brink in Game 6 before again making his mark.

▲ ▲ ▲

Warrener was dominating Lemieux and Jagr one-on-one. A five-minute review by the video replay judge went the Panthers way in the first period after Mellanby scored the first goal of the game. Yet, the Panthers were setting themselves up for a fall: they led by only 1-0 after the first period, despite spending most of the period in the Penguins' zone. Kevin Miller and Joe Dziedzic scored in the second period, and the Penguins had their first lead of Game 6 in Miami.

The Panthers, as desperate as they were in Game 4 of the Philadelphia series, tied the game when Lindsay banged home a rebound with 5:04 remaining in the second. Then, as if they were replaying Game 3, the Panthers outshot the Penguins, 15-3, over the next 11 minutes, while Barrasso turned away one shot after another. He was brilliant and threatening to become the star of the series when Straka, who was scratched in Game 5, showed his speed.

Using all the open ice the Penguins gave him, Straka thundered down the right wing and skated around J.J. Daigneault, who made the mistake of stepping up to meet him. Lindsay went to the net and Straka found him, then continued on for the return pass. With no time to waste, Straka lifted a shot over Barrasso's left shoulder and the Panthers had a 3-2 lead with 10:25 remaining in regulation.

On the bench, MacLean was wondering whether scratching Straka in the previous game was such a great decision.

"It's called shoving it up the coach's ass, and I like when they do it," MacLean said later. "I wish they'd continue to do it."

Straka's goal wasn't the winner because the Penguins came back. Lemieux skated around two defenders on a gorgeous play, and Tomas Sandstrom scored to tie the game with 8:43 remaining. Again, the Panthers were a goal away from elimination when Niedermayer lined up with Bryan Smolinski for a face-off to Barrasso's right.

Niedermayer, who hadn't scored a goal in the series, cleanly won the face-off back to Carkner at the left point. Smolinski made his second mistake, allowing Niedermayer a clear route to the net. Carkner shot. Barrasso made the save. Niedermayer, still by himself, whacked at the puck. Barrasso made another save. Niedermayer whacked again. This time it was in, and a wall of noise shook Miami Arena like never before. Marti Huizenga contributed to the rat storm by tossing one over the glass.

The crowd roared continuously through the final 6:02, and gasped when Nedved found Jagr bursting down the left wing with 35 seconds remaining. Vanbiesbrouck slid across the crease, Jagr made a return pass to Nedved as the play converged, but the puck bounced off of Carkner's stick. Vanbiesbrouck was going one way, the puck was going the other, and somehow it landed in his lap. The final score was 4-3 and the Panthers were going back to Pittsburgh for Game 7.

"At the start of the year, we never thought we'd be in Game 7 of the semifinals for the Stanley Cup," Fitzgerald said. "There's no pressure on us. We're not even supposed to be here."

This was more than anybody could've asked for, including the fans who came with "Thank You Panthers" banners, expecting Game 6 to be the season finale. There would be at least one more game and, this time, the pressure was on the Penguins.

"Defensively, they're the best team I've ever played against," said Lemieux, who still had only one goal in the series. Jagr, obviously feeling the stress of the series, refused to speak with reporters after the game. Asked why, Jagr snapped, "Because I said so." A day later, he talked about the challenge of Game 7 as if he feared the very idea. With the season on the line, Jagr was having a crisis of confidence.

The same couldn't be said about the Panthers.

"That's beautiful, isn't it?" MacLean asked. "All we want is a chance, and we've got our chance. We have nothing to lose and everything to gain."

Confidence was high. The Panthers were close enough to dream.

▲ ▲ ▲

On the afternoon of June 1 at the William Penn Hotel in downtown Pittsburgh, Tom Fitzgerald tossed around in his bed and tried to fall sleep. But his mind was racing, his heart was beating out of control, and his eyes were wide open.

Fitzgerald thought back to 1993, when he was with the Islanders and they eliminated the two-time defending Stanley Cup champion Penguins in Game 7 of the Conference semifinals. The Islanders' run ended with a loss to the Canadiens in the Conference finals.

Now Fitzgerald had another chance to get to the Stanley Cup finals and help the Panthers write a piece of history. The only third-year team to reach the finals was the 1970 St. Louis Blues, who played in a division with six other expansion teams; one of them had to make it, so the accomplishment was irrelevant. The Panthers could become the first third-year team to do it without the help of a favorable divisional alignment.

Then he thought about the upcoming game and his job of stopping the best players in the world, Lemieux and Jagr. That was enough to keep anyone awake nights, no less days, so he got out of bed and walked around the darkened room.

"You can turn on the TV," said Bill Lindsay, his roommate. "I'm not sleeping, either."

Fitzgerald couldn't wait for the opening face-off, but it was only 2:45, and the minutes were passing like hours. Would game time ever arrive? If he had followed his normal routine, Fitzgerald would've walked over to the Civic Arena at 5:00, but by 4:00, he figured there was no use hanging around his hotel room. Apparently, other players felt the same way, because Laus and Sheppard were already in the locker room when he arrived.

He measured and fixed the curves on his sticks, taped the blades, and then did a few interviews with ESPN and CBC. Time was moving faster now that he was occupied and, before long, it was 6:55 and the Panthers went out for the pre-game warmups. Another rush of excitement came over him, more anxiety. The meaning of this game was so clear.

We started this franchise three years ago, and now we're one game away from going to the Stanley Cup finals, Fitzgerald thought. *We beat two good teams to get where we are, and to get to the next level, we have to beat a great team.* He wasn't overwhelmed. He was confident, and so were his teammates. That 11 of them had been with him on that first night in Chicago in 1993 made this even more rewarding.

And then it was face-off time. Fitzgerald thought the game would rush right by and, before long, he'd know the outcome, but that didn't happen. Time was still passing so slowly, each second ticking down so vividly, and each play happening as if it were in slow motion. Hough slid a shot under Barrasso with 6:47 remaining in the first period, and Fitzgerald, knowing the Panthers were 3-0 during the playoffs when Hough scored, felt a little better.

"We play better with the lead, and we got it," Fitzgerald said. "We knew that if we could get the lead, we're a tough team to beat, but we're playing the Pittsburgh Penguins, they're a powerful team, and they can score three goals in 30 seconds."

Vanbiesbrouck turned away Lemieux on a shot from in front. Jagr circled the net on a wraparound and was stopped. One period ended and the Panthers still had the lead. The second period ended and it was still 1-0. But Nedved tied the game on a power play goal with 1:23 gone in the third.

The Penguins pressed for the winner. The Panthers were straying from their positions and letting the Penguins skate down the middle. Fitzgerald was tired, he had overstayed a shift, but the puck was on his stick and the neutral zone was wide open. Wilkinson back-pedaled. Fitzgerald, leading a three-on-three rush that wasn't going anywhere, crossed the blue line, took a slapshot, and headed for the bench. The puck ticked off Wilkinson's stick. Barrasso couldn't adjust to the change in direction.

Is it in? Fitzgerald asked himself.

The red light was on. The Panthers had a 2-1 lead with 13:42 remaining, and now time would pass even slower for Fitzgerald.

3:50, 3:49. 3:48. Garpenlov and Lindsay were racing in the other direction, and Fitzgerald, standing at his own blue line, was afraid to go any further. *God forbid it gets turned over and it's a three-on-one the other way,* Fitzgerald thought.

He was standing a hundred feet away, yet he could see the puck so vividly, even the writing on its side, as Lindsay passed to Garpenlov for a one-timer. The shot glanced off of Barrasso's shoulder, then high in the air, and behind him into the net. Fitzgerald looked up. There was 3:37 on the clock and Fitzgerald knew the Panthers were going to the Stanley Cup finals.

"It was so exciting," Fitzgerald remembered. "Even though we had two minutes left, there was no way in hell we were going to blow that two-goal lead. Then it felt like regular time. And then it ended and all hell broke out. It was something I'll never forget."

The Panthers mobbed Vanbiesbrouck and shook hands with the Penguins. Skrudland raised the Prince of Wales Trophy. Fitzgerald and his teammates gathered around the Trophy for a team photo and let the moment sink in.

My God, Fitzgerald thought. *We might be able to win the Stanley Cup!*

▲ ▲ ▲

Amid the delirium, MacLean walked toward the locker room and saw Bryan Murray standing in the runway, looking more excited than he had ever seen him. They had been through so much together — hired and twice fired, criticized for personnel decisions, losing with teams that maybe should've won, questioned when Murray hired him in Florida — and MacLean was as happy for Murray as he was for himself. MacLean walked up to his friend and wrapped his arms around him.

Then he saw his wife Jill, who had suffered with him through the hirings and firings. They were married 19 years ago, the first year he started coaching, and she had always helped him keep a level head.

Well, there was no need for that now. They were going to the finals!

And the Red Wings weren't. MacLean, Murray, Carkner, and Sheppard thought about that, too. Their former team had been eliminated two nights earlier by the Colorado Avalanche, and although they felt for the players, they didn't shed a tear for management. MacLean refused to call it poetic justice, but that's exactly what it was.

Fitzgerald, who, incredibly, outscored Lemieux and Jagr 3-2 in the series, phoned his father. Stu Barnes, the first-round bust whose career was saved by the Panthers, couldn't control his excitement. Teammates called their families on cellular phones, passed around victory cigars, and tried on their new Eastern Conference Champion T-shirts and hats. Barnes just looked around the locker room, shook his head in disbelief, and thought the simplest and most wonderful of thoughts: *Wow! We did it!*

▲ ▲ ▲

The celebration continued on the bus ride to the airport and 20,000 feet up in the Panthers' charter plane. Players were screaming and passing around the Prince of Wales Trophy. The assistant coaches joined the players at the back of the plane, and everyone was drinking and laughing. Some were chewing tobacco or smoking cigars, and others savored the victory simply by playing cards.

They drank beer, but not champagne, and the original Panthers reminisced about the past three seasons. The stories were happy, of course, because there had been so few down moments in the franchise's short history, and when the players thought about how far they'd come, they realized the trip wasn't all that long: 232 games, including playoffs, with the same captain, the same goaltenders, and the same leading scorer. Certainly none of this would've been possible without Ray Sheppard, Robert Svehla, Stu Barnes, and the other additions, but not much had really changed: The players selected in the expansion draft were the basis for a team that was going to the Stanley Cup finals.

The scene on the plane was joyous, not rowdy. All of the players wore their Eastern Conference Champion hats and savored the accomplishment. Watching highlights of the series on the TV monitors brought some of them close to tears. They had experienced it, lived it, and now they were getting to see it.

Down on the ground in South Florida, fans spilled onto the streets of Coconut Grove, South Beach, and Las Olas Boulevard in a wild celebration. Revelers packed the bars and people had already started camping out at Miami Arena, waiting for Stanley Cup finals tickets to go on sale. Some of these fans didn't even know the Panthers existed two months ago, but now they were diehards, acting like lifelong devotees.

The Panthers would've loved to go home and enjoy the celebration, but the plane was taking them to Denver, where the finals would open in just three days against the Western Conference champion Colorado Avalanche. When they arrived in Denver at 4 a.m., there was no welcoming committee awaiting them.

"If anything was disappointing, it's that we didn't get a chance to come home for a couple of days and really get focused on the series," MacLean said. "Maybe enjoy a bit of the celebration. Not enjoy by partying, but by being in the atmosphere, instead of getting on a flight and flying to Denver and having two days to prepare for the series. It would've been nice to have been able to do that."

Nice, but not realistic. The NHL was on a schedule dictated by television and the Panthers, who had entered prime time, would have to do as they were told. But the next 24 hours were not going to be easy. No rooms were available in downtown Denver that night, so at five in the morning, the Panthers checked into a hotel 10 miles out of town. Later, they switched to a hotel nearer McNichols Arena, a chore they could've done without in their physical state. In the late afternoon, MacLean gathered them for a light skate; anything harder and their bodies might have crumbled into little pieces. Although the players enjoyed taking the ice for the first time as Eastern Conference champions and were thrilled about being in the finals, they were feeling the after-effects of their celebration. The mile-high Denver air wasn't helping matters, nor were the constant distractions.

"Those days went by so quickly," Mellanby said. "We were still feeling a lot of the emotion of winning in Pittsburgh and guys were getting organized. Families were coming up to Denver and there was everything that goes with being in the finals."

Between ticket requests, the demands of the national media, the hoopla in Denver, and all the phone calls they were making and receiving, the Panthers never had the chance to focus on the enormous challenge they faced next.

The Colorado Avalanche's story was nearly as unique as the Panthers'. The franchise joined the World Hockey Association as the Quebec Nordiques in 1972 and was one of four WHA teams swallowed up by the NHL in 1979. After 16 NHL seasons in Quebec, the Nordiques were sold to COMSAT Entertainment Group after the 1994-95 season and moved from Canada to Denver.

Hockey fans in Colorado were the winners in this deal. The Nordiques, who had the best record in the Eastern Conference during the 1994-95 season before being eliminated by the Rangers, were a young, talented team on the rise. Peter Forsberg, the 22-year-old Swede who was one of five players traded to the Nordiques in the Eric Lindros deal, was establishing himself as one of the League's great all-around players, and Joe Sakic, who had scored 48 goals twice before, scored 120 points in 1995-96.

To this imposing duo of star centers, the Avalanche added a standout defenseman, Sandis Ozolinsh, acquired in a trade with the San Jose Sharks, and goaltender Patrick Roy, a two-time Stanley Cup winner with Montreal. The Avalanche had replicated the formula for a Stanley Cup champion: Great centers, Sakic and Forsberg, combined with a great defenseman, Ozolinsh, and one of the premier playoff goaltenders of all time, Roy, plus an outstanding supporting cast of forwards, Claude Lemieux, the 1995 playoff MVP with New Jersey, Adam Deadmarsh, Valeri Kamensky, Mike Ricci; and defensemen Adam Foote, Sylvain Lefebvre, and Uwe Krupp.

This team was loaded, and they had handled the Red Wings, the regular season champions, with relative ease in the Western Conference finals. The strategy of shutting down the other team's top two or three players, which worked so well for the Panthers during the first three rounds, just wasn't going to cut it this time.

"I didn't even want to watch the tapes, because it was kind of scary watching them," Ruff said. "We knew we were going to have to play just as well or better defensively, because you look at them: Sakic, Forsberg, Lemieux, Deadmarsh, they have all kinds of speed and players who can stickhandle. Forsberg could work his way out of a telephone booth. We knew we'd have to treat these guys like we treated Lemieux and Jagr. They were in the same class, but there were more of them. I had to give them the edge, but we still thought we could beat them."

Although the Panthers would later reflect upon the Eastern Conference series as their Stanley Cup, their only goal when the finals opened was finishing what they had started. The excitement of being in the finals was overwhelming. They were in it to win.

▲ ▲ ▲

Avalanche fans, neophytes like many Panthers fans and nearly as enthusiastic, arrived at McNichols Arena for Game 1 wearing and carrying rat traps. The Avalanche, concerned about being physically and emotionally ready after a five day layoff, had a secret weapon: the butt-end of Vanbiesbrouck's stick.

According to an obscure NHL rule, the knob of a goaltender's stick must be wrapped in white tape. Vanbiesbrouck had been covering the knob and blade of his stick with red tape for most of his three seasons in Florida, and nobody had said a word.

But 15 minutes before the start of Game 1, NHL Vice President Brian Burke got on his walkie-talkie and notified MacLean of the infraction. MacLean was incensed and made his feelings known in a loud, expletive-filled argument, but Burke wouldn't budge. Four minutes before game time, assistant equipment manager Tim LeRoy was delegated the unpleasant task of breaking the news to Vanbiesbrouck.

LeRoy's face was as white as a sheet. Vanbiesbrouck looked at him as if to say, *Why are you bothering me before Game 1 of the Stanley Cup finals?*

"John, some guy from the League said you have to change the tape on your stick," LeRoy said.

"I've had red tape on my stick for three seasons," Vanbiesbrouck said. "Why are they telling me this now?"

Vanbiesbrouck handed his sticks to LeRoy, who wrapped white tape over the red.

261

"John was pissed off," MacLean said. "I thought it was really poor judgment on their part. In fairness, it's a rule, but I thought it was unbelievably poor judgment that the League would do that to us 15 minutes before going on the ice, especially after three years."

The interruption to Vanbiesbrouck's pre-game routine left him angry when he should have been focusing on the game. MacLean hadn't calmed down by the time he took his spot behind the bench and the players sensed his tension. After the game, Avalanche Coach Marc Crawford wryly denied having played any part in the incident and MacLean believed him, but the players weren't so sure.

"It was a little bush, but you do whatever you can do to win," Mellanby said. "They said they didn't ask about it, but I think that's a crock of shit. The League noticed it and decided to change it? No way."

And if it wasn't off-ice referee Don Koharski who noticed the infraction, who was it? Mellanby suspected Patrick Roy.

"As a goalie, he would know something like that," Mellanby said. "He probably noticed during the playoffs. He's a goalie, he's looking for an edge, looking for controversy to rattle the team. I don't think it had that effect, though. We came out and played well and had control of the game."

The Panthers put the Tale of the Tape behind them and played a strong first period. Forsberg and Sakic couldn't go anywhere without getting hit, and the Panthers had the best scoring chances. Roy stopped Garpenlov on a breakaway and Lindsay on a second chance, before Fitzgerald took a pass from Lindsay and scored to give the Panthers a 1-0 lead with 3:09 remaining. On the bench, Lowry, Skrudland, and Hough loudly urged on their teammates, and Game 1 of this series was looking like Game 1 of the last three.

But the Avalanche improved their play in the second period. After Vanbiesbrouck stopped Forsberg on a break-in, Colorado scored three goals in 3:49 — one by Scott Young while skating into the high slot, the second by Ricci, and the third by Krupp at 14:21 off a brilliant cross-ice pass by Kamensky — to take a 3-1 lead. Skrudland pleaded with the Panthers to work harder, but work had nothing to do with what was happening. Roy turned away the Panthers for the final time in the third period, when Mellanby missed on a chance from in front of the net, and the Avalanche won, 3-1.

Although the Panthers didn't realize it at the time, they had wasted a chance to beat the Avalanche on a down night.

▲ ▲ ▲

MacLean had no idea how poorly his team played in Game 1 until he opened *The Denver Post* the next morning and saw a column by Mark Kiszla. The Panthers, he learned, were "a faceless team hiding behind Mickey Mouse tactics" and they had failed in an attempt to drag the game "down to the dark places where rodents thrive." Kiszla, a writer MacLean had never met, was carving up his hockey team, slice by slice.

> Dedicate this victory to the memory of Jean Beliveau, Wayne Gretzky, and every skater who has celebrated hockey as a game of skill and grace rather than 60 artless minutes of shameless clutching and grabbing. If hockey truly is to become a national passion, what the NHL needs is proof that hockey is more than mucking and grinding ...
>
> The Panthers are slaves to a marvelously effective defensive system that infuriates opponents and makes TV viewers from Montreal to Dallas want to reach for the remote control ...
>
> Florida turns hockey into a night to be endured rather than something to behold. The Panthers try to hide unspectacular, uninspiring talent behind their systematic de-evolution of the sport. They try to turn everything slick on the ice into ugly slush.

MacLean wasn't going to let this pass without saying something. His team hadn't been getting the respect they deserved, and he thought it was time to say something.

"It was brutally unfair after a game we easily could've won," MacLean said. "My philosophy has always been if I don't agree with something, I say it to people. The team deserved to have somebody take a stand."

That somebody was MacLean, who made copies of the column, left them in front of each player's stall, and spent the first two minutes of his morning press conference bashing Kiszla.

"This is a total insult to our organization and players, and a total embarrassment to the Panthers, the City of Denver, the Avalanche, and the NHL," MacLean said.

Kiszla, who arrived at McNichols Arena thinking the big story of the day would be the Vanbiesbrouck tape incident or Game 2, anything but a newspaper columnist, sat in surprised silence and listened to MacLean's tirade. Like it or not, he had just become a celebrity of the Stanley Cup finals.

When the press conference ended, Kiszla was surrounded by reporters shouting out every inane question that came to mind. A TV reporter from Miami accused, "You don't like rats, do you?"

"As a matter of fact," Kiszla replied, "I don't."

Later, Kiszla walked up to MacLean near the Panthers' team bus and introduced himself.

"Coach, I'm Mark Kiszla from *The Denver Post*."

"You were brutal in the newspaper today," said MacLean, who then unleashed an obscenity-laced diatribe.

"Is that the best motivational technique you can come up with?" Kiszla asked.

"Don't ever try to do that again," MacLean shouted.

"Are you done with me now?" Kiszla returned.

Finally, Bouris got between them and ushered MacLean onto the bus.

Kiszla wasn't done with MacLean. His column in the next day's paper concentrated on the coach, instead of the entire team:

> Maybe it's because MacLean knows a team doomed to lose any skill competition with Colorado is in desperate need of any motivational edge, no matter how contrived. Perhaps these lame inspirational stunts worked for MacLean when he coached the University of New Brunswick, but they won't make a difference in the big time. Me thinks I smell a rat wilting in the heat of an NHL championship.

MacLean had ignited an uproar that wouldn't stop. Kiszla was on every Panthers fan's enemies list, along with Joe Lapointe, Eric Lindros, and Jaromir Jagr. Mass playoff hype took over. Syndicated columnist Dave Barry roasted Kiszla in a column on the front page of *The Miami Herald*. A TV station revealed Kiszla's home phone number over the air and encouraged viewers to give him a call. They did, by the thousands, and some of the messages on Kiszla's answering machine were so threatening that his editor asked the NHL to intervene. MacLean offered to issue a public statement and when the series moved to Florida, Kiszla checked-in to his hotel under an assumed name.

What started as a rather amusing incident was building upon itself, and Kiszla's colleagues weren't helping. Walking with Kiszla to the press room between periods of Game 3 at Miami Arena, another writer announced, "This is Mark Kiszla from *The Denver Post*." Two well-dressed, middle-aged women cursed him the rest of the way down.

While the incident consumed Kiszla's life, MacLean was trying to figure out a way to win Game 2. He was far more concerned about his team's physical condition than anything Kiszla wrote. The Panthers were exhausted, and the only reason it didn't show in Game 1 was that they were riding the emotion and excitement of being in the Stanley Cup finals. For the first time since the playoffs began, MacLean didn't like his team's chances going into a game.

Ray Sheppard was thinking the same thing. The team was obviously tired after two exhausting, physical series and the defensemen were weary. The Panthers were relatively healthy for a team in the finals, but playing eight playoff games in 18 days had taken its toll.

"You could see it in practice," Sheppard said. "Guys were real excited about being there, but it was a struggle to get moving, to get your legs going. I felt that way. I was tired. And being in Colorado with the altitude didn't help at all."

The next day was a nightmare that started early in the morning, when the Panthers were awakened several times by a faulty fire alarm in their hotel. They apparently missed the wakeup alarm for Game 2. The Panthers were awful.

Forsberg scored three goals in the opening 15:05 and Vanbiesbrouck was pulled after 20 minutes with the Panthers trailing, 4-1. Mark Fitzpatrick, who hadn't played in five weeks, didn't fare much better against an Avalanche team that was as impressive as promised. How far did the Panthers stray from their game plan?

"I found myself playing forward a few shifts," Jovanovski said.

The Avalanche won, 8-1, and the final score was indicative of the game. Only five days after their victory in Pittsburgh, the Panthers were in trouble.

"It seemed like we were on a plane on the way home, down 2-0, before you could blink," Mellanby said. "Those days went by so quickly."

The Panthers, who had relied on character, hard work, and coaching, to get them through the first three rounds, were now relying on their fans. Home-ice, it seemed, was their only remaining advantage, and when they arrived back in Fort Lauderdale at 6 the next morning, hundreds of fans greeted them at the airport. It was June 7 now, and the last time the Panthers had seen Florida was a week ago, when they left for Game 7 of the Pittsburgh series.

"When you're down 2-0, home ice is a big advantage," MacLean cracked. "I found Denver not to be Doug MacLean friendly."

But the Avalanche were getting stronger, not weaker. Claude Lemieux, who had been suspended from the first two games for a hit on Detroit's Kris Draper in the previous series, would return to the lineup for Game 3. Forsberg, an outstanding player, was playing so well that he had people questioning who got the best of the Lindros trade. Roy was sharp, Vanbiesbrouck alarmingly shaky.

"It's always difficult to get throttled, but you can only look as far as yourself," Vanbiesbrouck said. "When you're in the Stanley Cup finals, you have to put things in perspective."

Keeping things in perspective was impossible for South Floridians, who were acting even crazier than before. Tickets for Games 3 and 4 sold out in two minutes and scalpers were selling upper level seats for $250. The Stanley Cup was on tour and fans lined up in hotel lobbies and malls for a view. Novelty stores, unable to keep up with the demand, were limiting rat sales to one box per customer. Television newscasters had lost all sense of journalistic responsibility. Many of them were wearing Panthers jerseys on the air. I-95 was lined with Stanley Cup banners and a life-sized replica of a Panther adorned the sidewalk in front of Miami Arena. Wayne Huizenga, a villain just a few months ago, signed autographs and shook hands like a celebrity. Anybody who didn't have a Panthers jersey, hat, or T-shirt, just wasn't dressed appropriately.

Lemieux — Claude, the one the Panthers couldn't stop — wasted no time quieting the fans. With 2:44 gone in Game 3, Kamensky outskated Svehla to the outside, circled the net, and made a perfect centering pass to Lemieux, who banged the puck past Vanbiesbrouck. The Avalanche knew the Panthers couldn't deal with their speed.

But Roy, who had never won a game in Miami in three seasons with the Avalanche and Canadiens, revealed his weakness: a five-hole that sometimes opens a little too wide. Lowry set up a screen in front and Sheppard threaded a shot between Lowry's legs, then through Roy's legs, to tie the score. A little over two minutes later, Niedermayer beat Ozolinsh to a long rebound and slipped a backhander between Roy's legs.

Roy leaned on his stick as rats showered down and clanked off his helmet. The Panthers had a 2-1 lead and were outplaying the Avalanche but, as they had learned, momentum was a fleeting feeling in Miami Arena. The rat storms after each home goal allowed the other team a chance to regroup. Even worse, in addition to the plastic rats, some fans were throwing coins and metal objects onto the ice. The Panthers wouldn't have minded seeing this tradition come to an end.

And it did: Niedermayer's goal was the Panthers' last of the season.

Hough nearly made it 3-1 early in the second when his shot from a sharp angle beat Roy, but the puck hit the post. Vanbiesbrouck stopped Mike Keane on a two-on-one at the other end but, with the Avalanche shortening their shifts to 30 seconds, Keane beat Vanbiesbrouck with a soft wrist shot that fluttered under Ricci's legs and into the net, tying the game. Two shifts later, Rhett Warrener stumbled over a broken Avalanche stick and Deadmarsh roared into the Panthers' zone. Sakic took the pass, skated in by himself, and fired a wrist shot over Vanbiesbrouck's glove for a 3-2 lead.

The Panthers would spend the summer dreaming about Roy's miracle save in the third period: Garpenlov skated to the side of the net and sent a cross-crease pass to Mellanby at the right post. The entire left side of the net was open, but Roy instinctively kicked out his left pad to make the save and preserve the win.

Down three games to none, the Panthers' survival instincts were all they had left.

▲ ▲ ▲

Sunday, June 9, was an off day and the weather fit the mood of the Panthers and their fans. Torrential rains, combined with gusty winds, fell from morning through night, flooding the parking lot at Gold Coast Arena. The Panthers returned to work on Monday for possibly their final morning skate of the season. They were hopeful, not optimistic.

"When my wife went skiing in Aspen," MacLean told the media, "I said, 'I'd really like to get to Colorado.' But not as much as I want to go tomorrow."

He said this with resignation, as if he knew there was no way it was going to happen. For most of two months, MacLean and his coaching staff had found ways to beat teams perceived as being better than the Panthers, but now they faced an impossible task.

"I suspect we'll play better tonight than in Game 3," MacLean said.

The previous night, the team met at the hotel, watched video clips, and discussed the challenge facing them. On Monday morning, the Panthers gathered again and encouraged each other to stay positive and not give up until the series ended. *One game at a time.* The old sports cliché was all the Panthers had left.

"We're not talking about winning four straight," MacLean insisted. "We're talking about winning tonight. We're concerned about winning tonight, bottom line."

Although MacLean couldn't guarantee victory, he was certain his team wouldn't go down without a fight. He laughed off the idea that Colorado, up three games to none, was under some pressure — "If that's pressure, I long for that type of pressure," he said — and finished his press conference by saying something he never thought he'd say to the media.

"I really hope that I get to talk to you guys tomorrow about going to Denver," MacLean said in a hushed tone. "I really do."

Hope was the theme for the Panthers. Lindsay managed to keep a straight face when he said, "It's a good situation for us." Skrudland, displaying the same stone face he shows after a win or a loss, talked about sticking with what got them there, even though what got them there obviously wasn't enough to get them further.

But Hough summed up the series and made it clear why there was really no hope at all. The Panthers had reached this point by concentrating on shutting down the other team's top two or three players and betting that their supporting cast was better than the other team's supporting cast. Against the Avalanche, that just wasn't so: Forsberg and Sakic were better than anyone on the Panthers, but so were Kamensky and Ozolinsh and Deadmarsh and Ricci and, most damaging of all, Roy.

"We thought coming in that we could beat them by stopping Forsberg and Sakic," Hough said. "We just didn't realize how deep they were. They've shown a lot of depth and character that we didn't expect."

The character the Panthers could deal with. The depth was another story.

▲ ▲ ▲

No one ever had confused the Panthers' character with that of South Florida's sports fans, who had a reputation for not showing up when their teams showed the slightest signs of slumping and giving up well before a game was over. As for Panthers fans, many of them weren't around when the season started, and they had taken their sweet time selling out the first two home playoff games. Now that the going was tough, these bandwagon-jumpers figured to disassociate with the losing team as quickly as possible. The Panthers would go out quietly and by themselves.

The local newspapers supported this theme with stories about ticket brokers practically giving away tickets for Game 4. People were calling to sell their tickets, and hardly anyone wanted to buy them. This behavior, the ticket brokers said, was predictable: South Floridians were fair weather fans.

But as game time approached and traffic increased around Miami Arena, it was obvious the Panthers were just as popular as they had been for the past two months. Hundreds of fans without tickets spent hours circling the Arena in a hopeless search. Anybody who suggested the possibility of a ticket for sale was immediately surrounded by dozens of prospective buyers. It was a seller's market; not even the scalpers had tickets.

Some fans carried signs reading, "Thank you, Panthers," and "Thanks for a great run." Pockets were stuffed with plastic rats and faces were painted in Panthers red, blue, and gold. Even if the fans were resigned to their team's burial in Game 4, this was one funeral they had every intention of attending. Loyalty would have its rewards.

▲ ▲ ▲

As much as he tried maintaining perspective, Vanbiesbrouck couldn't avoid the truth of what faced him that night. *If we lose today, we're done.*

Avoiding elimination was his first goal, avoiding history his second: Sakic had scored 18 goals in the playoffs, one short of tying the League mark, and Vanbiesbrouck was motivated by the idea of keeping him from a place in the record books.

Vanbiesbrouck liked what he saw when the game started. His team was playing well and taking the body. Jovanovski rammed into Deadmarsh. Ozolinsh was floored by Skrudland. They were getting scoring chances. Roy stopped Lindsay and Niedermayer on close-range chances, then Vanbiesbrouck got his turn and stopped Corbet on a rebound.

Here we go, Vanbiesbrouck thought. *It's going to be a battle.*

And it was, for 60 minutes of regulation time that seemingly passed in an instant. He stopped Ozolinsh on a shot from the high slot and turned away Ricci. Hough missed a chance to make it 1-0 when his shot sailed over a fallen Roy and the crossbar. The teams traded chances. Straka took a shot from the boards that slipped under Roy's pads, but missed going in by an inch. Vanbiesbrouck turned away a wrist shot by Sakic and Warren Rychel slid into him. Neither puck nor player went into the net, but Vanbiesbrouck needed a few minutes to recover. MacLean was up on the bench and screaming for an interference penalty, the intensity was building, and both goaltenders were in a groove.

With less than a minute remaining in the third period, Carkner's first shot was blocked, his second shot from the mid-slot was stopped by Roy. Sheppard collected the rebound at the left post. Roy stuck out his right pad. Sheppard tried to lift the puck into the top half of the net. Roy came across to make the save. The fans, seeing the outside of the net rippling and thinking the Panthers had scored, threw rats onto the ice, but it was a false alarm. Regulation time ended in a scoreless tie.

All right, Vanbiesbrouck thought, recalling the Panthers' 2-0 overtime record in the playoffs. *We're down to where we need it to be. One goal will get us the win. I'm not asking for two, or three.*

In the first overtime, Niedermayer avoided a check and tried jamming the puck past Roy, then Mellanby swooped in and somehow didn't score. Sheppard threw a pass in front of the net, but Warrener, moving in from the point, missed the one-timer. Ozolinsh had two incredible chances to end the game, first when he crept into the slot and fired a wrister that Vanbiesbrouck somehow gloved, and then on a redirection of a centering pass by Kamensky.

In the locker room after the first overtime, Vanbiesbrouck urged his teammates to be patient. "We're going to get our chances," he told them. But the Avalanche had the better scoring chances at the start of the second overtime, and Vanbiesbrouck made one of the most spectacular and luckiest stops of his career, flat on his back, as Scott Young tried and failed to shoot the puck through his body. Then Ozolinsh streaked down the right side and deflected a centering pass, but Vanbiesbrouck shot out his glove and kept the series from ending. At 10:06 of the second overtime, the game became the longest scoreless tie in finals history.

Be patient, Vanbiesbrouck told himself. *We're going to get our chances.* And then the Panthers got their chances and Roy stopped them. *Are we ever going to beat this guy?*

When the second overtime ended, Vanbiesbrouck had made 52 saves, Roy had made 60, and Vanbiesbrouck wondered if the game was ever going to end.

The Panthers returned to their locker room feeling totally exhausted. Some players laid on the floor with their legs perched on the bench. Others slouched in front of their stalls. Fitzgerald had gone through five shirts and three pairs of socks and every player did anything possible to keep dry. It was an impossible task. MacLean walked around trying to keep the players' spirits up. Vanbiesbrouck felt sweat draining through his skates. He was fighting dehydration and his voice was hoarse.

"Let's go guys!" Vanbiesbrouck tried to shout. The words came out sounding as if somebody else spoke them.

Skrudland tried to ease the tension.

"Hey, listen guys," he said. "I'm going to score."

Mellanby chimed in. "Hey, guys, it's after 12, I just turned 30!"

"Well, Jesus Christ!" Carkner said. "I hope somebody scores besides Screwy or Mell'll be 31 before this game's over!"

Vanbiesbrouck, trying to remain focused, heard this and laughed. *We can do it. We can do it,* he kept telling himself. He led his teammates out for the third overtime, feeling good about their chances.

The first four minutes passed quickly. Both teams were tired and scoring chances weren't coming easily. Mellanby battled for the puck along the side boards in the Panthers' zone. The puck came free, then bounced to Carkner in the left face-off circle. Sakic, in pursuit, reached out with his stick and Carkner's backhand clearing pass skittered toward the blue line. The puck ended up on Krupp's stick at the right point. Svehla pushed his man out of the crease, but into the path of the shooter.

Vanbiesbrouck saw Krupp wind up for a slapshot, then lost the puck through a maze of players and felt it glance off his pads. The crowd went silent.

He didn't even bother looking back.

Epilogue:
Going Home

T he puck was in the net, the clock read 1:06, and Doug MacLean, standing behind the Panthers' bench and realizing the season was finally
over, didn't notice the thousands of plastic rats pouring down from
the stands or hear the crowd's standing ovation. *Sixty-three shots on goal,*
he thought. *Why couldn't one of them have gone in?* The Avalanche piled
on top of Krupp and the Panthers consoled Vanbiesbrouck. Then the players lined up for the traditional series-ending handshake and MacLean felt
like he was dream-walking through the early morning.

He thought back upon the game, especially the two overtime intermis-
sions when his players sat on the floor in front of their lockers, legs spread
out, icepacks covering their feet. All of them were too physically and mentally drained to move or say a word, but somehow they were able to ignore
the hopelessness of winning the series and concentrate on the game. He
thought about the entire season: 82 regular season games starting in October,
followed by playoff games nearly every other night for two months. And
at first he was devastated because it didn't seem fair for all of the team's
hard work and dedication to end this way. His players wouldn't get the
chance to return to Colorado for Game 5 and then maybe even bring it back
for one more game at home and — who knows? — a miracle.

So he walked across the ice and through the maze of rats, oblivious to
the still-roaring crowd, but by the time he got back to the locker room, a
distance of no more than 150 feet from the bench, a completely different
emotion had overtaken him. The crushing disappointment over the result
of the game and the series had been replaced by pride in the team's accomplishments. No longer downcast, he stopped, dug his hands deep into his
pants pockets, and greeted each player as they walked into the room. Two
attendants wheeled a shopping cart full of champagne past where he was

standing and MacLean didn't want to notice them or think about where they were going.

He closed the locker room door one last time, gathered his players, and told them how proud he was of their great run. He didn't cry, although several of his players did, and he couldn't imagine how tired they must have felt; he was exhausted and he hadn't even been out there playing! His mind was working hard now, replaying the game, trying to think of a player who hadn't given his all or played his best on this night. Having failed to come up with even one name, he thanked them for making his first season as a head coach memorable, then walked around the dressing room and shook hands with every player.

Now it was time to face the press, and MacLean knew it would be easy because nobody could deny his team's effort or heart. All season, MacLean realized how tough it must be for a coach to face the press when his team doesn't give its all, and how lucky he was to not have that problem. He didn't have to think about what he would say; the words would come naturally when the questions were asked.

"I feel really proud," is what he said. "We played as hard as we're capable of playing. It's not hard to reflect back at all. Obviously, we're very disappointed, but I've got nothing but great feelings about the year."

But no sooner had he climbed into his car for the ride home than that melancholy feeling from after the game returned. He couldn't ward it off. The season was over. His team had lost its last game. Jill MacLean noticed her husband's mood changing and wasted no time snapping him out of his self-pity.

"You've had too good a year to be disappointed," she told her husband, lifting the mood for the rest of the ride.

They walked through their front door at about 3:30 Tuesday morning and saw their son Clark asleep in bed with the television still tuned to ESPN. He had obviously missed the end of the game and fell asleep not knowing whether his father's team won or lost. MacLean didn't have the heart to wake him, so he turned off the TV, tucked him in, and went to bed. He was tired, emotionally drained, and quickly fell asleep.

When the alarm rang three hours later, rousing him out of a deep, contented sleep, MacLean went to Clark's room and woke him for school.

"Did we win?" was the first thing Clark asked.

"No, honey, we lost," MacLean said.

"Awww, no!" Clark said. Then he got up, got dressed, ate his breakfast, and caught the bus, having already come to grips with his brief disappointment.

Kids are great, MacLean thought. *They don't get too uptight about something like this.*

He spent the day thanking well-wishers and speaking with a few reporters who dropped by the house. There was still work to do — on Friday, the family would board a plane back to Summerside, Prince Edward Island, for the shortest summer of their hockey lives — but right now, all he wanted to do was relax. A schedule that for nine months had been filled with practices, games, meetings, and flights, was now nearly empty. On Wednesday, he returned to Gold Coast Arena to take a team picture, meet with the players, and clean out his office. Wayne Huizenga called and offered to fly him home the next day.

"That's OK, Mr. Huizenga," MacLean said. "I'm flying out of Fort Lauderdale on Friday and I've already bought my tickets."

"Don't worry about it," Huizenga said. "I'm flying you home."

That night, MacLean and the players drove down to Miami Arena for what they assumed would be a sparsely attended rally. The team had lost, after all, and Game 4 ended so late that surely nobody would show up less than 48 hours later to cheer a losing hockey team. MacLean figured there might be six or seven thousand people in the building, but when he arrived, people were streaming out of the train station singing, "Let's Go Panthers!" and when he walked into the Arena, he was astounded.

The place was packed with fans, all chanting "Let's Go Panthers!" and acting as if their team had won the Cup. Fans held signs thanking the players. MacLean couldn't believe what he was seeing: The mass happiness, the joy on people's faces. He realized what this team had meant to the community and his emotions swelled. He felt like they had won.

And maybe this was the payoff. After all, the Panthers didn't have the chance to feel like champions after winning the Prince of Wales Trophy. Their plane left from Pittsburgh for Denver a few hours after Game 7 and, by the time the series returned to South Florida, the Avalanche led two games to none. Here was the sendoff to an incredible year. *A night to remember*, MacLean knew.

The fans shouted "Bee-zer! Bee-zer!" for John Vanbiesbrouck, "Ed-die, Ed-die!" for Ed Jovanovski. They cheered through a tape of playoff highlights, as if the moments were happening right before their eyes. MacLean, who earlier in the day was named Coach of the Year by *The Hockey News*, stepped to the podium to speak and received the kind of ovation usually reserved for Stanley Cup champions. He asked the crowd to stop cheering — he was embarrassed by the adulation — and felt something cold and wet rushing down his body. Jovanovski and Warrener had dumped a cooler of ice water over his head! MacLean felt too good to do anything but laugh.

"It's been a fun ride," he said later. "I hope it's like a ferris wheel that goes round and round that doesn't have any sudden stops."

The ride wasn't quite over.

▲ ▲ ▲

No roads lead to Summerside. You can get there by boat or you can get there by plane, and if you want to take a car, you're gonna have to hop a ferry. Take a plane from Fort Lauderdale and it's an all day affair with three stops, one in Newark, then another in Halifax, and, about 12 hours later, a final one in Charlottetown. Arrive at Charlottetown Airport and it's another hour by car to Summerside.

But this time, the MacLean family was going non-stop. On Friday, Doug, Jill, Clark, and MacKenzie boarded one of Huizenga's private jets and flew home in luxury. When the plane touched down at Summerside Airport at 3 p.m., Doug MacLean walked off and into a hero's welcome.

There must have been 300 people greeting them at the airport. A red carpet led from the plane to the small terminal. There were police cars, a fire truck with the Panthers' logo on one side, TV cameras, and reporters. His friends were there, and so were his parents. The Mayor of Summerside and the Premier of Prince Edward Island came out for the occasion. They were all cheering for Doug MacLean and, although he was touched by the reception, he also found it a little odd. These were people he had known all his life.

The MacLeans were escorted into a car and a procession of eight vehicles led them through town. People wore the Panthers hats and T-shirts that Huizenga had sent up for the celebration. Jill clutched a bouquet of flowers. Townspeople held banners that said things like, "Way to go, Doug!" Although there was no band — the band members were still in school — a lone bagpipe player led Summerside's version of a ticker tape parade. The parade route ended at the Silver Fox Curling and Yacht Club in downtown Summerside, where another 500 people assembled for a welcome home party.

"It makes you feel a little different," MacLean said. "But a lot of people got into the Panthers. There were no Canadian teams left after the second round and the notoriety we picked up was pretty unbelievable!

"It was an unbelievable day."

The MacLeans stopped in town on the way home to pick up a pair of baseball cleats for Clark — practice would start the next day — and arrived at their beachside cottage in the early evening. Summer was finally here and, with it, time to think about all that had happened.

"A third-year expansion team goes to the Stanley Cup finals and, to me, that's an unbelievable feat," MacLean decided. "What we accomplished may never happen again."

Two years ago, he had sat in this same cottage, suffering through the worst two weeks of his life, wondering if he'd ever again work in the NHL. This summer, there'd be no anxious walks along the beach. Only happiness.

Index

Anaheim Mighty Ducks, 15, 22, 55, 57-61, 63-65, 70, 87, 107, 206
Anaheim Arena, 15, 35
Arbour, Al, 30, 47, 67, 135, 144, 178
Arison, Micky, 186
Arnott, Jason, 24, 70-71, 73, 88
Baltimore Skipjacks, 175
Bancroft, Steve, 63
Barber, Bill, 38, 54
Barger, Carl, 17, 20, 28
Barnes, Stu, 103-05, 123, 144, 152, 157-59, 163, 167, 171, 189, 193, 199, 209, 212, 216, 220, 222, 226-27, 229, 233-34, 238-39, 241, 245, 251-53, 258-59
Barnett, Elliott, 6
Barnett, Mike, 86-88
Barrasso, Tom, 3, 250-53, 255, 257-58
Barrault, Doug, 64
Barrie, Len, 84
Belanger, Jesse, 64, 68, 85, 92, 100, 105, 111, 119, 127, 152, 163, 166-67, 193, 205, 207, 209, 216
Belfour, Ed, 26, 92, 183
Benning, Brian, 85, 92, 152-53, 155, 162, 189
Berard, Bryan, 191, 253
Bernfeld, Jerry, 21
Berrard, Steve, 146
Bertuzzi, Todd, 184
Bertuzzi, Larry, 181
Bettman, Gary, 27, 42, 54, 60, 70, 95, 125, 127, 202, 218; 1994-95 NHL lockout and, 141-43, 145, 149
Bielfield, Jay, 135
Billington, Craig, 26, 229
Blockbuster Entertainment Corporation, 6, 10-12, 18-19, 21, 23, 28, 41-42, 53, 58, 76-77, 106, 126, 139, 145-146, 160, 185, 203
Blockbuster Park, 18, 28, 106, 139, 146, 160, 185, 203
Blosser, Jim, 17, 22, 35
Bolger, Declan, 49
Bonk, Radek, 128-31, 151
Bossy, Mike, 30, 46
Boston Bruins, 7, 26, 63-64, 99, 107, 115, 117, 138, 174, 213, 217, 221, 224-32
Bouris, Greg, 32, 49-50, 53, 58, 60, 66, 69, 75, 89, 91, 99, 112, 172, 246, 264

Bourque, Ray, 225, 228-32
Bowman, Scotty 135-38, 178, 190, 214
Brind'Amour, Rod, 205, 233, 238
Broward County Commission, 185-86, 203, 218, 220
Brown, Keith, 84, 86, 91-92, 101, 102, 109, 152-53, 155, 159, 162, 190
Brown, Newell, 204
Buffalo Sabres, 26, 32, 46, 61, 117, 137, 166, 212, 214, 231
Burke, Brian 27, 71-73, 182, 221, 235, 261
Calgary Flames, 57, 65-66, 137, 162, 174, 196, 208
Campbell, Rob, 135, 138, 168
Candy, John, 16
Carbonneau, Guy, 56, 64, 68
Carkner, Terry, 2, 189-90, 193, 211, 226-27, 233-34, 249, 255, 258-70
Carolina Monarchs, 172
Chapman, John, 131, 175, 191
Chelios, Chris, 92
Cheveldayoff, Kevin 31
Chicago Blackhawks, 9, 26, 29, 32, 62, 82, 84, 91-93, 102, 135, 144, 213
Christiano, Jon, 114
Chynoweth, Dean, 31, 229-30
Chyzowski, Dave, 70
Ciccarelli, Dino, 134, 214
Cirella, Joe, 56, 63, 74, 85, 92, 101, 109, 152-53, 155, 162, 189
Clarke, Bob, 29, 37-42, 46-48, 51, 53-58, 60-65, 68-73, 79-88, 93, 99, 100, 102, 104-06, 109, 113-14, 119, 121-22, 129, 131, 138, 172, 174, 191, 197-98, 223, 235, 241
and departure from Panthers, 123-128
Sandy Clarke and, 39-40, 123, 125
Valeri Kharlamov and, 38
Coates, Al, 65
Coffey, Paul, 129, 134
Colangelo, Ron, 60
Colorado Avalanche, 31, 208, 258, 259, 260-63, 265-66, 268, 270-71, 273
Corkum, Bob, 64, 236
Cote, Greg, 173
Cowan, Scott, 185
Crawford, Marc, 262
Crispen and Porter Advertising Agency, 49, 76
Cunningham, Billy, 17

Daigle, Alexandre, 24, 70-73, 85-88
Daigneault, J.J., 56, 255
Dangerfield, Steve, 49
Daniels, Jeff, 152
Davydov, Evgeny, 84, 92, 96, 109
Deadmarsh, Adam, 73, 260, 261
DeJesus, Felix, 89
Demers, Jacques, 110, 133
Dennis, Ron, 49
The Denver Post, 263-64
Desjardins, Eric, 237-39, 241
Dessart, Kevin, 60, 111
Detroit Red Wings, 11, 47, 55, 117, 132-37, 174, 189, 204, 210, 214, 258, 260
Devellano, Jim, 133-39, 190
DiMaio, Rob, 242
The Disney Company, 12-13, 15-18, 21, 23-28, 34-35, 37, 106
Dombroski, Dave, 58
Domi, Tie, 47, 104, 113
Doubleday, Nelson, 33
Duchesne, Gaetan, 163
Dvorak, Radek, 190-91, 193, 200, 205, 227, 251
Dykhuis, Karl, 237
Dziedzic, Joe, 2, 255
Eakins, Dallas, 153
Edmonton Oilers, 7, 39, 61, 137, 141, 198
Ehman, Gerry "Tex," 31
Eisner, Michael, 15-19, 21-23, 25, 28
ESPN, 12, 232, 245, 251, 257, 272
Esposito, Phil, 8, 22, 25, 44, 61, 72, 78, 82-83, 88, 223
Farwell, Russ, 40, 124, 138
Fedorov, Sergei, 134, 163, 214
Fernandez, Manny, 208-09
Ferreira, Jack 29, 39, 55
Finley, Charles O. 30, 52
Firestone, Bruce, 24-25, 27
Fitzgerald, Tom, 3, 56, 64, 66-67, 80, 82-83, 85, 91-92, 94, 96, 99, 112-14, 121, 142, 144, 151-52, 155-56, 188-89, 193, 195, 199, 207, 213, 218, 225-26, 229-30, 234, 236, 238, 245, 249, 252, 255-58, 262, 270
Fitzpatrick, Mark, 26, 55-56, 61-62, 69, 79, 81-82, 85, 99, 116-18, 137, 152, 161, 164-65, 182, 192-93, 208-12, 265
    and Eosinophilia Myalgia Syndrome, 116
Fleet Center, 218, 229

Fletcher, Chuck, 23, 26, 42, 53-55, 60-64, 69, 71, 82, 86, 88, 104, 106, 114, 129-31, 149, 156, 163, 175, 181-82, 206
Fletcher, Cliff, 23, 26, 42, 62, 175
Florida Marlins, 11, 13-14, 16-17, 19-20, 23, 28-29, 43, 48-49, 51, 53, 58, 74, 76, 90, 96, 247
Florida Panthers
    arena search, 146, 185-87, 201-203, 218-220
    choosing uniform for, 50-54
    expansion bid of, 13-29
    first game of, 90-93
    first home game of, 95-97
    Miami Arena lease and, 35-37, 146-49
    and neutral zone trap, 85, 97-99, 112, 119, 152, 158-59, 194, 199, 248
    1996 Eastern Conference quarterfinals and, 224-232
    1996 Eastern Conference semifinals and, 232-245
    1996 Eastern Conference finals and, 245-258
    1993 Entry Draft and, 69-73
    1993 Expansion Draft and, 24-28, 54-57, 58-69, 73
    1994-95 NHL lockout and, 143-146, 149-50
    1996 Stanley Cup finals and, 260-272
    and Prince of Wales trophy, 258-59, 273
    rat craze and, 1, 195-96, 200, 227, 231, 235, 240, 243, 246, 251, 264, 266, 268, 269, 271
    Ryder Move of the Game, 111, 147
    team name, 43
Foligno, Mike, 99
Forsberg, Peter, 260-62, 265, 268
Franklin, Rob, 36
Friedland, Lloyd 160, 181, 184, 192
Ftorek, Robbie, 176, 179
Fuhr, Grant, 26, 137
Garpenlov, Johan, 3, 163, 193, 204, 210, 217, 221-22, 226, 257-58, 262, 267
Gartner, Mike, 45, 72
Gauthier, Pierre, 61, 65
Geris, David, 132
Gilhen, Randy, 56, 64, 80, 85, 92, 100, 105
Global Hockey League, 6
Godynuk, Alexander, 63, 85, 92
Gold Coast Ice Arena, 80-81, 87-88, 96, 111-13, 119, 144, 150, 159, 163, 167, 229, 245-46, 250, 267, 273

Goodenow, Bob, 142, 145, 149
Goring, Butch, 31, 66, 128, 179
Graves, Adam, 45, 72
Green, Gary, 48
Greenwood, Paul, 29, 32
Gretzky, Wayne, 5-6, 16, 70, 142, 201, 263
Halbrooks, Michael, 11
Hanbury, George, 218
Harkins, Todd, 66
Harkins, Brett, 189
Harris, Ron, 41, 54, 60, 131
Hartford Whalers, 10-11, 27, 55, 71-72, 88, 105, 142, 163, 193, 198, 213, 217
Hartsburg, Craig, 177
Hasek, Dominik, 26, 61
Hawerchuk, Dale, 233, 237, 242
Hawgood, Greg, 115, 154
Hayward, Rick, 82, 108
Healy, Glenn, 26, 55-56, 61, 69
Hebert, Guy, 56, 61, 107
Henry, John, 6-7
Henry, Paul, 191, 211
Hextall, Ron, 56, 233, 235, 238-39, 241-42, 244-45
Hill, Sean, 62, 107
The Hockey News, 58, 193, 273
Hockey Night in Canada, 196, 197
Hollywood Sportatorium, 14
Hough, Mike, 2, 56, 64, 80, 85, 91-92, 112, 152, 161, 170, 193, 205, 227, 240, 242-244, 252, 257, 262, 268-69
Howatt, Garry, 30, 38
Howe, Gordie, 38, 108, 135
Huizenga, Marti, 125, 255
Huizenga, H. Wayne, 9-11, 33-37, 40-43, 48-49, 51-54, 58, 60-63, 65, 83, 92-93, 96, 106, 111, 122, 124-27, 138-39, 145-46, 149-50, 159-60, 166, 170, 174, 178-80, 266, 273-74
  and *Forbes* magazine, 143
  and Major League Baseball, 7, 10, 16, 35
  and Marti Huizenga, 125, 255
  new arena search and, 185-87, 201-03, 218-20
  1990 expansion bid and, 6-7
  1992 expansion bid and, 13-29
Hull, Jody, 99-100, 112, 152, 170, 189, 193, 195, 205-06, 225, 227, 229, 230-232, 234, 236, 242-43
Hynes, Gord, 63
Ice Palace, Coral Gables, 14
Ilitch, Mike, 132-40, 178

International Hockey League, 62, 128
Jagr, Jaromir, 1-3, 95, 97, 107, 128, 163, 220, 245-46, 248-58, 261, 264
Jeremy Jacobs, 7, 26
Joe Robbie Stadium, 10-11, 16, 19-20, 33, 186
Johnson, Ryan, 131
Johnston, Ed, 97, 249
Jordan, Dean, 23, 29, 37, 48-50, 53-54, 58, 60, 62-63, 65, 76, 95-96, 111, 145, 185, 202, 218
Jordan, Michael, 90-91
Joseph, Dave, 21
Jovanovski, Ed, 129-32, 149-51, 155, 159, 163, 168-71, 173, 189-90, 193-95, 200, 204-05, 207, 209, 229, 234-35, 237-40, 244, 246, 265, 269, 273
Kamensky, Valeri, 260, 262, 266, 268-69
Kariya, Paul, 24, 41, 70-71, 73, 87
Keenan, Mike, 29, 33, 46, 120, 135, 138, 174, 178
King, Steven, 64
Kiszla, Mark, 263-65
Kozlov, Viktor, 24, 70, 71, 73, 134, 214
Kromm, Rich, 179
Krupp, Uwe, 260, 262, 270-71
Krushelnyski, Mike, 5
Kudelski, Bob, 109-10, 119, 152-53, 157-59, 161, 163, 166, 189-90, 193, 205, 216
Lacroix, Pierre, 29, 161
LaFontaine, Pat, 31-32
Lapointe, Joe, 250, 264
Laus, Paul, 62, 82, 107-109, 152, 171, 189, 193, 195, 207, 218, 229-30, 234, 237-38, 240, 257
Lebeau, Patrick, 66, 84
LeClair, John, 160, 233-34, 240-42, 245
Leetch, Brian, 211
LeFevre, David, 8
Leisure Management, 36, 187
Lemieux, Mario, 1-3, 70, 97, 142, 157, 220-21, 246, 248-50, 252-58
Lemieux, Claude, 166, 260-61, 265-66
Leroux, Francois, 2, 248
LeRoy, Tim, 144, 195, 261
Levins, Scott, 64, 83, 85, 92-94, 97, 109
Lewis, Bryan, 235
Linden, Jamie, 153, 190
Lindros, Eric, 40, 124, 127, 160, 232-38, 240-42, 244-46, 249, 260, 264, 265
Lindsay, Bill, 3, 57, 64, 80, 81, 83, 85, 91-92, 97, 112-13, 144, 152, 155, 161, 166, 171, 193, 195, 205-06, 209, 212, 216, 220-21, 225, 227,

230-32, 243-44, 255-58, 262, 267, 269

Linnemeier, David, 13

Lites, Jim, 134-36

Lomakin, Andrei, 64, 74-75, 85, 92, 152, 154, 163, 189

Lombardi, Dean, 71, 215, 216

Londono, Arley, 89

Los Angeles Kings, 5-6, 12-16, 31, 37, 134, 136, 158, 170, 179, 200, 206, 225

Lowell, Mel, 21

Lowry, Dave, 56, 64, 74, 80, 85, 91-94, 98-99, 102, 110, 152, 157, 161, 167, 193, 207, 226, 229-30, 239, 240, 243, 245, 249, 252, 262, 266

MacDonald, Todd, 73

MacLean, Clark, 200, 208, 212, 272, 274

MacLean, Doug, 132-35, 137-38, 188-95, 199-200, 203, 204, 206-13, 215, 217, 220-21, 225-26, 229-30, 233-35, 237, 240-42, 245-47, 250-52, 254-56, 258-63, 267, 269-74
   attends University of Prince Edward Island, 175
   and hiring by Panthers, 172, 174-81
   Mark Kiszla and, 263-65

MacLean, Jill, 200, 212, 258, 272, 274

MacLean, Jim, 207-08, 212

MacLean, MacKenzie, 200, 274

Madison Square Garden, 29, 47, 78, 108, 110, 120, 160, 181, 215, 217, 236

Maloney, Don, 32, 67, 184

Marchment, Brian, 92, 93

Mariner, Jonathan, 29, 60

Martin, Herbert U., 14

Martin, Jacques, 175, 177, 179

May, Brad, 231-32

McKee, Jay, 191

McLaren, Richard, 182-183

McLean, Kirk, 26, 55, 182

McNall, Bruce, 12-16, 21, 23

Meehan, Don, 42, 88

Meehan, Gerry, 32

Mellanby, Scott, 39, 56, 64, 67-68, 74-75, 80, 85-86, 91-93, 97, 99, 101-02, 111, 116, 119, 152, 157, 161, 189, 193, 195-200, 203-04, 206-08, 212, 215, 220-21, 226, 235-41, 246-47, 251, 253-54, 260, 262, 265, 267, 269-70
   attends University of Wisconsin, 197
   and incident at Steamer Jakes, 198
   Ralph Mellanby and, 196-97

Melrose, Barry, 67, 134, 136, 178

Messier, Mark 44-45, 211, 224

Miami Arena, 5, 11, 17, 35-36, 50, 54, 76, 81-83, 95, 97, 103, 111, 121-22, 128, 141-42, 146-48, 152, 164, 185-87, 193, 195, 200, 219, 226, 228, 230, 235, 237, 245-46, 250, 254-55, 259, 264, 266, 268, 273

Miami Dolphins, 51, 143, 246

Miami Heat, 17, 35-37, 49, 53, 107, 146-48, 186

Miami Sports and Exhibition Authority, 11, 21, 35-37, 147, 187

The Miami Herald, 5, 8, 14, 20, 43, 173, 264

Milbury, Mike, 138, 253

Miller, Kevin, 2-3, 254

Moller, Randy, 152, 162, 190

Montreal Canadiens, 2, 26, 56, 62, 65, 68, 100, 105, 107, 110, 176, 196-98, 256, 266

Montreal Forum, 100, 110, 161

Moore, Doug, 11

Moore, Chris, 157, 238

Morganti, Al, 232

Morrow, Ken, 30

Moynihan, John, 110

Muckler, John, 137-38

Murphy, Gord, 3, 63, 85, 92, 97, 99, 111, 116, 152, 162-63, 189, 193-94, 205, 208, 212, 220-22, 235, 237, 252-53

Murray, Terry, 175, 234, 246

Murray, Bryan, 47-48, 142-43, 149-51, 155-56, 158-59, 161-63, 166-81, 183-84, 189-94, 199, 213-16, 220-21, 223-24, 234-35, 246, 253-54, 258
   and Detroit Red Wings, 132-40
   and hiring by Panthers, 139-40

Murray, Andy, 47

Nashville, 201, 202

National Basketball Association, 17, 27

Nedved, Petr, 3, 248, 255, 257

Neely, Cam, 72, 225

Neilson, Roger, 44-48, 55-58, 60, 62-64, 78-82, 84-85, 87, 92, 96-105, 108-15, 117-19, 121, 124, 131, 139, 141, 144-45, 149, 151-53, 155-59, 163-65, 167, 188-89, 199-200
   fired by Panthers, 168-79

Nemirovsky, Dave, 189-90, 193

New Jersey Devils, 17, 26, 42, 45, 72, 85, 118, 151, 153, 165-66, 176, 179, 194-95, 201, 206-07, 209-10, 215-18, 241

New York Rangers, 2, 5, 6, 11, 26, 30-32, 42, 44-48, 55-56, 64, 75, 77-78, 99, 102-03, 107-08, 120-22, 138, 151, 153-54, 159-60, 161, 163, 166-67, 181-83, 198, 208-09, 211-15, 217, 220-21, 223, 232, 236, 245-50, 260

New York Islanders, 11, 22, 26, 29-34, 42, 46-47, 49, 55-56, 61, 66-67, 70, 81, 99, 114, 116-19, 121-23, 129, 134-35, 151-53, 156, 166, 174, 184, 203, 217, 220, 253-54, 256

NHL lockout, 12, 73, 143-46, 149-51, 159, 160, 163-64, 181, 183, 186, 189, 198

Niedermayer, Rob, 24, 70-74, 91-93, 99-104, 144, 152, 154-57, 159, 168, 170-71, 173, 188, 193-94, 200, 203-04, 209, 213, 217-18, 221-22, 226, 233, 237-38, 244, 252, 255, 266, 269
and first contract, 85-89

O'Dette, Matt, 131-32

Oates, Adam, 65, 225-30, 233

Obstruction, 194, 221, 249

Ogden Entertainment, 35, 37

Ontario Hockey League, 129-30

Osgood, Chris, 137, 210

Osterholt, Jack, 202, 218

Ottawa Senators, 22, 24-27, 59, 70-72, 79, 85, 87, 100, 109, 117, 166, 198, 217, 253-54

Otto, Joel, 238

Ozolinsh, Sandis, 260, 266, 268-70

Page, Pierre, 113, 120, 177

Paiment, Rosaire, 11

Palleschi, Ralph, 29, 32

Panther Pack tickets, 50, 110, 201

Patrick, Craig, 253

Patterson, Dennis, 41-42, 54, 60, 69, 71, 81, 129, 131

Philadelphia Flyers, 11, 17, 37-42, 51, 54, 63, 117, 123-28, 131, 133, 138, 151, 153, 160, 197-98, 200, 205, 210, 218, 223, 232-46, 248-49, 252
and Legion of Doom, 160, 232-34, 237, 245

Pittsburgh Penguins, 1-4, 17, 44-45, 64, 66, 78, 95-97, 108, 116, 128, 135, 152-53, 157, 167, 212, 220, 245, 247-58

Pocklington, Peter, 7, 28, 141

Podollan, Jason, 131

Poile, David, 29, 120, 127, 133

Potvin, Denis, 30, 63, 70, 91, 129, 138, 238

Poulin, Dave, 56, 64

Presley, Wayne, 56, 64

Primeau, Keith, 134, 137, 205

Pronger, Chris, 24, 70-71, 87, 88

Pulford, Bob, 26

Puppa, Daren, 26, 61, 69

Quinn, Pat, 55

Ramsay, Craig, 55-56, 60-61, 81, 101, 105, 113, 155-56, 167, 172, 174, 225

Redden, Wade, 191, 253

Redstone, Sumner, 106

Reich, Steve, 158

Renberg, Mikael, 160, 233-234, 238, 240

Ricci, Mike, 260, 262, 266, 268-269

Richer, Stephane, 63

Richter, Mike, 26, 55-56, 78, 103, 182-83, 192, 223

Ridder, Tony, 7

Rimer, Jeff, 91

Risebrough, Doug, 162

Robinson, Larry, 176, 179

Roche, Dave, 2, 252

Rochon, Rick, 7, 10, 17, 22, 35-36

Rodstrom, John, 203, 218

Roenick, Jeremy, 72, 93, 144

Rooney, Art, 30

Rosenthal, Robert, 29, 32

Ross, Karie, 90

Roy, Patrick, 100, 111, 182-83, 260, 262, 265-270

Rubin, Bob, 8

Ruff, Lindy, 81, 101, 105, 109, 113, 144, 149, 154, 156-57, 167, 171-72, 204-05, 225, 227, 233-34, 248, 261

Sakic, Joe, 260-62, 266, 268-70

Salerno, Pat, 218

Samuelsson, Kjell, 242, 244

Samuelsson, Ulf, 236

San Jose Sharks, 25, 39-40, 51, 71-72, 95, 137, 163, 214-16, 260

Saperstein, Jerry, 14, 23

Savard, Serge, 68

Schaffel, Louis, 17

Sean Michael Edwards, 51

Selanne, Teemu, 72, 191

Settlemyre, David "Sudsy," 42, 154

Severyn, Brent, 85, 109, 152, 189

Sheffield, Gary, 58, 90

Sheppard, Ray, 134, 214-17, 221-22, 226-29, 234, 236-37, 251-52, 257-59, 265-66, 269

Sinden, Harry, 26-27, 174, 225

Skrudland, Brian, 57, 64-66, 74-75, 80, 84-86, 89, 91-94, 100-03, 110, 112, 119-22, 143-45, 152-56, 161, 166, 170, 188, 193, 205, 207-08, 225,

229-30, 234, 242-43, 246, 249, 258, 262, 267, 269-270
and Selke Trophy, 155
Smiley, Don, 29
Smith, Mike, 103
Smith, Geoff, 152, 190, 193
Smith, Bill, 30, 44, 48, 59, 78, 81, 103, 114, 117, 137-38, 152, 164-65, 190, 193, 210, 212, 223-25, 228
Smith, Neil, 30, 44, 48, 78, 138, 223
Smolinski, Bryan, 252-53, 255
Smyth, Brad, 190
Smyth, Greg, 92
Snider, Ed, 124-27
Snider, Jay, 39-40, 123-25
Spano, John, 220
St. Louis Blues, 93, 138, 175, 213, 256
Stein, Gil, 12, 15-19, 21-23, 25-28, 47
Straka, Martin, 96, 216, 217, 251, 253, 254, 255, 269
Fort Lauderdale *Sun-Sentinel*, 21, 43, 185
Sunrise, City of 202, 218, 220
Sutter, Brent, 32, 92
Sutter, Duane, 30, 204
Svehla, Robert, 2, 162-63, 165, 170, 189, 190, 193-94, 199, 205, 222, 226, 234, 237, 240, 249, 259, 266, 270
Svehla, Robert, 2, 162-63, 165, 170, 189-90, 193-94, 199, 205, 222, 226, 233-34, 237, 240, 249, 259, 266, 270
Svensson, Magnus, 162-63, 170, 189, 193, 194-96
Svoboda, Petr, 237, 244
Sweeney, Tim, 64, 227
Sykora, Petr, 191
Szucko, Andre, 144
Tampa Bay Lightning, 21-22, 25, 27, 43, 59, 61, 71-72, 79, 83, 87-88, 94, 120-21, 142, 152-53, 218, 223, 232
Tavares, Tony, 60, 63, 70
Teale, Art, 186
Terranova, Kim, 49
Thibault, Jocelyn, 73, 161
Thomas, Steve, 67, 184
Thun, Anton, 150
Tichy, Milan, 62, 85
Tinkler, Scott, 144, 154, 190, 195, 196
Tkachuk, Keith, 67, 113
Tocchet, Rick, 115, 225-28, 233
Toronto Maple Leafs, 23, 26, 42, 46, 61-62, 175
Torrey, William, 22-23, 26-27, 41, 43, 46-49, 51-54, 56-61, 63, 66-70, 72, 80-82, 87, 96, 99, 100, 106-07, 121, 124-29, 131-32, 138-40, 142-43,

149, 156, 158, 160-61, 168, 170-72, 174, 178-81, 184, 187, 201-03, 218-19, 223
hired by Panthers, 33-35
and New York Islanders, 29-35
and Rich Torrey, 51
Tropical Ice Hockey League, 13
Tverdovsky, Oleg, 129, 131, 151
USA Today, 54
Vaisanen, Matti, 131, 191
Van Hellemond, Andy, 230
Vanbiesbrouck, John, 1-4, 26, 55-56, 60-63, 65, 68-69, 72-75, 77-79, 82, 85, 90-92, 94, 96, 99, 100, 103, 107, 110, 115-19, 121, 137, 142, 143, 145, 150, 152, 154, 164-67, 169, 187, 195-96, 199, 208-12, 216-17, 220-24, 227-30, 233, 235-38, 240-41, 244, 245-46, 249-53, 255, 257-58, 263, 265-67, 269-71, 273
and contract dispute, 159-61, 181-84, 191-93
and tape incident, 261-62
and Rosalinde Vanbiesbrouck, 78, 159, 193, 211
Vancouver Canucks, 26, 46, 55, 60-61, 114, 117, 125
Vernon, Mike, 137, 182
Viacom, 106, 146
Walsh, Stephen, 29, 32
Warrener, Rhett, 131, 190, 193, 253-54, 266, 269, 273
Washburn, Steve, 73, 190, 227
Washington Capitals, 11, 42, 132-133, 164, 166, 175-76, 208
Waste Management, 9, 19
Weekes, Kevin, 73
Wendt, Tim, 5, 11
Whitmore, Kay, 26, 55, 56, 60
Wiley, Jim, 215-16
Wilkinson, Neil, 3, 93, 248, 251, 257
Williams, Dave "Tiger," 46-47
Winnipeg Jets, 67, 84, 103-05, 137, 213, 274
Winter, Rich, 162, 191
Wirtz, Bill, 9-10, 12, 21, 26
Wood, Godfrey, 6-10, 14, 16, 23
Miami Hockey Inc. and, 6
Woolley, Jason, 163, 176, 189, 193-94, 237, 239
World Hockey Association, 14, 260
Wregget, Ken, 97, 250
Young, Scott, 262, 270
Ziegler, John, 8-10, 12